Belfast Studies in Language, Culture and Politics
General Editors: John M. Kirk and Dónall P. Ó Baoill

1: *Language and Politics: Northern Ireland, the Republic of Ireland, and Scotland* published 2000 ISBN 0 85389 791 3

2: *Language Links: the Languages of Scotland and Ireland* published 2001 ISBN 0 85389 795 6

3: *Linguistic Politics: Language Policies for Northern Ireland, the Republic of Ireland, and Scotland* published 2001 ISBN 0 85389 815 4

4: *Travellers and their Language* published 2002 ISBN 0 85389 832 4

5: Simone Zwickl, *Language Attitudes, Ethnic Identity and Dialect Use across the Northern Ireland Border: Armagh and Monaghan* published 2002 ISBN 0 85389 834 0

6: *Language Planning and Education: Linguistic Issues in Northern Ireland, the Republic of Ireland, and Scotland* published 2002 ISBN 0 85389 835 9

7: Edna Longley, Eamonn Hughes and Des O'Rawe (eds.) *Ireland (Ulster) Scotland: Concepts, Contexts, Comparisons* published 2003 ISBN 0 85389 844 8

8: Maolcholaim Scott and Roíse Ní Bhaoill (eds.) *Gaelic-Medium Education Provision: Northern Ireland, the Republic of Ireland, Scotland and the Isle of Man* published 2003 ISBN 0 85389 847 2

9: Dónall Ó Riagáin (ed.) *Language and Law in Northern Ireland* published 2003 ISBN 0 85389 848 0

10: *Towards our Goals in Broadcasting, the Press, the Performing Arts and the Economy: Minority Languages in Northern Ireland, the Republic of Ireland, and Scotland* published 2003 ISBN 0 85389 856 1

11: J. Derrick McClure (ed.) *Doonsin' Emerauds: New Scrieves anent Scots an Gaelic / New Studies on Scots and Gaelic* published 2004 ISBN 0 85389 860 X

12: Neal Alexander, Shane Murphy and Anne Oakman (eds.) *To the Other Shore: Cross-Currents in Irish and Scottish Studies* published 2004 ISBN 0 85389 863 4

13: *Legislation, Literature and Sociolinguistics: Northern Ireland, the Republic of Ireland, and Scotland* published 2005 ISBN 0 85389 874 X

14: Shane Alcobia-Murphy, Johanna Archbold, John Gibney and Carole Jones (eds.) *Beyond the Anchoring Grounds: More Cross-currents in Irish and Scottish Studies* published 2005 ISBN 0 85389 885 5

15: Dónall Ó Riagáin (ed.) *Voces Diversae: Lesser-Used Language Education in Europe* published 2006 ISBN 0 85389 886 3

16: William Lamb *Scottish Gaelic Speech and Writing: Register Variation in an Endangered Language* published 2008 ISBN 978 0 85389 895 2

17: Alasdair MacCaluim *Reversing Language Shift: The Role and Social Identity of Scottish Gaelic Learners* published 2007 ISBN 0 85389 897 9

18: Seán Mac Corraidh *Teaching through the Medium of the Irish Language: Beliefs and Practices of Immersion Teachers in Irish-medium Primary Schools in Belfast* published 2007 ISBN 0 85389 898 7

19: *Language and Economic Development: Northern Ireland, the Republic of Ireland, and Scotland* published 2009 ISBN 0 85389 910 X

21: Charlie Dillon and Ríona Ní Fhirghil, *Aistriú Éireann* published 2008. ISBN 978 0 85389 936 5

22 *Strategies for Minority Languages: Northern Ireland, the Republic of Ireland, and Scotland* published 2011 ISBN 0 85389 977 8

# Sustaining Minority Language Communities: Northern Ireland, the Republic of Ireland, and Scotland

Edited by

John M. Kirk and Dónall P. Ó Baoill

Cló Ollscoil na Banríona
2011

First published in 2011
Cló Ollscoil na Banríona
Queen's University Belfast
Belfast, BT7 1NN

Belfast Studies in Language, Culture and Politics
www.bslcp.com

© Cló Ollscoil na Banríona and contributors

The publication of this volume has been made possible through the financial support of Foras na Gaeilge and Colmcille.

British Library Cataloguing-in-Publication Data
A catalogue record for this book is available from the British Library.

ISBN 978 0 85389 976 1

The cover painting 'Looking Down on Tarbert', by Margaret Ballantyne, is reproduced with the kind permission of the artist and by courtesy of The Contemporary Fine Art Gallery, Eton.

Typeset by Nigel Craig in Granjon
Cover design by Colin Young
Printing by MPG Books, Bodmin, Cornwall

# Contents

Contributors

Acknowledgments

0. John M. Kirk and Dónall P. Ó Baoill
   *Réamhrá / Introduction*    1

**Part 1: Role of Education in Sustaining Minority Language Communities**
1. Dónall P. Ó Baoill
   *Introduction to Section*    9
2. John Harris
   *Minority Languages, Community and Identity in Ireland and Scotland*    11
3. Dónall P. Ó Baoill
   *Cultural, Social, Linguistic and Environmental Issues in Minority Language Development and Maintenance*    22
4. Morag MacNeil and Dónall P. Ó Baoill
   *Research Development and the Implementation of An Bradán Feasa Programme: Early Thinking of the Potential within a Social Issues / Applied Language Work-Stream*    29
5. John Galloway
   *Language Shift and Cultural Identity in the Gaidhealtachd: What Prospect for the Cultural Identity?*    36
6. Ian Malcolm
   *Young Protestants and Developing Irish in the Protestant Community*    44
7. Joe Mac Donnacha
   *The Role of the University in Sustaining Linguistic Minorities: An Irish Case Study*    53
8. Mary Delargy
   *Buíon dar Slua thar Thoinn do Ráinig Chugainn (Some Have Come from a Land beyond the Wave): Immigrant Learners of Irish in the North of Ireland*    65
9. Göran Wolf
   *Irish: Unfavourable Implications of Sociolinguistic Labels?*    69

**Part 2: Role of Policy in Sustaining Minority Language Communities**
10. Pádraig Ó hAoláin
    *Sustaining Minority Language Communities: Yin and Yang Juncture for Irish!*    81
11. Dónall Ó Riagáin
    *The Concept of Gaeltacht: Time to Revisit?*    89

12a. Laoise Ní Dhúda
*Pobal Gaeltachta an Bhreacbhaile: Cás-staidéar Sochtheangeolaíoch agus Eitneagrafaíoch sa Bheartas Teanga*   96

12b. Laoise Ní Dhúda
*The Breacbhaile Gaeltacht Community: A Sociolinguistic and Ethnographic Case Study in Language Policy*   114

13. Feargal Mac Ionnrachtaigh
*Ón Bhun Aníos: Resisting and Regenerating through Language in the North of Ireland*   132

14. John Walsh and Wilson McLeod
*The Implementation of Language Legislation in Dublin and Glasgow*   156

15. Douglas Chalmers and Mike Danson
*The Economic Impact of Gaelic Arts and Culture in Glasgow*   176

16. Matthew MacIver
*Sustaining Minority Languages*   188

**Part 3: Sustaining Scots-speaking Communities**

Introduction   192

17. John M. Kirk
*Scotland and Northern Ireland as Scots-speaking Communities*   193

18. Billy Kay
*Lowsin Time, Yokin Time: The Scots Leid in Twa Thoosan an Seiven*   206

19. †John Law
*The Scots Commonty*   212

20. Robert McColl Millar
*Linguistic Democracy?*   218

21. John Corbett and Wendy Anderson
*Using it or Losing it? Scots and Younger Speakers*   225

22. Christine Robinson
*The Role of Dictionaries in Sustaining a Language Community*   238

23. Ian Brown
*Drama as a Means for Uphaudin Leid Communities*   243

24. Gavin Falconer
*Hiberno-Central as an Unroofed Dialect of Scots*   249

**Part 4: Sustaining Minority Language Communities in Other Countries**

25. Andy Eagle
    *German-Speakin Swisserland: A Paitren for Dialect Uphaud* — 259

26. Bernadette O'Rourke
    *Sustaining Minority Language Communities: The Case of Galician* — 266

27. Judit Solymosi
    *Sustaining Minority Language Communities: The Case of Hungary* — 279

28. Tönu Tender
    *Sustaining Minority Language Communities: The Case of Estonian* — 284

29. Marina Solnishkina
    *Sustaining Minority Language Communities: The Case of Tatarstan* — 290

30. Alexander Pavlenko
    *Sustaining Minority Language Communities: The Case of Ukrainian in Southern Russia* — 298

**Editorial Disclaimer**

The views expressed in each paper are those of the author. Publication in this volume does not signify either editorial agreement or disagreement or editorial responsibility for these views.

**Publisher Disclaimer**

The publisher has used its best endeavours to ensure that the URLs for external websites referred to in this book are correct at the time of going to press. However, the publisher has no responsibility for the websites and can make no guarantee that a site will remain live or that the content is or will remain appropriate.

# Contributors

**Dr Wendy Anderson** is a lecturer in English Language at the University of Glasgow. She has written *The Phraseology of Administrative French: A Corpus-based Study* (Rodopi, 2006) and (with John Corbett) *Exploring English with Online Corpora* (Palgrave Macmillan, 2009).

**Prof. Ian Brown** is a Visiting Professor in Scottish Literature at the University of Glasgow and a Visiting Professor in Drama and Theatre Studies at the University of Glamorgan. He is General Editor of the three-volumed *Edinburgh History of Scottish Literature* (2007) and with Thomas Owen Clancy Series Editor of the *Edinburgh Companions to Scottish Literature* (Edinburgh University Press, 2008–).

**Dr Douglas Chalmers** is a lecturer in Media and Journalism at Glasgow Caledonian University. His many recent articles all deal with economic aspects of Scottish Gaelic.

**Prof. John Corbett** is Professor of Applied Language Studies at the University of Glasgow. His latest books are *Intercultural Language Activities* (Cambridge University Press, 2010) and (with Wendy Anderson) *Exploring English with Online Corpora* (Palgrave Macmillan, 2009).

**Prof. Mike Danson** is Professor of Economics at the University of the West of Scotland, Paisley. His latest books are *Employability and Local Labour Markets* (co-edited with Ronald W. McQuaid and Anne E. Green) (Routledge, 2006) and *Regional Development in Northern Europe: Peripherality, Marginality and Border Issues* (co-edited with Peter de Souza) (Routledge, due in 2012)

**Mary Delargy**, is an education officer with the Derry and Raphoe Library Project at the University of Ulster. At the time of the symposium, she was a research assistrant at the now-dissolved Academy for Irish Cultural Heritages at the University of Ulster.

**Andy Eagle** runs the popular Scots Online website (www.scots-online.org). He recently completed his monograph *Wir Ain Leed: An Introduction to Modern Scots*, now awaiting publication.

**Dr Gavin Falconer** completed a PhD on Scots language policy within the School of English at Queen's University Belfast in 2007. His publications include, with Ross G. Arthur, *The Bible in Plain Scots*, vol. 1: *Genesis,* vol. 2 *Exodus* (Alektryaina Press, Cambridge, ON, 2010) and, as Gabhán Ó Fachtna, three volumes of short stories in Irish: *Bás is Beatha ar an Bhóthar Chreagach* (Coiscéim 2007) *Na Réabhlóidí Datha agus Scéalta Eile* (Coiscéim, 2008) and *Snámhóirí Gaeltachta agus Scéalta Eile* (Coiscéim, 2010)

Dr John Galloway was a Post-doctoral Fellow in the Department of Celtic, University of Edinburgh, and subsequently a Research Associate of Leirsinn and Ionad Nàiseanta na h-Imrich at Sabhal Mòr Ostaig in Skye. Over the past twenty years he has carried out and reported on over forty studies and projects concerning language development, education and other aspects of Gaelic sociolinguistics for educational institutions, Gaelic organisations.

Dr John Harris is a senior lecturer in the Centre for Language and Communication Studies at Trinity College Dublin. His many publications deal with the teaching of Irish in the context of early learning and the primary school.

Billy Kay, who holds an honorary degree of a Doctor of the University of the West of Scotland, is one of Scotland's foremost broadcasters. His most recent books are *The Scottish World* (Mainstream, 2006, paperback 2008) and the third edition of *Scots: The Mither Tongue* (Mainstream, 2006).

Dr John M. Kirk is a senior lecturer in English and Scottish Language at Queen's University Belfast. His most recent edited books are (with Dónall Ó Baoill) *Language and Economic Development* (Cló Ollscoil na Banríona, 2009), and (with J. Derrick McClure and Margaret Storrie) *A Land that Lies Westward: Language and Culture in Islay and Argyll* (John Donald, 2009).

John Law, who sadly died in the Spring of 2010, was a teacher of English by profession, a Perth Town Councillor and General Secretary of the Scots Language Society. At the time of his death, he was working (with Caroline Macafee) on a translation of Gavin Douglas's *Eanados* into Modern Scots.

Joe Mac Donnacha is the Comhordaitheoir Acadúil / Academic Co-ordinator at Acadamh na hOllscolaíochta Gaeilge within the National University of Ireland, Galway. His brief concerns the development of a range of Irish-medium academic and research activities in academic areas that are seen as vital to the future of the Irish-speaking community. His main research interest is in the development of an organisational approach to language planning and in language planning as a strategic process. With Conchur Ó Giollagáin, he published the influential report *Staidéar Teangeolaíoch ar úsáid na Gaeilge sa Ghaeltacht / Comprehensive Linguistic Study on the Use of Irish in the Gaeltacht* (Dublin: Oifig an tSoláthair, An Roinn Gnóthaí Pobail, Tuaithe agus Gaeltachta, 2007).

Dr Feargal Mac Ionnrachtaigh is a product of Irish-medium education having attended Bunscoil Phobal Feirste and Meanscoil Feirste in West Belfast. He completed a PhD at Queen's University Belfast in 2009 on *Republican Prisoners and the Revival of the Irish Language in the North of Ireland*, upon which his contribution to the present volume is based. A founder-member of Gaeltacht Quarter GAA club, Laochra Loch Lao CLG, he is very active in the Irish language community revival in the city. He is chairperson of Upper Springfield Irish Language organisation Glór na Móna and works full-time as Project Worker with Gaeltacht Quarter Irish Language Development Agency, Forbairt Feirste.

**Prof. Matthew MacIver**, a native of the Isle of Lewis, who holds an Honorary EdD degree from the University of Edinburgh, is now an Honorary Professor at the University of the Highlands and Islands, where he is also Chair of the Board of Governors. He was General Secretary of the Council in Scotland until his retirement in 2009 and from 2006–2008 he was Chair of the Board of Bòrd na Gàidhlig.

**Dr Wilson McLeod** is a senior lecturer in Celtic and Scottish Studies at the University of Edinburgh. His most recent book is an anthology of medieval Gaelic verse, edited with Meg Bateman, *Duanaire na Sracaire: Songbook of the Pillagers* (Birlinn, 2007). He has published widely on language policy and planning issues in relation to Gaelic and is currently preparing a monograph on the evolution of Gaelic language policy and movements in Scotland.

**Dr Morag MacNeil** is a researcher in the Institute for Education, Teaching and Leadership at the University of Edinburgh. Her specialism is in evaluation. In previous posts, she has undertaken commissioned reports on a wide range of social and educational issues impacting on the Gaelic community. She is currently on secondment to the Scottish Government.

**Dr Ian Malcolm**, a journalist by profession, completed a PhD in Irish and Celtic Studies at Queen's University Belfast in 2007. A revised version of his thesis was published as *Towards Inclusion: Protestants and the Irish Language* (Blackstaff Press, 2009)

**Dr Robert McColl Millar** is a senior lecturer in Linguistics at the University of Aberdeen. His most recent books are *Northern and Insular Scots* (Edinburgh University Press, 2007) and *Authority and Identity: A Sociolinguistic History of Europe before the Modern Age* (Palgrave Macmillan, 2010). He has also revised R.L. Trask's *Historical Linguistics* (Hodder Educational, 2007), and *Why Do Languages Change?* (Cambridge University Press, 2010).

**Laoise Ní Dhúda** is a research student at the National University of Ireland, Galway, where she is working on a PhD on Irish language policy.

**Prof. Dónall Ó Baoill**, a native Irish speaker from Co. Donegal, is Professor of Irish at Queen's University Belfast. His most recent book is *Language and Economic Development*, co-edited with John Kirk (Cló Ollscoil na Banríona, 2009).

**Pádraig Ó hAoláin**, a native of Co. Tipperary, is the Chief Executive Officer of Údarás na Gaeltachta, the regional enterprise promotion agency for the Gaeltacht.

**Dónall Ó Riagáin**, who holds an honorary doctorate from Trinity College Carmarthen, where he is an honorary fellow, is one of the world's leading independent specialist consultants on language policy. He has edited *Language and Law in Northern Ireland* and *Voces Diversae: Minority Languages in Europe* for the present series and contributed to numerous of its other volumes.

**Dr Bernadette O'Rourke** is a lecturer in Spanish and Sociolinguistics at Heriot-Watt University, Edinburgh. Previously, she was a Lecturer in the School of Applied Languages and Intercultural Studies at Dublin City University and, between 1998 and 2000, a Language Assistant in the Department of English Philology at the University of Coruña. Her DCU PhD, which involved a cross-national comparative study of the Irish and Galician sociolinguistic contexts and an empirical study of young people's linguistic attitudes in each community, has been published as *Attitudes towards Weak and Strong Minority Languages: Irish and Galician in a European Context* (Palgrave Macmillan, 2010)

**Dr Alexander Pavlenko** is a senior lecturer in English Language at Taganrog Institute for Management and Economics, Russia. In 2006, he was an RSE/CRF Research Fellow at the University of Aberdeen and in 2010 a winner of an ESSE bursary, type B. His main research interest is in diachronic sociolinguistic studies and sociolinguistic comparisons. He has contributed to previous language and politics volumes in the present series.

**Dr Christine Robinson** is Director of Scottish Language Dictionaries and was an Honorary Fellow at the University of Edinburgh where she taught Scots. She recently published three small, popular, thematic dictionaries of Scots: *Scottish Wildlife*, *Wha's Like Us?* and (with Eileen Finlayson) *Scottish Weather* (Black & White, 2008)

**Dr Marina Solnishkina** is a senior lecturer in Linguistics at Tatar State Humanitarian and Pedagogical University, Kazan, Russian Federation. She graduated in 1994 with a PhD on professional sublanguages from Kazan State University. She contributed to the *Voces Diversae* volume in the present series.

**Dr Judit Solymosi** is Head of the International Department of the Office for National and Ethnic Minorities in Hungary. She was born and grew up in Budaopest and is a graduate of Eötvös Loránd University where she studied French and Russian Linguistics. She contributed to the *Voces Diversae* volume in the present series.

**Dr Tönu Tender** is an adviser to the Language Policy Department of the Ministry of Education and Research of the Estonian Government and author of numerous papers on Estonian language policy.

**Dr John Walsh** is a lecturer in Irish at the National University of Ireland, Galway. He spent 2009–10 as a Fulbright Irish Language Scholar at the University of California, Santa Cruz. His book, *Contests and Contexts: The Irish Language and Ireland's Socio-Economic Development*, based on his PhD thesis, was published by Peter Lang in 2011.

**Dr Göran Wolf** is a Wissenschaftlicher Mitarbeiter in English Linguistics at the Technische Universität Dresden. Previously, as a foreign language teaching assitant, he had taught German in Derry. He has co-edited (with Ursula Scaefer and Claudia Lange) *Linguistics, Ideology and the Discourse of Linguistic Nationalism* (Peter Lang, 2010) and his DrPhil thesis on the history of the English grammatical tradition has just been published as *Englische Grammatikschreibung 1600-1900: Der Wandel einer Diskurstradition* (Peter Lang, 2011).

# Acknowledgements

For financial support towards the publication of this volume, Cló Ollscoil na Banríona is most grateful to Foras na Gaeilge and Colmcille. The kind assistance of Pam McIntyre, Director of the Queen's University Language Centre, in arranging the translation into English of Laoise Ní Dhúda's paper is also gratefully acknowledged. The editors are indebted to the patience and co-operation of the contributors over what became an unexpectedly protracted editorial process.

This volume of papers arises from the Seventh Language and Politics Symposium on the Gaeltacht and Scotstacht, which was held from 7–9 November 2007, at Queen's University Belfast. The series of symposia forms a project within the AHRC Centre for Irish and Scottish Studies, in connection with which it has always been a pleasure to deal with Cairns Craig and Jon Cameron. This particular symposium received additional financial support from Foras na Gaeilge, Colmcille and the Ulster-Scots Agency. The organisers also received invaluable help and encouragement at various stages of planning from Deirdre Davitt, Dónall Ó Riagáin and Maolcholaim Scott. During the symposium, we received practical help from Máire Uí Bhaoill and Patrick McCafferty. For all this support, grateful acknowledgement is made.

# Réamhrá / Introduction

*John M. Kirk and Dónall P. Ó Baoill*

This volume of papers arises from the Seventh Language and Politics Symposium on the Gaeltacht and Scotstacht, which was held from 7–9 November 2007, at Queen's University Belfast.[i] The series of symposia forms a project within the AHRC Centre for Irish and Scottish Studies. This particular symposium also received financial support from Colmcille and Foras na Gaeilge, who have also helped fund these proceedings. For all this support we are most grateful.

The central theme of the symposium was concerned with policies for sustaining minority language communities and their implementation, with particular emphasis on Irish and Scottish Gaelic. The main focus was on identifying the role of language in forming and sustaining stabilised communities.

We devised several key questions at the outset, and each contributor was asked to address some or all of these questions in their contributions.

(a) What's wrong with current arrangements and practice? What research is needed to show what needs to be done?
(b) Are Irish and Gaelic self-sustaining to ensure their vibrancy and maintenance as community languages?
(c) How far is the sustaining of minority language communities conditional on infrastructure, environment, society, employment, urban renewal, culture, or anything else?
(d) What is the role of education in the sustaining of minority language communities – e.g. developing social skills, cultural identity or linguistic confidence?
(e) How far is the integration of language and culture into the community an environmental issue?
(f) Is the approach to such questions top-down or bottom-up? Whose task or responsibility is it ultimately to sustain a minority language community?
(g) What role can universities and other institutions of higher education play?
(h) With the arrival in Ireland and Scotland of significant numbers of speakers of Eastern European languages, how far have the future role and supporting mechanisms for Irish and Gaelic been undermined?
(i) Where are there communities where minority languages are being successfully sustained? What comparisons may be drawn with Irish and Gaelic, and what lessons are to be learned?
(j) In comparison with Gaelic, where does Scots stand with regard to its being a community language for much of the Scottish population, and what is or should be done for it? And for Scots speakers in Northern Ireland and the Republic of Ireland?

---

[i] A paper by Justin McCubbin has since appeared as 'Inimircigh in Éirinn agus an Ghaeilge: Ról na heitneachta agus na dteorainneacha eitneachultúrtha san aisghabháil teanga', *Taighde agus Teagasc* 6, 2008, pp. 48–63, and in English as 'Irish Language Policy in a Multi-ethnic State: Competing Discourses on Ethnocultural Membership and Language Ownership', *Journal of Multilingual and Multicultural Development*, 31.5. 2010. pp. 457–78.

For this publication, we have grouped the papers into four different sections:

- Role of Education in Sustaining Minority Language Communities
- Role of Policy in Sustaining Minority Language Communities
- Sustaining Scots
- Sustaining Minority Language Communities in Other Countries.

**Education and Minority Languages**

**Part 1**, the educational section focuses on the child's perception and experience in acquiring a minority language. From a larger research project emanating from Trinity College Dublin entitled 'Children's Voices' ('An Bradán Feasa'), there has emerged several sub-projects which are discussed under the following related topics: 'Minority Languages, Community and Identity in Ireland and Scotland', 'Family Language Policy and Immersion Education', and 'Beyond Language'. Each project in both parts of Ireland and in Scotland involves the investigation of both the indigenous as well as the recently introduced minority languages with the aim of gathering new and informative linguistic information about how plurilingual children function in multilingual societies.

**John Harris** sets out the above research context against prevailing knowledge. He finds the situation regarding Irish so different in Northern Ireland from the Republic of Ireland that each jurisdiction lends itself to very different techniques and measures of experimentation in language planning and language revitalisation. Levels of proficiency are different in each zone, although Harris argues that the recent increase in proficiency in the North may be due to measures and resources adopted in the South which have spilled over. But that speed of 'unprecedented change' in the North is also attributable to shifts in attitude arising in large measure from the *Belfast / Good Friday Agreement* of 1998, which, along with devolution in Scotland, have led to re-examinations and re-vitalisations of ethno-national sensibilities and identities and transformed them. Harris finds that although it is in the North that there is an appetite and a greater vitality for Irish despite the fact that the resources and infrastructure may be the poorer; at the same time, the status and position of Irish in the South have been reinforced by formal legislative measures, and long-term educational provision, which has produced an overall increase in the proportion of the population studying Irish at post-primary level, has been vindicated. Nevertheless, Harris concedes that more recent research into primary schools is showing that education is no longer playing that revitalisation and maintenance role it was doing only a generation ago.

At the same time, with immigration having risen 10% in the past ten years, there is now a new cohort of possible learners of Irish – through adaptation, accommodation, interaction and provision. Against this growing socio-political background of accelerated change, Harris calls for a new assessment of age-old issues such as language and identity and finds encouraging possibilities and prospects in immersion education for both natives and immigrants alike. For Harris, the starting point should be the embracing of changes to those concepts, paradigms and above all mindsets through which we currently seek to make sense of plurilingual individuals in a multi-lingual society.

**Dónall Ó Baoill** focuses on the crucial role of education and exposure in nurturing and developing a child's social and interactive abilities as well as its simultaneous acquisition of pragmatic skills. He raises questions about how such crucial skills are being conveyed through the immersion curriculum which forms part of the teaching of Irish. Ó Baoill emphasises the importance of integrating pragmatic skills through well-informed language teaching, and he urges the integration of language and social skills. Ó Baoill raises many questions and issues which Irish-medium educators have never considered in any great detail. Nevertheless, the success and potential survival of minority languages are intricately related to the outcomes of educational policies and their application. There is an urgent need for a re-assessment of curriculum content and language, culture and historical and environmental content need to be reconciled and integrated with children's learning and social integration.

**Morag MacNeil** and **Dónall Ó Baoill** stress the totality of the child's experience in its use of Gaelic in the context of other languages and the need for research to take a broader, interdisciplinary approach encompassing the impact on the child of the acquisition of more than one language. They feel that there is a need to look at the social community of the child, which begins with the social norms of the home and the home language and ends with the social norms of broader society, being mindful at all times of the child's linguistic competence in each environment. They put forward a model which links linguistic factors to social development, and in turn social development to cultural and ethnicity factors as these impinge on the child, on the one hand, and to an understanding of diversity in terms of the sense made of it by the child, on the other. Like John Harris, they further contrasts the situation of the autochthonous and allochthonous child and finds fresh common ground in each being 'the other'.

**John Galloway** looks at the inter-relationship between language, culture and identity in the Gaelic situation. Whereas he acknowledges that language may not be indicative of culture or identity, he does recognise that, if a language is once lost, there is usually less cultural identity. Although neither evidence-based nor speculative about the project to which Galloway is attached, he nevertheless constructs four cultural identities for possible future Gàidhealtachds: ' a strong and vibrant Gaelic identity', 'a Highland identity', 'an undifferentiated Scottish identity', and 'an undifferentiated British identity', all recalling to mind a similar set of possible identities investigated in MacCaluim (2007).

These opening papers are complemented by three papers which identify language communities and efforts to sustain or develop language confidence within them.

**Ian Malcolm** reports on his recent empirically-based doctoral research on the teaching of Irish in a number of Protestant post-primary schools in Northern Ireland. His results are fascinating, not least because it would appear that there may be real substance to the 'children of the ceasefire' concept. For many of the secondary school pupils interviewed, Irish amounted to an additional and potentially useful skill which could enhance their CVs. Irish-learning was only one part of a broader programme in Irish Studies developed by Gael-Linn. Malcolm concludes that his research shows that 'many young Protestants are ready and willing to learn the language [Irish] ... if they get the chance' and appeals to the authorities to give them that chance. Malcolm's paper is, of course, developed further in his monograph (2009), which shows that the depoliticisation agenda suggested by some is unlikely to work. Rather, he maintains that the way ahead is a sort-of 'multi-politicisation' of the language, which will require some radical thinking and fresh policies.

**Joe Mac Donnacha** reports on the Irish-medium tertiary level academy, *An tAcadamh*, in the Gaeltacht which is administered by the National University of Ireland, Galway. The academy has developed three undergraduate degree programmes, four full-time and seven part-time undergraduate diploma programmes, covering a broad range of courses and of research activities through the medium of Irish, with priority being given to the following needs of the Gaeltacht community: translation studies, language planning, education studies, information technology, communication studies, the arts, courses in applied Irish language skills, community development studies, studies in the development of natural resources, and managerial and business studies, each of which Mac Donnacha discusses briefly. Although the courses are delivered through the medium of Irish, the primary emphasis is on meeting the needs and requirements of the Irish-speaking community.

**Mary Delargy** reports anecdotally on her experience of teaching Irish to immigrants in Derry. In their different contexts and by their different means, these fresh initiatives are indicative of new approaches to the sustaining of Irish in response to changing needs and circumstances.

In the final paper in **Part 1**, **Göran Wolf** critiques the concepts of 'minority language' and 'national language'. By drawing on German scholarship, he unravels the contradiction regarding Irish as both a 'minority language' and a 'national language' and finds it more to be a 'nationalist language', not least because, for Wolf, it is Irish English (Hiberno-English, some might say) that is the 'national language'. If it is in need of safeguarding and maintenance, a language simply cannot be a national language, the inherent strength of which, through its mere existence, will maintain itself.

**Policy and Minority Languages**

The papers in **Part 2** address the need for clear policies for sustaining Irish- and Gaelic-speaking communities.

**Pádraig Ó hAoláin** critiques recent reports on the Gaeltacht and is very critical of their not having achieved or maintained the numbers of speakers or any other envisaged targets, and of their demonstration for Irish of steady decline. Despite numerous agencies and commissioned reports devoted to language survival, he is highly critical of the state for not playing its role, particularly through the public administration system. Although he lists the considerable body of individual pieces of support infrastructure now in place, he finds a serious lack of integration or co-ordination and also a lack of information particularly regarding speaker attitudes. So, for Ó hAoláin there is a serious language planning and language maintenance deficit with regard to Irish, and he calls for more co-ordination at central level and an integrated action policy.

**Dónall Ó Riagáin** urges a reconceptualisation of the 'Gaeltacht' as people or speakers, not as areas. Just as Irish speakers are to be found throughout the country, so, Ó Riagáin contends, public support and initiatives should be directed throughout the country too, and a nationwide approach adopted. The 'Gaeltacht' should be replaced by the notion of 'language development areas', where the use of the language should be revitalised in all transactions and exchanges of everyday life.

**Laoise Ní Dhúda** reports on her sociolinguistic and ethnographic doctoral case-study research within an unidentified Gaeltacht speech community (*An Breacbhaile*) somewhere in Ireland. Her paper addresses the aims and objectives of the study, the research questions being pursued and the proposed methodology which she intends to follow. A conceptual and empirical illustration of Spolsky's tripartite division associated with language policies are described for the communities which inhabit the 'Breacbhaile'. She summarises various approaches associated with language policy initiatives – outlining the success or otherwise of such initiatives. She outlines her methodology and gives a very full literature review section on the academic discourse associated with language planning, policy and management.

**Feargal Mac Ionnrachtaigh** finds that for some in the North of Ireland, particularly Republican prisoners, their interest in learning Irish grew through its being a useful even if largely symbolic weapon in their armory. Mac Ionnrachtaigh reports on his doctoral research, which involved his interviewing former Republican prisoners about their learning experiences. For those prisoners, Irish served as a badge of resistance against English, with all its cultural and hegemonic symbolism.

In the next paper, **John Walsh** and **Wilson McLeod** connect Ireland and Scotland by a critique of their separate language policies provided by Ireland's *Official Languages Act (2003)* and the *Gaelic Language (Scotland) Act 2005*. They begin by setting out the background both to language revitalisation, particularly in urban areas, and to each piece of legislation before going on to draw comparisons between the schemes and plans for Dublin (comprising those for Dublin City Council, Dún Laoghaire-Rathdown Council and South Dublin Council, and Fingal Council) and Glasgow. They provide much valuable, detailed information about each city. They conclude that direct comparison is difficult and parallels are few because of the differences in context and the separate requirements for each plan. In their comparison, however, Walsh and McLeod are invaluably instructive as well as beneficially critical. The paper updates the one presented at the symposium, which was largely based on Walsh and McLeod (2008).

**Douglas Chalmers** and **Mike Danson** also look at Glasgow's *Gaelic Language Plan* (2009) and do so alongside Glasgow's previous *Gaelic Arts Strategy* (2006–9). At the heart of the arts strategy was sustainability as well as value-addedness. To Chalmers and Danson, what is also important is the Gaelic labour market, for it is in Glasgow that there is a disproportionate share of the high quality jobs for which a working knowledge of Gaelic is essential. They explore the real impact of the annual Celtic Connections festival.

The final contribution on Gaelic is by **Matthew MacIver**, who, in his capacity of the then Chairman of Bòrd na Gàidhlig, sets out in an address his 'vision' for sustaining Gaelic and lays considerable importance on the Gaelic community seizing the unprecedented infrastructure now in place.

## Sustaining Scots-speaking Communities

In **Part 3**, the issue which is addressed is that of a Scots-speaking community, with Scots in Scotland and Northern Ireland being subjected to the same questions set out above as Irish and Gaelic were.

To these questions, **John Kirk** provides a set of answers; before that, however, he contextualises Scots-speaking communities by reviewing the prickly 'what-is-Scots?' question by explaining six factors or issues which underlie possible answers: the languageness of Scots, the apperception of Scots, the literariness of Scots, the medium issue (whether Scots is a matter of speech or writing or both), the legislative issue, and finally the issue of social need.

**Billy Kay**, well-known broadcaster and author of the highly-acclaimed book *Scots: The Mither Tongue*, now in a third edition (2006), provides in his highly vivid and accessible Scots a different set of answers to the set questions of sustainability by way of a valuable set of anecdotes and personal reflections to the questions set – albeit in the context of 2007 and not without serious challenge to the Scottish Executive prior to the 2007 election. As always, Kay provides many constructive suggestions for future action, some of which have come to fruition during the 2007–11 SNP Minority Government.

Another personal reflection to the questions is provided by the late **John Law**, a former editor of *Lallans* magazine, in a paper in a more traditional literary Scots. For many, Scots is first and foremost a literary language, and it was on that basis that Law and others succeeded in gaining recognition for Scots in the *European Charter for Regional or Minority Languages*. Like Kay, Law is highly critical of past Executive inaction but sees some hope with the SNP Minority Government.

**Robert McColl Millar** addresses the issue – much advocated by activists – of upgrading Scots to Part III recognition within the *European Charter for Regional or Minority Languages* – for many activists, a factor central to the sustaining of Scots at any level. Millar considers that many of the provisions simply could not be fulfilled, or even afforded. A huge burden would be placed on education, where Scots is already marginalised, and Millar's enthusiasm about the possibility is qualified by realism about the provision, cost-effectiveness and outcomes. More generally, he recognises that fragmentation and disconnectedness between – and even within – the parties mitigate against the formulation of a coherent policy for Scots or Part III recognition.

**John Corbett** and **Wendy Anderson** address the question of sustaining a Scots-speaking community by considering the potential uses of a corpus in creating teaching material for instruction in the language. Using data from their impressive Scottish Corpus of Texts and Speech, which has an unrivalled collection of current and authentic spoken and written Scots, they show how exercises on the use of the material can be applied to instruction about the language. Although the techniques are widespread in teaching English as a Foreign Language, until now they have not been applied to Scots. Corbett and Anderson thus offer a practical educational tool for increasing awareness of and increasing proficiency in Scots which is quite original.

It is often claimed that a historical dictionary is an indicator of language status, and that the two major historical dictionaries of Scots, the *Dictionary of the Older Scottish Tongue* and the *Scottish National Dictionary* are proof alone of Scots's languageness. **Christine Robinson** gives an account of the evolution of these dictionaries and of the on-going work of updating and revision, now happily funded directly by the Scottish Government. A language community cannot be maintained without a serious lexicographical record, and for Scots the historical dictionaries are the primary institution.

A language is also sustained through its literary *oeuvre*, and Scots has a literary output the equivalent of that in any standard language in sustained quality and quantity over a long period. **Ian Brown**, himself an accomplished dramatist in Scots, discusses several varieties of Scots which have appeared on the Scottish stage in the last half-century or so, constructing the argument – in his own style of effective and idiomatic Scots – that just by seeing and hearing Scots spoken on the stage and how the play shapes and crafts it into a form of an artistic expression is important for its sustaining.

**Gavin Falconer** considers the classification of Scots in Ulster by invoking the Klossian (1952, 1978) notion of 'unroofedness' whereby the formal functions of a variety of language are either not performed by that variety itself or are performed in another unrelated language. Applied to Scots, formal functions are performed by English, although the thrust of Falconer's paper is to show that Scots has had – and could still yet have – the functionality of a standard language, or 'roofedness'. He proposes the label of 'Hiberno-Central' for Ulster Scots, following the *Scottish National Dictionary*'s claim that Ulster Scots is a variant of West Mid Scots. Falconer argues against the notion that Ulster-Scots is a language, and also that it is as differentiated as Insular or Northern Scots.

These eight papers provide a useful snapshot of both the linguistic as well as political realities concerning Scots in 2007. The many anecdotes and personal observations provide useful documentation for garnering the many different attitudes towards Scots or levels of proficiency or awareness in the community or among politicians.

**Minority Languages in Other Countries**

In **Part 4**, we turn to how minority languages are being sustained in a number of comparable communities.

In a masterpiece of scholarly Scots, **Andy Eagle** looks at the situation in Switzerland. Swiss German is often compared as the closest comparable case with Scots, as a classic case of diglossia between Swiss German and standard German. Eagle reviews the functions performed by each before going on to discuss the threats to Swiss German, as well the motivations for its maintenance. Finally, Eagle teases out strengths and weaknesses in the situation, with valuable lessons for Scots.

**Bernadette O'Rourke** contends that Galician may be favourably compared with Irish. Although Galician has a reputation as a lost Celtic language, it is more usually compared with Spanish and other members of the Iberian language group. By moving away from each of those paradigms, O'Rourke attempts a fresh comparison with Irish with a macro-sociolinguistic approach involving socio-economic, socio-political and socio-demographic factors in each country. Her work is extended in O'Rourke (2010).

**Judit Solymosi** reports on linguistic diversity in Hungary, where no fewer than 13, mostly non-autochthonous, languages have state protection, each spread throughout the country. As no language predominates in any one area, sustainability takes on a different complexion in comparison with Scotland and Ireland, especially with regard to national minorities and their ethnicities.

**Tõnu Tender** reports on Estonia, another country where national minorities predominate, and where, since indepedence, reversing language shift and promoting ever-greater use of Estonian has been a major success. Tender recounts those developments and presents the various legislative acts which have bought about the sustaining of Estonian.

Like Estonia, Tatarstan, in its desire to establish its national identity, is seeking to assert that identity through its national tongue (Tatar). **Marina Solnyshkina** sets out the considerable ideologies which lie behind implementing greater use of Tatar and sustaining that use, albeit in a bilingual situation with Russian, which she describes.

Finally, **Alexander Pavlenko** describes the situation of Ukrainian in Southern Russia, where it remains only as a spoken language and in folksongs and folktales, but which is not otherwise being sustained, although serious efforts to do so were proposed as part of an ultimately rejected policy on Ukrainisation between 1925 and 1933. Despite these setbacks, Pavlenko describes how there remain some settlements where Ukrainian continues to be spoken and how these communities are being helped by a stronger, independent Ukraine.

In their different ways, these five case studies with their descriptions, reflections and insightful commentaries help us better to understand the situations in Ireland and Scotland, in what ways minority languages are being sustained, and in what ways politics, legislation and the State can intervene to help that process.

## References

Fishman, J.A. 1991. *Reversing Language Shift: Theoretical and Empirical Foundations of Assistance to Threatened Languages*. Clevedon: Multilingual Matters.
Kay, B. 2006. *Scots: The Mither Tongue*. Third Edition. Edinburgh: Mainstream.
Kloss, H. 1952. *Die Entwicklung Neuer Germanischer Kultursprachen*. München: Pohl.
Kloss, H. 1978. *Die Entwicklung Neuer Germanischer Kultursprachen seit 1800*. Second Edition, Düsseldorf: Pädagogischer Verlag Schwann.
MacCaluim, A. 2007. *Reversing Language Shift: The Role and Social Identity of Scottish Gaelic Learners*. Belfast Studies in Language, Culture and Politics 17. Belfast: Cló Ollscoil na Banríona.
Malcolm, I. 2009. *Towards Inclusion: Protestants and the Irish Language*. Belfast: Blackstaff Press.
O'Rourke, B. 2010. *Galician and Irish in the European Context: Attitudes towards Weak and Strong Minority Languages*. Houndmills: Palgrave Macmillan.
Walsh, J. and McLeod, W., 2008. 'An overcoat wrapped around an invisible man? Language Legislation and Language Revitalisation in Ireland and Scotland'. *Language Policy* 7: 21–46.

# Introduction to An Bradán Feasa

*Dónall P. Ó Baoill*

An Bradán Feasa, 'Children's Voices', was the name given to various initiatives being proposed to fill the many gaps that existed in the provision of Irish-medium Education especially at post secondary level, in third level institutions and in adult education generally in Northern Ireland. It arose from the work of Gaeloiliúint who were involved in setting up IME schools in Northern Ireland in the 1990s. When Comhairle na Gaelscolaíochta was established by the Department of Education in August 2000 to promote Irish-medium Education, Gaeloiliúint sought to extend its activities to adult and third level education through the medium of Irish. Its first initiative was a year long programme of lectures delivered at the Springvale Campus on the Springfield Road in West Belfast. At the end of this year funding ceased and the work at Springvale came to an end.

Following several meetings among former members of Gaeloiliúint and Ray Quinn of Texas who had financed the very successful initial year at Springvale, it was decided that we ought to initiate an integration programme involving Irish-medium Education and Gàidhlig-medium Education and to investigate the possibility of running a undergraduate or postgraduate degree which would be taught through the Medium of Irish and Gàidhlig. The difficulty was to find an agreeable location where instruction could take place and to find an interested cohort of students who were willing to take part in the degree programme. They would have to be competent in Irish and Gàidhlig from the beginning or take a crash course in their weaker language prior to beginning their degree programme. Some success was achieved in locating a possible site but securing the requisite financing to buy and renovate the identified site and building became the biggest stumbling block and ways had to be found to overcome this very real obstacle.

It was at this point that a set of meetings took place in order to prepare a proposal whereby various existing third level institutions and universities in Ireland and Scotland could co-operate in delivering a postgraduate Irish-medium Education/ Gàidhlig-medium Education educational programme for teachers, educationalists and planners. Subsequently, it became clear that, when such a programme came into being, it had to be accompanied by a well planned research programme which would focus on issues relating to education and training through a minority language.

During ongoing discussions and meetings, Ray Quinn met with Dr John Hegarty, Provost of Trinity College Dublin while on a tour of the United States. Dr Hegarty showed a keen interest in what we were trying to do and said he was willing to support our work in every way he could. On his return to Ireland, Dr Hegarty appointed Dr John Harris as research co-ordinator of the work being proposed from the different institutions. This resulted in our group having several meetings in the Provost's House in Dublin attended by representatives from various third level institutions in Ireland and Scotland.

There were two strands to the evolving programme of work – one educational, the other research based. The educational programme was to be based at Queen's University Belfast and consisted of an 18 month MA degree based primarily on peer education and learning. The School of Education and the School of Languages, Literatures and Performing Arts were to be the participants from Queen's University

Belfast. Prospective students would come from various social and governmental systems, health, education, law and the curriculum would cover a wide range of theme, including leadership, management change, sustainability, environment, culture and ethic , corporate responsibility and global business and national politics. All areas of study were to be made relevant to economic, social, religious, political, cultural and community interest. While the educational programme was open to all participating third level institutions, Sabhal Mòr Ostaig in the Isle of Skye one of the constituent college of the University of the Highlands and Islands was the only other institution which showed a keen interest in developing a parallel educational programme similar to what was being proposed at Queen's University Belfast.

An Bradán Feasa's research strand proposed to investigate and undertake minority language research in areas of relevance to the participating communities in Ireland, North and South, and in Scotland. All participating third level institutions were to be involved in this phase of the work, namely, Trinity College Dublin, Queen's University Belfast, University of Edinburgh and Sabhal Mòr Ostaig. The project was initially concerned with research that would help guide and illustrate successful ways in which we could support and sustain minority languages and their cultures. It was hoped that our work would include horizontal research on how different strategies could be replicated by other minority language communities engaged in reviving other endangered cultures. This was later extended to include both indigenous and immigrant minority languages. The future of An Bradán Feasa's work was thoroughly discussed at a pivotal meeting at Sabhal Mòr Ostaig on 18–19 June 2007, including strategies for developing funding bids. In this context the existing An Bradán Feasa document needed to be rewritten in order to be more useful in attracting research funds.

The next three contributions illustrate some of the proposed research questions and issues to be addressed and outline the advantages of examining minority language issues across the three jurisdictions and, in turn, open up interesting perspectives and discussion on familiar issues.

# Minority Languages, Community and Identity in Ireland and Scotland

*John Harris*

In the first three papers of this volume, we will talk about a project entitled *Minority Languages, Community and Identity in Ireland and Scotland* which has partners from the Republic, Northern Ireland and Scotland. We are concerned with both indigenous and immigrant minority languages. I lead the project on behalf of Trinity College Dublin and the other partners are Queen's University Belfast, the University of Edinburgh, and Sabhal Mór Ostaig, a constituent college of the University of the Highlands and Islands. I should emphasise that this is very much a work in progress and that we are still in the process of locating the project in the research literature and we welcome all feedback.[1]

While Dónall Ó Baoill, Morag MacNeil and John Galloway will each talk about their own aspect of the work, I will first try to set out some of the ideas that have motivated us. Inevitably, given my experience in language research in the Republic, I am clearer and can provide more detail from that perspective. The other speakers correspondingly will focus more on the Northern Ireland and Scottish perspectives. All of us, however, believe that examining issues of minority languages and multilingualism across the three jurisdictions offers many advantages and opens up interesting perspectives on familiar issues. I will begin with a sketch of the main features of the project and then look in a little more detail at the 'Children's Voices' theme within it and outline one particular study, 'Family language policy and immersion education', for which we are seeking funding.

## The Growth of Multilingualism: Minority Indigenous and Immigrant Languages

In recent decades the phenomenon of globalization/localization and increased mobility has meant that there has been an unprecedented rise in multilingualism around the world (Aronin, 2007; Singleton and Aronin, 2007). This development has at least three dimensions to it. One of these is the unprecedented spread and multiplication of functions of English as a world lingua franca. English is now very frequently acquired as an additional language, to such an extent that globally non-native speakers exceed native speakers – a development which of itself adds to the spread of multilingualism (Crystal, 2003; Singleton and Ryan, 2007). A second factor promoting multilingualism has been the success achieved in many parts of the world in revitalizing and extending the domains of use of minority, indigenous, local or non-international languages. Welsh, Basque, Irish and Maori immediately come to mind as examples of this phenomenon (Lewis, 2008; Cenoz, 2008; Harris, 2008; May and Hill, 2008). A third element in the growth of multilingualism has been migration, which of course has been particularly dramatic in the case of Ireland in recent years. The frequent effect of migration is that languages which are be widely spoken in one or more countries elsewhere in the world become minority community languages in the immigrants' adopted country.

In many communities, the form of multilingualism which develops will be determined by the relative strengths locally of the different kinds of forces and trends

---

[1] An alternative title for this paper might have been 'Multilingual Research on Autochthonous and Allochtonous Minority Languages in Ireland and Scotland'.

just noted. In Ireland and Britain, for example, minority indigenous language communities (such as Irish or Ulster Scots in Northern Ireland) and minority immigrant-language communities (such as Mandarin, Russian or Polish) live side by side with the majority-language English-speaking community. The need to investigate and understand the linguistic, social, educational and political issues which arise in living harmoniously together in such multilingual contexts, while according equal respect and esteem to different languages, speakers and identities is immediately clear.

**Identity and Indigenous Languages: Why Ireland and Scotland Just Now?**

A major motivation for the present study is the belief that at present, Northern Ireland, the Republic and Scotland together present us with a particularly interesting living laboratory for studying these different dimensions of multilingualism. For one thing, as we hope to illustrate briefly below, the contrasting but comparable linguistic, political and social circumstances obtaining in the three jurisdictions provide a number of naturally occurring experiments in sociolinguistics and language policy. In addition, because of the accelerated nature of the political, economic and linguistic changes which have been taking place in each of the three jurisdictions in recent times, we have an unprecedented opportunity to study the rapid growth of multilingualism and to consider its policy implications. Finally, there is an opportunity to decompartmentalise research on minority indigenous and minority immigrant languages, which have tended to occupy separate domains in the research literature (Harris, 2009). In doing so, we will be engaging with the real complexity of recent multilingualism, abandoning in the process the monolingual mindset which has often limited the investigation of the experience of multilingual learners and speakers.

In the three jurisdictions we are talking about, we can choose to observe indigenous languages and immigrant languages (autochthonous and allochtonous) either in their individual sociolinguistic contexts and/or in relation to each other. To take just one example: the three language areas in which Gaelic is spoken can be seen as representing three naturally occurring 'experimental-treatments' in sociolinguistic adaptation and change. The Republic, with an 85 year history post-independence of attempting to restore the language in a political context that has both interesting similarities and differences in terms of religion and identity with Northern Ireland, provides a rich basis for comparison and analysis. In Scotland, we have a society which is reconsidering, in a peaceful post-devolution context, issues of national identity, language maintenance and education.

One way illustrate the 'natural experiment' potential of this situation is to try to estimate in very rough and ready terms what impact political autonomy and the freedom to engage in long term language planning in the Republic has had on the subsequent revitalization of Irish (compared to Northern Ireland where until recently there was little institutional support for Irish). Almost from the moment of independence, the new Irish State quickly assigned significant social and legal status to Irish, and developed policies to maintain its use in existing Irish speaking areas and to revive its use elsewhere. In particular, it set about using the educational system to develop a basic proficiency in the general population. In a major sociolinguistic survey conducted simultaneously in the North and the Republic in recent years, Ó Riagáin (2007) asked representative samples of individuals to rate their ability to cope with normal conversations in Irish on a six-point scale, i.e. 'None', the 'Odd Word', a 'Few Simple Sentences', enough for 'Parts of conversations', for 'Most Conversations' or finally, if they regarded themselves as 'Native Speakers'. Combining the two highest categories of proficiency and the two middle levels, he found that while about 60% of those in the Republic of Ireland claimed high or partial levels of ability, only about one third of Northern Ireland Catholics claimed this level. Few Protestants in Northern Ireland reported any level of proficiency, even 'the odd word'.

Although information on religion in the Republic was not collected in this survey, the fact that people from Catholic backgrounds account for over 90% of the population means that the data for the Republic as a whole provides a reasonable approximation of the proficiency of the majority Catholic. As Ó Riagáin points out, other survey data would suggest that the Irish proficiency levels of Protestants in the Republic are lower than those of Catholics. The key point in the current context is that comparing proficiency levels in Northern Ireland (particularly in the Catholic Community) and the Republic in this kind of way allows us to benefit from what, in research terms, can be construed as an historic natural experiment in language planning and language revitalisation. The end result is clearly that the language planning and language revitalisation efforts in the Republic have produced substantial increases in proficiency levels in Irish in the general population compared to Northern Ireland. Indeed, as Ó Riagáin notes, the policies adopted in the Republic also had a material positive impact on language attitudes and behaviour even in Northern Ireland, simply because teachers and others promoting the language could benefit from corpus planning, educational resources in Irish, and facilities such as Irish summer colleges in Gaeltacht areas. Indeed, he argues that a full understanding of the operation of Irish language policy can only be obtained by extending the scope of the research to include all regions of the island of Ireland.

This kind of post hoc comparison between Northern Ireland and the Republic, however, is only one kind of research opportunity provided by a focus on minority languages in Ireland and Scotland at present. Another aspect which has considerable potential from a research point of view arises from the speed with which changes in the position of both minority indigenous and minority immigrant languages are occurring in each jurisdiction. In Northern Ireland, post Good Friday, there is an opportunity to study the role of language in community and civil society and in the longer term resolution of conflict. In the wake of Good Friday, and post devolution in Scotland, we have entered a phase of unprecedented change, in which language is likely to be a key element. The changes occurring grow from the dramatic movement in the political centre of gravity from states to communities which took place in recent years. Not only is political and civil society changing within Northern Ireland and Scotland, but the mutual sense of awareness and common cause in the three regions may be contributing, however slowly, to the transformation of ethno-national identities within each. Historical and linguistic connections between the Republic, Northern Ireland and Scotland are being re-examined, reclaimed and revitalised in a way that would have been inconceivable 10 or 15 years ago.

The change in political centre of gravity has also, however, transformed relations between the Republic and Northern Ireland, as well altering the agenda relating to many social, political and linguistic issues within the Republic itself. One recent example of this is how the resurgence of interest in Irish in Northern Ireland during the conflict and post-conflict period has affected the dynamics of language politics in the Republic. While the kind of widespread basic knowledge of Irish to be found in the Republic does not yet exist in Northern Ireland, and while the educational and language maintenance infrastructure which supports that competence has yet to develop (Nic Craith, 1999), it is Northern Ireland which recently seems to have the greater vitality in relation to the language and to have captured the leadership role in this regard on the island as a whole. This greater linguistic vitality north of the border, combined with the specific North-South structures that have emerged from the *Good Friday Agreement*, have enlarged the domain within which language planning in the Republic traditionally operated. It has also prompted perhaps some re-examination of the achievements of language planning south of the border (Harris, 2007) notwithstanding the real successes noted above.

On the positive side, nevertheless, the Republic can point to the consolidation of the position of the language in constitutional, legal and European contexts: the passing of the Official Languages Act, the appointment of an Official Languages Commissioner and the achievement of 'official working language' status in Europe. In more dynamic revitalisation terms, the expansion and continuing achievements of the all-Irish school movement and of TG4 (Irish language television) have to be counted as significant successes. Most important of all, perhaps, is the long-term continuing growth in the percentage of the population reporting some ability in Irish in the census (Ó Riagáin, 2001). Any interpretation of the latter as evidence of a more fundamental strengthening of the social or attitudinal base for Irish language revitalisation in the Republic, however, must be qualified by the knowledge that it appears to be largely due to the steady rise in educational participation rates in the wake of the introduction of free post primary education in the 1960s – and the consequent increase in the proportion of the population who now study Irish at post-primary level.

On the negative side, this very success of the education system in the Republic also seems for the first time to be threatened. For one thing, while the long-standing policy of teaching Irish throughout the primary and post-primary years has been periodically challenged without success, a considerably more sustained argument for optionality in the later years of post-primary education has been mounted in recent years by the main opposition party. Another concern is the evidence in a study by Harris et al (2006) showing that the education system is no longer playing the revitalisation and language maintenance role it traditionally did. The report shows that there has been a substantial, long-term decline in speaking proficiency in Irish in mainstream primary schools and to a lesser extent in Gaeltacht schools.

In Scotland too the dominant theme is one of continuing change. Many of the key political developments and government initiatives are still being piloted, or are only gradually becoming embedded in local decision-making. Language issues are no longer located on the periphery, but are increasingly contextualised within the broader themes of equity and the greater community integration. Language revitalisation is seen as part of both local community regeneration and cultural development at a national level. While many of the long term implications for language, culture, identity and ethnicity are still hard to predict, the impact on community cohesion and integration is not. To be successful, policy development must be based on a greater understanding of the associated processes and outcomes at individual and group levels.

**Immigrant Languages: A New Opportunity in Ireland to Study an Old Dilemma in Europe**

Superimposed upon these developments related to *indigenous* minority languages such as Irish and Ulster Scots, is another layer of change related to *immigrant* languages and peoples. Unlike most of Western Europe where immigrant communities and languages have long been a feature of life, the challenge of responding to new languages and cultures has been suddenly encountered, particularly in the Republic and Northern Ireland. To give an indication of the scale of recent immigration, it can be noted that the 2002 Census in the Republic showed that 7% of the population were non-nationals while the 2006 Census showed the figure was 10%. Barrett and McCarthy (2006) point out how exceptional this change is by referring to the fact that the non-national population of the UK grew by 2 percentage points between 1960 and 1990. This increase in the number of immigrants, allied with the gradual evolution of the experience of immigration itself over time, raises new issues both for immigrants and for the longer established community. Initially, the major linguistic challenge for immigrants may be the task of learning English. But later on, if the experience of other countries is anything to go by, issues of mother tongue teaching, early reading and many other issues will become important.

The very speed and recency of this development means that we have an opportunity – unlikely to be repeated elsewhere soon – to study the early stages of the linguistic and cultural adaptation of immigrant peoples and the interaction of these with the political, social and educational response of host countries/jurisdictions that have little or no significant previous history of immigration. The process of accommodation, provision and adaptation to immigrant speakers has proceeded too far in other western European countries to permit the kind of dynamic, real-time study that is still possible in the case of these three regions of Ireland and Scotland. This kind of research also opens up the crucial possibility of comparing issues of identity, Diaspora and migration in minority language immigrant communities with similar issues in the case of minority indigenous languages such as Irish, Ulster Scots, Scots and Scots Gaelic.

One of the many questions that arise is whether certain aspects of language and identity, and the motivation to learn Irish, may be changed by Irish-born children's engagement with newly arrived speakers of other languages. Part of the reality for many children in the North and the Republic now is that the chances of hearing Polish or Chinese on the street or in the school playground may be greater than the likelihood of hearing Irish. Another point worth noting is that the parallels between the linguistic experiences of new immigrants to Ireland in recent years, and the historical experience of migration and language shift in the country in the nineteenth and early-twentieth century, are real and direct. The fate of the Irish language in the nineteenth century was intimately tied up with economic migration. The imperative to leave Ireland, particularly in the wake of the famine, accelerated the pressures towards language shift from Irish to English. The fact of emigration itself, along with the anticipated probability of having to emigrate for economic reasons, combined to produce that shift. There is now an opportunity in these islands – both in society generally and in the context of research – to revisit these age-old issues of language, identity and migration, and to understand our national historical experiences in the light of the current reality of migration, linguistic change, and redefinition of identity for our new immigrants. The episodic public debate on language and identity issues in Ireland in recent years indicates the dynamic new context in which the oldest questions of indigenous languages and identity are being examined. Irish and Scottish researchers approach these questions, of course, with a special sympathy and interest. Emigrants from both Ireland and Scotland have made great contributions to the development of other countries, and we are increasingly conscious that new immigrants are now making a great contribution to ours. The growing awareness of these processes, augmented by the insights and information provided by research, has the potential to accelerate the post-conflict impetus for change and reconciliation in Northern Ireland.

## Research on Children's Voices in Minority Languages at Home and in School

We turn now to a discussion of one theme in the broader programme of research on minority languages envisaged above. It should be emphasised that this study is only at a planning stage and is discussed here simply to illustrate what we see as the potential value and scope of such work. The theme we will focus on is children's experiences of, and perspectives on, minority languages and identity in the three jurisdictions we have been talking about – the Republic of Ireland, Northern Ireland and Scotland.

Children are of particular interest because they are in the front line when it comes to engaging with language and identity issues and in negotiating responses to them. It is children who are most intensely engaged with the implications of home-school language change as they form peer relationships though a language that may be imperfectly mastered, while at the same time maintaining coherent relationships with languages and identities which they associate with home, siblings, parents and with their own personal past. It is important, therefore, to establish at first hand how personal, familial and ethnic identities are reexamined and remoulded by children as they learn and use new languages. Equally, we need to know how issues of identity, belonging, friendship and integration are understood by children when minority indigenous and immigrant languages come into contact at school.

This kind of information is crucially important in two ways. First, it is critical to the promotion of each individual child's personal growth and academic progress. But it is also central to effective language planning and policy development. Language planning in the past has often been about power (Baker, 2006). Adults – parents, civil servants or language planners – may make decisions about language, language promotion or language education. It is children, however, who often implement and are affected by these decisions. This is not to say that the child's best interests are not to the fore for parents and adults generally. Nevertheless, many language-related decisions may be made with relatively little independently-obtained information from the children who will be most affected, concerning their feelings or perceptions. Including children's perspectives on language and identity, particularly in a minority language context, is a contribution to making language planning/language management both more democratic – since it takes account of one of the main stakeholders – and more effective.

This focus on children's perspectives fits very well with a growing awareness more generally of the need to include children's views in making decisions about their lives. The importance of children's voices' in research in psychology and child development is by now well established (Greene and Hogan, 2005). In a number of areas of second language acquisition research, also, such as second language socialization (Duff, 2002), the emphasis is also on learners' experience. Second language socialization is the process by which non-native speakers of a language seek competence in the language and, typically, membership and the ability to participate in the practices of the communities in which that language is spoken. In the present study, the emphasis is on such issues as how learners construe language issues, how decisions about language use in the home and in school are arrived at, and how much input there is from the children versus adults. How do children in various kinds of challenging, difficult or 'transition' language situations at home, in school or with their peers, for example, understand these questions? What kinds of problems do they face in adjusting to changes in language; what are their preferences; what response would they like from adults?

The study of children's experience of language change and identity issues – whether minority indigenous or immigrant languages are involved – is crucial to understanding broader community relationships and the process of integration. By studying issues of minority languages, identity and community in children in Ireland and Scotland, we will be better able to respond to, support and integrate emerging minority language communities. Children's experience is also important at a societal policy level since if language shift occurs, it occurs in the childhood years. In the longer term we might also reasonably expect to be able to link information on early relationships between language and identity in children to the broader efforts in society to revitalise and maintain endangered languages.

**Family Language Policy and Immersion Education**

A particularly interesting study from the point of view of understanding and supporting the development and maintenance of different kinds of multilingual competence would be to compare the experiences of children and families who speak one of the indigenous (autochthonous) minority languages with those who speak one of the new immigrant (allochtonous) languages. For example, we could compare the experience of families who speak Irish at home to some extent versus those who speak languages such as Polish, Mandarin or Russian which are minority languages within the Republic and Northern Ireland.

Until recently, the most visible and institutionally distinct type of immersion in Ireland was represented by the Irish-medium sector outside Gaeltacht areas (Gaelscoileanna). Many children attending all-Irish schools come from primarily English-speaking homes, although in some cases a substantial amount of Irish would also be used. For the purposes of this study, it would be necessary to distinguish between Irish speaking families associated with immersion schools in the Republic and the North. In recent years, a greater appreciation has developed that models of multilingual education reflect linguistic and sociocultural histories and goals particular to each context Hornberger (2002, 2006, 2009; May, 1999; May and Hill, 2008). Hornberger (2009) contrasts, for example, the different place of English in M ori immersion and Canadian-French immersion. While the basic linguistic and educational approach of Irish immersion programmes in the North may be similar to there southern counterparts, the wider political, religious, sociolinguistic, and language policy context in which they are located, as we noted above, is critically different. Consequently, in a study of family language policy and immersion, the North-South dimension could be important if we are to understand the range of different sociolinguistic and policy contexts within which minority language use at home and in school occurs on the island of Ireland.

The other type of immersion education in Ireland is less visible and has not yet been explicitly defined in institutional terms as such. With the exception of some 'weekend schools', new immigrant communities in Ireland have so far made no organised attempt to establish their 'own' schools, and have decided to send their children to mainstream primary schools where English is the medium of instruction. To this extent, they are effectively receiving immersion type education, i.e. they are being educated in a language that is different from their home language, and in which they may initially have little competence.

In general terms, what we are interested in is how these different kinds of families develop strategies to accommodate their linguistic repertoires – in other words, how is family language policy (King and Fogle, 2006) explicitly or implicitly formulated by them, how is it implemented, and how does this process evolve over time? Are there differences in how children and adults see the linguistic issues with which they are confronted, and how do such questions relate to the role of the school and community and to issues of planning and policy at state level? The results should contribute to a better understanding of the kinds of sociolinguistic and educational support and provision required by different types of minority language speakers and provide the basis for more integrated and coherent language policy and planning by the state.

We would expect that while some of the experiences of the two kinds of minority language families might be similar, others could be quite different. Perceptions of the immersion education they receive might also be different for Irish and immigrant language speakers. Whether we consider Irish or immigrant minority languages, however, individual members of families may be fluent or native speakers of the minority language, bilingual to some degree, or may be primarily English speakers. In addition, the arrival of relatively large numbers of immigrants with the same language in a relatively short time period offers possibilities for the formation of minority-language networks which are likely to differ substantially from the case of Irish where the absolute number of speakers/families with a substantial command of the language may be relatively low.

Bearing these points in mind, we can give a few examples of research questions, issues and themes which might be pursued in the case of the three categories of family/immersion.

- How do minority indigenous and minority immigrant families in Ireland explain, frame, and defend (King and Fogle, 2006) their particular family language policies?
- What level of freedom do children from minority language homes feel about using their different languages?
- What is the relative contribution of parents and children, and of older versus younger children, in determining family language policy?
- Are there differences in the way parents and children see questions of minority language use, identity and community in relation to language.
- How adequate is school acquired language for use in the home or community?
- How are personal dilemmas of friendship, peer exclusion or conflict at school affected by immersion children's command of Irish (which is mainly acquired in a cognitive or academic context rather than in the relative intimacy of home)?
- Since many parents of children in all Irish schools rarely use Irish, how do children perceive the meaning and purpose of their Irish medium education vis a vis their home use of language?
- How important is the school in supporting home use of the minority language? What activities help?
- What aspects of state or local policy help or hinder greater home use of a minority language (Irish or immigrants' mother tongue)?
- How do immigrant language communities differ among themselves in terms of the extent of their use of the (minority) mother tongue and English?
- How do children whose home language is neither Irish nor English feel about their own language? What do they think of the future in terms of their language?
- What is the experience of immigrant children of becoming proficient at English while their parents continue to primarily speak their mother tongue? How do

language issues mediate parents' and children's understanding and perception of each others' worlds in a new country?
- How do minority immigrant language families feel about Irish, Irish speaking families or about learning Irish? Is acquiring Irish a factor in becoming an 'insider' in Ireland?
- Is there evidence of immigrant children attending Irish immersion as has happened in the case of French immersion in recent years (Swain and Lapkin, 2005).
- Are Irish immersion children's perception of Irish, and being part of an Irish speaking family, changed by meeting children whose home language is neither Irish nor English? Do children from different language backgrounds talk about language issues to each other?

## Embracing the Complexity of Multilingualism and Making it Manageable for Research

If the recent emphasis on multilingualism as a focus for study and research is to produce new insights into issues of identity, language learning and use, the concept should prompt us to define new areas of enquiry and even explore new research methodologies. To open our eyes to these new possibilities, it seems critical that we abandon a monolingual research mindset. This means working to decompartmentalise research domains such as minority languages and immigrant languages that we have kept rather too separate in the past. We need to do this irrespective of whether we are concerned with multilingualism as an individual characteristic or in terms of community.

Recently, I pointed out the need to decompartmentalise research in the case of early language learning (Harris, 2009). Research on early language learning tends to be confined largely to early *foreign* language learning. Yet, the informational base available for the comparative study of early language learning would be vastly expanded if research on 'foreign' and other target language types (minority, heritage, regional) were to be decompartmentalised. No doubt, what prompts many early foreign language learning researchers to tactically remove such minority language programmes from consideration is the belief that they are too different to foreign language learning contexts and that they raise idiosyncratic issues.

Taking the example of Irish in primary school, however, I show that early foreign language learning may not really be all that different to early minority, heritage or regional language learning, nor is foreign language learning immune from the influence of some of the variables that we associate with the added 'complexity' or supposed uniqueness of these minority language situations. Indeed, it can be argued that well functioning, long-established minority language programmes, such as the Irish one, can provide a particularly finished version of the early language learning 'treatment', as it were, something that is not always possible to obtain in the case of more recently established early foreign language programmes. Finally, in this regard, because early language learning programmes such as the Irish one have been monitored over a long period, they considerably expand the time frame within which we can examine the stability of programme effects and processes. All this seems to suggest, therefore, that there may be more continuity in the challenges, problems and nature of early language learning across different target language types – foreign, heritage, minority, regional or immigrant languages – than we have generally assumed in the past.

In conclusion, therefore, we propose that there is a similar need in other areas of multilingual research to re-examine earlier assumptions about the separation of research on different kinds of languages. We need to embrace what might initially seem to be the troublesome complexity of multilingualism. We believe that the troublesome aspects may in reality be the most interesting. We do not deny, of course, that all research requires us to set limits on the scale of an enquiry. In the project discussed here, we believe we have achieved a manageable level of complexity by limiting the study of minority immigrant and indigenous languages to Ireland and Scotland.

**References**

Aronin, L. 2007. *Current Multilingualism as a New Linguistic World Order*. Centre for Language and Communication Studies Occasional Paper. Dublin: Trinity College.
Baker, C. 2006. *Foundations of Bilingual Education and Bilingualism*. Clevedon: Multilingual Matters.
Barrett, A. and Y. McCarthy. 2006. 'Immigrants in a Booming Economy: Analysing their Earnings and Welfare Dependence'. Discussion Paper No. 2457. Bonn: Institute for the Study of Labour (IZA).
Cenoz, J. 2008. 'Achievements and Challenges in Bilingual and Multilingual Education in the Basque Country'. *AILA Review* 21: 13–30.
Crystal, D. 2003. *English as a Global Language*. Cambridge: Cambridge University Press.
Duff, P.A. 2002. 'The Discursive Construction of Knowledge, Identity, and Difference: An Ethnography of Communication in the High School Mainstream. *Applied Linguistics* 23: 289–322.
Greene, S. and D. Hogan. eds. 2005. *Researching Children's Experience: Approaches and Methods*. London: Sage.
Harris, J. 2007. 'Bilingualism and Bilingual Education in Ireland North and South', *International Journal of Bilingual Education and Bilingualism* 10.4: 359–68
Harris, J. 2008. 'The Role of Primary Schools in the Revitalisation of Irish'. *AILA Review* 21, 49–68.
Harris, J. 2009. 'Expanding the Comparative Context for Early Language Learning: From Foreign to Heritage and Minority Language Programmes'. In ed. Nikolov, M. *The Age Factor and Early Language Learning*. Berlin: Mouton de Gruyter. 351–76.
Harris, J., Forde, P., Archer, P., Nic Fhearaile, S., and M. O'Gorman. 2006. *Irish in Primary School: Long-term National Trends in Achievement*. Dublin: Department of Education and Science.
Hornberger, N.H. 2002. 'Multilingual Language Policies and the Continua of Biliteracy: An Ecological Approach'. *Language Policy* 1.1: 27–51.
Hornberger, N.H. 2006. 'Voice and Biliteracy in Indigenous Language Revitalization: Contentious Educational Practices in Quechua, Guarani, and Maori contexts. *Journal of Language, Identity, and Education* 5.4: 277–92.
Hornberger, N.H. 2009. 'Multilingual Education Policy and Practice: Ten Certainties (Grounded in Indigenous Experience)'. *Language Teaching* 42.2: 197–211.
King, K. and L. Fogle. 2006. 'Bilingual Parenting as Good Parenting: Parents' Perspectives on Family Language Policy for Additive Bilingualism'. *International Journal of Bilingual Education and Bilingualism* 9.6: 695–712.

Lewis, W.G. 2008. 'Current Challenges in Bilingual Education in Wales'. *AILA Review* 21, 69–86.
May, S. 1999. 'Language and Education Rights for Indigenous Peoples'. In ed. May, S. *Indigenous Community-based Education*. Clevedon: Multilingual Matters. 42–66.
May, S. and R. Hill. 2008. Maori-medium Education: Current Issues and Challenges. In ed. Hornberger, N.H. *Can Schools Save Indigenous Languages? Policy and Practice on Four Continents*. New York: Palgrave Macmillan. 66–98.
Nic Craith, M. 1999. 'Irish Speakers in Northern Ireland and the Good Friday Agreement. *Journal of Multilingual and Multicultural Development* 20.6: 494–507.
Ó Riagáin, P. 2001. 'Irish Language Production and Reproduction 1981–1996'. In ed. Fishman J. *Can Threatened Languages Be Saved? Reversing Language Shift Revisited: A 21st Century Perspective*. Clevedon: Multilingual Matters. 195–214.
Ó Riagáin, P. 2007. 'Relationships between Attitudes to Irish, Social Class, Religion and National Identity in the Republic of Ireland and Northern Ireland'. *International Journal of Bilingual Education and Bilingualism* 10.4: 369–93.
Singleton, D. and L. Aronin. 2007. 'Multiple Language Learning in the Light of the Theory of Affordances'. *Innovation in Language Learning and Teaching* 1.1: 83–96.
Singleton, D. and L. Ryan. 2007. 'Child Language Development in a Multilingual Environment'. Paper presented at the 10th Summer School in Psycholinguistics, Balatonalmadi, Hungary.
Swain, M. and S. Lapkin. 2005. 'The Evolving Socio-political Context of Immersion Education in Canada: Some Implications for Program Development'. *International Journal of Applied Linguistics* 15: 169–86.

# Cultural, Social, Linguistic and Environmental Issues in Minority Language Development and Maintenance

*Dónall P. Ó Baoill*

## 1. Introduction

It has been felt for some time that there is a need for a closer examination and analysis of the standard curriculum being taught in Irish/Gàidhlig-medium Education (IME/GME) schools and the development and classification of teaching materials for various cohorts of pupils in such schools. The IME schools tend to follow the same curriculum which is delivered in English medium schools. In almost all cases the curriculum in IME schools is an Irish language version which has been translated from an English original and this may be the same for Gàidhlig schools. Furthermore, there has been very little discussion of the content of the materials which are delivered in class, the methods of delivery, their cultural suitability or their environmental impact on the child's attitude and identity as envisaged for any future role (s)he wishes to fulfil within society.

This project is part of a much larger project called *Children's Voices / An Bradán Feasa*. The aims and focus of this project are to examine the impact of different types of linguistic teaching materials on cultivating an understanding of minority language culture, history and identity. Furthermore, it will focus of the social and linguistic development of minority language children whether from the Gaeltacht areas of Ireland and Scotland and in Irish/Gàidhlig medium schools in English speaking communities in Ireland both North and South and in Scotland. The research project can be divided into two core areas: (a) Integrated social and linguistic development in bilingual children; and (b) Cultural and environmental issues in minority language maintenance. The core questions pertaining to (a) will investigate the impact of the following factors on the acquisition of language and particularly social interaction and communication in different environments. Here follows some of the core questions that need to be addressed.

(a) How do children, who do not have the relevant competency in a language succeed in overcoming this barrier without recourse to English?
(b) Since the development of integrated social skills is of paramount importance in real communication, how do children begin to practise and acquire such skills within the school setting and elsewhere?
(c) How integrated in terms of their social, cultural and linguistic development should bilingual children be arising from their association with the minority language?
(d) How do the objectives of the curriculum and different syllabi being followed in schools prepare children for this integration of the necessary linguistic social skills? Does this mean a detailed examination of the available materials, teachers' understanding of their application and relevant teacher training (both pre- and post qualification)?
(e) What is the impact of language competence on the integration of language psychological/social skills? What happens in classes where there are mixed competencies? How are such classes handled in exposing all the children to supportive and stress-free contexts which develop and cultivate integrated skills?

(f) What constitutes 'successful integration' and how long does it take learners to reach an appropriate level? Are we talking about different periods up to the end of primary school and beyond?

(g) How different should the approach to integration be for the different groups from various linguistic backgrounds – native speakers from the Gaeltacht, native speakers from the Galltacht, children from an English speaking background only and children with a non-English speaking background at home?

It is necessary to discuss each of these questions in more detail in order to tease out some of the issues that are likely to arise. I will discuss each using summarised headings in the next few sections of the paper to bring related topics together for more integrated discussion.

## 2. Competency and Integrated Social Skills

There is very little known or written about integrated social skills in IME education as they do not seem to be a focused feature of teaching. Nevertheless, it appears from scrutiny of various research results that children acquire various social skills in their L2 slowly and that they are always limited in scope due to deficiencies in their language competence. A related set of question needs to be addressed, namely, who are the target speakers with whom we want to interact socially and how do children want to be integrated into such social groups, if at all? The answers to the last two questions need to be clearly iterated. Integrated and linked with curriculum design and proposed syllabi. The question of the target L1 community is a more complicated issue and one that has not received the attention and discussion that it warrants. This is of particular relevance to the IME school children outside the Gaeltacht speaking areas and impacts heavily on how we might approach the idea of 'integrational orientation' and its relevance to the L2 population in Ireland and Scotland.

We also need to formulate the various language levels appropriate to language usage at different stages in the development of L2 competency and show how they relate to the development of appropriate social skills. This will not be an easy task and a one-to-one relationship may not always be possible. There is also the question of the linguistic stages reached in both L1 and L2 and whether L2 learning is always going to lag behind and hence leaving a lacuna that never seems to be filled up. Is this one of the reasons that L2 learners reach a level/stage of interlanguage, which they seem unwilling to develop further and move towards the L1 model they should be aspiring towards, despite the valiant efforts of dedicated teachers and users of L2. It is necessary to investigate whether school settings and programme of instruction are sufficient for the acquisition of more advanced and pragmatically oriented social linguistic skills.

Children in IME interact with minority language communities and speakers in a variety of ways depending on their family background, their own competence in the language, the role schools play in bringing them into more continuous contact with native users in the Gaeltacht and outside. On the whole, they seem to be dependent to a large degree on the school domain and on their teachers. This curtails and restricts their use of more appropriate registers and intimate language with which they are familiar in their L1. There is a definite link between the acquisition of integrated social, cultural and linguistic skills and the level of language achieved by learners and their exposure to domains of usage which form a crucial bridge towards developing a healthy bilingual sociolinguistic and pragmatic competence. This is an area of study which needs more detailed study, analysis and investigation before any definite conclusions can ne reached and recommendations based on them can be made.

What constitutes 'successful integration' and how long does it take learners to reach an appropriate level? Are we talking about different periods up to the end of primary school and beyond? It would seem that linguistic integration is difficult to evaluate and takes various forms all through life. One might ask whether or not children in IME want to integrate in any 'real' way with children within the own age cohort in the Gaeltacht or elsewhere. What reasons would they give for having such ambitions – are they personal, social, linguistic, based on mutual interest on a multiplicity of factors? The Gaeltacht seems a long way off for many children in IME and their parents – the amount of time they can spend there is going to be limited. How, then can the gaps in linguistic interaction with their peers be filled outside of the school domain? There is an urgent need to undertake research to identify these gaps and make practical recommendations on how they can be remedied through learning and practice.

## 3. Curricula and Syllabi

How do the objectives of the curriculum and different syllabi being followed in schools prepare children for this integration of the necessary linguistic social skills? Does this mean a detailed examination of the available materials, teachers' understanding of their application and relevant teacher training (both pre- and post qualification)? The type of social interaction under discussion probably means a greater emphasis on speech and on colloquial usage – something which is difficult to acquire outside the classroom situation. There is a tendency among learners in general to focus on a particular restricted set of usages for particular constructions and idiomatic phrases. This leads to an overkill at times and produces many ungrammatical forms and correct pragmatic use of language is seldom met with in ordinary speech. Things are slightly better in the written norm as this receives particular attention or focus within almost all teaching approaches. There is a certain kind of middle class standardised language to be acquired as the essential ingredient for future success at all levels of the educational system. Teachers are trained and well prepared to deliver the inner core of language which is so essential for all learners with every ambition of reaching set standards and objectives. Here again we know little of the linguistic content of texts and other resources used in IME classrooms which strive to achieve these goals.

In overall summary terms, this research would involve different methods and approaches – gathering of statistics via questionnaires, direct observation, analysis of available teaching and instructional materials, information on pre- and in-service training for teachers dealing with instruction through the medium of a minority language, the setting of achievable objectives and developing parents' understanding of minority language maintenance and the role of minority language medium education in cultivating and supporting this objective.

## 4. Cultural and Environmental Issues in Minority Language Maintenance

The focus of this project lies in investigating the content of all materials to which children being taught through the medium of a minority language are exposed at different periods of their learning careers. It is imperative that the following areas at least be investigated by the research programme.

## 4.1 Linguistic Content and its Appropriateness.

While much has been achieved within IME programmes, there has been little discussion of the 'real' content of extant teaching materials and on how they promote the learners understanding of culture and the importance of environmental issues in promoting minority language culture and identity. There is a basic question that needs to be fore grounded, namely, what do we mean by culture in the Irish or Scottish context? How is it different from the English language culture of the two countries? What significant part does Irish/Gáidhlig as languages play in cultivating and promoting new imaginative and innovative approaches to the maintenance and extension of a minority culture under threat from a dominant world language and its accompanying influences? Unless we succeed in developing our thinking in this important area which should form the foundation of our future teaching, then we will have failed in realising one of our core objectives. Learners need to be fully aware of the living realities which every vibrant minority language community is exposed to on a daily basis. This training is a prerequisite in order to assist speakers and users of minority language to engage meaningfully with the constant cultural and linguistic tensions and contradictions pertaining to sociolinguistic realities of bilingual communities.

## 4.2 Cultural Content and its Nature.

What exactly should be the cultural content of teaching and other materials that children are exposed to through Irish or Gàidhlig medium education and teaching? This is a subject that has not been discussed very much in any research literature – much is taken for granted. However, in light of the development of modern societies and children's exposure to global culture and exchange, there is a greater need than ever to outline and clarify our approach to all matters related to this issue.

There is a genuine and urgent need to look afresh at how cultural concepts can be extended to newer and modern contexts and modified in innovative ways to express emerging ideas, concepts and understandings. The necessity to do this results in the majority of cases to unceasing exposure to a macro world culture which is at times very alien to the genius and make up of minority languages whose domains of usage have been curtailed and reduced. Unless we succeed in convincing learners and adult speakers alike that this is a worthwhile and achievable objective, we will have little chance in arranging and promoting materials which will cultivate and enhance a mutual identity and a proper understanding of our common cause.

## 4.3 Exposure to Environmental and Historical Materials.

Teachers when relating their experiences about teaching certain subjects often mention the teaching of history, geography and religion as particularly difficult. When asked why, one almost always receives very general answers – devoid of specifics and therefore hard to pin down. Dialectal material unfamiliar to learners is often blamed as are translations of English texts used into Irish which are blamed as being unnatural in expression and devoid of imaginative methods of presentation and delivery in class. They do not interact personally with the learners and their experiences which they have acquired through the medium of English and/or other languages. While it is obvious that there is a question of language usage and difficulty of expression, there is also an urgent need to look at what knowledge and information is being transferred to the learners or native speakers and what from such information should take. This requires us to dig deeper in order to explain in a more meaningful way what constitutes culture at present for Irish or Gàidhlig speakers. This also imposes certain language restrictions on how such information is being imparted. This is the weak link in the chain and until we get to the core of the matter, our efforts at teaching indigenous minority languages and converting them into an efficient tool to prepare minority communities to acquire the essential skills and education required for full participation in minority language maintenance.

Both Irish and Gàidhlig have at their disposal a rich and varied cultural tradition in written form as well as a strong oral component of storytelling, folklore and singing which should form the basis on which teaching and instructing materials should be based. There is a need of course to bring successful modern methods of teaching as well as developing the required interactive tools and resources that children and learners have become used to and expect to have available to them in the context of both school and home. This would help bring the subject to life and convey to children the importance of language not just for communication purposes but as a tool that carries old and living traditions to future generations and when this is made more attractive and interesting through the minority language, it leaves a lasting impact on their own linguistic development and prepares them to become better citizens in the future. This requires detailed planning of interesting syllabi and teaching materials to instil in children the worth associated with their minority language and how it can contribute to new and innovating developments which contribute to the economic and cultural development of the people and the environment in which they live. Above all, all of our endeavours to promote and maintain minority languages must at all time focus on presenting the minority language as a living modern culture which can contribute substantially not only to its own survival but enhance and enrich other languages and cultures which they come into contact with through a wide range of human interaction. Therefore, there is a great onus on the educational system to bring minority language children to high interactive linguistic levels in order to equip them for full participation in maintaining and cultivating their minority language and its culture to the highest possible degree.

### 4.4 Science, New Technology and Indigenous Minority Languages

There has been much talk and debate among teachers about imparting essential knowledge to children and the teaching of specific subjects. The debate seems to revolve around the linguistic content of different subjects and teaching packages as I have already alluded to. It definitely also applies to the teaching of scientific information where the focus is on the indigenous culture and its general environment. Once more there is an urgent necessity to define the meaning of 'indigenous' in our present context and to outline broadly what the main lines of approach should be in trying to reach our target outputs. The power and availability of computers, the internet and mobile phones for example as means for modern communication and interaction with people of your own age, with people with similar or different lifestyles and cultures is very attractive to young people. If this is done through the medium of your own minority language, then it demonstrates the power and usefulness of language, its capacity as a vehicle for high level communication across a wide spectrum of people. This widens children's horizon and instils in them a pride in their own language, culture and experience.

The first step is to analyse the content of the materials available vis-à-vis language, culture and historical/environmental content. Science presents us with a particular challenge in developing out minority language resources by inventing new linguistic creations bases on native structures and understandings and applying these in the preparation of teaching materials, through computer study programmes and integrative scientific/cultural advances where the minority language is being stretched to newer limits and cultivated in new and challenging ways.

This should be done with the help and assistance of teachers and other educators who have realised concerns about such matters.

Secondly, there is a need to isolate the major strands running through the presentation of materials and how these impact on learning and social integration by children in Irish/Gàidhlig medium schools. Unless they can be identified and further refined, then setting of achievable objectives and outputs will still be out of reach.

The linguistic debate continues and seems to revole around issues relating to national versus local language/dialect, the use of idiomatic language, cultural content and expression which some learners find difficult to conceptualize. It is difficult to get practitioners to focus on these specific issues and to propose solutions.

Furthermore, there is an urgent need for teachers and parents to reflect on their role in understanding how minority medium education cultivates, supports and sustains minority language communities and their cultures. All of this must involve issues of curriculum, teaching orientation and training, family/school liaison programmes to help integrate the work of schools with the immediate localities in which the children live , environmental interaction relating to history, geography, place-names, lore, cultural behaviour as well as integrational orientation and citizenship in young children.

### 4.5 Research Issues

The research would involve different methods and approaches among different subgroups. We need detailed factual statistical information collected through questionnaires, analysis of available instructional materials, the relevance of in-service training for teachers in the Irish/Gàidhlig-medium sector and the role of parents and other providers in developing children's competence and confidence to interact and integrate through the medium of a minority language.

We need to show a great deal more in terms of detailed description about the nature of the 'cultural elements' to be taught, how best to integrate environmental and historical information, the language content (national versus local, idiomatic expression, cultural expressions, etc.), setting of achievable objectives and developing parents' understanding of minority language maintenance and the role of minority language medium education in cultivating and supporting this objective and a cross-comparison with other minority languages in similar contexts.

### References

Brooks, N. 1986. 'Culture in the Classroom'. In ed. Valdes J.M. *Culture Bound: Bridging the Cultural Gap in Language Teaching*. Cambridge: Cambridge University Press. 123–8.

Byram, M. 1986. *Minority Education and Ethnic Survival: Case study of a German School in Denmark*. Multilingual Matters 20. Clevedon: Multilingual Matters.

MacCaluim, A. 2007. *Reversing Language Shift: The Social identity and Role of Adult Learners of Scottish Gaelic*. Belfast Studies in Language, Culture and Politics 17. Belfast: Cló Ollscoil na Banríona.

Mac Corraidh, S. 2008. Ar thóir an dea-chleachtais: *The Quest for Best practice in Irish-medium Primary Schools in Belfast*. Belfast Studies in Language, Culture and Politics 18. Belfast Cló Ollscoil na Banríona..

Ó Baoill, D.P. 1999. 'Social cultural distance, integrational orientation and the learning of Irish'. In eds. Chambers A. and D.P. Ó Baoill, *Intercultural Communication and Language Learning*. Dublin: IRAAL. 189–200.

Walsh, R.B. 1976. 'Difficulties encountered by Hiberno-Irish Speakers in Using the Sound System of Irish and French'. Text of a Lecture Given on 24.4.1976 under the auspices of IRAAL.

# Research Development and the Implementation of Am Bradán Feasa Programme: Early Thinking of the Potential within a Social Issues / Applied Language Work-Stream

*Morag M. MacNeil and Dónall P. Ó Baoill*

Introduction

The conference paper on which this contribution to the Proceedings is based sits within the research strand of the work programme being developed at the time under the auspices of Am Bradán Feasa and its theme of 'Researching Children's Voices'. It reflects early exploratory thinking within the work-stream which focused on issues associated with the social and educational development of children living in the three jurisdictions of Northern Ireland, the Republic of Ireland and Scotland, and who could be defined by, or associated with, minority languages and cultures.

At the start, the thinking was influenced by three social trends. Across Scotland, Northern Ireland and the Republic of Ireland, there were (and still are) concerns about the diminishing numbers of speakers of the autochthonous lesser-used languages of Gaelic and Irish.[1] This has highlighted the need for enhanced understanding of the key structural, socio-linguistic and family-based factors associated with revitalisation of the more fragile languages and cultures which co-exist with a world language such as English.

Quite separately, the impact of the enlargement of the European Union on immigration had created new language communities (and combinations of language communities) again across the three jurisdictions.

There were also major changes being implemented which influenced how services were to be delivered to children, particularly in education. This incorporated changes in the curriculum;[2] integrated service provision to take account of the child beyond attainment indicators and across a much wider range of measures of achievement and well-being than was previously the case.[3] The trends have been similar across the three jurisdictions.

None of the above trends were in themselves new, but taken together they were new at the time and they raised new questions to be considered and explored both in the context of sustaining minority language communities and in the context of developing a base-line understanding of social issues within our diverse communities.

This work-stream enhanced the range of broadly social issues for potential inclusion in the multi-disciplinary programme being taken forward by the development team of An Bradán Feasa in place at the time. It was being explored in order to assess the potential for expanding the frameworks and projects being developed concurrently around the critical socio-political and socio-linguistic areas into enquiries focused on individual and group experiences of children whose association with a minority language or culture highlighted one kind of difference from the mainstream, one kind

---

[1] See for example the work of MacKinnon (e.g. 2010) on Gaelic in Scotland and the work of Ó Riagáin (e.g. 2001) on Gaeilge.

[2] See for example the documentation in place for implementation of the Curriculum for Excellence in Scotland.

[3] The *getting it right for every child* approach developed by the Scottish Government is a good example of this.

of potential groups of factors which could impact, positively or negatively, on normative aspects associated with attainment, achievement, social inclusion, well-being and general social and emotional health.

The issues discussed here emerged from the consideration of three key questions:

- What difference is a minority language likely to make for the child in holistic terms, strengthening or weakening the body of factors which influence the extent to which the potential of the child can be optimised in terms of potential for achieving and also in terms of general well-being and resilience in a changing world?
- What can be learned from an enhanced understanding of the impact on individual children which could be used at language community levels to support and sustain minority languages and their culture?
- And what elements of knowledge transfer (already known understanding in the field and new research findings) have the robustness to transfer horizontally across the different kinds of minority languages which form part of the social fabric in the three jurisdictions which could most effectively be incorporated into the initial and ongoing course development addressing the main work activity of An Bradán Feasa?

From these key questions, interest began to focus on the way language communities were currently operating and how they were impacting on every aspect of children's lives. In short, the overarching question boiled down to what being part of a specific language community might actually mean for a child.

**Ideas for Taking Forward**

Two clusters of ideas emerged from the early thinking, both exploring a range of potential impacts and outcomes and both beginning to map out the key areas from which relevant data could be obtained.

The first looked at what would be involved in a detailed consideration of the inter-relationship between levels of language competence and evidence of the development of age-appropriate social skills in children who speak a minority language. It was also felt that issues of identification and integration with a minority language community was also likely to impact on social development within and beyond the home setting. This emerged from the ideas pulled together by Professor Dónall Ó Baoill of Queen's University Belfast around how issues associated with language competency and associated social skills were associated with the broader issues associated with language development, revitalisation and maintenance at community levels (see Ó Baoill in this volume).

A second cluster of ideas focused on relevant sets of questions arising from an enquiry on how bilingual or multilingual children structured their concepts of their communities, how they learned to operate within these constructs, their understanding of them and the extent to which this impacted on their sense of belonging. Here it was felt that more could be learned about how children were able to do this with language skills still in development (as is predictably the case in immersion contexts) and the extent to which language competence levels influenced the attainment of the necessary levels of age-appropriate understanding, and associated patterns of behaviour, in these areas. Initial thoughts around these issues were pulled together by Dr Morag MacNeil at the University of Edinburgh's School of Education. The two areas shared a great deal in common.

## General Approach Taken

Both sets of ideas were embedded in an applied and reality-based approach throughout the discussions. In this work-stream, the main focus was on considering language and cultural factors in terms of potential correlations with social outcomes (though the impact of social factors on language issues was also kept in the frame). The aim was to keep the focus on the whole child and the totality of environments likely to be part of the entity of the child's social world.

## Multi-disciplinary Positioning

It was recognised that the thinking of how to operationalise these ideas in research terms would need to take account of a number of disciplines and indeed work towards an appropriate interdisciplinary framework. Initial thinking had identified the need to explore how belonging to both discrete minority language communities and operating within broader multi-language communities could be conceptualised within disciplines associated with social and language development such as sociolinguistics, education and child development.

## The Types of Data to be Accessed or Collected

It was recognised that large data sets, already in place or obtained regularly on a statutory basis, could provide strong contextual background for any work undertaken as part of this work-stream. For example, national or large group normative statistics, applicable to all children, could provide base-level indicators, including impact and outcome patterns against which children defined by linguistic and cultural descriptors could be compared.

Though much was known about some of the language elements relating to the autochthonous languages in the three jurisdictions, it was acknowledged that more needed to be known, linking to what also would help enhance levels of understanding of the position of all the minority languages present across the locations in question. Updates on numbers of speakers and their key descriptors such as age, gender and other markers were felt to be important in understanding the family context and the language parameters surrounding the child. Domains of language usage were felt to be part of the linguistic influences determining the sociolinguistic footprint of the language communities inhabited by the child. In addition, the broader socio-political reviews and updates of the range of languages spoken in the multi-linguistic communities of the three jurisdictions were also considered an important background context in looking at the child's relationship to language and perception of belonging.

Of course, the social communities which children inhabit are likely to be broader than their language communities. But it is language which is likely to link the various entities of the child's world. It is language which provides the synaptic links which gives a child the understanding of what is expected, which carries the explanations of positions taken, which demonstrates patterns for negotiating social issues and provides cultural and ethical rationales.

---

[4] Examples here could include centrally held Government statistics, HMI reports in Education and in Children's Services, and specially commissioned reviews of outcomes such as that undertaken by Johnstone et al, 1999.

Because of this, aggregated data sets on measures of language competence at all developmental stages were felt to be a critical area for data gathering, across all the work streams of Am Bradán Feasa, particularly where language could be seen to impact on understanding the social norms in the range of social communities across which all children navigate. This would be equally appropriate for attainment data and could greatly facilitate the analysis of patterns associated with different groups of interest across different language communities and in different educational contexts.[4]

**Potential Groups of Interest**

In each of the three jurisdictions, children from two main categories were of interest. The first was based on the kind of communities in which the children live and could include communities autochthonous to the location or region, other well-established ethnic communities and also the more newly formed communities, encompassing the new wave of European immigrants.

A second categorisation could focus on the language of instruction at school, and whether it is the first or second (or indeed third) language of the children sampled. (There are of course further variations on potential additional groups, such as children whose first language is English, taught through English, but the main focus of An Bradán Feasa Programme was to focus on the smaller language groups, though comparative projects may become of interest as the shape of the Programme and how it will be implemented becomes more clear.)

Stages and transitions were felt to be central to this work-stream. An early years focus incorporating pre-school, transition to school and the first stages of primary schooling can be expected to produce rich data in terms of socialisation and patterns of language use. It is anticipated that older children will be of particular interest as broader social and linguistic factors come into play, particularly around the transition phase of moving into secondary education and the teenage years.

Other factors of interest influencing decisions about what kind of data bases to build up could be structured around gender, social background and of course language. Patterns of language use at home and language of instruction in school could be of value in understanding the social milieu in which children operate.

Outcome data was also seen to be needed, for example across cognitive and attainment measures, and though much in this area is continuously and routinely collected, a marker was put down for reviewing what was actually in place, how it was aggregated and the extent to which there was any potential for breaking down what was aggregated in order to explore cross-linkages with new data obtained from smaller studies incorporating specific issues building from measures of interest around the individual child. For example, in this context, indicators could be used to identify particular social skills and levels of maturity in understanding social concepts and constructs which support learning and development, and can in turn be analysed by key descriptors associated with a range of language factors.

**Potential Methods**

Though some thought had been given to methods which would be applicable within this work-stream and the two sets of ideas forming the basis for project development within it, it was too early in the process to do more than explore a range of potential ways of accessing and collecting the data which would be required.

There was a recognition that the questions of interest to this work-stream could best be answered from mixed method frameworks. This could include, as mentioned above, secondary analyses of databases. Documentary analysis was also felt to be important for providing a structural background for what was likely to be in place in the classrooms of interest. Structured and semi-structured observations schedules could be used, to establish reference points for language capacity, social skills and understanding of the social milieu and ethos in which children must learn to survive and develop. Various real or constructed scenarios could be explored in workshops to capture the thinking of the younger children. Interviews and surveys with key stakeholders would help in exploring ideas in this context, though initial testing of how this would work would of necessity need to be with small numbers.

**Additional Questions Emerging from Early Discussions**

Some very broad areas for question development had emerged at the time of writing, for example:

- What transition strategies/tactics do children employ in ordering their social world before they are competent in the language of instruction?
- What elements of the curriculum help children to integrate their linguistic and social skills?
- What are the indicators of successful integration of these skills and how alike are they for all groups?
- What is currently in place for helping children to consider issues of complex identity and citizenship, at all stages of education (including curriculum content, language of delivery, classroom ethos and implicit and explicit social values being transmitted) in order to explore the potential for helping children value cultural and ethnic diversity and understand that diversity need not undermine the cohesion of communities?
- How is this interpreted in the social management and the teaching styles, particularly in terms of how children are helped to develop ideas about equality, inclusion and fairness and practise ways of sharing, taking turns, negotiating and similar social skills?
- How do teachers address the language development areas needed to encourage the behavioural and attitudinal outcomes associated with social cohesion, inclusion, resolution of conflict, respect for difference and development of shared values as children grow?
- How do levels of language competence impact on the behavioural and developmental indicators associated with the above social actions and how do children use their communicative competences (English, Gaelic, Gaeilge, and immigrant languages) to develop the way they shape their relationships with others?
- How do groups of children regard their cultural and community identities, particularly where these are in shift and how does this impact on their sense of wellbeing and integrated developmental needs as a whole?
- How do schools, teachers, families and community leader transmit the most appropriate ethos in multicultural and multilingual communities, particularly around establishing a balance between supporting and valuing each of the cultures in question while promoting a sense of belonging to a broader and more diverse community?

These were the broader of the research questions and many other questions are subsumed within them, to work towards helping our understanding of how children use language to order and define their social space and make sense of their social world.

**Knowledge Transfer**

It was anticipated that developments here could support knowledge transfer particularly for teacher education, support for parents and on a broader basis, contributing to the understanding of what enhances how minority groups, new and autochthonous, can operate to the social good in our diverse community landscapes.

**Some References**

Baker, C. 2000. *The Care and Education of Young Bilinguals*. Clevedon: Multilingual Matters.
Baker, C. 2006. *Foundations of Bilingual Education and Bilingualism*. Fourth Edition. Clevedon: Multilingual Matters.
GRSO (General Register Office Scotland). Various Census Reports.
Harris, J., Forde, P., Archer, P., Nic Fhearaile, S. and S. O'Gorman. 2006. *Irish in Primary Schools: Long-term National Trends in Achievement*. Dublin: Department of Education and Science.
HMIE (Her Majesty's Inspectorate of Education). 2009. *Improving Scottish Education 2005–2008 (Gaelic)*. Edinburgh: HMIE.
Johnstone, R. et al. 1999. *The Attainments of Pupils Receiving Gaelic-medium Primary Education in Scotland*. Stirling: Scottish CILT University of Stirling.
Learning and Teaching Scotland. 2002. *Education for Citizenship for Scotland*. Dundee: Learning and Teaching Scotland.
Macdonald, S. ed. 1997. *Inside European Identities*. Oxford: Berg.
MacKinnon, K. 2010. 'The Gaelic Language Group: Demography, Language-Usage, Transmission, and Shift'. In eds. Watson, M. and M. Macleod, *The Edinburgh Companion to the Gaelic Language*. Edinburgh: Edinburgh University Press. 128–145.
MacNeil, M. and R. Stradling. 2000. *Emergent Identities and Bilingual Education*, Isle of Skye: Leirsinn Research.
MacNeil, M.M. 2003. 'The Education and Training of Teachers of Lesser Used Languages: Working Towards a Template for Progress'. In ed. Schiavi-Fachin, S. *L'Educazione Plurilingue* (Plurilingual Education). Udine: University of Udine Press. 193–212.
MacNeil, M., Schiavi-Fachin, S. and L. Nicoloso. 2009. *Guide for Teachers / Guide pai insegnants / Guida per gli insegnanti*, Udine: Agjenzie Regjonal pe Lenghe Furlane.
Ó Riagáin, P. 2001. 'Irish language Production and Reproduction, 1981–1996'. In ed. Fishman, J. *Can Threatened Languages Be Saved?* Clevedon: Multilingual Matters. 195–214.
Osler, A. and H. Starkey. 2005. *Changing Citizenship: Democracy and Inclusion in Education*. Maidenhead: Open University Press.
Robinson, J.B. 1996. 'Falling between Schools: Some Thoughts on the Theory and Pactice of Interdisciplinarity'. In eds. Salter, L and A. Hearn, *Outside the Lines:*

*Issues in Interdisciplinary Research*. Montreal: McGill-Queen's University Press. 85–93.

Scottish Executive. 2002. *National Priorities in Education*. Edinburgh: The Scottish Executive.

Scottish Government. 2008. *A Framework for Learning and Teaching*. Edinburgh: The Scottish Government.

Scottish Government. 2009. *Building the Curriculum: Skills for Learning, Skills for Life and Skills for Work*. Edinburgh: The Scottish Government.

Stradling, R. and M. MacNeil. 2000. *Home and Community: Their Role in Enhancing the Gaelic Language Competencies of Children in Gaelic-medium Education*. Isle of Skye, Leirsinn Research.

Stradling, B and MacNeil, M. 2007. *Delivering Integrated Services for Children in Highland: An Overview of Challenges, Developments and Outcomes*. Inverness, UHI Millennium Institute.

# Language Shift and Cultural Identity in the Gàidhealtachd: What Prospect for the Cultural Identity?[1]

*John Galloway*

The Highlands and Islands enjoy the popular reputation of being culturally distinct and for some ninety percent of the area – most of the Highland mainland and the Hebrides – this is represented by the Gaelic heritage. Features of Gaelic culture have been documented in this area over some six centuries since a Highland/Lowland divide became apparent with the spread of English language and cultural influences across the Lowlands; Fordoun's chronicle of the 1380s distinguished the Gaelic world across geography, language and way of life (Skene 1880). Distinct cultural elements cited in more recent times include language and literature; music, song and dance; a notable appreciation of ancestry, kinship, community and a 'sense of place', vernacular architecture, food and drink, work associated with the land and the sea, folklore, entertainments, sport and pastimes.

This cultural distinctiveness is often invoked by local authorities and a variety of organisations in claiming special status for the area: as an attraction for tourists, as a unique and rich heritage which can be enjoyed by the employees of relocating companies; as the basis for establishing regular cultural exchange visits and cooperative ventures with Ireland and Nova Scotia; and as a reason for special consideration of applications for funding (Visit Scotland 2005; Visit Highlands 2007; Visit Hebrides 2007; Highlands and Islands Enterprise 2007; Government of Nova Scotia 2007). The advantages gained have been held to benefit the population in general: "(T)he Highland Council recognises the educational, artistic, cultural, social and economic importance of Gaelic in underpinning our place in the modern world" (Highland Council 2007). The undoubted importance of Gaelic culture to Scotland as a whole has been officially acknowledged as a cultural expression which "is significantly in excess of what one might expect from a fragile minority community" (Scottish Executive 2003), attracting an international appreciation disproportionate to the country's size and population. This widespread interest applies to the language itself (Galloway 1995) and has been shown to represent an economic resource (Sproull and Ashcroft 1993; Chalmers 2003).

However, the increased recognition, celebration and economic benefit of this cultural distinctiveness over the past fifty years has coincided with a continued decrease in the number and proportion of Gaelic speakers in the population of the Gàidhealtachd (Census 1991/2001). Causal factors are commonly acknowledged: continued out-migration, language shift within the remaining native population, in-migration of monoglot English-speakers, the influence of the mass media. Less commonly perceived are the questions raised by the effect: what part does the Gaelic language play in Gaelic culture; can the celebrated cultural distinctiveness survive a continuing diminution of the Gaelic-speaking population; what are the prospects for maintenance of the cultural identity of the Highlands and Islands?

## Concepts of Culture and Cultural Distinction

The term 'culture' is popularly used in a loose, inexact manner; in more serious considerations, academics across several fields have proposed over a hundred definitions according to the needs of particular studies. For simplicity and practical relevance, two

---
[1] This paper was first published in *Scottish Gaelic Studies*, vol. XXIII, 2007, pp. 201–12.

general definitions are helpful: one by Edward Sapir in 1921: culture is "what a society does and thinks", and that formulated by UNESCO in 1982 and adopted by the past Scottish Executive, which is more specific about what the doing and thinking encompasses:

> ... in its widest sense, culture may now be said to be the whole complex of distinctive spiritual, material, intellectual and emotional features that characterize a society or social group. It includes not only the arts and letters, but also modes of life, the fundamental rights of the human being, value systems, traditions and beliefs.

Cultures are distinguishable by their discreteness: human societies have at least some ways of 'doing' and 'thinking' which are different to others. Inevitably, this is linked to different senses of identity, as the people in these societies are aware of their own ways of doing and thinking and in many cases prefer them to other ways and are hence wary of external cultural influences. Such sensitivity is often particularly well developed in smaller societies which feel under the threat of cultural 'swamping' by larger ones. While larger and/or economically dominant societies are usually able to maintain their own ways of doing and thinking, and to initiate, choose and drive forward such cultural change as members of the society desire, smaller societies often lack the requisite size of population, the economic strength, and the political clout to promote their own ways of doing and thinking, and to exercise choice to the same degree. We often find, amongst such smaller societies, members who are in a state of resistance to changes induced or imposed by the encroachment of dominant cultures.

Cultures have always borrowed from each other, and all ways of doing and thinking are subject to change. Yet, where it has been historical, the sense of a cultural distinction often remains strong, especially between adjoining societies, even where objective analysis can find few elements of difference in people's lives. An explanation of the persistence of such feeling was given by Barth (1969), who proposed that metaphysical 'boundaries' between groups are the important factor in maintaining their identities, rather than the 'cultural content' which the boundaries enclose. Such mental boundaries may sometimes be the main factor, but there are many cases where the 'cultural content' appears to have a key significance; groups whose cultural distinction is, for the most part, compromised, may deliberately nurture traditional elements of their culture to confirm the integrity of the group. (This nurturing of the identity may be reinforced by the re-modelling of tradition: in the Scottish context, distinctive and accessible Gaelic cultural symbols have been adopted as pan-Scottish ones – hence the wearing of Highland dress at Burns Suppers, rather than the eighteenth century Lowland 'hoddin grey' jacket and breeks which Burns himself wore.)

In this context of 'cultural content' we should note Jerzy Smolicz's (1981, 1992) introduction of the idea that 'core values' – for example, language, religion, music, attention to traditions of kinship – maintain groups' cultural distinction. These core values may not be the same for all cultures, but within each group, Smolicz reckoned, they are the foundation of the sense of separate identity, and their demise hastens the loss of that sense and the merging of the group with another. This is an attractive explanation, although it has to be borne in mind that Smolicz drew on the specific cases of immigrant communities at a particular time in a particular plural society (Australia). Nevertheless, the theory's application to many threatened cultures in their homelands seems apt, and if we consider the range of 'core values' which appear to be cherished amongst cultures in general, no core value seems to be so widely regarded as vital to cultural individuality as language.

## The Role of Language in Culture

At a fundamental level – the evolution of human culture in general – the biologist Allott (1999) perceived the faculty of language as the 'missing link' which facilitated cultural development: "the foundation of culture ... the source of the human cultural potential ... the mode of transmission and of change of cultural systems ... the form through which cultural systems are originated".

Such a view is consistent with one of the founding ideas in the field of modern sociolinguistics, the Sapir-Whorf or Whorfian hypothesis, which, based on studies of differences between North American and European languages, proposes that people who speak different languages are likely to have different cultural outlooks, because the particular structure of each language induces a different cultural structuring of reality. This was not an original idea: Schlesinger (1991) summarised commentators on the perceived correlation between linguistic and culture differences from Francis Bacon (1561–1626) onwards, but Sapir, and later Whorf, articulated it in the context of modern research, as 'linguistic relativity'.

The stronger interpretations of the Sapir-Whorf hypothesis – the implication of an acquired immutability of mindset, with the language of upbringing inducing a fundamentally discrete mentality – is nowadays regarded as insufficiently supported by evidence. Many millions throughout the world are bilingual, and effectively bicultural from an early age, and it is clear that the human mind can understand and adapt to concepts prevalent in other cultures. However, there is evidence of some sort of connection between language, culture and thought (Cooper and Spolsky, 1991).

A less prescriptive, but more plausible general theory in the 'language begets culture' vein was suggested by Joshua Fishman (1991): that particular languages are linked to particular cultures; that a language "is, at any times during which that linkage is still intact, best able to name the artifacts and to formulate or express the interests, values and world-views of that culture". He proposed that 'language-based culture' – comprising elements such as oral history, genealogy, folklore, customs, seasonal observances, music and song etc – does not survive language shift, and in the event of a language falling into disuse – a process to which minority language speech-communities are susceptible when in contact with a majority language society – the residual culture is different to that associated with the language. He did not, however, cite particular evidence.

Fishman felt that language and culture are also linked because most of the culture is expressed in the language and because, for its speakers, language represents or symbolises their culture (Fishman 1996). Very often this seems true: time and again we come across instances of the value placed on language, especially by speakers of minority languages. To give a few reported examples, we find it amongst the Sorbs (Stephens 1976), the Sami (Eidheim 1969), the Faroese (Sandoy 1992), the Galicians (Pedersen 1989), the Frisians (Van der Plank 1987), the Irish (Ó Riagáin and Ó Gliasáin 1994), Romansh-speakers (Camathias 1971), and the Welsh (Osmond 1988). There is also no doubt as to the eagerness with which groups such the Basques, Catalans, Indonesians, Koreans, Latvians, and Lithuanians moved towards legislation supportive of their language when they achieved partial or full political autonomy. Smolicz (*ibid.*) reported that Ukranian-Australians' continued use of their language is the main plank of their self-perceived cultural distinction and sense of identity.

There is thus wide support for the idea of language being a vital part of culture.

Taking a global perspective, proponents of this link often cite the dangers attending the loss of individual languages and also languages in general, in respect of the linguistic – and hence cultural – diversity they represent, which is sometimes held to be as important for humanity and the planet as biodiversity (Woodbury 1993, 1998; Krauss 1992; Skutnabb-Kangas 2000). These arguments would appear to support the interests of minority language activists, whose anxiety is easy to understand, as many minority languages, long-established in use across everyday domains and held in affection by their speakers as a professed symbolic and emotional link to their cultural identity and heritage, have become increasingly threatened by language shift.

However, instances where language is not thought so important have to be acknowledged. Some groups do manage to discontinue language use while retaining other 'core values' on which they base their cultural distinction. For example, Pandharipande (1992) reports speech communities in India who are not concerned about losing their language, because they feel they can preserve their cultural identity through their traditional rituals, dress patterns, food habits, and their "unique values." Jerzy Smolicz (*ibid.*) cited Italian-Australians – in contrast to Ukrainian-Australians – as showing little interest in retaining everyday use of their language, but maintaining their integrity as an identifiable group through retention of their bonds of kinship as the key marker. It is also true that the argument for the uniqueness and preciousness of the knowledge imbued by each linguistic 'window on the world' can be pursued too far, as in the supposition that this knowledge cannot be expressed or fully understood in any language except the original, and that it will pass from human experience with the last speaker. Translations may lack the art of the original expression, but they can certainly convey knowledge: when Whorf himself wished to explain the expression of time in the languages he studied, he was able to translate them into English, and thereby give his readers a good understanding of another way of thinking. Moreover, language does not always reflect a native wisdom as profound, nor a cultural resource as invaluable, as is sometimes perceived: for example, the oft-quoted claim that the Inuit language has words for 400 different kinds of snow, reflecting a unique knowledge of particular environmental conditions, is reportedly false (Pullum 1991). There are, apparently, just two 'root' words for snow, which can be combined with other words to make compounds – just as English uses 'snow' in snowflake, snowstorm, snowdrift, snowhole, snowman, snowball, snowshoe etc.

On balance, however, language has widespread acknowledgement as a fundamental component of culture. Perhaps its role was well summarised thus: that language does not determine what can be thought, but it influences routinely what *does* get thought (Leowenstein and Ocasio, 2005). Returning to the idea of 'a culture' being 'a way of doing and thinking', the linguistic requirement for the framing of thoughts and consideration of familiar knowledge, practices and actions presents an arguable case for the importance of language.

**Language Shift and the Particular Case of Gaelic**

The present significance of a fundamental link between language and culture lies in the implication that language shift will affect other aspects of culture. Here, it has to be acknowledged that a 'chicken and egg' argument might be made: the intrusion of external cultural influences can be held to induce language shift. However, it has to be considered that – as Fishman (1991) proposed – certain language-specific elements must decline with the language itself. Language shift can proceed to language death in a locality within two generations, with dramatic effect: Fishman concluded that the cultural change thus induced is "a sudden and catastrophic separation from the communal cultural achievement"; Crystal (2000) observed that "(T)he loss of a language is certainly the nearest thing to a serious heart attack that a culture can suffer", while Dorian (1987) proposed a universal pattern:

"Quite typically the threatened language community is also dispossessed of its heritage, often astonishingly ignorant of such basic information as where the ancestral population came from, what the original nature of their means of livelihood was, how their cultural institutions functioned, and what their traditional lore (songs, stories, proverbs, humour, satire or invective, artwork, crafts) was like."

Dorian wrote with regard to the Gaelic of East Sutherland, and her comments find support in observations of trends concomitant with the decline of other local Gaelic speech- communities: the loss of cultural knowledge passed on by Gaelic-mediated oral tradition (Grant 1961; Shaw 1986; Dorian 1981; Bennett 1989; MacArthur 1990; Watson 1992); lack of traditional entertainment skills (MacKinnon and MacDonald, 1980); and changes in traditional music (Shaw 1991; MacDonald 1994).

**Speculating on the Future**

To summarise answers to the first two of the questions posed at the beginning of this paper: the Gaelic language seems to be a vital part of certain aspects of Gaelic culture; cultural knowledge and skills mediated by the language do not survive intergenerational shift to English. Together, the potential loss of the language and language-based knowledge and skills at community level would appear to substantially undermine the Gàidhealtachd's cultural distinctiveness, as many non-language-based aspects of culture in the domains of work, home life and recreation have been supplanted by others from the dominant English-language world. In such circumstances, it might be increasingly difficult for claims for a separate cultural identity to be made with much evidence of validity.

Against that, it may be argued that Gaelic-medium education is a social, educational and cultural success, and while it cannot replace the lost Gaelic-speaking majority, it maintains a Gaelic presence and related cultural activities in many communities where they would otherwise have been lost. In addition, it might be expected that traditions such as folklore, storytelling and crafts would be replaced in the course of communities' accommodation to newer forms of entertainment and technology, and in more recent years – in contrast to the decline in the number of Gaelic-speakers – traditional song, music and dance have flourished with encouragement from public and private funding. It seems possible that these and other elements of Gaelic culture could – granted sufficient popular support – survive and function as 'core values' (as proposed by Smolicz) which are sufficient to continue the area's cultural distinctiveness.

Concluding: in the long term four broad scenarios may be postulated for the future linguistic and cultural identity of the Gàidhealtachd:

- A strong and vibrant Gaelic identity which is supported by a majority of the population, whether speakers or not;
- A 'Highland' identity which is maintained by popular support for some 'core value' features of Gaelic culture, but not for the language itself, which is known only as the interest of a few academics;

- An undifferentiated 'Scottish' identity, characterised by widespread acceptance of Lowland speech and cultural icons, in place of Gaelic tradition;
- An undifferentiated 'British' identity, in which the Highlands and Hebrides are culturally distinguishable from the Lowlands by being noticeably less Scottish, having lost markers of Gaelic tradition and not substituted Lowland markers in their place.

Much will dependent on local and national policies and plans, and their success. If, however, the four possibilities outlined above are accepted as a plausible range, only the first two offer a distinct cultural identity which would validate the claims to special regional status cited at the beginning of this paper, and it is arguable that the 'core values' which would support the second are currently strongly associated with individuals and organisations supportive of the language. At present it would seem that the ways of 'doing and thinking' which have given the Highlands and the Hebrides – and the Highlands and Islands overall – the reputation of being culturally distinct are still dependent on the nurture of the language, and it is a matter of conjecture as to whether this is, in official circles, fully acknowledged.

## References

Allott, R. 1999. 'Evolution and Culture: The Missing Link'. In eds. van der Dennen, J.M.G., Smillie D. and D.R. Wilson. *The Darwinian Heritage and Sociobiology*. Westport, CT: Praeger. 67–81.
Barth, F. ed. 1969. *Ethnic Groups and Boundaries*; Boston: Little, Brown.
Bennett, M. 1989. *The Last Stronghold: Scottish Gaelic Traditions of Newfoundland*. Edinburgh: Canongate.
Camathias, F. 1971. 'Pertgei nus vulein restar Romontschs: Ovras' ['Why we want to remain Romontsch'. Text and Translation] ed. by Alfons Maissens. In ed. Grigor, D.B. *Romontsch: Language and Literature: The Sursilvan Raeto-Romance of Switzerla*. Cambridge and New York: Oleander Press. 336–41.
Census 1991. *1991 Census Gaelic Language*, Table 1. Edinburgh: HMSO [1994].
Census 2001. *Gaelic Speakers by Council Area*.
Chalmers, D. 2003. *The Economic Impact of Gaelic Arts and Culture*. Unpublished PhD Thesis, Glasgow Caledonian University.
Cooper R.L. and B. Spolsky, eds. 1991. *The Influence of Language on Culture and Thought*. Berlin: Mouton de Gruyter.
Crystal, D. 2000. *Language Death*. Cambridge: Cambridge University Press.
Dorian, N. 1981. *Language Death: The Life Cycle of a Scottish Gaelic Dialect*. Philadelphia, PA: University of Pennsylvania Press.
Dorian, N. 1987. 'The Value of Language Maintenance Efforts which are Unlikely to Succeed'. *International Journal of the Sociology of Language* 68: 57–67.
Eidheim, H. 1969. 'When Ethnic Identity is a Social Stigma'. In ed. Barth, F. *Ethnic Groups and Boundaries*. Boston: Little, Brown. 39–57.
Fishman, J. 1991. *Reversing Language Shift*. Clevedon: Multilingual Matters.
Galloway, J.M.K. 1995. *The Role of Employment in Gaelic Language Maintenance and Development*. Unpublished PhD Thesis, University of Edinburgh.
Grant, I.F. 1961. *Highland Folk Ways*. London: Routledge and Kegan Paul.
Krauss, M. 1992. 'The World's Languages in Crisis'. *Language* 68: 1–42.

Loewenstein. J. and W. Ocasio. 2005. *Vocabularies of Organizing: How Language Links Culture, Cognition, and Action in Organizations*. McCombs Research Paper Series No. OSSM-03-05, University of Texas.
MacArthur, E.M. 1990. *Iona: The Living Memory of a Crofting Community, 1750–1914*. Edinburgh: Edinburgh University Press.
MacDonald, A. 1994. 'Reclaiming the Tradition. Interview in *Am Braighe* [Mabou, Nova Scotia]. Spring Issue. 12–13.
MacKinnon, K. and M. MacDonald. 1980. *Ethnic Communities: The Transmission of Language and Culture in Harris and Barra*. Report to the Social Science Research Council; Hatfield Polytechnic Social Sciences Reports Series No. SSR 12. Hatfield: Hertis Publications.
O Riagáin, P. and M. O Gliasàin. 1994. *National Survey on Languages 1993: Preliminary Report*. Dublin: Institiúid Teangeolaíochta Eireann.
Osmond, J. 1988. *The Divided Kingdom*. London: Constable.
Pandharipande, R. 1992. 'Language Shift in India: Issues and Implications'. In eds. Fase, W., Jaspaert K. and S. Kroon. *Maintenance and Loss of Minority Languages*. Studies in Bilingualism Series 1. Amsterdam: John Benjamins. 253–75.
Pedersen, R. 1989. Report on Study Visit to Galicia 1989. Inverness: Highlands and Islands Development Board.
Pullum, G. 1991. *The Great Eskimo Vocabulary Hoax and other Irreverent Essays on the Study of Language*. Chicago: University of Chicago Press.
Sandøy, H. 1992. 'Faroese: A Minority Language or a National Language?'. In eds. Blom, G., Graves, P., Kruse, A. and B.J. Thomsen. *Minority Languages: The Scandinavian Experience*. Oslo: Nordic Language Secretariat.
Sapir, E. 1921. 'Language, Race and Culture'. In his *Language: An Introduction to the Study of Speech*. New York: Harcourt, Brace and World, 207–20.
Schlesinger, I.M. 1991. 'The Wax and Wane of Whorfian Views'. In eds. Cooper, R.L. and B. Spolsky. *The Influence of Language on Culture and Thought*. Berlin: Mouton de Gruyter. 7–44.
Scottish Executive. 2003. *The Gaelic Language Bill Consultation Paper*. Edinburgh: The Scottish Executive.
Shaw, J. 1991. 'Language, Music and Local Aesthetics: Views from Gaeldom and Beyond'. *Scottish Language* 11/12: 37–61.
Shaw, M.F. 1986. *Folksongs and Folklore of South Uist*. Third Edition. Aberdeen: Aberdeen University Press. [First Edition 1955]
Skene, W.F. 1876–80. *Celtic Scotland, a History of Ancient Alban*. 5 vols. Edinburgh: David Douglas.
Skuttnabb-Kangas, T. 2000. *Linguistic Genocide in Education: or Worldwide Diversity and Human Rights?* Mahwah, NJ: Laurence Erlbaum Associates.
Smolicz, J.J. 1981. 'Core Values and Cultural Identity'. *Ethnic and Racial Studies* 4.1: 75–90.
Smolicz, J.J. 1992. 'Minority Languages as Core Values of Ethnic Cultures'. In eds. Jaspaert, K., Fase, W. and S. Kroon. *Maintenance and Loss of Minority Languages*. Studies in Bilingualism 1. Amsterdam: John Benjamins. 277–305.
Sproull, A. and B. Ashcroft, B. 1993. *The Economics of Gaelic Language Development*. Glasgow Caledonian University.
Stephens, M. 1976. *Linguistic Minorities in Western Europe*. Llandysul: Gomer.
UNESCO. 1982. Mexico City Declaration on Cultural Policies World. Presented at the World Conference on Cultural Policies, Mexico, 26 July – 6 August 1982.

Van der Plank, P.H. 1987. 'Frisian Language Use and Ethnic Identity'. *International Journal of the Sociology of Language* 64: 9–24.
Watson, M. 2003. *Being English in Scotland*. Edinburgh: Edinburgh University Press.
Watson, S. 1992. 'Scottish and Irish Gaelic: The Giant's Bedfellows'. In ed. Dorian, N.C. *Investigating Obsolescence*. Cambridge: Cambridge University Press. 1–59.
Woodbury, A.C. 1993. 'A Defense of the Proposition, "When a language dies, a culture dies"'. *Texas Linguistic Forum* 33: 101–29. [Proceedings of the First Annual Symposium about Language and Society, Austin, TX]
Woodbury, A.C. 1998. 'Documenting Rhetorical, Aesthetic and Expressive Loss in Language Shift'. In eds. Grenoble, L.A. and L.J. Whaley, *Endangered Languages*. Cambridge: Cambridge University Press. 234–58.

**Websites**

Government of Nova Scotia. 2007.
www.gov.ns.ca/dtc/culture/culture_gaelic_memorandum.asp
Highlands and Islands Enterprise, 2007. www.hie.co.uk/about-our-area.html
Highland Council. 2007. http://www.highland.gov.uk/leisure/gaelic
Visit Hebrides, 2007. www.visithebrides.com
Visit Highlands, 2007. www.visithighlands.com/about/culture
Visit Scotland, 2005. www.visitscotland.com

# Young Protestants and Developing Irish in the Protestant Community

*Ian Malcolm*

## Introduction

Northern Ireland has made tremendous advances in recent years as a result of the peace process which culminated in the *Belfast / Good Friday Agreement* of 1998 (GFA, 1998). This broadly but not universally welcomed accord provided the foundation for devolution and the new Stormont administration, a system of mandatory coalition, which has given important powers back to local politicians after a long period of sectarian violence and direct rule from Westminster.

The mandatory nature of the power-sharing executive means that bitter political rivalries have been tempered by the need to work together. The current iteration (in 2010) effectively means government through a partnership involving the staunchly unionist Democratic Unionist Party (DUP) and the strongly republican Sinn Féin. Although this is an uncomfortable juxtaposition (to call it an 'alliance' would be stretching a point), politicians have demonstrated an ability to co-operate, notably agreeing the devolution of policing and justice powers in March 2010 after protracted negotiations (BBC, 2010).

Decommissioning by all of the major terrorist groups has strengthened community confidence that the peace is 'for real'. Although attacks by so-called republican dissidents occasionally shake this belief, politicians on both sides unite to condemn dissident activity, and the Police Service of Northern Ireland is welcomed in areas where the pre-Agreement Royal Ulster Constabulary used to be rejected by nationalists and republicans.

Despite the positiveness of the overall picture, major fault lines persist including, without doubt, the question of language in what is still effectively a divided society. The *Belfast / Good Friday Agreement* itself acknowledges the importance of language issues and promises to:

> Recognise the importance of respect, understanding and tolerance in relation to linguistic diversity, including in Northern Ireland, the Irish language, Ulster-Scots and the languages of the various ethnic minority communities, all of which are part of the cultural wealth of the island of Ireland. (*Belfast Agreement*, 1998:19)

Interpretation of this, however, has proved difficult. One manifestation of continuing hostility to Irish during the lifetime of the current Assembly was the attempt by an Ulster Unionist MLA (Member of the Legislative Assembly) to curtail the use of Irish in chamber proceedings in 2007 (McNarry, 2007). The language, McNarry claimed, was being forced down unionists' throats by republicans 'in an uncompromising and adversarial way'. This debate in its entirety provides a concise – if depressing – summary of contemporary unionist attitudes to the issue of language.[1]

Calls for an Irish Language Act (see Pobal, 2010), supported by nationalists but opposed by unionists, have been highly contentious and one DUP member described

---

[1] I would highly recommend that readers of this paper read the full debate as recorded in Hansard (Vol. 24 *Northern Ireland Assembly Debates*. 9 October 2007. pp. 280–93) to gain an overview of where Northern Ireland's political parties stand on the issue.

efforts to introduce legislation as an 'expression of anti-British malice' and 'alienating and intimidating' (Shannon, 2007). Subsequently, the then DUP Culture Minister Edwin Poots decided not to proceed with legislation, citing costs and the potential to 'increase polarisation and entrench suspicions and patterns of antipathy' (Poots, 2007).

On the surface and on the basis of this evidence, it would seem that the stereotyped view of negative Protestant and unionist attitudes towards Irish remains undiminished. Indeed, when the question is raised on Northern Ireland's phone-in radio shows, the depth of hostility shown by some from the Protestant/unionist tradition might seem to indicate that nothing has changed.

But do the breathlessly-expressed views of 'Thomas from North Belfast' or 'David from Portadown' represent the opinions of Northern Ireland's young people, the generation which has grown up in the more peaceful period engendered by the Good Friday Agreement? Until the research that provided the foundations for *Towards Inclusion* (Malcolm, 2009), none had chosen to challenge this perception, perhaps accepting that anti-Irish (language) sentiment transferred from generation to generation, as it appears to have done in the past.

**Research Background**

It seemed timely to ascertain the views of young Protestants and unionists by developing a research package that would include quantitative and qualitative techniques. A triangulated methodology, therefore, included a 52-item questionnaire, focus groups and one-on-one interviews. The research sample involved more than 130 A-Level students (16–18-year-old) attending 'Protestant' schools in which the Gael-Linn *Aspects of a Shared Heritage* programme has operated for a number of years.

Gael-Linn, a voluntary organisation founded in 1953, is devoted to the promotion of the Irish language on an all-Ireland basis. The *Aspects* programme was conceived in the mid–1990s as a way to dispel some of the many misconceptions among young Protestants about the Irish language. According to Ó Ciaráin (2004):

> It was believed that unionists and Protestants felt alienated from the language and associated it with the IRA, 'Tiocfaidh Ár Lá' and so on. We did a little market research ... and we put this scheme together.

Gael-Linn's *Aspects* initiative takes Irish to places where it has not gone before, introducing young Protestants to facets of language and culture over an 8–10-week course which covers topics including surnames, place-names, Hiberno-English, history and more (Gael-Linn, 1997). At its core is a basic introduction to the language itself. Using these schools as the research vehicle, it was possible to achieve a sample including pupils who had taken the course and others who had not. This permitted a valuable opportunity to contrast the views of 'takers' and 'non-takers'. It should be understood, however, that this essay is concerned only with some 'headline' findings and does not explore 'taker' –vs.– 'non-taker' comparisons, which are fully explored in *Towards Inclusion*.

There is a certain bittersweet irony that Northern Ireland's segregated education system (see Kernohan, 1995) was of valuable benefit to this research, given that it made it relatively easy to access a predominantly Protestant cohort.[2]

---

[2] There were also a handful of Catholic participants in the questionnaire, but their responses were eliminated from statistical enquiry as the opinions expressed therein were beyond the research remit.

## Insights from the Data

Analysis of questionnaire returns centres on statistical techniques such as Chi-Square and Analysis of Variance. Other methods (correlation and $t$-tests) were also employed, but time constraints and sample size meant that more complex regression modelling was not used. The qualitative dimension was at all times underpinned by the principles of reflexivity to evaluate – and hopefully minimise – one's own potential impact on the information-gathering process (Coolican, 2004: 235).

The questionnaire first ascertained certain basic facts about participants, regarding age, gender, religion and political beliefs. These represent a sound starting point and form the 'key variables', important as standalone factors and also significant in the interpretation of attitudinal positions adopted by participants.

Gender was found to be of no significance in determining attitudes towards the language among the sample. On some attitudinal questions females were slightly more positive about Irish, on others males were slightly more positive but differences were never significant.

In Northern Ireland, it could be assumed that religion will be a definitive marker in terms of how one views the Irish language, with Catholics almost guaranteed to be more sympathetic to the language than their Protestant counterparts. For over a century or so, the equation has been simple: Protestants/unionists dislike the language, while Catholics/nationalists hold it in high esteem:

> Catholic nationalists speak easily of 'our language', whether they speak Irish or not, while most of the Protestant and unionist community regard that language as alien, even when they have obviously Gaelic surnames ... (Mac Póilin, 1990: 1)

Mac Póilin adds that Protestants and unionists 'often find themselves choking on the political package that goes with the word [Irish]'. This would seem to be borne out by some of the comments referenced in the introduction above.

As this research excluded Catholics, evaluation of the religion variable, therefore, centred on the difference in views between three main Protestant groups: Presbyterian, Church of Ireland (the predominant Protestant denominations), and Other, which is an amalgamation of participants belonging to smaller faith groups, including Methodist, Free Presbyterian, Baptist and Pentecostal. Taken individually, their small numbers would have violated the parameters of valid statistical enquiry, but the disparate nature of the combined group does perhaps have an inherent if unintentional natural balance.

Religion was found to be a statistically significant factor. There was a clear difference between Church of Ireland and Presbyterian respondents. Taking the statement-question *'Everyone should have the chance to learn Irish'* as an example, 71% of Church of Ireland respondents agreed, compared to 62% of Presbyterians. The Other group recorded 52%. This pattern was pleasingly consistent, in that Church of Ireland participants were always more positive towards the language than their Presbyterian counterparts.

The position of the Other group wavered, sometimes falling between Church of Ireland and Presbyterian and sometimes recording the lowest percentage – but at no stage did their views overtake those of the Church of Ireland respondents. Only on one

---

[3] Why this is so is discussed in Malcolm, 2009: 199.

attitudinal item did the Presbyterian group score a higher percentage than Church of Ireland students – and that related to whether or not they felt they had benefited from doing the Gael-Linn course.[3]

Religion clearly remains an important factor in determining attitudes towards the language and the research sample confirmed – as may have been pre-supposed – that politics also remains a statistically significant factor in attitudinal determination. For the purposes of statistical validity, political groups were conflated into Unionist/Loyalist and Other/None. Taking the statement/question 'Irish is a dead language' as an example, the agreement level among Unionist/Loyalist was 71%, compared to 29% for Other/None.

This pattern was repeated in every attitudinal variable, those describing themselves as Unionist/Loyalist consistently taking a darker view than their Other/None peers. Politics seemed to define respondents' views with even greater clarity than the religion variable.

While the importance of religion and politics as attitudinal determinants could possibly have been predicted, the age variable threw up some fascinating results. Given that the range was 16-year-old to 18-year-old, the scope for variance seemed limited. However, a clear and statistically valid pattern emerged, in that younger respondents were consistently more positive in their views of Irish.

The statement/question '*Everyone should have the chance to learn Irish*' provides a typical example of responses. 85% of 16-year-olds were in agreement, while 17-year-olds recorded 71% and 18-year-olds registered 50%. The pattern was statistically significant and consistent throughout all attitudinal variables. In some ways, one might have expected that older respondents would take a more 'mature' view of the language debate and be more open-minded than their younger counterparts. Clearly, this was not the case.

It opens up an intriguing possibility: is this the 'Children of the Ceasefire' factor, in that younger respondents had suffered less exposure to the latter stages of the 'Troubles', or indeed the difficult 'birthing' process of the new peaceful Northern Ireland, than their older brothers and sisters? Might it be the product of what was happening at the proverbial 'mother's knee' level as their parents reacted to contemporary political and terrorism-related events at a formative stage in their personal development?

One must be wary of drawing conclusions based on this variable, but it would be fascinating to repeat the research today as – given that all 16–18-year-olds have had mercifully limited but equal exposure to terrorism and its effects – results across the age spectrum should indicate no difference in attitudes towards Irish if the 'Children of the Ceasefire' theory is correct.

### The Living Irish Concept

Figure 1 shows how course-takers rated elements of the Gael-Linn programme as operated in their schools.[4] The popularity of certain items is immediately obvious. Learning Irish was the most popular component of the course, followed closely by place-name study, music and the two traditions and Gaelic surnames in English. By contrast, those elements of the course which dealt with historical aspects of the language were considerably less popular.

---

[4] A *céilí* (Irish music and dancing) is an optional part of the course, but only where facilities permit. It was not, therefore, part of this study.

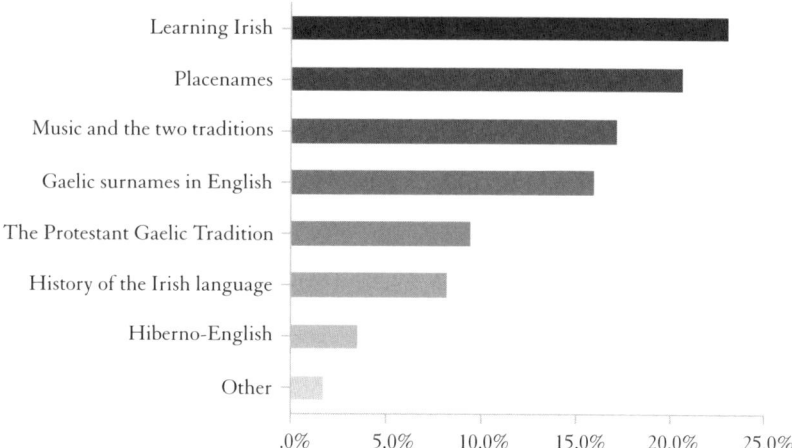

Figure 1: How Students Rated Course Elements

This introduces the 'Living Irish' concept, in that students appeared to be responding favourably to those items which were of particular relevance to them as individuals. Place-names, for example, relate directly to the everyday environment around them. Most place-names in Northern Ireland have origins in Irish and people are naturally curious about their own personal spaces. Furthermore, even a cursory examination of place-names can reveal many interesting things about the history, geography or mythology of a place. Place-names have a value-added component in that they not only show the continuing relevance of Irish today but also offer information which is 'hidden' from those who know nothing of the language.

The same is true of surnames. Many in Northern Ireland have names derived from Irish or Scots Gaelic. Even if they don't, they inevitably have friends and relatives with Gaelic name origins. Furthermore, the Gael-Linn course shows that even what might at first glance appear to be quintessentially 'English' names often have well-concealed Irish origins. Indeed, students are generally fascinated to find that well-known unionist politicians in Northern Ireland have names whose origins can be traced to Irish and/or Scots Gaelic. Examples include Donaldson (< Sc.G. *Mac Dòmhnall*), McCrea (a personal name, not a patronymic, Gaelic *Macrath* 'son of grace', but earliest record is from an ogham inscription from Co. Cork *Magi Rati*), Campbell (< Sc.G. *Cambeulach*), Simpson (son of *Sim*, of English origin and use as well as of *Mac Shímídh*, an Anglo-Scottish patronymic surname, from the medieval masculine given name 'Simme') and Paisley (cf. *Pàislig*, 'of local origin from that town'),[5] prominent elected members of the DUP ... a party with little time for the 'language of leprechauns' (Wilson, 2002).

The surnames and place-names elements undoubtedly cash in on the curiosity factor and the point was reinforced in the focus groups, where these course components were discussed in a positive manner.

Learning Irish also fits into the 'Living Irish' framework, as the language is shown

---

[5] According to the *Wikipedia* entry on Paisley, 'the burgh's name, formerly known as Paislay, is of uncertain origin; some sources suggest a derivation either from the Brythonic word, *pasgill*, 'pasture', or more likely, *passeleg* 'basilica', (i.e. major church), itself derived from the Greek *basilika*. However, some Scottish place-name books suggest 'Pæssa's wood/clearing', from the Old English personal name *Pæssa* and *leah* – 'clearing, wood'. Pasilege (1182) and Paslie (1214) are recorded previous spellings of the name.'

to be contemporary and vibrant, relevant not to past generations but to the young people of today. Even though the course could offer no more than the briefest of introductions to the language, many respondents welcomed this opportunity to learn a little Irish.

Despite experiencing understandable initial difficulties with the phonetic system of Irish and struggling with what some described as the 'strange' pronunciations, a majority of students enjoyed the language lessons. Another aspect of this core course element is the opportunity to dispel the myth that Irish is a 'republican' language, a belief that is widely and deeply held by many from the Protestant/unionist community. Irish is essentially presented as just a language, like any other, which can be used to express any idea, concept or thought.

Some examples help place Irish in an entirely different context for the participants. The expression *Tiocfaidh Ár Lá* is a rare example of an Irish phrase that most unionists and Protestants do understand because of its unpalatable political connotations. It means 'Our Day Will Come' and is often seen as a battle-cry of militant republicanism, used to irritate unionists and loyalists. However, pupils are intrigued to discover that the phrase has a 'unionist antidote': *Ní Thiocfaidh Bhur Lá* ('Your Day Will Not Come').

Other examples provide reinforcement, by signalling what may be key points of political/cultural reference for many Protestants/unionists: *'Dia Leis An Bhanríon'* ('God Save The Queen'); *Ar Son Dé agus Uladh* ('For God and Ulster') and *Ní Sinne An Bhrasaíl ach Tuaisceart Éireann* ('We're Not Brazil, We're Northern Ireland'). This last example refers to the Northern Ireland soccer team's unofficial anthem; support for the team is often a *de rigueur part* of 'being unionist'. Nationalists and republicans are much more likely to support the Republic of Ireland team.

The popularity of the 'Living Irish' elements must be contrasted with the frosty response to the historical components. *The Protestant Gaelic Tradition*, *History of the Irish Language* and *Hiberno-English* were not rated highly in the questionnaire returns and focus group discussions confirmed that students had comparatively little interest in the historical dimension. History shows that Protestants figured prominently in efforts to preserve and promote the Irish language over the centuries and many speakers of Gaelic settled in the north of Ireland during the Plantation period – but this failed to cut much ice with students.

For them, the historical element was of little relevance today. It was not believed that figures such as Robert Shipboy Mac Adam (a Presbyterian pioneer of efforts to preserve and promote Irish in the nineteenth century (see Hughes, 1998), were likely to serve as role-models for young Protestants in the twenty-first century. Similarly, Gusty Spence, a senior loyalist who learned Irish while in prison in the 1970s (Garland, 2001: 222), was not considered a useful example. While his unionist/loyalist credentials are certainly not in doubt and Spence is a 'contemporary' figure for many in Northern Ireland, seen through the eyes of today's teenagers, he, too, is simply a figure from a distant past.

### Defining Depoliticisation

A recurring theme in both questionnaires and focus groups was the word 'depoliticisation', a term frequently used by unionist politicians to keep potential Protestant engagement with Irish at a safe distance. Many students said that the language must be depoliticised before Protestants would take an interest in Irish. Certainly, the term is a tricky one and really needs to be decoupled from the broader language debate. The difficulty is that while a language itself is probably not a political entity, any language can be used in a political way. And Irish has undeniably been used in a very political way on many occasions.

Even Chris McGimpsey, a unionist politician who strongly advocated Protestant re-engagement with the language, believed that 'a neutral stance' was essential to increase its credibility and potential acceptability. McGimpsey however, was doubtful whether help from 'a large number' within the Irish language movement in Northern Ireland would be forthcoming (1994: 15–6). Conversely, O'Reilly notes that there may be dangers for nationalists and republicans in 'depoliticising' the language (1998: 177).

The implicit meaning of depoliticisation in the Northern Ireland language debate is that Irish carries an inherent political message. Therefore, to depoliticise the language might mean, for example, that members of Sinn Féin stop using Irish, or that use of the language be censured in contexts where it could be seen as inflammatory. If unionists are correct and Sinn Féin does use the language 'as a kind of warped ideological jihad' (Kennedy, 2007), it's not terribly likely that the party will happily or readily 'decommission' Irish to facilitate its political opponents.

And the counter-argument is, of course, that English too can be seen in the same light, with unsubtle political overtones carried in a variety of terms. For Protestants, the name of Northern Ireland's second city is 'Londonderry'; for Catholics, it is 'Derry'. The term 'Ulster' means the historic nine counties for Catholics, but the post-Partition six for Protestants. The term 'Province' also carries the same ambiguity.

In Northern Ireland, therefore, all language has the potential to be divisive ... even without taking into account the recent importation of 'new' languages by migrants from inside and outside the European Union.

**Finding a Way Ahead**

Probably more than anything else, this research is about opening the debate on Protestant engagement with the Irish language in Northern Ireland. The statistics and focus group material show that there is a curiosity about the language among young Protestants. It may be the case that this is an inherent curiosity or, alternatively, something which only comes to the fore when there is some sort of 'trigger', in this case the *Aspects* course. Further research could clarify this point.

The Gael-Linn programme is clearly a valuable instrument in awakening – or perhaps even creating – young Protestant/unionist interest in Irish but unfortunately timetabling constraints in schools brought about by curriculum/examination changes mean that the course does not have the same 'reach' it enjoyed several years ago. The result is that fewer young people from the Protestant community now have the chance to engage with Irish in their schools.

Whatever the method of developing and structuring the debate, some factors are clear. For example, trying to 'sell' Irish by using historical facts will not work. The argument that Protestant engagement with Irish goes back centuries and that many Plantation settlers were Gaelic speakers carries little weight. Using historical figures as role-models is also unlikely to work. Language proponents often 'helpfully' point out that Douglas Hyde, the first president of Ireland, was a Protestant and an Irish speaker. True, but his politics were essentially nationalist, ruling him out as someone with whom unionists could happily identify (Malcolm, 2009: 31–2).

Better outcomes are likely from marketing Irish as a living, vibrant language with a role in the twenty-first century, seen in the context of other useful modern European languages. Even more important, perhaps, is promoting the language as a useful part of one's skill set. Some respondents thought Irish would 'look good' on their CVs but most were unaware of the burgeoning range of job opportunities open to those with qualifications in Irish. This would promote the language as relevant and as something that can offer potential economic benefits.

Another interesting point to emerge is that respondents believed that young Protestants should have the opportunity to engage with the language. There were some codicils, explored in the main research, but essentially all participants – even those who were dubious about Irish – believed that the language should be available to all in 'Protestant' schools as an option. And no-one thought that learning Irish might turn them into Catholics, nationalists or republicans – the old 'bogeyman' fear of unionist politicians.

Many students who had done the Gael-Linn course talked of their willingness to learn more Irish were the opportunity available and some even expressed sadness that it had not been offered at an earlier stage in their school lives. However, all were agreed that Irish must be a choice and not compulsory. Any attempt at compulsion would surely be counter-productive given the political sensibilities that are only likely to change gradually in a society emerging cautiously from the dark years of sectarian conflict.

In conclusion, the research has provided a primary assessment of the views of young Protestants and unionists towards the language. Gael-Linn deserves praise for its short but effective course. Many young Protestants are ready and willing to learn the language ... if they get the chance. But it must be made available early enough in their school lives to be worthwhile.

The challenge now for others is to take the steps to ensure that they do indeed get that chance. Yet there has been a distinct lack of interest from the Department of Education and Foras na Gaeilge, the all-Ireland body charged with the promotion of the Irish language, when it comes to making the language available and appealing to young Protestants.

Perhaps it is time for the statutory agencies to learn from the experience of Gael-Linn, a voluntary organisation which has done what they have singularly failed to do – give young Protestants the chance to learn something about their rich Irish language heritage.

**References**

Bardon, J. 1992. *A History of Ulster.* Belfast: The Blackstaff Press.
BBC. 2007. 'Poots opposes move on Irish act'. <http://news.bbc.co.uk/1/hi/northern_ireland/7046117.stm> [accessed 26 May 2010]
BBC. 2010. 'PM hails 'historic' NI justice vote'. <http://news.bbc.co.uk/1/hi/northern_ireland/8558466.stm> [accessed 26 May 2010]
Coolican, H. 2004. *Research Methods and Statistics in Psychology.* Fourth Edition. London: Hodder and Stoughton.
Gael-Linn. 1997. *Aspects of a Shared Heritage.* Dublin: Gael-Linn.
Garland, R. 2001. *Gusty Spence.* Belfast: Blackstaff Press.
Good Friday Agreement (GFA). 1998. *The Agreement: Agreement Reached in the Multi-Party Negotiations.* Belfast.

Hughes, A.J. 1998. *Robert Shipboy MacAdam (1808–1895): His Life and Gaelic Proverb Collection*. Belfast: Queen's University Institute of Irish Studies.
Kennedy, D. 2007. In *Northern Ireland Assembly Debates*. Vol. 24, 9 October 2007, p. 291.
Kernohan, Harry. 1995. *A General Introduction on Education in Northern Ireland*. <www.batod.org.uk/index.php?id=/batod/regions/northernireland.htm> [accessed 27 April 2005]
Mac Póilin, A. 1990. *The Protestant Gaelic Tradition*. [pamphlet] Belfast: ULTACH Trust.
Malcolm, I. 2009. *Towards Inclusion: Protestants and the Irish Language*. Belfast: Blackstaff Press.
McGimpsey, C. 1994. [Untitled article]. In ed. Mistéil, P. *The Irish Language and the Unionist Tradition*. Belfast: Ulster People's College / ULTACH Trust. 7–16.
McNarry, D. 2007. In *Northern Ireland Assembly Debates*. Vol. 24, 9 October 2007, pp. 280–1.
Ó Ciaráin, R. 2004. Based on interview with subject held in Gael-Linn's Armagh office, 29 January 2004.
O'Reilly, C, 1998. *The Irish Language in Northern Ireland: The Politics of Culture and Identity*. Houndmills: Macmillan.
Pobal. 2010. 'Work on the Irish Language Act'. <www.pobal.org/english/irishlanguageact.php> [accessed 26 May 2010]
Poots, E. 2007. In *Northern Ireland Assembly Debates*. Vol. 24. 16 Oct 2007. pp. 364–5.
Shannon, J. 2007. In *Northern Ireland Assembly Debates*. Vol. 24. 9 Oct 2007. p. 287.
Wilson, S. 2002. Speaking on *Eorpa*. BBC Scotland (TV). 19 November 2002.

# The Role of the University in Sustaining Linguistic Minorities: An Irish Case Study

*Joe Mac Donnacha*

## 1. Introduction

The National University of Ireland, Galway (NUI, Galway) has had a statutory obligation to provide third level courses through the medium of Irish since 1929. In the period 1929–2003 this obligation was fulfilled by encouraging and facilitating staff members who were competent in Irish to teach their courses through the medium of Irish where demand existed among the student body. In addition, a small number of scholarships were provided to high achieving students who opted to follow their course through the medium of Irish. By the year 2000, the University had a total of 204 students following courses or part of their course through the medium of Irish in the faculties of Arts, Science and Commerce. In addition, the University provides undergraduate and postgraduate courses in Irish language and literature and provides a diploma course in applied Irish language skills that students can take on a voluntary basis.

In the year 2000, the University decided to review its approach to the provision of third level courses through Irish. In undertaking this review, it was decided to adopt an external customer-led approach and to review the current needs of the Irish-speaking community and how NUI, Galway, as a third level institution, could best meet these needs. The result of this review was the adoption by the University of a development strategy for Irish-medium University Education (NUI, Galway 2000), and the establishment of a new Irish-medium Academy – *Acadamh na hOllscolaíochta Gaeilge* (NUI, Galway 2003).

The underlying philosophy of the new development strategy and of *Acadamh na hOllscolaíochta Gaeilge* is:

> the desire of NUI, Galway to provide for the specific needs of Irish speakers and Gaeltacht [Irish-speaking districts] communities, through the promotion of academic programmes, courses and research activities in subject areas that are seen as being of over-riding importance to their future development, and through initiatives in other related areas. The Development Strategy aims to increase the Irish-medium educational opportunities available to Irish speakers, in the Gaeltacht and throughout the country, and to contribute in a positive manner to the social, economic, cultural and linguistic life of their communities and of the country. (NUI, Galway 2003: 44–5).

A key part of the University's approach in this area is its desire to create stronger educational linkages with other institutions working with linguistic and other minorities. Within this context one of the objectives of its new approach is the creation of 'a third level education model that can be emulated by other minority language communities as a vehicle for their sustainable development.' (NUI, Galway 2003: 45)

This paper will review the background that led NUI, Galway to adopt this particular third-level Irish-medium model. It will include a brief introduction to the current status of the Irish language and the history of NUI, Galway's promotion of Irish-medium studies. The paper concludes with an outline of the main principles which *Acadamh na hOllscolaíochta Gaeilge (An tAcadamh)* sees as central to its future success and development.

## 2. The Irish Language

With the establishment of the Irish Free State in 1922, the Irish Language was accorded the status of 'national language' (with English being equally recognised as an 'official language') under Article 4 of the Constitution of the Irish Free State (*Saorstát Éireann*) Act, 1922. A new constitution, *Bunreacht na hÉireann*, enacted in 1937, declares that 'The Irish language as the national language is the first official language', with English being declared as 'a second official language'.

However, by 1926, the number of Irish-speakers in the Irish Free State was only 543,511 (18.29%), out of a total population of 2,971,992. By 1936, a year before *Bunreacht na hÉireann* was enacted, the number of Irish-speakers had increased to 666,601 (23.75%), out of a total population of 2,806,741. This dichotomy between the constitutional status of Irish and its de facto position as a minority language is, perhaps, best explained in a reference from a 1934 court case in which Justice Ó Cinnéide, in referring to the constitutional status of Irish in the 1922 constitution, stated:

> The declaration by the Constitution that the national language of Saorstát Éireann is the Irish language does not mean that the Irish language is, or was at that historical moment, universally spoken by the people of the Saorstát, which would be untrue in fact, but it did mean that it is the historic distinctive speech of the Irish people, that it is to rank as such in the nation and, by implication, that the State is bound to do everything within its sphere of action ... to establish and maintain it in its status as the national language and to recognise it for all official purposes as the national language. (Ó Foghludha V McClean (1934) IR 469 68 ILTR 189 (1934)).

And indeed the Irish State has invested heavily in the intervening years in efforts to maintain Irish as a living language in those areas where it is still spoken and to revive it in the rest of the country. This investment has had mixed results. Census returns show that language ability amongst the population, when defined as the number of people who can speak the language to some degree of competence, has increased steadily, from 18 per cent in 1926 to almost 42 per cent in 2006 (Census 2006). In one sense this represents quite a considerable achievement. However, the census returns of the number of Irish-speakers, are an insufficient indicator with which to analyse the success or otherwise of any language planning effort. A clearer indication of the sustainability of language planning outcomes can be achieved by looking at the census data relating to language usage. Census 2006 reported that of the 42% of the population age 3 years and over who were reported as being able to speak Irish, just over 72,000 persons, representing 4.4 per cent of all those who could speak Irish, spoke it on a daily basis outside school.

These numbers include a large number of people living outside the traditional Irish-speaking (Gaeltacht) districts who are capable of speaking Irish to various levels of competence. While some of these participate in various social and organisational language networks, Irish has not taken hold again as a social and community language in any place outside of the traditional Gaeltacht districts. Within the Gaeltacht districts it appears that the pattern of language shift to English continues unabated and is now at a critical stage (Ó Giollagáin and Mac Donnacha *et al.* 2007).

## 3. National University of Ireland, Galway

The National University of Ireland, Galway (NUI, Galway), was founded in 1845 as Queen's College Galway. It was one of the three Queen's Colleges founded under the provisions of *The Queen's Colleges (Ireland) Act*, 1845, the others being located in Belfast and Cork. The College was opened for students in 1849 and functioned as a constituent college of the Queen's College from 1850 until that institution was dissolved in 1882, with the establishment of the Royal University. The Royal University was dissolved under the provisions of the *Irish Universities Act*, 1908, which created two new universities: The Queen's University of Belfast (into which Queen's College, Belfast was converted) and the National University of Ireland – a federal University with its seat at Dublin and with three constituent colleges, at Dublin, Cork and Galway. Thus, under a new charter issued in December 1908 the College became University College, Galway. Under the *Universities Act*, 1997 University College Galway was reconstituted as a University under the name of *Ollscoil na hÉireann, Gaillimh* / National University of Ireland, Galway and became a constituent University of the National University of Ireland (together with the National University of Ireland, Dublin; the National University of Ireland, Cork; and the National University of Ireland, Maynooth).

## 4. NUI, Galway's Commitment to the Irish Language.

Under the *University College Galway Act*, 1929[1] the Governing Body of the College committed to providing an increasing proportion of its courses through the medium of Irish and to making better provision for the study of the Irish language and literature in return for a commitment by the Government to provide extra resources for such activities. This Act also made it incumbent on the College authorities to appoint people to positions in the College who are 'competent to discharge the duties thereof through the medium of the Irish language: provided a person so competent and also suitable in all other respects is to be found amongst the persons who are candidates or otherwise available for such appointment.'

With this legislative provision in mind, the College in the intervening years committed itself to increasing the use of Irish across a broad range of its administrative and academic activities. In pursuit of this aim the University provided courses through the medium of Irish in a number of disciplines and provides a broad range of courses in the Irish language for members of staff and students.

However, the development of Irish-medium courses in the University did not keep pace with the development of the range of English-medium courses and the number of students taking them. This was particularly so in the period of the late 1980s and early 1990s, when the number of students attending Irish universities increased rapidly, but when no 'strategic plan was implemented, nor even outlined, to ensure that third-

---

[1] This Act was amended in 2006. The amended act now contains a provision to ensure that the 'governing authority of the College shall ensure that one of the principal aims for the operation and development of the College set out in each strategic development plan prepared after the commencement of this section is the provision of education at the College through the medium of the Irish language.'

level education through Irish would be developed proportionately, concurrently and in parallel with third-level education through English.' (Ó Cinnéide 2004).

## 5. Strategic Review

In the year 2000, the University decided to review its approach to the provision of courses through the medium of Irish. This review was brought about partly by the movement towards a strategic approach to planning in Irish Universities generally.

Underlying this review, was the knowledge that although the University had continued to provide courses through the medium of the Irish language in the period since 1929, the responsibility for this activity was left mainly at the departmental level and, in many cases, the commitment to Irish language provision was dependent more on the commitment of individual members of staff than on any coherent strategy at University level. Within this context, the provision of courses through the medium of Irish within the University had become *ad hoc* and, while courses were being provided through the medium of Irish in a range of academic departments, it had become increasingly difficult for students to access a sufficient number of Irish-medium modules/courses to allow them to complete a full degree course through the medium of Irish.

Under this system, for teaching staff, the decision to teach through the medium of Irish was in the main a personal commitment that invariably led to an extra workload, and often the decision to teach through Irish was seen to be in conflict with the need to commit time to academic research. Within academic departments, debates regularly ensued around the issue of whether staff should be using scarce departmental resources to teach a small number of students through the medium of Irish, when those same resources might be better utilised teaching a much larger body of students through the medium of English.

This *laissez faire* approach to Irish-medium studies within the University also meant that no structure existed to support staff committed to teaching through the medium of Irish. Very little was done in developing Irish-medium teaching resources, or in providing training for staff teaching through Irish, or to ensure sufficiently attractive career paths existed for staff wishing to commit to teaching through Irish on a long-term basis. Neither could it be claimed that what was being provided was 'an Irish-medium university' model, as, with a small number of notable exceptions, the Irish-medium activities were, in the main, restricted to the provision of courses only, with very little provision for encouraging research and facilitating publication of academic material through the medium of Irish. These misgivings culminated in the knowledge that although the University was providing a reasonably broad range of services through the medium of Irish it did not add up to a coherent strategy for meeting the needs of the Gaeltacht and Irish-speaking community.

Some considerations were foremost in underpinning the University's review of 2000. These included issues related to:

- The role of the University in Society.
- The needs of the Gaeltacht/Irish-speaking community with regard to the third-level sector.
- Current developments within the Gaeltacht.

## The Role of the University in Society

The University was concerned that one of its primary roles was to serve the needs of the society of which it is part. This role has been given a legislative basis in Section 12 of the *Universities Act*, 1997, which states, for example, that the objects of Universities shall include the promotion of learning in society generally; the promotion of the cultural and social life of society; and the promotion of the official languages of the state, with special regard to the preservation, promotion and use of the Irish language.

Within this context, the University felt, that given its obligations under the *University College Galway Act*, 1929, and in view of its location in proximity to one of the strongest Irish-speaking Gaeltacht districts, that it should play a leading role in facilitating the sustainable development of the Irish-speaking community.

## The Needs of Gaeltacht/Irish-speaking Community with regard to the Third Level Sector

The review identified several specific issues relating to the Gaeltacht and Irish-speaking community generally which it felt were relevant and should be the focus for the development of Irish-medium studies in the future:

- The large number of Irish language and Gaeltacht institutions/organizations involved in various aspects of language planning has led to a corresponding need to educate and train students and language planning practitioners through the medium of Irish in a broad range of related linguistic, administrative, planning and managerial disciplines.

- The continued development of Gaeltacht based business organizations and the shift from manufacturing to knowledge based industries within the Gaeltacht required the University to provide degree level and life-long learning opportunities through the medium of Irish in related disciplines for individuals working or available to work in these sectors.

- The development of Irish-medium education at primary and second level in the Republic of Ireland and in Northern Ireland.

- A predicted increase in demand from all public sector organizations for fully qualified employees who are competent in Irish, as a result of the enactment of the *Official Languages Act*, 2003.

## Current Developments within the Gaeltacht

Major changes have taken place in the Gaeltacht in recent years. A 1997 ESRI report (Watson and Fahy 1997), showed that those sectors with obligations in relation to planning and policy issues in the Gaeltacht (including the third level sector) faced many new challenges if we were to provide Gaeltacht communities with the instruments in terms of education, skills and leadership, necessary to enable them to fulfill their personal, social and cultural aspirations, while at the same time maintaining Irish as the primary home and social language of the community.

One of the main points highlighted by the Report was the number of young people leaving the Gaeltacht in search of employment opportunities elsewhere which were commensurate with their educational qualifications and with their aspirations. Referring to this the Report stated:

> Recent emigrants from the Gaeltacht over five years numbered in the region 6,000 in total, or 1,200 per year…These emigrants are heavily comprised of well-educated young people who get good jobs elsewhere in Ireland or abroad. Gaeltacht students coming to the end of their education number up to 1,500 per year…over half of these say that they expect to leave the Gaeltacht to find jobs, even though the majority say they would be happy to live in the Gaeltacht on social grounds. (Watson and Fahy 1997).

The Report also stated that:

> The groups who depart are a major loss to Gaeltacht economic and social life, particularly when the cumulative effect over the years is taken into account. (Watson and Fahy 1997).

This report suggests that although young people in the Gaeltacht were availing of the third level opportunities available to them, this is happening in a social and economic context, which results in young Gaeltacht people being educated for employment opportunities that exist mainly outside of their own communities. Thus Gaeltacht communities, despite having invested heavily in their youth, end up being deprived of the input of these young people in the social, economic, and cultural life of the community. This further reduces the viability of these communities and increases the likelihood that the Gaeltacht will not survive as a distinct language community unless these issues, which are essentially planning issues, can be resolved.

In this context, NUI, Galway, came to the conclusion that there was a need for a third level education strategy for the Gaeltacht:

(i) Which could deal with the challenges facing the Gaeltacht of today and in which the Irish language is seen as a central factor.
(ii) Which could be integrated with an appropriate economic development strategy.
(iii) Which would ensure that a high proportion of Gaeltacht students have access to third level education which is being delivered within the Gaeltacht, thereby increasing the likelihood that they will undertake a venture or a profession within the Gaeltacht at the end of their third level education period.

## 6. Strategic Development Plan

The University published its *Strategy for the Development of Third Level Education in the Gaeltacht* in May 2000 and started the process leading to the establishment of *Acadamh na hOllscolaíochta Gaeilge* (Academy for Irish-medium University Studies), a new academic and administrative structure charged with the future development of Irish-medium University Studies under the auspices of NUI, Galway. *An tAcadamh's* brief would include three distinct elements:

- The development of a broad range of University courses through the medium of Irish, with priority given to meeting the particular needs of the Irish-speaking/Gaeltacht community.

- The development of a range of research activities through the medium of Irish, again with priority being given to covering the research needs of the Irish-speaking community.

- The development and implementation of a capital investment programme that would allow an *tAcadamh* to deliver on its academic commitments on campus and within the Gaeltacht. This includes a proposal to develop five Irish-medium university centres – one of which is located on the University campus, with two located in the Connemara Gaeltacht and with one each located in the Gaeltacht districts of Donegal and Kerry.

Within this context, the following ten academic areas were proposed for prioritization in relation to course development and research activity:

- Translation Studies.
- Language Planning.
- Education Studies.
- Information Technology.
- Communication Studies.
- The Arts.
- Courses in applied Irish language skills.
- Community development studies.
- Studies in the development of natural resources.
- Managerial and business studies.

In the next section I give a brief introduction to the first six areas of priority identified above, with an outline of the reasoning that lies behind their identification as areas of priority and the type of activity being undertaken in relation to each area.

## 6.1 Translation Studies

The demand for translation services from English to Irish, and for other services in which a high standard of written Irish is required has grown considerably in recent years. The existing companies providing translation services have experienced a large increase in demand for their services as a result of the provisions of the *Official Languages Act* enacted in 2003, which places an onus on all public sector organizations to produce a range of documents and reports bilingually, and the decision to recognize Irish as an official language of the European Union with effect from January 2007. There is, therefore, a high level of demand for qualified translators and good employment opportunities exist for young graduates as well as opportunities for young entrepreneurs who want to start their own business. *An tAcadamh's* current suite of courses in the discipline of translation studies includes a degree programme, two MA programmes (one in text based translation studies and one in Conference Interpreting) and a part-time Diploma (see Table 1).

## 6.2 Language Planning

The Irish State has invested a lot of effort in the preservation and promotion of Irish over the past 80 years. As a result of this a lot of experience and expertise has been developed in relation to many aspects of language planning. A broad range of organizations are involved in language planning of one kind or another. These include public sector organizations, voluntary organizations, private sector organizations, third level institutions and other organizations in the education sector. The number of individuals working in the public sector with direct responsibility for various aspects of language planning shall increase significantly as a result of the Government's recently enacted language act, as all public sector bodies will have to develop a strategy that will enable them to ensure that their services meet the needs of Irish speakers and can be delivered through the medium of Irish. *An tAcadamh* is of the view that a key element in ensuring the overall effectiveness of the language planning effort lies in the education and training of both current and future language planning practitioners.

*An tAcadamh* is already active in research into language planning issues in Ireland and have been successful in winning a number of major research commissions, leading to the publication of two important research reports: a baseline study of Gaeltacht schools (Mac Donnacha *et al.* 2005) and a sociolinguistic study of the Gaeltacht (Ó Giollagáin and Mac Donnacha *et al.* 2007).

An tAcadamh currently provides an MA in Language Planning which is run on a part-time basis and is targeted at professionals currently working in the sector. Further developments currently being planned include the provision of a fulltime MA programme and a new diploma programme in Language Planning.

## 6.3 Education Studies

The Irish-medium education sector has grown considerably since the early seventies. In addition to the 171 Gaeltacht schools, there are 168 Irish-medium primary schools and 43 Irish-medium secondary operating in non-Gaeltacht areas. As evidenced by the continuous growth of new Irish-medium schools over the past twenty years, this sector is likely to continue to grow. Despite this growth there is still a huge gap between the level of supply and potential demand. Currently only c. 6% of primary school children are receiving their education through the medium of Irish. However, research by Institiúid Teangeolaíochta Éireann (Ó Riagáin and Ó Gliasáin, 1994), shows that up to 30% of parents would be willing to send their children to an Irish-medium school if such a school was available locally. Given these figures it seems likely that there will be a continuous demand for teachers and services in this sector in the foreseeable future.

*An tAcadamh's* objectives in this area are to support the continued development of Irish-medium education by providing support services and by ensuring that teachers are available who are qualified to teach through the medium of Irish in gaelscoileanna (Irish-medium schools in non-Gaeltacht districts) and in Gaeltacht schools. The University currently provides a postgraduate diploma in education through the medium of Irish. In addition *An tAcadamh* has developed a part-time Diploma in Language Acquisition and Child Development for people working as language assistants in Gaeltacht schools and a part-time MA in Language Teaching for teachers already working in the sector. Further courses envisaged in this area include teacher training programmes at degree level, and courses in preschool education, remedial education, career guidance and school management and development.

## 6.4 Information Technology

In order to ensure that the Gaeltacht and the Irish language can take advantage of the information era, continuous investment is necessary to ensure that the necessary information, concepts and skills are available in Gaeltacht communities to enable them to avail of the opportunities that new information and communication technologies provide. *An tAcadamh* has already invested successfully in this area, through projects initiated on its Gaeltacht campuses. Projects undertaken to date include a post-graduate course in software development, and two diploma courses in Applied Computer Skills.

## 6.5 Media and Communications

The Irish-speaking community currently has access to a broad range of Irish language media, which includes broadcast and print media. These play an important role in sustaining the future of the Irish language and of the Gaeltacht. They provide recreation, education and information for the community through the medium of their own language, and they act as a forum in which community organizations, elected representatives, journalists and other experts can communicate and debate their views and opinions on various issues which relate to the life of the Gaeltacht and of the country. They provide a platform for Gaeltacht and Irish speaking artists – actors, writers, musicians, dancers etc. – which enables them to perform and celebrate their art. It is estimated that between them Irish language broadcast and print media provide fulltime employment, of a kind attractive to young graduates, for in excess of 500 people.

A broad range of professional skills is needed by these media services. In addition they need professionals who have excellent spoken and written Irish and they also need access to people with the necessary management and strategic planning skills. *An tAcadamh* currently offers a BA in Communication Studies, a Higher Diploma in Applied Communications and diploma courses in radio and television broadcasting. We have also established a television production company on one of our Gaeltacht campuses, which has produced programmes for TG4, the Irish language television service.

## 6.6 The Performing Arts

The arts are an important element in the life of all communities. This is especially so in the case of a linguistic community like the Gaeltacht and Irish speaking community. The arts provide them with an opportunity to enquire into and make sense of their own lives, their own imaginations and their own concepts of identity and spirituality and to open them up for examination by the community and the rest of the world. Heretofore, Gaeltacht communities have held onto their traditional art forms as a defense and as an escape from the constant stream of global cultures and linguistic pressures to which they are exposed through the access which they have to national and international media. Performance arts which are seen as being of particular importance in their own right and which have an important role in sustaining the community identity of the Gaeltacht include:

- The Performing Arts:   Drama, *agallaimh beirte*, work songs.
- Music:   Traditional and modern music, singing and dancing.

- Literature: Prose, poetry, radio and television writing.
- Folklore: Storytelling.

The support structures for these Gaeltacht art forms are to be found in voluntary/community organisations such as: *An Comhlachas Náisiúnta Drámaíochta*, *An tOireachtas*, *Pléaráca*, *An Cumann Scoildrámaíochta*, and *Comhaltas Ceoltóirí Éireann*. Raidió na Gaeltachta has been a champion of Gaeltacht art forms since its establishment in 1972, and TG4 represents new opportunities for their exposition, development and presentation. An important factor in the value of these arts is their facilitation of the development of relationships between artists from the Gaeltacht and other Irish speaking artists, with artists from other linguistic and minority communities.

An tAcadamh is currently developing its suite of programmes in this area and currently provides a Higher Diploma in Drama Studies, a Diploma in the Staging of Traditional Music and a part-time Diploma in Acting.

**Table 1: Current Suite of Programmes Offered by Acadamh na hOllscolaíochta Gaeilge (as of September 2008)**

| Courses offered by Acadamh na hOllscolaíochta Gaeilge |
|---|
| MA/Dioplóma Iarchéime i Léann an Aistriúcháin *(MA/Posgraduate Diploma in Translation Studies)* |
| MA in Ateangaireacht Chomhdhála *(MA in Conference Interpreting)*. Commencing September 2008. |
| MA i dTeagasc Teangacha (An Ghaeilge) *(MA in Language Teaching)*. Part-time programme. |
| MA sa Phleanáil Teanga *(MA in Language Planning)*. Fulltime and Part-time programme. |
| Ph.D/M.Sc. (trí thaighde) sa Teicneolaíocht Faisnéise *(Ph.D/M.Sc. (by Research) in Information Technology)* |
| Dioplóma Iarchéime san Oideachas *(Postgraduate Diploma in Education)* |
| Ard-Dioplóma i gCumarsáid Fheidhmeach *(Higher Diploma in Applied Communications)* |
| Ard-Dioplóma sa Dramaíocht *(Higher Diploma in Drama Studies)*. Part-time programme. |
| BA sa Chumarsáid *(BA in Communications Studies)* |
| BA i Léann an Aistriúcháin *(Translations Studies as part of Omnibus BA programme)* |
| BA (Gaeilge agus Léann an Aistriúcháin) *(BA in Irish and Translations Studies)*. Denominated degree programme commencing in September 2008. |
| BA sa Riarachán Gnó *(BA in Business Administration)*. Commencing in September 2008 in collaboration with Letterkenny Institute of Technology. |
| Dioplóma sna Dána (Scileanna Raidió) *(Diploma in Radio Broadcasting)*. Full time programme. |
| Dioplóma sna Dána (Scileanna Teilifíse) *(Diploma in Television Broadcasting)*. Full time programme. |

| | |
|---|---|
| Dioplóma sna Dána (Ríomhaireacht don Riarachán Gnó) *(Diploma in Business Computing)*. Full time programme. | |
| Dioplóma sna Dána (Cóiriú agus Stáitsiú an Cheoil Thraidisiúnta) *(Diploma in the Staging of Traditional Music)* | |
| Dioplóma sna Dána (Scileanna Aistriúcháin) *(Diploma in Translation Studies)*. Part-time programme. | |
| Dioplóma i dTeicneolaíochtaí Gnó *(Diploma in Business Computing)*. Part-time programme. | |
| Dioplóma sna Dána (Aisteoireacht) *(Diploma in Acting)*. Part-time programme. | |
| Dioplóma sa Ghaeilge (C1) *(Diploma in Irish (Level C1))*. Part-time programme. | |
| Dioplóma sa Ghaeilge (B2) *(Diploma in Irish (Level B2))*. Part-time programme. | |
| Dioplóma sa Ghaeilge (A2) *(Diploma in Irish (Level A2))*. Part-time programme. | |
| Dioplóma i Léann an Traidisiúin *(Diploma in Folklore))*. Part-time programme. | |

## 7. Conclusion

As of September 2008, *an tAcadamh* provides a total of seven postgraduate programmes, three undergraduate degree programmes, four full-time undergraduate diploma programmes and seven part-time undergraduate diploma programmes. In the current Academic year (2007–08) *an tAcadamh* has 78 postgraduate students and 119 fulltime undergraduate degree and diploma students. In addition a total of 797 students are registered on *an tAcadamh*'s suite of part-time diploma programmes.

For the future we see several principles as being critical to the way in which we wish to develop An *tAcadamh*. Firstly the focus of *An tAcadamh* will not be on the provision of courses through the medium of Irish. Our focus will be on providing courses that meet the needs and requirements of the Irish-speaking community. By definition, this means that the courses will be delivered through the medium of Irish – and this is not a debatable issue. However, a focus on meeting the needs of the language community rather than focusing on providing courses in the target language, in our view, allows for a more strategic approach to the provision of university education in lesser-used languages and results in more sustainable outcomes.

Secondly, the focus of *An tAcadamh* will not be limited to the provision of university courses through the medium of Irish. A key element of its development will be the nurturing of research activity and the development of consultancy type services which allow *An tAcadamh* to share its expertise with other public, private and community organizations active in the Irish-speaking community. We want to be an Irish-medium university institute in the broadest sense of what a university should be – encompassing both research and teaching activities.

Our purpose, as an Irish-medium institute is not simply to ensure that the major ideas, issues, theories and practices of the day are borrowed from the rest of the world and considered, discussed and debated in Irish, important and all as this may be. Our major challenge is to ensure that we as an Irish-medium university academy have the self-confidence to create, develop and inspire new ideas, theory and practice and thereby contribute to the intellectual diversity of the world rather than simply borrowing from it.

An *tAcadamh* will provide a significant proportion of its courses on our Gaeltacht campuses, thereby ensuring that a significant proportion of Gaeltacht residents have access to third level education without having to leave their own community – to ensure that they are educated to benefit their own community rather than being educated out of their community.

Finally, *An tAcadamh* will seek to make a difference – and that is how we shall measure our success in the future. Have we made a difference? Have we made a significant contribution to the creation of a sustainable future for the Irish language community? Have we made a significant contribution to the development of language planning theory and practice – not just in Ireland but internationally? And have we created a university model that can be emulated in other places as a means of ensuring that other indigenous communities have access through the medium of their own language to the full range of benefits that a university can bestow?

**References**

Census of Population. 2006. Dublin: Central Statistics Office.
Mac Donnacha, S., F. Ní Chualáin, A. Ní Shéaghdha, and T. Ní Mhainín. 2005. *Staid Reatha na Scoileanna Gaeltachta*. Dublin: An Chomhairle um Oideachas Gaeltachta agus Gaelscolaíochta.
National University of Ireland, Galway. 2000. *A Strategy for the Development of Third Level Education in the Gaeltacht.*
National University of Ireland, Galway. 2003. *Strategic Plan for NUI, Galway: 2003– 2008.*
Ó Cinnéide, M. 2004. 'University Education in Irish with Particular Emphasis on the Requirements of the Gaeltacht'. In eds. Nic Pháidín, C and D. Uí Bhraonáin, *University Education in Irish: Challenges and Perspectives*. Dublin: Fiontar Dublin City University. 107–23.
Ó Giollagáin C., S Mac Donnacha, F. Ní Chualáin, A. Ní Shéaghda and M. O'Brien. 2007. *Staidéar Teangeolaíoch ar Úsáid na Gaeilge sa nGaeltacht*. Dublin: An Roinn Gnóthaí Pobail, Tuaithe agus Gaeltachta.
Ó Riagáin P. and M. Ó Gliasáin, 1994. *National Survey on Languages 1993: Preliminary Report*. Dublin: Institiúid Teangeolaíochta Éireann.
Watson D. and T. Fahey, 1997. *Survey of Employment Needs in Gaeltacht Areas: Report to Údarás na Gaeltachta*. Dublin: ESRI.

# Buíon dar Slua thar Thoinn do Ráinig Chugainn (Some have Come from a Land beyond the Wave): Immigrant Learners of Irish in the North of Ireland

*Mary Delargy*

Recent events surrounding the potential introduction of an Irish Language Act for Northern Ireland have raised a number of important issues. In particular the decision by the DUP Minister for Culture Arts and Leisure not to proceed with it on grounds of cost led to accusations of sectarianism since the debate seemed to divide along party political lines.[1] This is despite the fact that the last twenty years have seen a growth in the number of members of the Protestant community choosing to learn Irish. Moreover, there is evidence of some interest among members of the new immigrant communities in learning more about their country of adoption through learning the language. This paper is a very personal one insofar as the issues discussed in it all came about as a result of my involvement with and passion for the Irish language. It explores two different groups of learners of Irish, one members of the 'indigenous ' Protestant community the other a group of members of the 'new communities' living in Derry. 'New communities' refers to members of the various communities recently arrived in Ireland. Each of the groups had a different emphasis on the aspect of Irish in which they were interested, and this is explored in the essay.

In the early 1970s, I started secondary school in Derry. My education was received against a backdrop of the Troubles, internment was introduced three weeks before the new term began, my first year punctuated by Bloody Sunday and the subsequent events for which it was a catalyst. Irish was taught only in the Catholic secondary schools in Northern Ireland and was seen by some, despite its associations with poverty and backwardness, as a way in which we could assert our identity. To those with political aspirations, it was another way in which separateness from England could be demonstrated, to those with less overt political beliefs it was a cultural identifier which marked out our unique position of having the oldest vernacular literature in Europe after Latin and Greek. Moreover, the majority of the textbooks used at the time the twin traditions of faith and fatherland with their emphasis on saints, scholars and Celtic mythology.

At the same time, in Belfast, Bunscoil Phobail Feirste, the first Irish medium primary school opened its Portakabin doors to five children. The school received no funding from the Department of Education but was funded by the dedicated parents who had established the Shaw's Road Gaeltacht – or Irish-speaking district – some years previously.

Thirteen years and several hundred children later, the school was finally awarded recognition by the Department of Education in 1984. There are currently [in 2007] 33 primary schools and three secondary schools in Northern Ireland providing Irish-medium education.[2]

A trip to the Gaeltacht or Irish-speaking area was a most enjoyable three-week summer break. Although teachers encouraged us improve our skills in speaking and writing the language, even they seemed to feel it was destined to end its days as a

---

[1] For examples of the debate, see www.dcalni.gov.uk
[2] Comhairle na Gaelscolaiochta website, www.comhairle.org

forgotten tongue since long before Reg Hindley strode on to the scene with his *Death of the Irish Language*.² The topic for debate in the class was frequently a variant on the theme of 'Nach bhfuil i ndán don Ghaeilge ach an bás' or, translated, 'the fate of the Irish language is its demise'. It is ironic, therefore that almost 30 years later the number of people learning to speak Irish from within the Nationalist community may not be significantly different, but people from a greater diversity of backgrounds are now choosing to learn the language.

My own interest in the language grew and continued right through to a degree in Celtic Studies from Queen's University. Although I remained passionate about the language my linguistic skills were not as competent as I might have wished and I realised that talents lay in a different direction.

In 1987, I was appointed as a library assistant in the renowned Linen Hall Library in Belfast. As an Irish speaker, one of my duties was to bring together the library's assorted books and periodicals in Irish to form the nucleus of a collection. This was combined with regular counter duties so on many an occasion I found myself standing at the library desk carrying on a conversation in Irish. Over a period of time I was approached by a number of people who told me that they had always wanted to learn Irish but never had an opportunity-most of them were from a Protestant background and would not have learnt it at school. According to the most recent Census figures available (2001), just under 11,000 persons from the Protestant community in Northern Ireland have 'some knowledge' of the language, with the highest proportion in the 40–59 age group and around 60% of the total being female. Gradually the idea formed that the library might be a suitable setting in which to hold classes particularly since the library with its historical connections with the United Irishmen and the concepts of liberty, equality and fraternity, and its more recent role as the repository for material from all possible political opinions, made it a perceived 'neutral' venue where people from diverse backgrounds could study the language. I was fortunate in having an understanding boss who agreed to allow classes to be held on the premises. These began with a small group of ten people meeting once a week for half an hour and gradually grew to three classes per week at beginners' intermediate and advanced levels and teachers recruited from beyond the library thanks to the generous support of Iontaobhas ULTACH / ULTACH Trust an organisation whose stated aim is 'to promote the Irish language throughout the entire community of Northern Ireland' and equally generous funding and support from the Community Relations Council. The question of whether a member of the class was Catholic or Protestant never arose overtly and unlike one of the other classes which I taught, no-one ever attempted to find out whether anyone else belonged to a particular group or not. What was evident, however, was that there was a difference in the topics which were of interest to the different sections of the community. As I knew many of the students in the class personally, I had a reasonable idea as to their religious background. I became aware that one section – mainly those from a Protestant background – were much more interested in place names and surnames than other aspects of the language. I spent a considerable amount of time not only discussing the origin of the main towns and cities but also much smaller places – right down to townland level, where I was often forced to thumb my way through the volumes on the place names of various counties in Northern Ireland issued by the place-names project at Queen's University in order to find the meaning of some long-forgotten townland in Antrim or Down. Why precisely they had such an interest in these details is a matter of speculation – there will undoubtedly be those who see in it legacy of the coloniser wanting to maintain his hold on the land.

³ Reg Hindley, *Death of the Irish Language*. London: Routledge. 1990.

In an article published in 1979 at the time when the Post Office first tried to replace townland names with postcodes the late Deirdre Flanagan wrote:[4]

> At a social level, one's identity is one's forename and surname. In civic terms, however, the address is an essential part of the identity. The urban address is normally house-number and street-name; nevertheless the town-dweller tends to identify, on a personal level with the area he lives in rather than the street. [...] People identify with their town lands whether they stay in them or go from them. It is equally true of Planter and of Gael. The identity of people with their place is instinctive, traditional and deep-rooted. It applies at all levels from tenant to lord. (A peer of the realm must express his toponymic identity in his title, e.g. Lord O' Neill of the Maine.)

My first experience of teaching Irish to those from outside the island came in 2006. The Academy for Irish Cultural Heritages at the University of Ulster attracts researchers and postgraduate students from around the world and that year's cohort was no different. Included among them were a German, an American, a Canadian, two Italians, a Lithuanian and a Kenyan.

Not everyone, as may be obvious from the above, had English as their first language. On occasion, normally when in contact with the home country, it was normal for people to revert to using their first language. As someone who speaks Irish, I have on occasion used the language with colleagues with whom I work on specific projects.

I had not anticipated the amount of interest which speaking Irish provoked in my colleagues. At first it was the usual questions about how long I had been learning to speak Irish, how many people spoke it, etc. Gradually this developed in enquiries about where Irish could be learned. It became apparent that rather than have people trying to find beginners' classes starting midway through the year my best plan was to organise the classes myself. When preparing for the classes I had put together material which was very similar to that which I had used for my previous classes as I anticipated that the students would have similar interests. I was surprised, therefore to discover that the topics on which the new students wanted to spend most time were quite different. Possibly because they did not have – or need – the same sense of rootedness to the locality, they showed little interest in finding out about the origin of the place names. Rather, they preferred to find out as much as possible about the customs and folklore associated with Ireland which could be understood through learning the language. These included discussion on the festival of *Samhain* or Halloween both in Ireland and in other European countries which arose out of the students learning the names of the months of the year. This grew into a wider discussion about not only the celebration of Halloween with its associations with the two worlds but also commemorating the Day of the Dead on the following day and symbolism and rituals surrounding death and burial – a discussion which we probably would have felt was too sensitive to have had without the catalyst of the language lesson. Similarly the word *Bealtaine*, the name for the month of May opened up discussions about the symbolism of bonfires in festivals throughout Europe and further afield.

The concept of members of the new communities choosing to learn Irish is one which has been gaining momentum over the last few years.

There is already one organisation, iMeasc, dedicated to people from outside Ireland who wish to learn the language. Formed in 2005 by Ariel Killick, an Australian

---

[4] Flanagan, D. 'Place-Names: A Matter of Identity'. *Bulletin of the Ulster Place-Name Society*, ser. 2, vol. 1 (1978), 1–2.

translator, and Alex Hijmans, a journalist, and former editor of *Foinse*, the group is an 'informal network and lobby group for immigrants with an interest in speaking Irish. There was a fear that the 'influx of foreign nationals' would be used as an excuse for downgrading the status of the language, particularly after the requirement of fluency it Irish was removed from *An Garda Síochána* (the Irish police force) to allow more people from ethnic minority communities to join the force. The group was awarded the TG4 (Irish Language Television) prize for Outstanding Services to the Irish Language in 2006. Accepting the award, Ariel Killick said:

> The number of highly-fluent Irish speaking immigrants and the range of ways they are actively contributing to strengthening and diversifying this most central aspect of Irish culture ... is astounding'[4]

More recently an article in the *Irish News* drew attention to an initiative by Gael-Linn, an organisation for Irish-language speakers in Armagh. The aim is to encourage interaction between members of the Polish community living in Armagh and Irish speakers in the city. The Poles will learn a little Irish and the Irish-speakers a few words of Polish as well as each gaining some understanding of the other's culture. A series of events have been organised including a lecture looking at links between Ireland and Poland and a trip to the Gaeltacht is planned for later in the year. This type of event has been particularly successful in bringing together men from the locality and newcomers who might have been self-conscious about ways to get to know one another without the excuse of the language classes.

A further event forging links between the Irish-speaking community and the new communities was organised by Irish-language umbrella organisation *POBAL* in February 2008. The press release for the event described a range of activities:

> On this day, POBAL are organising a Celebratory Parade in support of the Irish language and diversity to the city centre. In addition, there will be a rich mix of multi-cultural activities for all ages before the parade. The event is part of POBAL's new project, 'Tá: 'Say yes to the Irish language', and Irish language and English groups from all over the country are supporting the initiative. Now the innovative campaign is being joined by ethnic minority and arts groups to raise the positive profile of our shared cultural wealth. Cultúrlann McAdam Ó Fiaich will be the venue also for workshops and taster sessions from 11 am with an International Food Fayre, music and storytelling, Chinese arts, songs from south America, poetry from Africa, face-painting and henna hand painting and Indian Head Massage.

Julius Anakaa of the Afro-Community Support Organisation said:

> 'It is good that POBAL have taken this initiative to bring people together, recognising the Irish language as well as other communities that live here. This can only increase and add to the richness of the culture here and make it a better place.'[5]
>
> Perhaps the future of the language lies not only with Irishmen and women but with those who 'have come from a land beyond the wave'.

---

[4] *ITIA* [Irish Translators' and Interpretors' Association] *Bulletin*, November 2006; see www.translatorsassociation.ie

[5] Quoted at http://www.pobal.org/english/ta.php

# Irish: Unfavourable Implications of Sociolinguistic Labels?[1]

*Göran Wolf*

## Preliminary Contextualisation

Before embarking on this article's actual content, I should like to highlight an omnipresent aspect of Irish life and culture as it presents itself in the Northern Ireland: murals – a topic about which, unfortunately, little academic interest has been shown. In discussing two notably important and compelling Belfast murals, my argument becomes apparent. The two murals to which I refer were photographed in Belfast in November 2007. At that time, the Irish Gaelic mural, as I shall refer to it (Figures 1a and 1b), was situated in the Falls Road area; the other mural, referring to Ulster Scots (Figures 2a and 2b), was to be found in the Albertbridge Road area.

With reference to fundamental human rights, the Irish Gaelic mural bears the message *An Ghaeilge thart timpeall orainn*, followed by a translation, *Irish is all around us*. This points, first of all, to a truism. In Belfast, as anywhere else on the island of Ireland, Irish is of course all around us, since the majority of place-names, family-names and other nomenclature is of Irish origin. Yet that obvious fact implicitly calls for action. It seems to stand for: 'If Irish is all around us, why do you not speak it?' or 'Why do you pretend it is something foreign and try to prevent others enjoying it?'.[2] I take the mural to be a comment on language awareness (and ethnic language use), which is surely the first step towards maintaining a language.

The mural related to (Ulster) Scots can be read in a similar fashion. Although some factual references are questionable, the linguistic aspect is once again important. This mural almost beseeches a recourse to shared traditions in approaching well-known Northern Irish disputes. Linguistically, this culminates in the given Scots phrases: *Dinnae houl yer wheest – houl yer ain!* Again, this can be interpreted as an act of raising awareness for a speech variety: 'If you have a high opinion of common ground with Scotland and/or Britain in general, you ought to have a high opinion of Scots.'

Regardless of the political outlooks that they express, the messages of the two murals support their respective speech varieties by implicitly calling for active use. What is more, language issues are public and, literally, visible, a fact that this short excursus is intended to illustrate. If we take the assertions presented in these murals to extremes, we may conclude that both opinions refer to the sentiment that people make out a desirable unifying form of speech.

## Preliminary Remarks

This contribution is based upon the following line of thought. Language maintenance can no doubt be described, discussed and supported by academic work. Yet language maintenance has to happen in the 'real world' beyond scholarly considerations. Sustaining a (minority) language is therefore a matter of its corresponding speech community. That speech community is where maintaining a language is publicly and

---

[1] This article is dedicated to those two people who introduced me to Irish affairs: Bernadette Ferguson and Kevin Dobbins.

[2] I owe the latter reading to Gavin Falconer, to whom I am greatly indebted for some very valuable comments and remarks on an earlier draft of this paper.

Figure 1a: Irish Language Mural

Figure 1b: Irish Language Mural, Detail

officially communicated. Here, 'public communication' should be understood as communication within the speech community and through any of its media; 'official communication' refers to communication of politicians and other decision-makers. It goes without saying that the latter type of communication especially is not always characterised by accurate and factual usage of terminology or neutral argumentation. More often than not, an ideological bias creeps in. Ideology should not be deemed wrong, however, since that is how awareness can best be raised. At the same time, ideological bias can also veil the truth. It is therefore clear that public and official discourses cannot get around the necessity of using terminology correctly.

*Irish: Unfavourable Implications of Sociolinguistic Labels?* 71

**Figure 2a:** Ulster Scots Mural

**Figure 2b:** Ulster Scots Mural, Detail

## Introduction

Regarding the symposium to which the present volume's authors were invited, a great deal of relevant terminology is sociolinguistic terminology. One very prominent term is given in the symposium's title: 'minority language'. Some of the languages dealt with in November 2007 in Belfast have become minority languages as a result of language contact. As is evident all over the world, language contact is a process without predictable outcomes.

One language that has gone through just such an unpredictable process of language contact is Irish, and it was Irish that inspired my review of sociolinguistic terminology. The reason is that, I believe, to the interested outsider – i.e., an outsider in relation to Ireland as well as to linguistic matters – the terminology used to refer to the Irish language might seem ambivalent.[3] Irish Gaelic is given a number of labels depending on the context. Of course, *Bunreacht na hÉireann* refers to Irish as a 'national language'. In other places, Irish is called 'community language' (e.g. *Ráiteas i leith na Gaeilge* 2006), 'endangered language' (e.g. Fennell 1985), 'lesser-used language' (Antonini, Corrigan and Wei 2002), 'minority language' (e.g. Ó Corráin and MacMathúna 1998), 'official language' (e.g. *Bunreacht na hEireann*), 'threatened language' (e.g. Ó Riagáin 2001), or 'working language' (e.g. *Ráiteas i leith na Gaeilge* 2006). At first glance, all of those labels reflect specific angles – all of them justifiable – from which Irish can be viewed.

Taken literally, however, and judging from a perspective that takes those sociolinguistic labels seriously, some of the given notions are contradictory, and some may even be mutually exclusive. The terms that, in my opinion, are mutually exclusive are 'national language' and 'minority language', and it is the former of them that this article seeks to explore in relation to its repercussions for maintaining Irish Gaelic as a minority language.

In order to adumbrate my argument within the limits of a contribution such as this, I shall proceed as follows. I shall first introduce selected contributions to the discussion of the sociolinguistic concept of 'national language'. This concept will be treated in relation to its sociological cognate term 'nation'. Secondly, I shall challenge the applicability of the terms with regards to the linguistic situation in Ireland. The article will conclude with critical notes on the terminology that result from questions of their applicability. By returning to one contribution to the field of sociolinguistics in particular – as far as I can tell, a lesser-known one – I hope to give fresh impetus to discussion about maintaining minority-language communities.

## Terminological Considerations

The context in which any present-day language must be viewed is globalisation. Referring to globalisation, some scholars question the validity of concepts such as 'nations' and 'national language' and, indeed, deem those terms obsolete (cf. Smith 2001: 92). Yet globalisation is a de-traditionalising force that brings about reversals. Regionalisation or localisation is therefore a resort to that which is just around the corner. Nations, national identities and national beliefs are certainly not yet anachronistic.

---

[3] It is important to stress that, in this paper, I am dealing with Irish Gaelic irrespective of the two political entities – the Republic of Ireland vs. Northern Ireland as part of the United Kingdom – that exist on the island. I am fully aware that this would require a more complex analysis. Yet the facts that the political entities do not coincide with the boundary of Ulster as historical province, and that languages go beyond state borders, justify my approach, which, in this respect, is disconnected from political considerations.

In the following, the important concept of 'nation' is taken for granted. This concept, as well as all related ideas, has been treated by a large number of scholars from fields such as anthropology, history, politics or, obviously, linguistics. A nation is a highly abstract unit, and, in Anderson's terms, a nation is 'imagined' (1991 [1983]). It is imagined because of one very obvious fact:

> [T]he members of even the smallest nation will never know most of their fellow-members, meet them, or even hear of them, yet in the minds of each lives the image of their communion. (Anderson 1991: 6)

Not only are nations imagined communities at a given point in time, they are also historically constituted communities, because '[a] nation is by its nature a transgenerational entity' (Shils 1995: 100). This historicity of nations confirms Hobsbawm's well-known postulate that 'the real 'nation' can only be recognised *a posteriori*' (1990: 9; Hobsbawm's italics). In sum, Smith's definition still stands the test of time:

> A nation can therefore be defined as a named human population sharing an historic territory, common myths and historical memories, a mass, public culture, a common economy and common legal rights and duties for all members. (Smith 1991: 14)

Disregarding different facets that may find different emphases, one should not underestimate the fact that nations are aggregates of personal and communal *will*. Members of any nation must have the will to imagine their national community and to accept their belonging to specific national territories, myths, histories, cultures, economic and legal units. Reichmann's comments below are very much along those lines:

> Betrachtet man Gegebenheiten des Typs 'Gemeinschaft', 'Nationalsprache', 'Volk' als genuin historisch, dann sind sie per definitionem Konstrukte, Entwürfe, Ideen, Bilder, Glaubensinhalte, Zielvorstellungen, Sinnstiftungen geschichtlich Handelnder; sie existieren nur, indem sie von einer Gruppe von Menschen als existent behauptet und behandelt werden.[4] (Reichmann 2000: 420–1)

Eventually, we should like to see the concept of 'nation' on a 'desirable' basis: communication networks, educational systems, language planning are usually limited within that aggregate (cf. Ferguson 1996: 269).

The concept of 'national language' is just as basic: language seems to be the 'supreme [...] human symbol system' and it is 'more likely than other symbol-systems to become symbolic' (Fishman 1987: 639). And even though the nation-language nexus is not without dispute (cf. Hutchinson 1987: 9), there is scholarly and lay agreement about the importance of languages to national identities. Discussing ambiguities and obscurities in relation to the concepts 'dialect', 'language' and 'nation', Haugen (1996) introduced a straightforward imperative:

---

[4] Considering realities such as 'community', 'national language', 'people' as genuinely historical, these are *per definitionem* constructs, frameworks, ideas, images, beliefs, objectives, meaningful foundations of historical agents; these realities only exist because people consider them to exist and treat them accordingly. (translation G. Wolf).

> Every self-respecting nation has to have a language. Not just a medium
> of communication, a 'vernacular' or a 'dialect', but a fully developed
> language. Anything less marks it as underdeveloped. (p. 927)

Less demanding, Fishman considers language 'a defining characteristic of a nationality' (1972: 49). He points out that '[t]he ideological pinnacle of language nationalism is not reached until language is clearly pictured as *more* crucial than the other symbols and expressions of nationality' (*ibid.*). Fishman's understanding, which has been widely acknowledged, has recently been matched by the general remark that:

> Nationalism is the doctrine that requires the congruence between the
> political and the cultural (ethnic) group. The motto of modernity is one
> state, one culture. (Llobera 2004: 84)

However, even if relevant terminology is touched upon in all quotes above, they still do not provide us with a concise definition of the concept 'national language'.

In the following, I should like to examine a number of approaches offered in handbooks on sociolinguistics and other relevant publications in the field, and I should like to start with one with which I am both content and discontent. Approaching the term 'nationalist language', which in my opinion should be kept separate from 'national language',[5] Fasold established six sociolinguistic criteria for 'national language' status:

1) 'symbol of national identity for a significant proportion of the population';
2) '*widely* used for some *everyday* purposes';
3) '*widely and fluently* spoken within the country';
4) 'no major alternative nationalist languages in the country';
5) '*acceptable* as a symbol of authenticity';
6) 'link with the glorious past' (Fasold 1984: 77; my italics).

In a different, but nonetheless concrete conceptualisation, by Ising (1987), we read:

a) *Standard* bzw. *Literatur-*, *Hoch-* oder *Schriftsprache* einer nationalen Sprach- und Kommunikationsgemeinschaft (unter Ausschluß von Dialekten und Soziolekten).
b) Gesamtheit der historischen, regionalen, sozialen und funktionalen (situativen) *Varietäten* einer Sprache, die von einer Sprach- oder Kommunikationsgemeinschaft in der Epoche ihrer Herausbildung und Existenz als Nation gesprochen und geschrieben werden.[6] (p. 335)

---

[5] The reason why I want to differentiate clearly between 'national language' and 'nationalist language' is their different connotations: a language is a nationalist language if it helps to support nationalist views, if it helps to implement *nationalist* concerns, and if it aids the pursuit of identity nationalism.

[6] a) *Standard or literary language* of a national speech and communication community (excluding dialects and sociolects). b) Sum of all historical, regional, social and functional *varieties* of a language that are spoken and written by a speech and communication community during its stages of development and existence as a nation. (translation G. Wolf).

I should like to draw attention to the notion of a 'Kommunikationsgemeinschaft' ('communication community'). It emphasises that a national language is used habitually and extensively.

Other attempts to come to terms with 'national language' offer us the following. Matthews considers a national language '[o]ne which is a source or sign of identity for a nation [which should be] distinguished from an official language' (Matthews 1997: 238). Both Trask and Trudgill offer concise definitions that exhibit the same line of thought: a national language is the 'single principal' (Trask 1999: 198) or the 'main' language of a country/state (Trudgill 2003: 91). Giving a varied and lengthy definition, Barbour presents us with national languages that are the 'majority language of the nation' (Barbour 2004: 291), 'core defining characteristic of the nation' (Barbour 2004: 292), that have a 'symbolic, identity-forming role' (*ibid.*) and that 'have little to do with utility' (*ibid.*). Obviously, all attempts have their origin in very particular standpoints, and there is no right or wrong with any of them. However, language is about speaking, writing and communicating, and it is only in actual communication that one can exhibit signs of identity. A symbol that is not used extensively may become even more symbolic, and this can possibly be problematic. The more symbolic an entity is, the more it is apt to become random and replaceable.

**Challenge of Applicability**

If we now hold the minority language Irish Gaelic up against what has just been presented, one would have to stress what has been said probably more than once: the official classification in the *Bunreacht* does not seem to reflect the (socio)linguistic reality on display in Ireland (cf. Ó Murchú 1993: 471). Ideologically as well as politically, it is, no doubt, unfavourable to say that Irish is not a national language. That is why I should like to recapitulate a number of implications that are strongly related to all of the above. Yet they are not necessarily voiced when discussing any of these issues. To repeat, I should like to recapitulate some implications that result from the conferral on a minority language of the label 'national language'.[7]

The first and much too obvious implication I derive from the notion 'minority language' itself. The term 'minority' comes from the Latin word *minor* (cf. *minoritas/minoritatem*), which in turn is related to the Latin words *minuere* 'to reduce', 'to diminish', 'to lessen', *minutia* 'smallness' and *minus* comparative of *parum*: 'less', 'fewer'. Given that etymology, a minority language is inherently weak. It is weak in many respects, whereas 'national language' as a term bears the connotation of a strong and vital language. That might create a contradiction for its actual as well as potential speakers: a strong language or – to illustrate the point that I should like to make much better – national language is not necessarily one that has to be safeguarded or maintained. A strong language will maintain itself through its mere existence. A minority language, however, is associated with language maintenance, language revival, language revitalisation or even with the threat of language death. All of those notions have an uneasy feel to them, and their unquestionable relevance with regard to the language situation in Ireland has been addressed more than once (e.g. Ó Béarra 2007).

Another point that, as far as I have been able to find out, has not been addressed by studies concerned with the terminology discussed here is that a language can be

---

[7] Whether this official labelling coincides with views held by (all) individual members of the corresponding speech community is not discussed and would of course be a legitimate objective of a study of language attitudes.

exclusivist or inclusivist. It goes without saying that any language is always both exclusivist and inclusivist, i.e. a language includes those who speak it and excludes those who do not. However, that must be seen in a different light if we are concerned with specific language functions. In that way, I maintain that a national language, if held against its corresponding speech community, must be inclusivist.

A third point of discussion once again raises issues of what is implied by terminology. As stated above, the label 'national language' is a sign of the soundness and vitality of a language, and at the same time, it suggests that the (national) speech community should be under the obligation to use the language extensively (cf. once again Fasold 1984: 77), which is why I should like to suggest the following. If the maintenance of languages is discussed, the question of language loyalty and language disloyalty should be addressed too, since language disloyalty is a fact of life yet hardly attracts any attention (Kramer 1990: 16). I am not sure whether language disloyalty has been studied with regard to Irish (or any other language among those discussed at the symposium), but I should like to see whether Kramer's conception will hold its own in the Irish situation, which has been influenced by migratory and economic necessities. Kramer says:

> Sprachilloyalität liegt vor, wenn Angehörige einer Sprachgemeinschaft statt der eigenen [eine] fremde Sprache bevorzugen, weil sie ihre Muttersprache entweder als zu wenig geeignet für bestimmte Zielsetzungen oder als nachteilig für ihre politischen Überzeugungen ansehen.[8] (p. 16)

He continues:

> Sprachloyalität und Sprachilloyalität sind Reflexe ideologisch-politisch-gesellschaftlicher Prozesse, die sich außerhalb des Rahmens der von einer eng definierten Systemlinguistik beschriebenen Phänomene abspielen und doch eine entscheidende Auswirkung auf das Sprachleben haben.[9] (p.21)

Questioning loyalty and disloyalty as well as their influence upon the life of a language also leads us to address whether, in the case of Ireland, we are still dealing with English as a foreign language, because simple observations, such as the one given by Safran about Dublin (1999: 87), can and must be extended to the conclusion that 'for most Irish people, life in Ireland is interpreted through English rather than Irish Gaelic'. Given that simple truth, I believe that we must approach the idea that, at least potentially, Irish English is able to take over all characteristics of a national language, as given by Fasold's matrix.[10] In my view, its course has taken off from its state of contradiction along the ideological and the material axis (Kallen 1988: 137), as can be

---

[8] There is language disloyalty if members of a speech community prefer a foreign language to their native tongue because they consider the latter either less suitable for certain objectives or disadvantageous for their political convictions. (translation G. Wolf).
[9] Language loyalty and language disloyalty reflect ideological and political processes in society. Those take place beyond those phenomena that can be described within the framework of narrowly defined linguistics. Yet reflections of societal processes exert a decisive influence upon the course of languages. (translation G. Wolf).
[10] Intriguing arguments that would support this view are given in Fennell 1985 (especially pages 252–5).

seen in one of the recent studies by John Kirk and Jeffrey Kallen. There the authors identify features of Irish (Standard) English capable of creating cohesive identity:

> [W]e point out that lexical and syntactic markers have more than referential or propositional value alone, since they serve both to point to wider cultural values associated with Ireland and the Irish people and to create solidarity between speakers who share these values. Such Celtic features in discourse have the function of establishing and defining a speech community[.] (Kirk and Kallen 2006: 108–9)

If that view is verified by future studies,[11] we shall have to accept the following: Irish as a minority language is functionally a nationalist language along the lines described above. Irish is functionally a *ceremonial* national language, which is, I believe, in the present context of globalisation the only *national language* status a minority language can take on. Irish is, at best one of two national languages – in order to do justice to a situation unique to Ireland, we might want to distinguish between an *endoglossic* national language and an *exoglossic* national language[12] or, from a slightly different angle, a *native* national language and a *nativised* national language. Thus, sociolinguistic as well as dialect studies, in a co-operative effort, will have to produce more attitudinal studies to verify or falsify a statement that Barbour, in my view, wrongly attributes to Ó Laoire, in whose article we do not find mention of it: 'Most Irish people seem happy with a linguistic identity focused on Irish varieties of English.' (Barbour 2000: 38; cf. Ó Laoire 1995). Irish English, if it is able to gain in cultural as well as societal acceptance, if it will meet standardising activities, is a more than likely candidate as a national language. Linguistically, it certainly expresses Irish identity, i.e. it provides clearly Irish features, as numerous studies have been able to show (e.g. Bliss 1977, Hickey 1986, Kallen 1989, Mac Mathúna 1990a, Odlin 1991, Ó hÚrdail 1997, Dolan 1998, Filppula 1999, Kirk and Kallen 2006).

## Conclusion

The term 'national language' should be used dispassionately to refer to that common language which is used *habitually* and *naturally* as an all-purpose medium of communication by all members of a national community and which creates feelings of solidarity amongst those members and characterises those members as belonging to their national unit. This appeal to neutrality finds its corroboration in the following statement, which was, of course, not intended as neutral when first stated more than 100 years ago:

> [E]ine Sprache [muß] als nationale Besonderheit anerkannt werden, sobald sie von einem Volke als dessen Familiensprache gesprochen wird.[13] (Böckh 1866: 309)

Accepting that line of thought, it is very difficult to justify the acceptance of Irish as a

---

[11] One such study is Falconer 2010.
[12] Those notions lean heavily on Kloss's terminology, referring to endoglossic and exoglossic countries, i.e. countries with indigenous and imported languages (1968: 71).
[13] A language must be acknowledged as a national characteristic as soon as it is spoken by a community as its family language. (translation G. Wolf)

national language. Irish is a minority language, not a national language in the sense of the above. It is understood that this is a controversial and unfavourable statement. Yet this provocative statement reflects linguistic realities. If an issue is not put in a favourable light, the public is usually given to doing something about it, as can be seen currently with bad news on the destruction of natural resources and other ecological matters. Suzanne Romaine has recently suggested treating language in exactly the same way we treat nature, natural resources and ecological trends. Romaine explains:

> [Languages] are vital parts of complex local ecologies that must be supported if global biodiversity, as well as human cultures and even humanity in general, are to be sustained. (2007: 130)

In that sense I believe that presenting linguistic realities could help make it clear to the public that some languages are weaker than generally perceived – even though for Irish there are good reasons to be in an upbeat mood (see Ó Riagáin 2007) – and that this, in the course of time, should provoke public and societal support. It is that kind of support that is needed for language maintenance, as was shown with reference to Ireland and Wales many years ago by Williams (1987). Such support is needed because all elaborate language planning is in vain if it does not reach the speech community. Yet if controversial, unpopular labels provoke public action, they are a good way to raise language awareness and, ultimately, to instigate language maintenance.

**References**

Anderson, B. 1991. *Imagined Communities. Reflections on the Origin and Spread of Nationalism*. Second Edition. London and New York: Verso. [First Edition 1983]
Antonini, R., Corrigan K. and L. Wei. 2002. 'The Irish Language in the Republic of Ireland and in Northern Ireland'. *Sociolinguistica* 16: 118–28.
Barbour, S. 2000. 'Britain and Ireland: The Varying Significance of Language for Nationalism'. In eds. Barbour S. and C. Carmichael. *Language and Nationalism in Europe*. Oxford: Oxford University Press. 18–43.
Barbour, S. 2004. 'National Language and Official Language'. In eds. Ammon, U., Dittmar, N., Mattheier, K.J. and P. Trudgill. *Sociolinguistics. Soziolinguistik. An International Handbook of the Science of Language and Society. Ein internationales Handbuch zur Wissenschaft von Sprache und Gesellschaft*. vol. 1, Second Edition. Berlin: de Gruyter. 288–95.
Bliss, A.J. 1977. 'The Emergence of Modern English Dialects in Ireland'. In ed. Ó Muirithe, D. *The English Language in Ireland*. Cork: Mercier. 7–19.
Böckh, R. 1866. 'Die statistische Bedeutung der Volkssprache als Kennzeichen der Nationalität'. *Zeitschrift für Völkerpsychologie und Sprachwissenschaft* 4: 263–402.
Dolan, T.P. ed. 1998. *A Dictionary of Hiberno-English: The Irish Use of English*. Dublin: Gill and Macmillan.
Falconer, G. 2010. 'A Second National Language? Substrate and Standard in Irish Parliamentary Transcription'. In eds. Lange, C., Schaefer U. and G. Wolf. *Linguistics, Ideology and the Discourse of Linguistic Nationalism*. Frankfurt/Main: Peter Lang, 175–99.
Fasold, R. 1984. *The Sociolinguistics of Society*. Oxford: Blackwell.

Fennell, D. 1985. 'The Relationship of the New Irish Nation to Gaelic'. In ed. Ureland, P.S. *Entstehung von Sprachen und Völkern. Glotto- und ethnogenetische Aspekte europäischer Sprachen*. Tübingen: Niemeyer. 247–59.
Ferguson, C.A. 1996. 'The Language Factor in National Development'. In ed. Huebner, T. *Sociolinguistic Perspectives. Papers on Language in Society, 1959–1994*. Oxford: Oxford University Press
Filppula, M. 1999. *The Grammar of Irish English: Language in Hibernian Style*. London: Routledge.
Fishman, J.A. 1972. *Language and Nationalism: Two Integrative Essays*. Rowley, Mass.: Newbury Publishers.
Fishman, J.A. 1987. 'Research on National Languages'. In eds. Ammon, U., Dittmar, N., Mattheier, K.J. and P. Trudgill. *Soziolinguistik. An International Handbook of the Science of Language and Society. Ein internationales Handbuch zur Wissenschaft von Sprache und Gesellschaft*. vol. 1. Berlin: de Gruyter. 638–46.
Haugen, E. 1966. 'Dialect, Language, Nation'. *American Anthropologist* 68: 922–35.
Hickey, R. 1986. 'Possible Phonological Parallels between Irish and Irish English'. *English World-Wide* 7: 1–21.
Hobsbawm, E.J. 1990. *Nations and Nationalism since 1780: Programme, Myth, Reality*. Cambridge: Cambridge University Press.
Hutchinson, J. 1987. *The Dynamics of Cultural Nationalism. The Gaelic Revival and the Creation of the Irish Nation State*. London: Allen and Unwin.
Ising, E. 1987. 'Nationalsprache/Nationalitätensprache'. In eds. Ammon, U., Dittmar, N., Mattheier, K.J. and P. Trudgill. *Sociolinguistics. Soziolinguistik. An International Handbook of the Science of Language and Society. Ein internationales Handbuch zur Wissenschaft von Sprache und Gesellschaft*. vol. 1. Berlin and New York: de Gruyter. 335–44.
Kallen, J.L. 1988. 'The English Language in Ireland'. *International Journal of the Sociology of Language* 70: 127 42.
Kallen, J.L. 1989. 'Tense and Aspect Categories in Irish English'. *English World-Wide* 10: 1–39.
Kirk, J.M. and J.L. Kallen. 2006. 'Irish Standard English: How Celticised? How Standardised?' In ed. Tristram, H.L.C. *The Celtic Englishes IV. The Interface between English and the Celtic Languages*. Potsdam: Universitätsverlag. 88–113.
Kloss, H. 1968. 'Notes Concerning a Language-Nation Typology'. In eds. Fishman, J.A., Ferguson C.A. and J. Das Gupta. *Language Problems of Developing Nations*. New York: John Wiley. 69–85.
Kramer, J. 1990. 'Sprachilloyalität'. In ed. Nelde, P.H. *Language Conflict and Minorities. Sprachkonflikte und Minderheiten*. Bonn: Dümmler. 15–22.
Llobera, J.R. 2004. *Foundations of National Identity: From Catalonia to Europe*. Oxford: Berghahn Books.
Mac Mathúna, L. 1990. 'Contrastive Aspects of English and Irish'. In ed. Bramsback, B. *Homage to Ireland: Aspects of Culture, Literature and Language*. Uppsala: Acta Universitatis Uppsaliensis. 81–98.
Matthews, P.H. 1997. *The Concise Oxford Dictionary of Linguistics*. Oxford: Oxford University Press.
Ó Béarra, F. 2007. 'Late Modern Irish and the Dynamics of Language Change and Language Death.' In ed. Tristram, H.L.C. *The Celtic Languages in Contact. Papers from the Workshop within the Framework of the XIII International Congress of Celtic Studies, Bonn, 26–17 July 2007*. Potsdam: Universitätsverlag. 260–9.

Ó Corráin, A. and S. Mac Mathúna eds. 1998. *Minority Languages in Scandinavia, Britain and Ireland*. Uppsala: Acta Universitatis Uppsaliensis.
Odlin, T. 1991. 'Irish English Idioms and Language Transfer'. *English World-Wide* 12: 175–93.
Ó hÚrdail, R. 1997. 'Hiberno-English: Historical Background and Synchronic Features and Variation'. In ed. Tristram, H.L.C. *The Celtic Englishes*. Heidelberg: Carl Winter. 180–99.
Ó Laoire, M. 1995. 'An Historical Perspective on the Revival of Irish Outside the Gaeltacht, 1880–1930, with Reference to the Revitalization of Hebrew'. *Current Issues in Language and Society* 2.3: 223–35.
Ó Murchú, M. 1993. 'Aspects of the Societal Status of Modern Irish'. In eds. Ball, M.J. with J. Fife. *The Celtic Languages*. London: Routledge. 471–90.
Ó Riagáin, P. 2001. 'Irish Language Production and Reproduction, 1981–1996'. In ed. Fishman, J.A. *Can Threatened Languages Be Saved? Reversing Language Shift, Revisited: A 21st Century Perspective*. Clevedon: Multilingual Matters. 195–214.
Ó Riagáin, D. 2001. 'Irish: New Perspectives for the Future'. In ed. Ammann, A. *Linguistics Festival. May 2006, Bremen*. Bochum: Brockmeyer. 79–96.
*Ráiteas I Leith na Gaeilge 2006*. 2006. Rialtas na hÉireann, Dublin. [accessed via http://www.taoiseach.gov.ie]
Reichmann, O. 2000. '*Nationalsprache* als Konzept der Sprachwissenschaft'. In ed. Gardt, A. *Nation und Sprache. Die Diskussion ihres Verhältnisses in Geschichte und Gegenwart*. Berlin: de Gruyter. 419–69.
Rolston, B. 2003. 'Changing the Political Landscape: Murals and Transition in Northern Ireland'. *Irish Studies Review* 11.1: 3–16.
Romaine, S. 2007. 'Preserving Endangered Languages'. *Language and Linguistics Compass* 1.1–2: 115–32.
Safran, W. 1999. 'Nationalism'. In ed. Fishman, J.A. *Handbook of Language and Ethnic Identity*. Oxford: Oxford University Press. 77–93.
Shils, E. 1995. 'Nation, Nationality, Nationalism and Civil Society'. *Nations and Nationalism* 1: 93–118.
Smith, A.D. 1991. *National Identity*. Reno: University of Nevada Press.
Smith, A.D. 2001. *Nationalism*. Cambridge: Cambridge University Press.
Trask, R.L. 1999. *Key Concepts in Language and Linguistics*. London: Routledge.
Trudgill, P. 2003. *A Glossary of Sociolinguistics*. Edinburgh: Edinburgh University Press.
Williams, C.H. 1987. 'The Land in Linguistic Consciousness: Evidence from the British Isles'. *Sociolinguistica* 1: 13–29.

# Sustaining Minority Language Communities: Yin and Yang Juncture for Irish!

*Pádraig Ó hAoláin*

The *Coimisiún na Gaeltachta / Gaeltacht Commission Report*[1] published in 2002 stated bluntly that Irish in the Gaeltacht was facing a crisis due to both external and internal factors. Anecdotal evidence gathered through Comhar Naíonraí na Gaeltachta, the administrative body responsible for 80 Irish-medium preschool groups *(naíonraí)* and from primary school sources in the interim years strongly indicate that there is an ongoing current of language shift occurring in the Gaeltacht. According to these sources the number of children entering the *naíonraí* and primary schools with Irish as their first language has shown a steady decline. Obviously such a continuing process of language shift, as highlighted in the Coimisiún Report, seriously threatens the survival of the Gaeltacht as a distinct speech community. The completion and publication of the *Comprehensive Linguistic Study of the Use of the Irish in the Gaeltacht,*[2] carried out by the National University of Ireland, Galway, in association with the National University of Ireland, Maynooth, on behalf of the Department of Rural, Community and Gaeltacht Affairs, makes available up-to-date, scientifically-based data on the use of Irish as a home and community language in the Gaeltacht. The results are expected to confirm the anecdotal evidence gathered since 2002.

Predictions about the imminent extinction of the Irish language, and particularly of the Gaeltacht, have a long history.[3] Of course, the erosion or decline of Irish as a community language, or, indeed of any minority language, is not a random process. It follows a clear pattern in which the trend begins with the introduction of the dominant language, English in this case, through non-traditional contexts. These non-traditional contexts include the media, modern forms of entertainment, pop culture, and the internet. Given the pervasive role of the state in the Gaeltacht many of these contexts are generated or controlled by state agencies and public services – although a number of these have begun to deliver a greater level of services through Irish since the enactment of the *Official Languages Act* 2002 and its vigorous implementation by the Language Commissioner since 2004.

The industrialisation process, which has been in train since the late 1960s and which gathered significant momentum in the early 1990s, has been a contributor to this process of language shift but to date there has been no scientific study of the extent of that impact. In my view, the industrialisation process, which directly impacts on approximately 10,000 of the working population of the Gaeltacht (total population 95,000 people, according to the Census of Population in 2006, who are employed by grant-assisted businesses has a lesser impact on the erosion of the language as a home and community language than the plethora of state agencies delivering a range of

---

[1] *Coimisiún na Gaeltachta / The Gaeltacht Commission Report*, The Department of Arts, Heritage, Gaeltacht and the Islands, 2002.

[2] Ó Giollagáin C., S Mac Donnacha, F. Ní Chualáin, A. Ní Shéaghdha and M. O'Brien. *Staidéar Teangeolaíoch ar Úsáid na Gaeilge sa nGaeltacht. / Comprehensive Linguistic Study of the Use of Irish in the Gaeltacht.* Dublin: An Roinn Gnóthaí Pobail, Tuaithe agus Gaeltachta, 2007.

[3] See Breandán Ó hEithir, Unpublished Report, Board na Gaeilge, 1990; Reg Hindley, *The Death of the Irish Language: A Qualified Obituary*, London: Routledge, 1990; and Máirtín Ó Cadhain, *Páipéir Bhána agus Páipéir Bhreaca*, An Clóchomhar Tta, 1996.

services mainly through English to these communities. Most of the grant-aided for-profit businesses have middle-management personnel who have a reasonable competency in the language, and most of them participate in the language promotion initiatives of the grant-aiding agency, Údarás na Gaeltachta. They are for the most part favourably disposed towards, if not always proactively enthusiastic, about the language. Grin[4] states that economic activity and minority language vitality are not necessarily antagonistic.

**Historical Background**

The pervasive influence of the system of public administration had established English as the passport to advancement long before the achievement of independence by the 26 county Irish Free State. By the time the Irish Free State was established in 1922, English had replaced Irish as the dominant language throughout most of the country. Irish had ceased to be the community language in all but a number of both small and large dispersed areas, together with six offshore islands, mainly along the western coast. This resulted in a region comprising a fragmented population base geographically dispersed over seven local authority counties which was predominantly rural in character with a high dependency on subsistence farming and fishing. As maintenance of the national language became an integral part of the policies of successive governments the survival of the these Irish-speaking areas as distinct speech communities came to be a major focus of state intervention.

The districts concerned were officially designated "Gaeltacht areas" and, while the first forty years after independence were characterised by population haemorrhage through constant emigration and by what was described by Ó Tuathaigh as "economic retardation"[5] for the next half century, these received a substantial level of state aid towards their economic, social and cultural development, mainly through a dedicated Department of State (Roinn na Gaeltachta) and a dedicated regional development agency (Údarás na Gaeltachta / the Gaeltachta Authority). We have to remember that modern industrialisation did not reach the Republic of Ireland until the 1960s. When the process gathered momentum a wide spectrum of funded schemes and industrial projects were put in place. While some schemes were designed expressly to encourage greater use of the language itself, the major emphasis was on improving the economic opportunities and the standards of living of the Gaeltacht people – in effect, population maintenance as the platform for language maintenance.

Up until the late 1970s language decline in the Gaeltacht was associated with the region's history of depopulation and, conversely, language maintenance was perceived mainly as a problem of stabilising population numbers. The Minister for the Gaeltacht in the period 1973–5, Mr. Tom O'Donnell, uttered the since much-quoted statement "no jobs, no people; no people, no Gaeltacht; no Gaeltacht, no language", and that succinctly captures the essence of the official view on the relationship between the socioeconomic development, demographic viability and linguistic conservation. In short, it was believed that putting an end to involuntary emigration from these areas by providing worthwhile employment half the battle would be won.

---

[4] François Grin, 'Promoting Language Through the Economy: Competing Paradigms', in eds. Kirk, J.M. and D.P. Ó Baoill, *Language and Economic Development: Northern Ireland, the Republic of Ireland and Scotland*. Belfast Studies in Language, Culture and Politics 19, Belfast: Cló Ollscoil na Banríona, 2009, pp. 1–12.

[5] M.A.G. Ó Tuathaigh, *The Development of the Gaeltacht as a Bilingual Entity*, Dublin: Institiúid Teangeolaíochta Éireann, Occasional Papers 8, 1990.

## The Role of the State

Since there is a continuing process of language shift occurring in the Gaeltacht, the three core questions we have to address are: how can the Irish-speaking communities be sustained, what is the role of the state in this process; and to what extent can the economic development role of the State be harnessed to ensure the conservation of the language? In my view, the state has a central role to play in terms of setting out a clear policy and action-plan, creating the environment for popular support, ensuring that the public administration system proactively implements the policy and action plan, and formulating incentive schemes to effect the active participation of the business sector in the project. A major problem in the Gaeltacht is that many of the arms of public administration do not consciously function in line with the stated current language maintenance policy of the state or with the language maintenance objectives entrusted to the regional development agency for the Gaeltacht, Údarás na Gaeltachta / The Gaeltacht Authority. State-sponsored programmes of industrialisation, while having a significant degree of success as a population maintenance policy since the 1970s, do not of themselves ensure language maintenance but they have the potential to be a major contributor to the process through the 'normalisation' of the use of Irish in the business domain. They must be an integral part of an integrated language plan. However, the attaching of certain language conditions to grant-aid and equity investments approved to new and expanding businesses has at least negativised or reduced the impact of these modernising forces on the language in the communities in which they are located, and they are a major contributor to population stabilisation and maintenance which is the platform for language maintenance. The bottom line, however, is, as Grin has stated,[6] *the business of business is business.*

It can be contended that because of the convention of linking economic development and language survival, state language policy has been too narrowly entrusted in the past to special state development agencies – a situation which does not address the wider role of the state through the general expansion of the public administration system.

There is a wide spectrum of state agencies or bodies which, although having jurisdiction in the Gaeltacht, operate as regional or area-specific branches or parts of more extensive and predominantly English-using systems. Since the majority of these services have historically been provided in the Gaeltacht through English only a pattern has been established on both sides of the counter which is difficult to reverse, except in cases where the state agency or service is proactive in creating an awareness of the availability of the service in Irish on an equal basis with English. This situation is being addressed vigorously by the Language Commissioner's Office through the implementation of the provisions of the *Official Languages Act 2003*. As far as the attainment of the state's linguistic objectives is concerned, there are anomalies and contradictions in the role of the state in the Gaeltacht which facilitate and expedite the rate of language shift because they reinforce the native speaker's embedded perception that English is the norm for accessing a wide range of state services, entitlements or benefits except those provided by the Department of Rural, Community and Gaeltacht Affairs and Údarás na Gaeltachta. These latter two prove the point that, where the services are provided *ab initio* through Irish, they are fully availed of as the norm by Irish speakers in the Gaeltacht. Normalisation of usage must be a core objective of all language promotion and maintenance initiatives for minority languages, otherwise they become marginalised and confined to certain traditional domains.

---

[6] Grin, François, *ibid*. p. 5.

## State Language Policy

While Irish is the first official language of the state according to the constitution, and while successive governments since the foundation of the state have stated their commitment to maintaining the Gaeltacht and supporting the language in the Gaeltacht and nationally, the language policies of the state have swung between the revival of Irish, the promotion of language awareness campaigns focused on the role of Irish in ethnic identification (e.g."its part of what we are" advertising campaign of the 1990s) and the promotion of bilingualism. From the late 1970s / early 1980s onwards the state adopted a *laissez faire* attitude to language use. As stated by Pádraig Ó Coimín:[7]

> explicitly or implicitly [the state] has moved to a position where the choice of language is now more a matter of individual initiative and performance rather than an outcome of the way opportunities to improve abilities and usage are deliberately organised through state action. Our view is that, as well as having an ideological rationale and philosophical basis, the promotion of Irish needs active leadership, commitment, and action by the state and its institutions ... passivity or neutrality on the part of the state is in effect a stance favouring the dominant language.

That discussion document focused on the influence of media and public institutions as well as the role of the state itself in the maintenance of the language. Arising out of that analysis possible policy directions towards the aim of achieving increased use of Irish within a coherent bilingual policy were indicated. The report strongly posits the view that "current trends can be altered by popular will complemented by State action". This is the key to achieving sustainability. Twenty years later, notwithstanding the further erosion that has occurred in the Gaeltacht in the interim, popular will complemented by State action is a formula that must be at the core of the government's response to the conclusions and recommendations of the *Comprehensive Linguistic Study on the Use of Irish in the Gaeltacht*.

## Stocktaking: Future Direction Emerging

Much of the stocktaking necessary to inform a new strategic initiative has been done by *An Staidéar Cuimsitheach Teangeolaíochta ar úsáid na Gaeilge sa Ghaeltacht / A Comprehensive Linguistic Study on the Use of Irish in the Gaeltacht*, carried out between 2005–7. This is the most comprehensive linguistic survey of the use of Irish ever carried out throughout the Gaeltacht. It not only details the level of Irish language usage in every part of the Gaeltacht but also gives us a clear read of those factors that are the most powerful and pervasive eroding agents operating both at the edges and at the heart of the Irish-speaking communities in the Gaeltacht. The government's immediate response to the Linguistic Study was to establish a Cabinet Sub-Committee chaired by *An Taoiseach* "to agree," as stated by Minister Ó Cuív, "an integrated action plan to secure the future of Irish as the community language of the Gaeltacht". The future of the last surviving communities where Irish is the communal and home language through historical transmission rather than the language chosen through ideological

---

[7] Pádraig Ó Coimín, *The Irish Language in a Changing Society: Shaping the Future*, Dublin: Bord na Gaeilge, 1988.

commitment depends on that government decision being actioned and implemented.
   I believe that Irish speakers in the Gaeltacht and throughout the State are ready for the challenge of doing whatever is necessary to match and implement state action to maintain the language and increase the level of usage; and the number of speakers of the language provided the Government sets out a clear strategy accompanied by an integrated action plan, as well as an appropriate means of facilitating community involvement in a language planning process in the Gaeltacht. Community ownership, or "buy-in" is an ingredient which will be vital to the success of any new initiative. Fragile though it may be, I believe that we still have a sufficiently robust level of Irish-language usage in the Gaeltacht on which to build a platform for sustainability and growth which we will not have twenty years hence unless proactive state intervention in key domains is initiated now. The fact that we have such a foundation – i.e. that approximately 30% of the overall population of the Gaeltacht are habitual Irish speakers (accortding to *A Comprehensive Linguistic Study of the Use of Irish in the Gaeltacht*, 2007) – is a modern-day miracle in itself when one considers the enormous pressures, both internal and external, over the past 150 years, the deficiencies in current arrangements and practices, and the huge sociocultural and socioeconomic pressures of the mainly English-speaking world we live in. Though under constant pressure from within and without the Irish-speaking community in many parts of the Gaeltacht is resilient and tenacious.

**Sustaining Irish-speaking Communities**

The Gaeltacht areas are essentially rural communities although there are a number of densely populated urban-type settlements and small towns in the region. Community and economic development experts generally agree that while employment creation constitutes a key element to any development strategy, employment creation for rural areas is a particularly complex task due to the variety of economic, social and environmental situations found in these areas. The element of a minority language added to the profile of those communities provides a major challenge to government agencies with responsibility for the economic, social and cultural development of these areas. It is in this context that one realizes the extent of the challenge associated with endeavouring to provide the economic conditions that will buttress sustainable language communities *i.e.* in a manner that embeds the language as a core component of the developmental process. The proactive involvement of both the community development organisations and the for-profit sectors as partners in this process is vitally necessary in order to ensure its success.

**The Platform for Sustainability**

We already have in place many of the major elements of the grid of supports which are crucial to language maintenance and the increase of Irish Language usage in the Gaeltacht and beyond:

- a dedicated Department of Rural, Equality and Gaeltacht Affairs with a Senior Government Minister
- a dedicated regional development agency with a wide range of powers and functions relating to economic, social and cultural development
- a Gaeltacht-based dedicated national Irish language radio service, RTÉ Raidió na Gaeltachta.

- a dedicated Gaeltacht-based national TV Service, TG4.
- The *Official Languages Act 2003* which is being rolled out on a planned basis by the Department of Rural, Equality and Gaeltacht Affairs and focusing particularly on those branches or departments of the Public and Civil Service providing services to the Gaeltacht community
- The Language Commissioner's Office based in the Gaeltacht, which is very proactive in ensuring compliance with provisions of the *Official Languages Act 2003*
- 30 funded community groups which have a language promotional and management function in their areas
- 35 Irish Language Service Centres throughout the Gaeltacht which provide facilities for those wishing to learn Irish
- 80 Irish-medium pre-school groups and 25 youth clubs funded by Údarás na Gaeltachta
- a range of language-based businesses and organisations providing educational, training and advisory services through Irish throughout the Gaeltacht.

The most important non-government initiative taken in recent years – though with substantial support-funding from exchequer sources, including Údarás na Gaeltachta, – was the establishment of Irish-medium third level education outreach centres in three Gaeltacht areas by *Acadamh na hOllscolaíochta Gaeilge* / the National University of Ireland, Galway. These centres now provide accredited third level courses to in excess of 500 students, they have a substantial socioeconomic and linguistic impact in the areas in which they are located and are strong agents of language sustainability.

**Return on Investment**

You may well ask: why, if so much was done, has the return on investment through these initiatives not been greater in terms of the sustainability of the language? In general terms one can say, with the benefit of hindsight, that little thought was given by the policymakers to the concepts of integrated language planning and language management when these initiatives and projects were introduced. Schemes were introduced to meet a particular pressing need but were, in the main, uncoordinated. Important components of the scaffolding necessary to ensure sustainability were always missing. Integrated planning was a concept demanded and expected in the economic development sphere but unfortunately was not recognised until recent years as being necessary in relation to addressing the needs of, and securing the future of, the Irish-speaking communities in the Gaeltacht. There was always an underlying assumption that once the service was provided or the scheme initiated that the hearts, minds and feet of Irish speakers in the Gaeltacht would follow.

However, contemporaneous to the establishment of all of the above-mentioned schemes, Irish-medium instruction in primary and postprimary schools in the Gaeltacht was gradually regressing, English was becoming more and more the lingua franca of the social networks of Gaeltacht youth and the number of families with Irish as their first or principal language was gradually declining. I believe that this pattern goes to the core of the challenge facing Údarás na Gaeltachta, the Department of Rural, Community and Gaeltacht Affairs, and that whole plethora of community-based organisations in the Gaeltacht which have maintenance of the Irish language as a core objective – to contain and revert this decline which has been occurring progressively and inexorably over the past 150 years.

**Achieving Sustainability**

All commentators, practitioners and language planning specialists are agreed that the first step in language revitalisation or rescue is information gathering i.e., information assessment of a language's current situation. Equally important as facts about the numbers of speakers are facts about the *attitudes of the language speakers* themselves and of the larger community of which they are part. When it comes to addressing the problem of language shift *attitude* is critical – how people look at their language and what they feel about it. Do the speakers take pride in their language, enjoy listening to others using it well, use it themselves whenever they can and provide occasions when the language can be heard? According to Crystal,[8] the conditions are favourable for maintenance when this positive, supportive mindset exists, and languages decline when these positive attitudes are missing. Apathy is the big enemy and is as erosive and corrosive an agent as antipathy.

**The Planning and Management Deficit**

I believe that we have not made the progress we might have made, nor achieved the return on investment in linguistic terms that we could have and should have, because these initiatives, schemes and projects were introduced in a language planning and language management vacuum. While very worthy in themselves, and immensely valuable elements of the grid of services to which the Irish-speaking Gaeltacht communities were entitled, they lacked integration and cohesion. They were introduced independently of each other to address a particular deficiency or need at a particular time and in particular sectors rather than being informed by a holistic view of the needs of the language community and what was required to secure community "buy-in". This could be called the 'famine relief' approach. It is an approach that has resulted in sufficient sustenance being provided on an ongoing basis to keep the recipient language community alive on the linguistic equivalent of one meal per day, but not sufficiently nurtured to generate full health leading to natural or organic growth. Organic growth is critical to the survival prospects of a minority language community. That organic growth can only be achieved on the basis of an integrated development plan, of which the language needs forms a core element, which gives ownership to the community of those vital components of managing language maintenance, promotion and development at local level – the means of expressing local pride in the language. However, a popular movement to proactively engage with the process of language shift and revitalise usage in domains where it has become underutilised or redundant can only be generated by a fundamental change of strategy by the State which includes not only institutional changes but also motivational and awareness-raising initiatives aimed at galvanising popular support.

We are optimistic that an integrated action policy will emerge from the deliberations of the Cabinet Sub-Committee working under the chairmanship of *An Taoiseach*. We have reached a critical crossroads, a defining juncture, where the chosen way forward will determine the future of the Gaeltacht areas as distinct language communities. We have reached a Yin and Yang juncture! In their terminological context Yin and Yang are the two complimentary principles of Chinese philosophy:

[8] David Crystal, *Language Death*, Cambridge: Cambridge University Press, 2000.

Yin being the negative dark and feminine and Yang the positive bright and masculine. Their interaction is thought to maintain the harmony of the Universe and to influence everything within it. In the context of the sustainability of minority languages, and the defining crossroads which we have reached, I refer particularly to Arnold Toynbee's discussion in his *"A Study of History"* on the alternating rhythm of movement and pause in the history of mankind as the Yin and Yang – Yin being the static and Yang being the dynamic.

To remain in Yin is to remain at peace. It is also to remain primitive, unchanged and uncivilised – static. Yang represents activity – the origin of man's achievements in civilisation. The movement from Yin to Yang occurs when a society is presented with a major challenge. There is no peaceful or easy transition to a higher endeavour. Rather, does a society find itself confronted with a challenge which it must either accept and overcome or succumb to and lose something extremely valuable which will result in that society becoming something quite different?

There are those who will drift before the challenge and continue to live much as before, and there are those who will face the challenge even though the barriers to surmount will seem immense because they believe they can discover in themselves that immense act of human genius required to establish a new platform on which to grow out of and beyond the challenge or crisis.

I believe that we face such a challenge as far as sustaining Irish as a community language in the Gaeltacht is concerned. When faced with such a challenge the first step is stocktaking. Where do we stand now? What is the challenge facing us? What are the obstacles to be overcome? What are the core issues to be addressed? The stocktaking has been done in *An Staidéar Cuimsitheach Teangeolaíochta ar úsáid na Gaeilge sa Ghaeltacht/ The Comprehensive Linguistic Study on the use of Irish in the Gaeltacht*. The new strategy and action-plan promised by the government Sub-Committee, which will eventually become government policy will, I believe, address all these questions and grasp the opportunity to adopt an integrated radical language maintenance and development plan which will provide all the major stakeholders with the opportunity to secure the future of Irish as a home and community language in the Gaeltacht and as the habitual language of communication of growing numbers of people throughout the State.

# The Concept of Gaeltacht: Time to Revisit?

*Dónall Ó Riagáin*

On 31 October 2007, a major sociolinguistic study on Irish in the Gaeltacht was launched.[1] It was commissioned by the Department for Community, Rural and Gaeltacht Affairs and was prepared by Acadamh na hOllscolaíochta Gaeilge, NUIG and the National Institute for Regional and Spatial Planning, NUIM. Undoubtedly, it is the most comprehensive and detailed study of the Gaeltacht ever undertaken. It would be invidious of me to attempt to give a resumé of its 567 pages. Suffice it to say that it paints a picture of decline – one might say of terminal decline – in the use of Irish as a community language in the Gaeltacht. One might reasonably conclude that its findings suggest that the Gaeltacht, as a substantially Irish-speaking entity will have ceased to exist in about 20 years time if there is not a marked sea-change in language usage practices.

The report or its contents will not come as a surprise to the people of the Gaeltacht or to those who take an active interest in Gaeltacht affairs. Indeed FOINSE, the Irish-language weekly newspaper published a leak on the report in its edition of 15 July 2007. Irish has been under siege for over 300 years although paradoxically there were probably more Irish speakers on the eve of the Great Famine than at any time in the history of the language. All the indicators over the decades since the establishment of the independent state in 1922 have suggested an unrelenting pattern of decline. Indeed, the selected accounts on the position of Irish, contained in the report of the Commission of Inquiry into the Preservation of the Gaeltacht, established in January 1925, and quoted in John Walsh's *Díchoimisiúnú na Gaeltachta,*[2] give one a horrible sense of *déjà vu*.

This should not come as a surprise. The Gaeltacht as we know it today was first defined following on the publication of the aforementioned report. This led to the adoption of the *Housing (Gaeltacht) Act* of 1929. This was (in some ways) a peculiar piece of legislation intended to support the erection and improvement of dwelling houses and also ancillary accommodation for poultry and pigs in the Gaeltacht. The Gaeltacht then consisted of a number of remote districts, mostly on the west coast where Irish was still spoken as the normal vernacular by at least a considerable minority of the inhabitants. Those listed in the schedule that accompanied the *Housing (Gaeltacht) Act, 1929* included districts in Cavan, Leitrim, Roscommon, Sligo, Louth, Tipperary, Clare and Limerick now no longer deemed to be in the official Gaeltacht. The survival of Irish in Gaeltacht areas was not the result of an inspired patriotic decision taken by the inhabitants. It was simply a case of these districts being so remote and underdeveloped that English had not yet penetrated them. And remoteness was a key factor!

If one looks at a map of Gaeltacht districts based on the 1891 or even 1926 Census data, it is interesting to note the preponderance of English around railway lines. A contributor to *An Claidheamh Soluis* in 1899, writing under the nom-de-plume, Donnchadh Rua, commented on Irish in County Wexford:

---

[1] *Staidéar Teangeolaíoch ar úsáid na Gaeilge sa Ghaeltacht / Comprehensive Linguistic Study on the Use of Irish in the Gaeltacht*. Dublin: Oifig an tSoláthair, An Roinn Gnóthaí Pobail, Tuaithe agus Gaeltachta, 2007).http://www.pobail.ie/ie/AnGhaeltacht/AnStaidearTeangeolaioch/file,8677,ie.pdf

[2] John Walsh, *Díchoimisiúnú na Gaeltachta – Coimisiún na Gaeltachta 1926*, Dublin: Cois Life, 2002.

I may here remark that the W.D. and L. Railway seems to have trailed something of English taste right through the county, and the influence is felt on both sides of the line to a breadth of some miles ... There is nothing necessarily English about a railway of course, but 'tis a mark of progress, and so is English thought to be unfortunately.

Dr. Pádraig Ó Riagáin has done more research on the patterns of language use over three decades than probably any other person. In his seminal work, *Language Policy and Social Reproduction*,[3] Ó Riagáin observes that:

> Bilingualism in Ireland always had a territorial or regional dimension. But it would seem that the linguistic distinctions between the Gaeltacht and the rest of the country are disappearing.

This he attributes to changing occupational patterns, increased access to higher education and changes in shopping and recreational patterns. In short the people of the Gaeltacht have become much more mobile as communications have improved. We read in Peig Sayer's autobiography[4] that she spent four years working in An Daingean as a domestic servant without visiting her family in Dún Chaoin, only about 14 kms away. Young people from there would think nothing nowadays of making the return trip twice or even three times in the one day! Until around 1940 people from the Iorras Gaeltacht travelled by sea to Sligo or Ballina to do their Christmas shopping or conduct other business because of the appalling state of the roads in West Mayo. In contrast, the youth of Conamara today seek recreational and social outlets in Galway city and Salthill. Housewives from Gaoth Dobhair think nothing of doing their weekly shopping in the Letterkenny Retail Park. All of this contributes to an increased use of English, more linguistically mixed marriages and the weakening of Irish even in the core Gaeltacht areas. I am not bemoaning improved communications but simply pointing out that factors that led to the demise of Irish in other parts of the country are now at play even in the Gaeltacht heartland.

Writers like Pearse (in Irish) or Synge (in English) painted a romanticised picture of the Gaeltacht. There was nothing exceptional about this. Romantic nationalism and the glorification of peasant lifestyles, inspired by thinkers and writers like Von Herder, were in vogue at the end of the nineteenth century. However, far from being a kind of Garden of Eden, the Gaeltacht districts in the late nineteenth and early-twentieth centuries were for the most part overpopulated, underdeveloped areas of poor land where poverty, underemployment, emigration, poor education, ill-health (especially tuberculosis) were features of everyday life.

The independent Irish state rightly perceived the importance of the Gaeltacht as a repository of oral Irish, unbroken in tradition and rich in idiom. For this reason and for general humanitarian reasons it seemed only right to support the Gaeltacht socially and economically.

However, no Irish government implemented a coordinated, consistent Gaeltacht policy. While schemes were established to assist certain aspects of Gaeltacht life, the state at the same time continued to send public servants to Gaeltacht areas who were incapable of, or even unwilling to, deliver public services through Irish. There never was and still is no policy for delivering education through Irish in the Gaeltacht. I

---

[3] Pádraig Ó Riagáin, *Language Policy and Social Reproduction,* Oxford: Oxford University Press, 1997.
[4] Peig Sayer, *Peig: the Autobiography of Peig Sayers of the Great Blasket Island,* Dublin: Talbot Press, 1983.

organised a major conference on Gaeltacht education for An Chomhairle um Oideachas Gaeltachta agus Gaelscolaíochta [COGG] in April 2007. I confess to being appalled by the official attitude to the issues raised. Education in the Gaeltacht was seen as no more than an extension of countrywide English-medium education.

Furthermore, it is painfully evident that whenever the interests of big business and linguistic or cultural considerations clashed, big business always won out. The construction of new housing schemes in Gaeltacht areas, mostly for non-Irish speakers, is a glaring example. Because of its proximity to Galway city, the Cois Fharraige Gaeltacht has come under heavy siege. An Rinn, the only surviving Gaeltacht in East Munster, has recently come under severe threat from a housing development, totally unrelated to local needs. Government quotas on Irish speakers applying for such housing accommodation is little more than a fig-leaf and a shrivelled one at that. The 'Shell to Sea' campaign in Ros Dumhach has an interesting linguistic aspect that the media have so far missed. Although the affected area is in what is left of the Iorras Gaeltacht, the protesters, even when speaking in Irish on TG4 or Raidió na Gaeltachta, made their case on safety or environmental grounds only. There was here an implicit recognition that linguistic or cultural arguments would count for nothing at the Cabinet table, not to mention the boardroom of a multi-national oil company.

In 2002, a Commission, established by the Minister to review the state of the Gaeltacht made a number of recommendations.[5] One of them was that linguistically weak areas should be given a certain period within which to strengthen the position of Irish or face having Gaeltacht status withdrawn. While such a strategy might bring about improvements in some cases it is inherently flawed. 'Expelling' areas from the official Gaeltacht would do nothing to improve the position of Irish but would almost certainly undermine the confidence of those who remained loyal to the language. Extensive areas in West Clare and Cork, for instance, were removed from the official Gaeltacht in 1956, some for dubious party political reasons, one might add. Native Irish has all but disappeared from these districts now.[6]

**Where Stand We?**

Is Irish then in a 'melt-down' situation? Looking at the position of the language holistically, the answer has to be a resounding 'no'. The 2006 Census[7] shows that there are 1,656,790 Irish speakers in the Republic. Add around 160,000 from Northern Ireland and one arrives at a total of more than 1.8 million. Only 64,265 of these live in officially designated Gaeltacht areas.

There are obvious signs of increased use of Irish and of its vigour. Literary output is always an interesting tool with which to access the health of a language. Alan Titley[8] observes:

> The Irish literature of the twentieth century has been richer and more plentiful than any previous century. In the first instance this is a question of volume. There is simply more Irish writing and more Irish books in the last hundred years than in all previous centuries put together.

---

[5] Coimisiún an Gaeltachta 2002. Report/Tuarascáil. 2002.
[6] Máirtín Ó Cadhain, 'The Death of the Clare Gaeltacht'. In ed. Seán Ó Laighin, *An Ghaeilge Bheo: Destined to Pass*, Dublin: Coiscéim, 2002.
[7] Census Statistics Office, 2007. *Census 2006, Volume 9: The Irish Language* [Online]. Available at: http://www.cso.ie/census/census2006results/volume_9/volume_9_irish_language_entire_volume.pdf
[8] Alan Titley, *A Pocket History of Gaelic Culture*. Dublin: O'Brien Press, 2000.

This growth is also evident in radio broadcasting. Besides Raidió na Gaeltachta there are two private radio stations broadcasting in Irish: Raidió na Life in Dublin and Raidió Fáilte in Belfast.

Referring to the Irish-speaking communities James McCloskey, Professor of Linguistics at the University of California, Santa Cruz, observed:

> It occurs to me first that, for a linguistic community that has been told over and over again that it is as good as dead, this is a most lively, interesting and enjoyable network to be part of [ ... ][9]

One may point out that the vast majority of these Irish speakers nationally are only L2 speakers – people who acquired Irish at school, many of whom aspire to their children becoming L1 users. The most important steps forward for Irish over the past three decades must surely have been the phenomenal growth of Irish-medium education (the *gaelscoileanna*), the establishment of TG4, the enactment of the *Official Languages Act, 2003* and the according of status as an official and working language to Irish by the European Union at the beginning of 2007. What is striking is that all of these developments have come about, not as a result of government initiatives, but rather as a response by government to popular demand.

One fascinating figure that one finds in the Census data is the number of Irish speakers in the 3–4 year old age-group. These are children whose Irish was acquired in Irish-speaking homes. The figure is 14,773. But how many of these are Gaeltacht children? Only 1,226 or slightly over 8%. This clearly indicates that there are far more Irish-speaking families scattered around the country than in the Gaeltacht.

The real problem with this large group of Irish speakers is that they have little opportunity to use Irish on a daily basis. This is largely because Irish is effectively excluded from certain key domains, the most obvious of which is economic activity. Although only a small minority of people use Irish on a daily basis outside of the education system, very substantial numbers use it occasionally. The problem seems to be one of opportunity rather than one of willingness. Language use is largely dependent on domains where the use of the particular language is normal and unhindered, or on institutions in which the language is dominant. e.g. in the case of Irish we might immediately think of *gaelscoileanna*, festivals or Irish-language clubs.

In short, the problem lies not with the language but with our concept of 'Gaeltacht'. Making minor adjustments to the model that has inspired official thinking for over eight decades will cure nothing. Had the deck-chairs on the Titanic been rearranged, the ship would still have sunk!

**A New Proposition**

In *Cruthú na Gaeltachta 1893–1922*,[10] Caitríona Ó Torna reminds us that the Gaeltacht was not always perceived as a geographical entity but rather as the Irish–speaking people as opposed to the English-speaking community: na Gaill. The geographical definition seems to have been largely a product of the early days of the language and cultural revival. I suggest that we need to re-evaluate our perceptions accordingly.

What then am I proposing? I am proposing that we change our concept of

---

[9] James McCloskey, *Guthanna in Éag: An Mairfidh an Ghaeilge Beo? / Voices Silenced: Has Irish A Future?* Baile Átha Cliath: Cois Life. 2001.
[10] *Caitríona Ó Torna. Cruthú na Gaeltachta 1893–1922.* Dublin: Cois Life, 2005.

'Gaeltacht' from a geographical one – one of scattered semi-Irish speaking districts, mostly on the western seaboard – to one of an Irish-speaking community wherever that community may reside. With this definition Irish speakers living in the existing Gaeltacht would remain in the Gaeltacht: those who did not speak Irish would not. The same criteria would apply to all Irish citizens living in Ireland, irrespective of whether they lived in West Belfast, Dublin, Cork or wherever. In short, think of people rather than places.

### An Imperative First Step

The census questions on Irish in the Republic provide us with invaluable information, not only on the number of Irish speakers on a geographical basis but also on the age, sex and occupation of these speakers. What is amazing is that, census after census, this information has been presented to the public in tabular form only. It is critical that it be also presented in cartographical form so that we see clearly where Irish speakers who pursue a particular way of life (e.g. as farmers, teachers, civil servants) live.[11] Equally, it is imperative that we know where Irish-speakers in certain age-groups live. [We know already that people in the 10–14 and 15–19 age-groups have the highest ability in Irish, and that Irish is strongest among the higher socioeconomic classes.] If we can clearly visualise where certain groups reside, we can start linguistic planning with confidence, not just on a geographical, but also on an age-related and occupational basis. We can then confidently start 'growing' the language in a sharply focused manner. This would mean that even the scarce public resources available would be utilised in a targeted manner thus ensuring maximum effectiveness.

### Creation of Irish-speaking Urban Communities

Attempts have been made over the years to develop urban Gaeltacht districts. There was an effort to develop such a Gaeltacht in the 1920s – Páirc na Gaeltachta in Whitehall, Dublin. Smaller efforts were made in Glanmire, Cork and in Naas, both with modest success. The most successful of all was the Shaw's Road Gaeltacht in West Belfast. In the *Sunday Tribune* of 4 November 2007 there was an interesting report on a new organisation called *Baile* which aims at establishing urban *Gaeltachtaí*. While this is very exciting and commendable, it is unlikely that a major breakthrough could be made without official backing. And there should be official support for this initiative!

Having said that, we must be aware that social interaction in urban settings may differ considerably from traditional models with which we are familiar. Fishman's GIDS may need revisiting. 'Neighbourhood', for instance might be replaced by, or understood as, social networks. People who live in apartment blocks may barely know those living on either side of them and prefer to interact socially with friends and acquaintances acquired through work, recreation, family contacts or cultural and educational activities. A degree of geographical proximity is undoubtedly necessary in order to enjoy normal community life but in present-day society there often is a scope for other factors to come in to play.

---

[11] I understand that Acadamh na hOllscolaíochta Gaeilge, with support from An Roinn Gnóthaí Pobail, Comhionannais and Gaeltachta, is now going to address this issue.

[12] An excellent description of the latter can be found in Pavel Stranj, *The Submerged Community: An A to Ž of the Slovenes in Italy*, Trieste: Slovene Research Institute, 1992.

Public support should be focused on the creation and development of largely Irish-speaking institutions that could give the language a firm footing in urban as well as rural settings. Interesting models can be found in bilingual cities throughout Europe e.g. the Dutch-speaking community in Brussels or the Slovene-speaking community in Trieste.[12] I am thinking in particular of businesses that would operate largely but not exclusively through Irish. I stayed in a hotel in Conamara in 2007. Although located in the heart of the Cois Fharraige Gaeltacht I failed to find any member of staff who was able (or maybe willing) to speak to me in Irish. I am informed that this hotel received financial support from Údarás na Gaeltachta. Around the same time, a young Dublin woman, Irene Ní Mhuireagáin, received the annual award of The Irish Marketing Institute in respect of her graphic design and marketing company, Cumarsáid Creative. Although the company provides a full service through Irish it does not qualify for support from Údarás na Gaeltachta because it is based in an inner Dublin suburb rather than in the official Gaeltacht. If effective language planning is our objective, this is surely daft! An tÚdarás is not to blame: our concept of Gaeltacht is.

**A Blueprint for the Future**

What then am I proposing? I am suggesting that, as part of the new proposed national plan for Irish, Ceantair Forbartha Teanga [CFT] , 'language development areas', should be chosen and every effort made to facilitate people living in these areas to convert their ability in Irish into active daily usage. I think that three or four pilot areas should be chosen, and that somewhat different strategies might be employed in the different areas so that the efficacy of each strategy might be evaluated. One area might be a large urban conglomeration, such as the designated 'Gaeltacht Quarter' in West Belfast. Another might be adjacent to one of the Gaeltacht 'colonies' in County Meath. (With the new M3, access to Dublin would be comparatively easy.) Another might be a provincial market town, such as Abbeyfeale in County Limerick, which has consistently performed well in the Glór na nGael competition, and where there are strong Irish-speaking networks.

The choice of the initial pilot CFTs should be decided on their suitability, based on Census data. Towns with existing Irish-medium institutions (e.g. a *gaelscoil*) should be prioritised. A key element in developing a CFT should be economic activity. [The Irish language movement has for decades been obsessed with recreational activities.] We are living in the age of the knowledge economy. This means that a person can be gainfully employed, without heavy capital outlay, if s/he has the skills to perform effectively and competitively. Thanks to ICT, location also has become a lot less important than hitherto. Údarás na Gaeltachta should be allowed to financially support Irish-speaking enterprises irrespective of their location. Only public servants (e.g. Gardaí, district nurses, local government officials) with good active ability in Irish should be appointed to a CFT. Banks, shops, the clergy and other operators in the services sector (e.g. doctors, dentists, hairdressers) should be approached with a view to their offering their services in Irish. Acadamh na hOllscolaíochta Gaeilge should be encouraged to offer courses in their locality. A steering committee, with local representation as well as representatives from responsible state agencies, should be set up in each case. Ongoing monitoring from the very start would be an essential element in order to evaluate the effectiveness and cost-effectiveness of different measures.

## The Nua-Ghaeltacht and the Existing Gaeltacht

Would such a conceptual shift as I propose not herald the death of what is left of the traditional Gaeltacht? On the contrary, I am convinced that it would have a positive effect. Being part of a growing, dynamic, nationwide linguistic community would surely be a more attractive proposition for a young person living in a Gaeltacht area than being defined in terms of residency in an ever-shrinking 'reservation for Irish-speaking natives'. The growth of Irish nationwide certainly slowed the decline of the Gaeltacht. [Conradh na Gaeilge in its early days could be credited with pioneering cultural tourism, although the term was then unknown.] A planned approach to converting latent ability in Irish into active use nationwide would, I am convinced, be highly effective and certainly cost-effective. Nothing is static: anything not growing is going to wither. Developing, rather than merely sustaining, our language communities has to be the way forward.

# Pobal Gaeltachta an Bhreacbhaile: Cás-staidéar Sochtheangeolaíoch agus Eitneagrafaíoch sa Bheartas Teanga

*Laoise Ní Dhúda*

## Brollach

Fáiltíonn an taighdeoir go mór leis an seans seo iniúchadh a dhéanamh ar an gcaoi ar féidir pobail na dteangacha mionlaigh a chothú. Tá súil aici solas a chaitheamh ar chineál amháin taighde a léireoidh an réamhobair atá le déanamh ina thaobh sin.

'Pobal Gaeltachta an Bhreacbhaile:[1] Cás-staidéar Sochtheangeolaíoch agus Eitneagrafaíoch sa Bheartas Teanga'[2] is teideal don pháipéar seo. Ar an ábhar sin, beartaíodh gan ainm nó suíomh tíreolaíoch na láithreach taighde a nochtadh agus ainm cleite (An Breacbhaile atá lonnaithe i gceantar Gaeltachta in Éirinn) a thabhairt uirthi chun ardleibhéal rúndachta agus anaithnidithe a bhaint amach. Ní ar mhaithe le mioneolas ar phobal an Bhreacbhaile a thuairisciú agus a scaipeadh a tugadh faoin taighde áirithe seo ach ar mhaithe le hiniúchadh a dhéanamh ar ghnéithe de chleachtas teanga, creideamh teanga agus bainistíocht teanga a dhéanamh.

Tabharfar blaiseadh sa pháipéar seo de thaighde atá á dhéanamh faoi láthair. Tá an obair seo mar chuid de thráchtas PhD atá ar siúl go leanúnach. Tá bliain caite ag an taighdeoir ag plé leis. Dá bharr sin, ní hé seo an focal deireanach ar an scéal ach roinnt tuairimí ar an ábhar agus sampla den réamhfhiosrú atá á dhéanamh. Feartar fáilte mhór roimh mholtaí a chuirfidh leis an taighde.

## Aidhm an Pháipéir

I dtús báire cuirfear an taighde i láthair go hachomair. Pléifear aidhmeanna an tráchtais, ceisteanna taighde agus an mhodheolaíocht a ghabhann leo.

Tabharfar léargas gearr ar shuíomh an togra taighde sa réimse léinn ansin. Déanfar machnamh ar an dioscúrsa a phléann an phleanáil teanga, an beartas teanga agus an bhainistíocht teanga. Is riachtanach an cúlra seo a lua chun comhthéacs do chreatlach theoiriciúil an staidéir a sholáthar. Tabharfar blaiseadh de smaointe bunaidh na pleanála teanga. Cíorfar coincheap an bheartais teanga. Mar chuid den scagadh sin, díreofar ar an mbainistíocht teanga ach go háirithe. Déanfar idirdhealú chomh beacht agus is féidir idir pleanáil teanga, beartas teanga agus bainistíocht teanga in ainneoin na doiléire téarmaíochta atá forleathan sa litríocht.

---

[1] Ceantar tuaithe seachas ceantar uirbeach atá i dtéis. Ar an ábhar sin, tá an aidiacht 'breac' feiliúnach agus sofaisticiúil sa chomhthéacs seo toisc go gcuimsíonn sé an éiginnteacht chultúrtha agus teanga sin a ndéanann Nic Eoin cur síos chomh críochnúil sin uirthi sa leabhar *Trén bhFearann Breac* (2005).

[2] Labhair an taighdeoir go pearsanta le Fidelma Ní Ghallchobhair ón gCoiste Téarmaíochta chun na téarmaí 'polasaí teanga' agus 'beartas teanga' a phlé. Theastaigh ón taighdeoir an téarma atá ag an gCoiste ar *language policy* a dheimhniú agus an téarma is ceart don taighdeoir seo a úsáid i gcomhthéacs an staidéir atá beartaithe aici a chinntiú. An bhfuil difríocht idir beartas teanga agus polasaí teanga? Níl freagra deifnídeach ag an gCoiste ar na ceisteanna seo. Is iondúil go sonraítear 'beartas' sa reachtaíocht agus go mbíonn 'polasaí' i mbéal an phobail / na meán dar le Ní Ghallchobhair. Sa litríocht, braitheann an leagan ar an údar. Baineann Ó hIfearnáin (2006), Ó Flatharta (2006) agus Ó Torna (2005) leas as beartas teanga. Moladh don taighdeoir a rogha féin a dhéanamh faoin leagan is fearr ar *language policy* ach na cúiseanna ina leith a léiriú. Bheartaigh an taighdeoir an leagan *beartas teanga* a roghnú sa chás seo toisc go bhfuil saothar foilsithe ag Ó hIfearnáin (2006) ar an ábhar le déanaí. Gort léinn ann féin é beartas teanga (Fidelma Ní Ghallchobhair, teagmháil phearsanta, 05/06/07).

Scrúdófar rangú triarach Spolsky[3] i leith an bheartais teanga ansin agus déanfar luacháil ar a fheiliúnacht mar bhunchloch theoiriciúil an togra. Pléifear trí dhlútheilimint an rangaithe sin, mar atá; cleachtas teanga, creideamh teanga[4] agus bainistíocht teanga ina rainn féin agus mar aonad iomlán. Féachfar leis na príomhphointí teoiriciúla a ríomh faoi dheireadh an pháipéir, in ionad cur síos cuimsitheach a dhéanamh ar an ábhar téagartha seo.

Mar cheangal, cuirfear teoiric na bainistíochta teanga i láthair roimh chonclúidí a tharraingt le chéile.

### Cur Síos Gairid ar an Togra

Déanfar grinnstaidéar sochtheangeolaíoch ar an gcaoi a bhfeidhmíonn an beartas teanga i gceantar Gaeltachta trí mheán na heitneagrafaíochta. Tabharfar léargas coincheapúil agus eimpíreach ar rangú triarach Spolsky i leith an bheartais teanga (.i. cleachtas teanga, creideamh teanga, bainistíocht teanga) sa Bhreacbhaile. I bhfocail eile, is mian leis an tráchtas dochtúireachta seo staidéar sainiúil sochtheangeolaíoch agus eitneagrafaíoch a dhéanamh ar an mbeartas teanga i bpobal comhaimseartha Gaeltachta.

Féachfar le dinimicí teanga nó beartas teanga intuigthe an phobail a iniúchadh ag leibhéal an bhaile i gceantar an Bhreacbhaile. Scagfar an cás sochtheangeolaíoch sa dúiche trí mhionscrúdú a dhéanamh ar rangú triarach Spolsky agus cuirfear bonnlíne taighde ar fáil dá réir. Go sonrach, tabharfar cuntas ar chleachtas teanga phobal Gaeltachta an Bhreacbhaile le huirlisí na heitneagrafaíochta. Scrúdófar creideamh teanga i measc an phobail. Fiosrófar cúrsaí cumhachta agus a nasc le bainistíocht fhollasach teanga agus bainistíocht neamhfhollasach teanga araon (Shohamy, 2006). Déanfar plé ar an nasc intreach idir an bhainistíocht shimplí agus an bhainistíocht eagraithe mar chuid den iniúchadh ar theoiric na bainistíochta teanga (Jernudd agus Neustupný 1987; Nekvapil 2006).

Déanfar dianstaidéar sochtheangeolaíoch ar an gcaoi a bhfeidhmíonn an beartas teanga i gceantar Gaeltachta trí mheán nótaí taighde agus agallamh. Ar bhealach eile, is é aidhm an tráchtais seo scagadh a dhéanamh ar chuid de na gnéithe is suntasaí a bhaineann le beogacht agus leochaileacht teanga i bpobal comhaimseartha Gaeltachta. Tógfar an phríomhcheist taighde seo a leanas: cén chaoi a bhfeidhmíonn beartas teanga sa Bhreacbhaile de réir rangú triarach Spolsky? Sa tslí sin, tabharfar léargas uathúil ar an bpróiseas a leantar chun beartas teanga a scagadh agus a dhearadh ag an micrileibhéal áitiúil. Feicfear céard é ról mhuintir na háite le hais cúraimí an taighdeora sa phróiseas sin. Ar bhealach eile, ceisteofar céard í feidhm an bheartais teanga i gceantar comhaimseartha Gaeltachta in Éirinn?

Dar le Crystal, tá trí mhórchúram le cur i gcrích má tá bearta i bhfabhar thodhchaí teanga a chothú ar intinn: (i) fáthmheas agus measúnú (ii) cur síos agus anailís (iii) idirghabháil agus athmheasúnú (2000: 145). Baineann an tráchtas seo le léargas a thabhairt ar an gcéad agus an dara pointe ach go háirithe, aidhm a thagann le comhairle Spolsky (2004: 218). Ar an ábhar sin, insíonn Ó hIfearnáin nach féidir aon idirghabháil chiallmhar nó 'aon phleanáil teanga chumasach', a mbeidh toradh fónta uirthi a thosú, gan an taighde ceart oiriúnach a dhéanamh roimh ré (2006: 3).

Pléifear na difríochtaí idir pleanáil teanga, beartas teanga agus bainistíocht teanga,

---
[3] Is sochtheangeolaí clúiteach é an tOllamh Bernard Spolsky (tuilleadh eolais ag http: //www.biu.ac.il/faculty/spolsb).
[4] D'fhéadfaí idé-eolaíocht a úsáid sa chás seo ar aon oiread. Is fearr le Spolsky 'creideamh teanga' toisc go seachnaítear na macallaí polaitiúla atá inchurtha leis an bhfocal 'idé-eolaíocht' (2007: 3).

más ann dóibh, mar chuid den tráchtas seo. Is leor a rá anois go mbaineann pleanáil teanga leis na hiarrachtaí teanga-lárnaithe a bhíodh ar bun le linn tréimhse ar leith, ón mbarr anuas nó ag an rialtas de ghnáth. Is nós le Jernudd agus Neustupný pleanáil teanga a úsáid chun tagairt don saghas gníomhaíochta (rialachán smachtach, aontaobhach aonchineálach) a thit amach i gcaitheamh tréimhse ar leith. Ina dtuairim sin, seasann an téarma 'bainistíocht teanga' do réimse níos leithne a tháinig chun cinn comhthreomhar le forbairt sa litríocht Cheanadach Fhrancach:

> The use of this term, language management, in lieu of the currently widely used language planning *will leave the latter term free to refer to the particular phase of the 'linguistics of language problems' which developed in the 1970s*. This usage coincides with the Canadian French use of the term *aménagement linguistique* [...] (1987: 71, liomsa an bhéim).

Ar an láimh eile, tá réimse níos leithne ag roinnt leis an mbainistíocht teanga a chuireann maicreaghnéithe (reachtaíocht, cearta) agus micreaghnéithe (tuairimí an phobail) san áireamh (Nekvapil, 2006: 99). Mar chuid den iniúchadh, déanfar machnamh ar theoiric na bainistíochta teanga (Jernudd agus Neustupný 1987; Nekvapil 2006). Tabharfar aird ar leith ar choincheap na mbainisteoirí teanga. Tógfar ceisteanna cosúil le: Céard is bainisteoir teanga ann? Cé hiad na bainisteoirí teanga? Cé atá freagrach as bainistíocht teanga?

Go han-simplí, is ionann beartas teanga agus na haidhmeanna ginearálta teanga a leagtar síos chun idirghabháil a stiúradh. Ag an am céanna, ní hionann beartas ginearálta náisiúnta agus beartas sainiúil an phobail. Déanfar idirdhealú chomh beacht agus is féidir idir na coincheapa seo bíodh is go bhfuil an t-uafás siar is aniar eatarthu sa litríocht fós.

Cuirfear torthaí an taighde agus na moltaí a thagann chun solais ar fáil don phobal taighde, agus thiocfadh leo iad a úsáid chun dlús a chur lena bpróiseas bainistíochta teanga féin. Tógfar ar an litríocht reatha trí iniúchadh a dhéanamh ar iarrachtaí bainistíochta teanga ag an micrileibhéal áitiúil. Leis sin, déanfar anailís ar fheidhm an bheartais teanga i gceantar comhaimseartha Gaeltachta. Ar shlí eile, tabharfar léargas coincheapúil agus eimpíreach ar réiteach beartas teanga do phobal Gaeltachta, gné den dioscúrsa nach bhfuil pléite go dtí seo in Éirinn.

**Modheolaíocht**

**Tairbhe na Heitneagrafaíochta**

Is mian leis an staidéar seo beartas teanga intuigthe an phobail a chíoradh de réir rangú triarach Spolsky (2004) bunaithe ar obair cháilíochtúil ghoirt. Chuige sin, tograíodh nótaí taighde agus agallaimh a úsáid mar uirlisí eitneagrafaíochta chun próifíliú a dhéanamh ar chás sochtheangeolaíoch an phobail. Mar a dúirt Wates:

> Community profiling involves building up a picture of the nature, needs and resources of a community with the active participation of that community. It is a useful first stage in any community planning process to establish a context which is widely agreed (2000: 42).

Cuireann Canagarajah leis an bpointe sin. Is dóigh leis-sean go bhfuil rochtain ag eitneagrafaí ar eolas luachmhar ón taobh istigh faoi ghréasáin teanga nach bhfuil teacht ag gachuile thaighdeoir air. Ní mór tuiscint a fháil ar an bpobal ina maireann an teanga chun anailís agus fiú athruithe a dhéanamh ar bheartas teanga an phobail sin. Thiocfadh leis an eitneagrafaí moltaí a chur ar fáil i dtaobh réiteach nó athbhreithniú an bheartais teanga:

> Whatever the type or level of policy-making addressed, ethnography can bring out surprising findings about language relationships that elude those acting from outside the community. On the basis of their findings, ethnographers may offer recommendations that can make an important contribution to the formation or revision of language policies (2006: 159).

Insíonn Ricento go dtugann an eitneagrafaíocht léargas dúinn ar shaol an ghnáthdhuine le gur féidir tuiscint níos fearr a fháil ar ról teangacha ina saol agus tionchar na mbeartas follasach agus neamhfhollasach[5] orthu:

> Ethnography can provide insights about life at the grass-roots level and lead to better understanding of the role of language(s) in the lives of people directly affected by overt or covert language policies or regimes (Ricento, 2006: 130).

Sa chaoi chéanna, tá ardluach ag roinnt le cur síos leanúnach taighde cosúil le dialann taighde mar is trí na nótaí sin a éiríonn leis an taighdeoir an ní intuigthe nó eolas neamhinste a iompú ina ní follasach (Maykut and Morehouse, 1994: 33). '(A)ll understanding is tacit knowing, all understanding is achieved by indwelling' dar le Polanyi (luaite ag Grene 1969: 160).

### Lochtanna Féideartha na Modheolaíochta

Ar an láimh eile, áfach, ceaptar go coitianta go mbíonn taighde cáilíochtúil agus an eitneagrafaíocht ach go háirithe ró-shuibiachtúil. Múineann an eitneagrafaíocht chriticiúil gur chóir don eitneagrafaí gluaiseacht ón éisteacht fhulangach go machnamh aisfhillteach (Canagarajah, 2006: 164). Sa tslí sin, déanann an taighdeoir gach iarracht láimhseáil chriticiúil a dhéanamh ar bhreathnóireachtaí agus cothromaíocht a aimsiú idir an ghné scolártha acadúil, toil an phobail agus mianta pearsanta (Ó Laoire, 2003: 127).

Maidir le múnla an cháis-staidéir, luaitear go minic ina choinne nach féidir ginearálú a dhéanamh ar na torthaí. Nuair nach bhfuil ach ceantar amháin nó suíomh beag faoi staidéar, seans go gcuirfear ina leith go bhfuil sé áitiúil agus sainiúil (Bryman 2004: 51). Níl an taighdeoir seo ag súil le ginearálú a dhéanamh ar thorthaí an cháis-staidéir. Gach seans go mbeidh na torthaí seo fónta do ghrúpaí agus coistí áitiúla teanga eile (Bell, 1999: 13), ach is riachtanach do gach pobal a chúinsí féin a scrúdú sula dtéann siad i mbun gníomhaíochta. 'There is no one-size-fits-all solution for revitalisation and preservation' a mheabhraíonn Romaine (2007: 122).

---

[5] Tagraíonn beartas follasach do bheartas ginearálta náisiúnta na críche a bhíonn i bhfoirm scríofa go hiondúil. Seasann an beartas neamhfhollasach do bheartas intuigthe na sochaí nó is éard a thiteann amach ag leibhéal an bhaile gach lá (Schiffman 1996; Shohamy 2006). Pléifear na téarmaí seo sa rannóg faoi bheartas teanga.

Agus an comhthéacs sin ar intinn, cuirfear modhanna fiosrúcháin i láthair anseo thíos roimh dhíriú ar chreatlach theoiriciúil an staidéir.

## Modhanna Fiosrúcháin

Faoi láthair, tá breathnóireachtaí comhthitimeacha á mbailiú go rialta sa láthair taighde .i. am ar bith a théann an taighdeoir chuig ionad poiblí (m.sh: siopa, garáiste, teach tábhairne, séipéal) scríobhtar tuairiscí ar an eachtra de réir chritéir Berg i ndialann taighde (2007: 197–104). Tá tagairt sna nótaí do dháta, am, ábhar, suíomh agus fad na heachtra. Déantar cur síos ar an méid a thit amach agus pléitear cúrsaí teanga. Is ar chúrsaí teanga agus iompar teanga i measc phobal an cheantair a dhíríonn an cuntas scríofa ach go háirithe.

Go minic, scríobhtar nótaí lámhscríofa ar dtús i leabhar nótaí an taighdeora. Breactar an cuntas chomh luath agus is féidir i ndiaidh na heachtra ar fhaitíos go ndéanfaí dearmad ar shonraí. É sin ráite, bíonn an taighdeoir ag brath go mór ar an gcuimhne chomh maith lena cumas aireachtála agus tabhairt faoi deara. Scríobhtar an cuntas seo chomh luath agus is féidir i ndiaidh na heachtra agus déantar tagairt d'ord na n-imeachtaí, líon na ndaoine a bhí i láthair, príomhshonraí / cainteoirí an chomhrá, sleachta cainte / focail a sheas amach agus mar sin de. Tá tuairiscí rialta laethúla á gcoinneáil ag an taighdeoir agus tugtar uimhir thagartha do gach eachtra. Ní bhactar le mionchur síos a dhéanamh ar an suíomh fisiciúil ar mhaithe le cúrsaí rúndachta.

Bíonn rangú triarach Spolsky mar threoir don taighdeoir nuair a scríobhann sí sa dialann taighde .i. tá cúrsaí teanga agus iompar teanga mar phríomhfhócas an taighde. Ar na príomhcheisteanna a ritheann leis an taighdeoir agus í ag scríobh sa dialann taighde tá: Cé hé/hí cainteoir(í) an chomhrá? Cé a labhair ar dtús? Cén teanga / leagan a bhí á úsáid aige/aici? Ar tháinig athrú ar theanga an chomhrá? Céard is cúis leis an athrú? Cén teanga a labhraíonn na cainteoirí seo le chéile de ghnáth? Cén teanga a labhraíonn an taighdeoir leis an duine sin go hiondúil? Cén chaoi ar chuir an taighdeoir aithne ar an gcainteoir? Cathain ar chuir an taighdeoir aithne ar an gcainteoir? Cá bhfuil cónaí air/uirthi? Cén gairm bheatha atá aige/aici? An bhfuil baint ag an gcainteoir le gnólacht / institiúid Gaeilge?

Déantar idirdhealú idir an bhreathnóireacht féin agus athmhachnamh nó tuairimí an taighdeora, mar a mholann Berg, Maykut agus Morehouse. Déantar athmhachnamh ar phríomhtharlúintí na n-iontrálacha dialainne chun tuiscint a fháil ar a bhfuil ag titim amach sa cheantar faoi láthair agus chun bunchreatlach an phatrúin úsáide teanga a rianadh. Bíonn rangú triarach Spolsky mar threoir don taighdeoir nuair a dhéanann sí machnamh aisfhillteach ar eachtraí na dialanne taighde. Ceistítear cén tionchar a bhí ag láithreacht an taighdeora ar an teanga a labhraíodh? Cén fáth ar roghnaíodh teanga amháin thar teanga eile? Cén impleacht a bhí ag an suíomh ar an teanga a roghnaíodh? Cén impleacht a bhí ag an ábhar cainte ar an teanga a roghnaíodh? Cén impleacht a bhí ag rannpháirtithe an chomhrá ar an teanga a roghnaíodh? Cén teanga a labhraítear san áit seo go hiondúil? Cén fáth ar chuir na daoine seo comhrá ar a chéile? Cén fáth go labhraíonn duine le duine eile? Cé na cineálacha éagsúla comhráite atá le sonrú? An bhfuil foghrúpaí le sonrú i measc muintir na háite? Baineann próiseas leanúnach aisfhillteach leis an saghas seo taighde.

Comhlánófar an t-eolas seo le hagallaimh leathstruchtúrtha. Reáchtálfar seasca agallamh ar a laghad le muintir an cheantair. Chuile sheans go gcuirfear a thuilleadh agallamh i gcrích ag brath ar dhul chun cinn na hoibre agus cúrsaí ama.

Déanfar códú oscailte agus ansin códú fócasáilte (de réir rangú Spolsky) ar na sonraí. Ní léir fós cé mhéad den anailís sin a bheidh sa tuarascáil deiridh áfach. Cuirfear sleachta (leasuithe) éagsúla ón dialann taighde sa tráchtas chun tacú leis na hagallaimh a dhéanfar i measc an phobail (.i. eolas a forlíonadh). Déanfar chuile iarracht léargas cothrom a thabhairt ar an gceantar taighde. Cabhróidh an dá uirlis taighde (dialann, agallamh) go mór leis an taighdeoir an cuspóir sin a bhaint amach. Cíorfar na ceisteanna agus na téamaí céanna ( .i. bunaithe ar chleachtas teanga, creideamh teanga agus bainistíocht teanga an phobail) le huirlisí difriúla chun torthaí taighde a chomhdhearbhú agus a chóineartú .i. bainfear leas as dhá uirlis taighde chun muinín a chothú sna torthaí a fhaightear.

Ag críoch an taighde cuirfear torthaí na hoibre i láthair an phobail ag seisiún aiseolais. Tabharfar deis do mhuintir an cheantair a dtuairimí agus a moltaí a léiriú faoin staid reatha sochtheangeolaíoch agus bearta don todhchaí. Cineál scrúdú bailíochta é an seisiún faisnéise seo.

I ndiaidh taighde cáilíochtúil bunaithe ar nósmhaireachtaí teanga mhuintir an cheantair a phlé, molfar cur chuige cuimsitheach do bheartas teanga nua a bheidh infheidhmithe tríd an gcomhpháirtíocht. Tá gach cás teangeolaíoch agus pobal taighde sainiúil ann féin. Is ceart an próiseas a bhunú ar an mbonn indibhidiúil sin dar leis an taighdeoir seo.

**Litríocht na Pleanála Teanga, an Bheartais Teanga agus na Bainistíochta Teanga**

**Réamhrá**

Tabharfar spléachadh ar an dioscúrsa acadúil a roinneann leis an bpleanáil teanga, an beartas teanga agus an bhainistíocht teanga sa chuid seo den pháipéar. Is i gcomhthéacs na litríochta seo a fhorbrófar an tráchtas.

Le gairid, tá bláth agus borradh tagtha ar réimsí léinn na pleanála teanga, an bheartais teanga agus na bainistíochta teanga. Is de dheasca leathnú fhorlámhas an Bhéarla (nó teangacha domhanda eile) agus bás teangacha bundúchasacha na cruinne a spreagadh suim an athuair i dtéamaí na pleanála teanga agus an bheartais teanga dar le Hornberger (2006: 24). Tagraíonn sí do ghort na pleanála agus an bheartais teanga amhail is nach féidir an dá choincheap a scarúint óna chéile (2006: 24). Tá díospóireacht shaibhir leathan ar siúl idir scoileanna smaointeoireachta éagsúla faoi na difríochtaí, más ann dóibh, idir pleanáil teanga agus beartas teanga (Spolsky 2004; Ó hIfearnáin 2006). An cosúil go bhfuil réimse na pleanála teanga agus an bheartais teanga ag comhtháthú le chéile? Nó, an dá scoil smaointeoireachta difriúla iad? Más ea, an gá meascán den dhá theoiric a ionramháil? Nó, an tairbheach tarraingt ar théamaí *l'aménagement linguistique* don chineál seo togra? Is ionann *l'aménagement linguistique* agus bainistíocht teanga.[6]

Béimníonn Nekvapil an t-athrú téarmaíochta atá le sonrú sa litríocht ó phleanáil teanga go bainistíocht teanga (2006: 94). Míníonn Jernudd agus Neustupný go dtagann an téarma 'bainistíocht teanga' le brí an choincheapa Cheanadaigh / Fhrancaigh *l'aménagement linguistique* (1987: 71). Leis sin, tráchtann Grin ar *gouvernance linguistique* agus *gestion linguistique* (2005). Is cosúil nach athrú foclaíochta amháin atá tugtha faoi deara ag Nekvapil agus gur fiú tuilleadh suntais a thabhairt do theoiric na bainistíochta teanga. Tá sé ar intinn na saincheisteanna seo a spíonadh amach i gcomhthéacs an tráchtais agus idirdhealú coincheapúil a lorg idir pleanáil teanga agus bainistíocht teanga. Tabharfar blaiseadh beag de na tuairimí seo sa pháipéar. Mar sin, díreofar ar an bpleanáil teanga amháin anois.

[6] Ar an ábhar sin, ní miste a mheabhrú gur fiúntach litríocht lasmuigh de dhomhan an Bhéarla a scrúdú chun léargas níos cuimsithí a fháil. Is minic a bhíonn claonadh Eura-Meiriceánach an Bhéarla le brath sa litríocht seo.

## An Phleanáil Teanga

Is ionann pleanáil teanga agus gníomhaíocht a fhéachann le tionchar a imirt ar chleachtas teanga an phobail ag brath ar aidhmeanna réamhshocraithe (Swann *et al.*, 2004: 173). Is gá aidhmeanna teanga agus seach-theanga a shoiléiriú agus cruth a chur ar smaointe faoin bpróiseas roimh dhul i mbun ghníomhaíocht na pleanála teanga. Meicníocht atá sa phleanáil teanga dá réir sin. Stiúrann an rialtas nó eagraíocht údarásach eile an próiseas seo de ghnáth (Kaplan agus Baldauf 1997: xi). Baineann fréamhacha réimse na pleanála teanga le gníomhaireacht aontaobhach an rialtais amháin agus go dtí seo rinneadh formhór an staidéir ag an maicrileibhéal seo. Go tráthrialta smaoiníonn scoláirí de chuid na pleanála teanga ar iarrachtaí an mhórscála nó i dtéarmaí náisiúnta amháin, an cineál pleanála a bhíonn ar bun ag leibhéal an stáit (Baldauf, 2006: 148). Seo é cur chuige clasaiceach na pleanála teanga, nuair a shamhlaítear an chumhacht ar fad a bheith i lámha na n-údarás. Féachann an tráchtas seo le gníomhaíochtaí teanga ag micrileibhéal an phobail a léiriú, áfach.

Tugann Ó Riain tús áite do chomhthéacs náisiúnta na pleanála teanga chomh maith: 'gníomhaíocht eagraithe chun fadhbanna teanga a réiteach, ar an leibhéal náisiúnta de ghnáth…' (Ó Riain, 1994: 1). Tagann an méid seo le tuairimí Fishman:

> Most scholars limit the term language planning to 'the organised pursuit of solutions to language problems, typically at the national level' (Fishman, 1973: 23/4 luaite ag Bratt Paulston, 1994: 5).

An ionann sin agus dearbhú go mbaineann gníomhaíochtaí na pleanála teanga leis an maicrileibhéal amháin? An leor pleanáil teanga ag an leibhéal náisiúnta amháin i sochaí an lae inniu? An bhfuil ionad do ghluaiseachtaí an phobail sa phleanáil teanga? Déanfar plé ar na ceisteanna seo agus ar chineálacha difriúla pleanála teanga (agus saghasanna éagsúla gníomhaireachta) anois díreach.

### Cineálacha Difriúla Pleanála Teanga

#### Réamhrá

Tugann Baldauf le fios go nglactar leis go coitianta anois go dtarlaíonn an phleanáil teanga agus go ndéantar teanga a phleanáil ag an iliomad leibhéal .i. micrileibhéal (coistí áitiúla teanga, an duine aonair, tuismitheoirí, gnólachtaí), maicrileibhéal (rialtas náisiúnta agus ollnáisiúnta) agus méisileibhéal (rialtas áitiúil, na meáin) (Baldauf, 2006: 147). Sa chaoi chéanna, roinntear an phleanáil teanga ina dá cuid go minic; micriphleanáil teanga (a tharlaíonn ag an micrileibhéal go hiondúil) agus maicriphleanáil teanga (a bhíonn ar bun ag an maicrileibhéal de ghnáth).

Ní mór a cheistiú an ceart scoilt chomh simplí sin a dhéanamh idir cineálacha éagsúla na pleanála teanga? Sa saol idéalach, nach ceart próiseas pleanála teanga uilechuimsitheach a dhearadh a chuireann micrileibhéal agus maicrileibhéal san áireamh?

#### Barr Anuas / Maicriphleanáil

Tarlaíonn maicriphleanáil teanga i gcomhthéacs níos fairsinge de ghnáth, agus go hiondúil bíonn an cineál seo pleanála ar siúl ag an maicrileibhéal amháin (.i. leibhéal an rialtais / an stáit). Seo é cur chuige clasaiceach na pleanála teanga a luadh níos túisce:

Most general frameworks (...) and much of the exemplary literature cited to support them suggest that language planning is a large scale activity, i.e. it occurs mainly at the macro level (Kaplan agus Baldauf 1997: 52).

Spreagann an cineál seo pleanála ceisteanna riachtanacha faoi ghníomhaireacht dar le Baldauf (2006). Cé aige / aici / acu a bhfuil an chumhacht dul i gcion ar chleachtas teanga an phobail nó athruithe pleanála teanga (ón mbarr anuas) a mholadh ag an micrileibhéal a cheistíonn sé? Déantar teanga a phleanáil ach bíonn duine nó eagraíocht nó lucht cumhachta ag stiúradh an phróisis de ghnáth. Ní ann don phleanáil teanga gan pleanálaí. Áitíonn Ó hIfearnáin go mbaintear úsáid as téarma na pleanála teanga nuair atá smacht agus údarás i gceist agus socruithe á gcur i bhfeidhm, córas atá cáinte aige (2006: 7). Dar le Kaplan, is ionann é sin agus pleanáil teanga ón mbarr anuas (1997: 55) (nó cur chuige clasaiceach na pleanála teanga). Sa chás áirithe sin, is minic a dhéanann grúpaí cumhachtacha roghanna ar son pobail teanga beag beann ar thuairimí na ndaoine sin. Bíonn ról an phobail tánaisteach. An bhfuil neamhleanúnachas agus fiú baol tromaíochta bainteach le cur chuige an bhairr anuas?

Tá ról fíorthábhachtach ag na húdaráis sa phróiseas pleanála teanga leis an gcur chuige seo. An ceart a rá áfach go bhfuil an mheá go hiomlán ina bhfabhar? An coincheap líneach, diúltach agus údarásach é mar sin, toisc go dtugtar easpa airde ar thuairimí an phobail urlabhra? Ar shlí eile, an iondúil go mbíonn neamhréireacht idir *macra* agus *micrea* leis an gcur chuige traidisiúnta seo de chuid na pleanála teanga?

**Bonn Aníos / Micriphleanáil**

Tá borradh faoin bpleanáil teanga i gcomhthéacsanna áitiúla ag an micrileibhéal i litríocht an Bhéarla le gairid (Baldauf, 2006: 147). Tagraíonn micriphleanáil teanga do phleanáil a dhíríonn ar aidhmeanna teoranta ar scála beag (ag an micrileibhéal go minic). Leis sin, tugtar pleanáil teanga ón mbonn aníos ar an sórt pleanála a chuireann rannpháirtíocht an phobail mar chuid den phróiseas pleanála (Kaplan agus Baldauf, 1997: 52).

Is gnách go ndíríonn micriphleanáil ar chineál eile gníomhaireachta a bhíonn ar bun ag gnólachtaí, institiúidí, coistí áitiúla agus mar sin de. Sa chás seo réitíonn an gníomhaire (nó an bainisteoir teanga) an bóthar do phróiseas pleanála teanga ag an micrileibhéal le gur féidir teanga(cha) a fhorbairt ag an leibhéal sin agus earraíocht a bhaint as acmhainní teanga. Is amhlaidh gurb inmhianaithe go dtuigfeadh an bainisteoir teanga nósmhaireachtaí nó rialacha intuigthe na sochaí le gur féidir an beartas is dual don phobal a dhearadh. Tá go leor solúbthachta ag roinnt leis an gcur chuige seo. Tugtar tosaíocht do thoil agus do rannpháirtíocht an phobail. Freagraíonn an cineál seo pleanála do riachtanais agus fadhbanna sainiúla an tsuímh, gá sonrach na háite sin do ghníomhaíochtaí teanga (Baldauf, 2006: 155).

**Tátal**

I dtuairim Baldauf is cuid chomhlántach den mhaicriphleanáil iad gníomhaíochtaí ag an micrileibhéal. Ní dóigh leis gur leor an mhicriphleanáil nó an mhaicriphleanáil amháin (Baldauf, 2006: 165). Ar shlí eile, is dócha go mbraitheann an cineál pleanála ar aidhmeanna an togra agus comhthéacs an staidéir. 'Every group must decide what can best be done realistically for a particular language at a particular time' a mholann

Romaine (2007: 122). Leis sin, braitheann rath na pleanála teanga ar rannpháirtíocht agus tacaíocht an phobail ach go háirithe (Kaplan agus Baldauf, 2003: 201). Ar an iomlán, próiseas uileghabhálach atá sa phleanáil teanga dar leis an taighdeoir seo. Bheadh sé earráideach díriú ar ghné amháin den phleanáil teanga (.i. an mhicriphleanáil, cuir i gcás) gan léargas a fháil ar an mórphictiúr. Ní mór do ghníomhaíocht pleanála teanga ar bith dul i gcion ar an micrileibhéal agus an maicrileibhéal ar bhonn comhtháite. Ag an am céanna, ní leor go mbeadh an dá chineál pleanála teanga ag feidhmiú taobh le chéile, caithfidh go mbeadh teagmháil choibhneasta chomhthuilleamaíoch eatarthu dar leis an taighdeoir seo. Níl aon chinnteacht go dtarlóidh sin le haon chur chuige amháin den phleanáil teanga ámh.

Áitíonn Blommaert go bhfuil scóip na pleanála teanga teoranta do chineál ar leith gníomhaíochtaí agus idirghabhálacha a bhíonn faoi anáil na polaitíochta agus á stiúradh ag an rialtas de ghnáth:

> The scope of the term 'language planning' is often intuitively confined to a particular type of activities: consciously planned, politically inspired but rationally implemented forms of language treatment in a multilingual context in third world or emergent states (Blommaert, 1996: 206).

Is amhlaidh atá an cineál seo pleanála aontaobhach ar son an luchta rialacháin agus cumhacht-lárnaithe dá réir. Is dócha, mar sin, go bhfuil an chontúirt ann go bhfuil smacht éigin agus baol tromaíochta le tuiscint ó ghníomhaíocht seo na pleanála teanga nuair a bhrúnn na húdaráis rialacha ar an bpobal ón mbarr anuas. Cáintear a leithéid de phleanáil:

> [...] governed by their (.i. governments or leading elites) self-interests and reproducing rather than overcoming sociocultural and econo-technical inequalities (Fishman, 1994: 94).

Díríonn Blommaert ar pholaitíocht na pleanála teanga arís is arís eile agus feictear dó nach bhfuil aon éalú ón gcur chuige traidisiúnta seo den phleanáil teanga. Tagraíonn sé don chosc a chuirtear ar nósmhaireachtaí teanga ar leith de dheasca na pleanála teanga, do ról an stáit mar phríomhghníomhaire sa phróiseas nó cothromaíocht na cumhachta i lámha na n-údarás agus do bhaol na claontachta agus an easpa daonlathais atá mar chuid lárnach den phleanáil teanga (Blommaert, 1996: 206). Soiléiríonn na tuairimí seo ar fad go bhfuil ualach idé-eolaíochta á iompar ag an bpleanáil teanga, go bhfuil tuiscintí ar leith intuigthe le próiseas na pleanála teanga agus nach bhfuil an cur chuige seo ar leas an phobail de ghnáth:

> [...] language planning itself appears to be ideologically burdened. It carries implicit assumptions about what a 'good' society is, about what is best for the people, about the way in which language and communication fit into that picture, and about how language planning can contribute to a social and political progress (Blommaert, 1996: 215).

An tátal is mó atá le baint ón iniúchadh seo ar an bpleanáil teanga ná go bhfuil údair áirithe a luann an éagmais dhaonlathais a roinneann léi, constaic a chruthaíonn fíoramhras i leith chur chuige na pleanála teanga don togra seo. Ní léir go bhfuil cothrom na féinne ag baint leis an bpleanáil teanga mar is iondúil go mbíodh cóimheá na cumhachta ag claonadh i dtreo na gcinnteoirí go dtí seo. An amhlaidh atá beartas teanga (agus/nó cur chuige na bainistíochta teanga) níos rannpháirtí agus daonlathaí mar choincheap nó mar chur chuige? Déanfar iniúchadh ar choincheap an bheartais teanga anois.

### Beartas Teanga: Réamhrá

Go han-simplí, is ionann beartas teanga agus na haidhmeanna ginearálta teanga a leagann an rialtas síos i bhfoirm scríofa scaití chun idirghabháil a stiúradh (.i. beartas ginearálta náisiúnta). Ar bhealach eile, seasann croí an bheartais teanga de ghnáth do chreidimh agus cleachtais an phobail i leith na dteangacha atá acu (.i. beartas sainiúil an phobail).

Baineann teacht chun cinn an bheartais teanga leis na hathruithe atá tagtha ar nádúr na sochaí sibhialta. Ar ndóigh, tá iompraíocht an stáit i leith an phobail ag athrú le glúin anuas sna tíortha daonlathacha. Is amhlaidh atá na húdaráis ag tarraingt siar ón idirghabháil idir an saoránach agus a chuid roghanna pearsanta, cúrsaí teanga san áireamh (Ó hIfearnáin, 2006: 7). Is dealraitheach go bhfuil an stát ag súil le deireadh a chur leis an méirínteacht sin i saol an duine (Ó hIfearnáin, 2006: 7). Más ea agus ar an modh sin, tá an phleanáil teanga ag géilleadh a háite do choincheap úr seo an bheartais teanga dar le Shohamy (2006: 49). An amhlaidh atá coincheap na pleanála teanga seanchaite mar sin?

Léiríonn an sainmhíniú ar bheartas teanga i bhfoclóir na sochtheangeolaíochta go dtagraítear go minic don bheartas teanga agus don phleanáil teanga go comhchiallach (Swann et al. 2004: 173). Is coincheapa gaolta ach difriúla iad i dtuairim Kaplan agus Baldauf. Bíodh is go bhfuil go leor cosúlachtaí eatarthu ní hionann an dá phróiseas dar leo (1997: 14). Is riachtanach do ghníomhairí pleanála teanga nó bainisteoirí teanga an t-idirdhealú seo a fhiosrú dar le Baldauf (2006: 149). Tá dlúthnasc idir pleanáil teanga agus eolas ar thréithe an bheartais teanga dar le Ó hIfearnáin. Sonraíonn sé go gcaithfear nádúr an bheartais teanga a thuiscint chun pleanáil fhiúntach teanga a chur i gcrích (2006: 5). An cosúil go bhfuil gá leis an dá eilimint mar sin?

Bíonn go leor siar is aniar idir pleanáil teanga agus beartas teanga sa litríocht fós, tagairtí acadúla agus neamhacadúla san áireamh. Tá an doiléireacht agus cineál neamhchinnteachta seo forleathan. Seo roinnt samplaí den éidearfacht seo, nó nós na n-údar pleanáil agus beartas a lua taobh le chéile in aon abairt amháin, gan scoilt ghlan eatarthu: 'language policy and planning (LPP)' (Hornberger, 2006: 24); 'micro policy and planning' (Kaplan agus Baldauf, 1997: 52); 'language planning policy' (Moal, 2007); 'Welsh planning and policy' (Williams, 2000: 1); 'language policy and planning (Ricento, 2000: 196); 'policy and planning' (Spolsky agus Shohamy, 1999: 46); 'Language policy, or language planning' (Grin, 2003: 27). Is geall gur comhlogú iad pleanáil agus beartas teanga i litríocht an lae inniu. Díreofar ar chineálacha difriúla beartas teanga anois.

### Céard í an Difríocht idir Beartas Scríofa agus Beartas Intuigthe?

Tugann Swann et al le fios go bhfuil dhá chineál bheartas teanga ann, beartas follasach agus beartas intuigthe (2004: 173). Aontaíonn Spolsky leis an áiteamh seo agus tagraíonn sé do bheartas scríofa soiléir chomh maith le beartas neamhscríofa intuigthe (2004: 11). Is éasca an beartas scríofa soiléir a aithint dar leis (2004: 11). Tá teacht ar an gcineál seo beartais sna ráitis fhoirmiúla atá mar chuid de dhoiciméid oifigiúla.

Ar an láimh eile, bíonn an beartas neamhscríofa ach intuigthe don phobal le feiceáil in iompar agus i ndearcadh an phobail i leith na dteangacha a labhraítear sa tsochaí (Ó hIfearnáin, 2006: 6). Insíonn Schiffman go dtugtar neamhaird go minic do ghnéithe neamhfhollasacha an bheartais teanga (nó séard a thiteann amach ag leibhéal an bhaile gach lá), modh oibre atá lochtach dar leis toisc go bhfuil dlúthbhaint ag an mbeartas seo leis an bpobal (1996: 13).

Lena chois sin, is ann don bheartas teanga fiú mura bhfuil ráiteas scríofa soiléir ar fáil. Ní minic a scríobhann aon phobal a bheartas síos mar a bheadh cáipéis pholasaí ann (Ó hIfearnáin, 2006: 1). Fiú nuair a bhíonn beartas teanga scríofa soiléir ar fáil, ní féidir i gcónaí a éifeacht ar chleachtas an phobail a dheimhniú (Spolsky, 2004: 8). Nuair nach bhfuil aon tagairt phoiblí don teanga sa cháipéisíocht oifigiúil, is féidir an beartas a dhéanamh amach ó chleachtas an phobail nó cleachtas na n-údarás i leith na teanga dar le Ó hIfearnáin (2006: 6). Seachadtar agus cothaítear an beartas intuigthe seo gan cheist i dtuairim Schiffman (1996: 13). Níl sé furasta teacht ar an mbeartas intuigthe mar go mbíonn sé lonnaithe go smior in aigne an phobail agus is minic i bhfolach é dá bharr (Ó hIfearnáin, 2006: 6). Ar an láimh eile, is minic a bhíonn beartais éagsúla le sonrú i measc an phobail. Bíonn nádúr an bheartais teanga casta agus níos caolchúisí (Ó hIfearnáin, 2006: 6).

Tuigtear do Spolsky go mbaineann beartas teanga le húsáid na teanga ó thaobh an phobail de, agus an bealach a ndéantar an t-iompar teanga sin a bhainistiú. Tugann sé 'beartas teanga' ar na creidimh uilig agus ar na cleachtais uile atá ag pobal teanga nó stát agus ar na socruithe bainistíochta a dhéantar ar an gcleachtas agus ar na creidimh sin. Admhaíonn Ó hIfearnáin gur fearr an téarma 'bainistíocht' ar phleanáil sa chomhthéacs seo toisc go dtugann sé tús áite d'iompar an phobail teanga seachas do thoil na n-údarás pleanála (2006: 7).

Más ag iarraidh beartas teanga an stáit nó aonad eile a mheas, comhairlíonn Spolsky gur cheart díriú isteach ar a staid chasta teangeolaíoch ar dtús (Spolsky, 2004: 218). Áitíonn sé gur féidir beartas teanga an phobail a thuiscint agus meabhair a bhaint as cineálacha difriúla sonraí faoi theanga nuair a dhírítear ar a thrí chomhábhar, mar atá, cleachtas teanga, creideamh teanga agus bainistíocht teanga.

Molann Spolsky go gcaithfear léirsmaoineamh a dhéanamh ar chleachtas, creideamh agus brúnna seanbhunaithe na háite chun cur le beartas teanga ginearálta agus céimeanna speisialta a thógáil i dtreo bainistíocht teanga:

> To go from a general language policy to specific plans for language management, one must respect established practices and beliefs and pressures within the constituent social groups that make up the nation (...) (2006: 17).

Feicfear anois an buntús maith é rangú triarach Spolsky chun beartas teanga a iniúchadh ag leibhéal an phobail nó chun fáthmheas a dhéanamh ar chás sochtheangeolaíoch an Bhreacbhaile i bhfoclaíocht Crystal (2000: 145). Tabharfar sracfhéachaint ar nasc gach comhábhair leis an obair pháirce anois.

## Cleachtas Teanga

Is ionann cleachtas teanga agus na roghanna comhfhiosacha agus neamh-mheabhracha a dhéantar idir teangacha na sochaí agus cineál na teanga sin nó an gnáthphatrún a bhaineann le roghnú idir leaganacha an stóir theangeolaíoch (mar shampla; Gaeilge v. Béarla, réim ard v. réim íseal, canúint áitiúil v. teanga chaighdeánach). Tá cleachtas an duine aonair, cleachtas an phobail agus cleachtas na n-údarás (bainistíocht) le cur san áireamh. Leis sin, tá rangú do chainteoirí comhaimseartha Gaeltachta ag teastáil, chun ilghnéitheacht na gcomhchainteoirí Gaeltachta a léiriú agus chun comhdhéanamh an phobail Ghaeltachta seo a mheas. Caithfear a dhéanamh amach ansin cé na cineálacha éagsúla leaganacha teanga atá le sonrú sa cheantar (.i. Béarla na háite, canúint áitiúil na Gaeilge, teanga na scoile agus leaganacha inmheánacha eile).

Is gá cineálacha teanga atá á labhairt nó leaganacha an stóir theangeolaíoch a rangú. Beidh léargas luachmhar ar fáil ar chúrsaí teanga na háite san fhaisnéis seo. Cuir i gcás, an bhfuil lorg nó fianaise den iompú teanga (msh: códmheascadh) le sonrú sna leaganacha teanga? Ní fios fós cén chaoi is fearr na leaganacha teanga a rangú. Ar bhealach eile, bíonn cineálacha difriúla pobal chun cinn go sochtheangeolaíoch ag staideanna éagsúla an iompaithe teanga (Haugen, 1953: 370; Baker agus Prys Jones, 1998: 151). Bíonn tionchar ag an gcomhthéacs sochtheangeolaíoch ar leaganacha an stóir theangeolaíoch, cineálacha cainteoirí, deiseanna úsáide teanga, an leibhéal seachadta teanga agus cleachtas teanga an phobail. Faoi réir ag torthaí an taighde, déanfar cur síos ar staid teangeolaíoch phobal an Bhreacbhaile agus a áit ar chontanam an iompaithe teanga.

Éilíonn cur chuige éiceolaíoch Spolsky go gcuirfear athróga neamhtheangeolaíocha agus a mbaint le hathróga teangeolaíocha san áireamh (.i. athróga sóisialta, polaitiúla, eitneacha, reiligiúnda, eacnamaíochta agus cultúrtha agus mar sin de) (2004: 218). Tabharfar cuntas ar luach chumarsáide na leaganacha teanga agus oiriúnacht na dteangacha ag brath ar an gcomhthéacs tríd an anailís sin.

### Creideamh Teanga

Is ionann creideamh teanga an phobail agus meonta nó tuairimí atá in uachtar i measc na ndaoine sin faoi theanga agus faoi úsáid teanga. Bíodh is go n-imríonn creideamh teanga tionchar díreach ar an gcleachtas teanga, ní dhéantar i gcónaí de réir mar a chreidtear (Ó hIfearnáin, 2006: 11). Ní miste, mar sin, creidimh an phobail i dtaobh luachanna na leaganacha teanga a mheas. Is cóir tuiscint a fháil ar na díospóireachtaí agus na comórtais idé-eolaíochta i measc an phobail nó soiléiriú idé-eolaíochta a lorg más mian le sprioc an taighde dea-thionchar a imirt ar chleachtas teanga an phobail (Ó hIfearnáin, 2006: 12). Tugann Dauenhauer agus Dauenhauer insint shimplí ar a bhfuil i gceist leis sin agus iad ag moladh iniúchadh macánta a dhéanamh ar staid na teanga:

> This calls for an open, honest assessment of the state of the language and how people really feel about using and preserving it, replacing wishful thinking and denial of reality with an honest evaluation leading to realistic recommendations (1998: 63).

Ó thaobh creideamh teanga, mar sin, scrúdófar dílseacht, spreagadh agus gradam na leaganacha teanga. Féachfar le scagadh a dhéanamh ar luach siombalach na teanga náisiúnta agus luachanna féiniúlachta na teanga mionlaigh mar chuid den iniúchadh.

### Bainistíocht Teanga

Is ionann bainistíocht teanga agus idirghabháil ar an teanga, nó iarrachtaí sainiúla dul i gcion ar chleachtas teanga agus creideamh teanga. Go hiondúil bíonn duine nó grúpa laistiar den iarracht seo agus tugann Spolsky 'bainistíocht teanga' ar a leithéid d'idirghabháil. Tá baint ag cúrsaí cumhachta leis an gcomhábhar seo mar go mbíonn bainistíocht fhollasach (dlíthe, cearta) agus bainistíocht neamhfhollasach (comharthaí bóthar, scrúdú iontrála scoile, cáipéisíocht an rialtais) i gceist (Shohamy, 2006). Dá réir sin caithfear ról an duine, ról an phobail, ról na n-údarás agus ról an taighdeora ar chleachtas agus creideamh an phobail a scrúdú mar chuid den anailís. Léireofar an tionchar atá ag cinneadh an duine aonair i dtaobh roghnú teanga ag leibhéal an chomhrá agus na himpleachtaí atá ag roghanna an duine ar chás teangeolaíoch an phobail. Tógfar ceisteanna cosúil le: Cé hiad na bainisteoirí teanga? Cén ról atá ag na bainisteoirí teanga sin i gcur chun cinn agus i múnlú na Gaeilge (an Bhéarla) i measc an phobail? Cé do atá an bhainistíocht teanga á dhéanamh? Cé atá freagrach as bainistíocht teanga?

Castacht eile sa scéal seo go mb'fhéidir go bhfuil beartais dhifriúla a easaontaíonn le chéile ag páirtithe éagsúla na sochaí. Ní hionann an staid inmhianaithe teangeolaíoch agus an fíorstaid agus caithfidh an bhainisteoir teanga nó an taighdeoir an iomlatáil idir an dá chás seo a fhiosrú.

Déanfar iarracht anois soiléiriú coincheapúil a dhéanamh ar an mbainistíocht teanga. Chuige sin, díreofar ar theoiric na bainistíochta teanga ach go háirithe (Jernudd agus Neustupný 1987; Nekvapil 2006). Níl anseo ach creatlach an scéil.

**Fréamhacha na Bainistíochta Teanga**

Ní hé Spolsky a chéadcheap téarma na bainistíochta teanga. Liostálann Cooper an focal ar cheann de na téarmaí féideartha don réimse ina shaothar clasaiceach ar an bpleanáil teanga (1989: 29). Tugann Kaplan agus Baldauf cuntas níos faide ar a rogha téarmaíochta siúd (1997: 27, 207–109):

> In this book we use 'language planning' as the generic term for the discipline and use it to encompass everything from government macro-level national planning to group or individual micro-level planning. While language planning initially referred to government planning for national situations (eg Fishman *et al.*, 1968), the term has been used for many years to reflect a much broader range of issues and approaches to language planning, as we believe this volume demonstrates.
> However, Jernudd (1993: 133) among others, has argued that as 'language planning… takes decision makers, for example governments, specification of language problems as their axiomatic point of departure' and therefore a new term, language management, is needed to describe 'bottom-up' and discourse based planning. Reflecting this argument, language management or aménagement linguistique has begun to appear to a limited extent in the literature (Jernudd agus Neustupn , 1987) (Kaplan agus Baldauf, 1997: 27).

Is dóigh le Kaplan agus Baldauf gurb ionann an bhainistíocht teanga agus an téarma Fraincise 'l'aménagement linguistique' mar sin[7] (Kaplan agus Baldauf, 1997: 207). Ag an bpointe seo, ní miste a lua gur roghnaigh Nelde (2003) an téarma Fraincise 'l'aménagement linguistique' nuair a theastaigh uaidh deileáil le saincheisteanna bainteach le beartas teanga an Aonais Eorpaigh. Is é a bharúil gurb é an téarma Fraincise an leagan is feiliúnaí, nua-aoisí agus is Eorpaí (Nekvapil, 2006: 94). Meabhraíonn Nekvapil gurb iad Jernudd and Neustupn (1987) a tharraing an téarma 'bainistíocht teanga' isteach i litríocht na sochtheangeolaíochta ar dtús, i ndiaidh dóibh páipéar comhdhála a thabhairt i Québec, Ceanada (2006: 94).

---

[7] Ní bheidh deis 'l'aménagement linguistique' a dhianchíoradh sa pháipéar seo cheal ama.

Tugann Calvet (1996) tosaíocht don bhearna sa litríocht Fhrancach. Tagraíonn sé don easpa tráchta ar ghníomhaíochtaí teanga de chineál eile atá pobal nó grúpalárnaithe. Roinneann Le Blanc réimse *l'aménagement linguistique* i dtrí chuid, an phleanáil stádais, an phleanáil chorpais agus tionscnaimh phobal-lárnaithe nó *les initiatives émanant des communautés* (LeBlanc, 2003: 8).[8] Lé déanaí, tugtar aitheantas do ghné eile den bhainistíocht teanga sa litríocht Cheanadach mar sin agus is é sin gluaiseachtaí nó tionscnaimh phobal-lárnaithe (LeBlanc, 2003: 7/8). Seo athrú fócais ó choincheap traidisiúnta na pleanála teanga chun sórt eile gníomhaireachta a chur san áireamh. Bronntar creidiúnacht agus admháil ar ghníomhaíochtaí an phobail. Glactar leis gur féidir le grúpa a ghluaiseacht teanga féin a cheapadh agus a riaradh. Ní gá go mbeidh an rialtas i gcónaí laistiar de.

Le cur chuige na bainistíochta teanga, déantar anailís ar dtús ar idirghníomhaíochtaí an duine le daoine eile agus fiosraítear cén chaoi a láimhseálann an duine teanga sa ghnáthchaint laethúil. Tugann an léargas seo comhthéacs nó bunús do bhainistíocht teanga i measc an phobail. Tá dúil ag an taighdeoir seo leas a bhaint as cur chuige na bainistíochta teanga don togra, go mór mór toisc go bhfuil áit ag idirghníomhaíochtaí an duine ann. Sa chéad rannóg eile beidh tuilleadh tráchtaireachta ar theoiric na bainistíochta teanga chun an pointe seo a fhorbairt (Jernudd agus Neustupný 1987; Nekvapil 2006).

**Teoiric na Bainistíochta Teanga**

Baineann an teoiric go dlúth le hidirdhealú a dhéanamh idir dhá phróiseas a rialaíonn úsáid teanga, mar atá:

(i) giniúint agus glacadh le caint nó '*production and reception of discourse*' (Nekvapil, 2006: 95).
(ii) na gníomhaíochtaí a mbíonn tionchar acu ar ghiniúint agus glacadh le caint .i. gníomhaíochtaí meititheangeolaíocha (Nekvapil, 2006: 95). Is ionann 'meititheangeolaíoch' agus feasacht shoiléir teanga dar le Swann *et al* (2004: 204/5).

Tugtar 'bainistíocht teanga' ar an dara pointe, iompar ar leith dírithe ar theanga (Nekvapil, 2006: 95). Tarlaíonn an bhainistíocht teanga ag dhá leibhéal (atá éagsúil ach nasctha) dar leis an teoiric seo: an bhainistíocht shimplí agus an bhainistíocht eagraithe. Tabharfar aghaidh ar na coincheapa sin anois.

**An Bhainistíocht Shimplí**

Tig le cainteoir bainistíocht a dhéanamh ar ghnéithe éagsúla dá c(h)uid chainte féin le linn comhrá (nó idirghníomhaíocht éigin), mar shampla, leagan áitiúil cainte a athchur (nó a cheartú dar leis/léi) le leagan caighdeánach den teanga. Tarlaíonn an bhainistíocht seo láithreach agus bíonn duine aonair amháin i gceist (Nekvapil, 2006: 96). Déanann sé(í) machnamh aisfhillteach ar a p(h)íosa cainte, cuir i gcás, agus ceartaíonn sé(í) é(í) féin dá réir. Tá feasacht áirithe teanga nó cumas éigin tabhairt faoi deara intuigthe.

Ina theannta sin, is féidir le cainteoir bainistíocht a dhéanamh ar thréithe éigin de chaint a chomhchainteora (an té lena bhfuil sé(í) ag caint) i gcaitheamh comhrá, mar

---

[8] Tá deighilt Spolsky ar an mbainistíocht teanga difriúil. Luann sé an phleanáil stádais teanga, an phleanáil chorpais teanga agus pleanáil an insealbhaithe (2006: 8). Céard faoi phleanáil an ghradaim a luann Baldauf? (2006: 147).

shampla, Gaeilge a athchur le Béarla, nó a mhalairt. Bíonn tionchar dearfa díreach ag an mbainisteoir teanga ar rogha teanga an chomhchainteora sa chás sin. Fágann sin go mbíonn an cinneadh (chomh maith leis an údarás agus an chumhacht a ghabhann leis) faoin teanga roghnaithe i seilbh an bhainisteora. Seo fíorghníomhaíocht aistreach na bainistíochta teanga, dar leis an taighdeoir seo, toisc go dteastaíonn bainisteoir agus comhchainteoir ar a laghad. Ar ndóigh, ní ann don bhainistíocht teanga gan bhainisteoir. Caithfear a bheith in ann an bainisteoir a ainmniú nó a dhéanamh amach, dar le Spolsky:

> The third component is language management, the *explicit* and *observable* effort by someone or some group that has or claims to have authority over the participants in the domain to modify their practices or beliefs (Spolsky, 2007: 4, liomsa an bhéim).

An cinneadh comhfhiosach a spreagann an bainisteoir teanga? I gcás an togra seo, fiosrófar an ndéanann muintir (nó bainisteoirí) an Bhreacbhaile cinneadh comhfhiosach Gaeilge nó Béarla a labhairt? Cén fáth? An gá? (Tá creideamh teanga fite fuaite leis an gcomhábhar seo chomh maith). Cén chaoi a n-éiríonn le Béarlóir amháin grúpa Gaeilgeoirí a thiontú ar an mBéarla go hiondúil? An amhlaidh atá forlámhas bainistíochta ag an mBéarla? Má tá, cén fáth? Cén chaoi ar féidir an nós seo a athrú? (ag brath ar mhianta an phobail dar ndóigh)

Tugtar 'bainistíocht shimplí' ar a leithéid de tharlúintí, bainistíocht a tharlaíonn i rith dioscúrsa nó cainte beo (Nekvapil 2006: 96). Thiocfadh le duine ar bith a bheith ina b(h)ainisteoir teanga ar an mbonn sin, ag brath ar an gcomhthéacs agus an tarlúint. Dá réir sin, is léir tábhacht na bainistíochta simplí nó na n-idirghníomhaíochtaí indibhidiúla (Nekvapil 2006: 98). Dá réir sin, tá áit ag ról an duine agus eachtraí an phobail sa phróiseas seo.

**An Bhainistíocht Eagraithe**

Níl an bhainistíocht eagraithe teoranta d'idirghníomhaíocht amháin (Nekvapil 2006: 96). Stiúirtear an bhainistíocht seo atá córasach a bheag nó a mhór. Caithfear eagrú éigin a dhéanamh ar an gcineál seo bainistíochta toisc go bhfuil go leor leibhéal ag roinnt léi, mar shampla, bainistíocht ag leibhéal an phobail, bainistíocht ag leibhéal an rialtais, bainistíocht ag leibhéal na scoile agus mar sin de. Is gá go mbraitheann an bhainistíocht eagraithe ar an mbainistíocht shimplí a mhéid agus is féidir, dar le teoiric na bainistíochta teanga (Nekvapil 2006: 96). Éilíonn an teoiric seo teagmháil choibhneasta idir bainistíocht eagraithe agus bainistíocht shimplí.

Mar chuid den iniúchadh ar an mbainistíocht eagraithe, tá an taighdeoir seo ag súil le hagallamh a chur ar údaráis an Bhreacbhaile .i. príomhoide na bunscoile, oifigigh Údarás na Gaeltachta, coisteoirí an chomharchumainn agus mar sin de.

**Iarmhairtí Macra agus Micrea i Dteoiric na Bainistíochta Teanga**

Leagann lucht na bainistíochta teanga béim ar chumas theoiric na bainistíochta teanga toisí ag an micrileibhéal agus ag an maicrileibhéal araon a chur san áireamh (Nekvapil, 2006: 99). Treisíonn Kuo agus Jernudd an pointe seo agus meabhraíonn siad gur chóir d'anailísithe agus gníomhairí teanga an mhicreapheirspictíocht agus an mhaicripheirspictíocht a ionramháil ar bhealach cothrom (Nekvapil, 2006: 99/100) .i.

cothrom na féinne a thabhairt do mhianta an phobail agus tuairimí na n-údarás. Go bunúsach, ba cheart go mbeadh gaol dialachtaiciúil (nó teagmháil choibhneasta) idir *macra* agus *micrea* nó fairsingíonn siad a chéile, de réir theoiric na bainistíochta teanga (Nekvapil, 2006: 100). Ionannaítear an mhicriphleanáil teanga le bainistíocht shimplí (bunaithe ar ghnáth idirghníomhaíochtaí / caint), agus aithnítear an mhaicriphleanáil teanga le bainistíocht eagraithe (Nekvapil, 2006: 101). Is iondúil (go hidéalach) go mbíonn comhshnaidhm idir an dá chineál bainistíochta teanga go dialachtaiciúil .i. bíonn tionchar ag bainistíocht eagraithe ar an mbainistíocht shimplí ach ar bhealach eile bíonn an bhainistíocht eagraithe mar thoradh ar an mbainistíocht shimplí (Nekvapil, 2006: 101).

Tá sé d'aidhm ag an taighdeoir seo a oibriú amach an bhfuil an cás sin fíor do Ghaeltacht an Bhreacbhaile agus mura bhfuil, cén chaoi ar fearr é a thabhairt ar bord. Beidh le feiceáil an bhfuil sé réalaíoch nó praiticiúil é sin a shamhlú.

## Tátal

Is féidir a áiteamh go bhfuil cur chuige na bainistíochta teanga daonlathach mar go bhfuil guth an duine agus imeachtaí an phobail lárnach sa phróiseas. Dá bhrí sin, cur chuige uilechuimsitheach atá i gceist toisc gur féidir *macra* (údarás) agus *micrea* (pobal) a áireamh.

Is mian leis an taighde seo rangú triarach Spolsky maille le teoiric na bainistíochta a ionramháil chun an togra taighde a stiúradh. Féachfar le múnla don phobal a cheapadh bunaithe ar obair cháilíochtúil ghoirt. Forbrófar an teoiric agus an rangú faoi réir ag torthaí taighde.

## Tagairtí

Baker, C. and S.P. Jones, 1998. *Encyclopedia of Bilingualism and Bilingual Education.* Clevedon: Avon.
Baldauf, R.B. 2006. 'Rearticulating the Case for Micro Language Planning in a Language Ecology Context'. *Current Issues in Language Planning* 7.2/3: 147–70.
Baldauf, R.B. Jr. and R.B. Kaplan. 2003. 'Who are the Actors? The Role of (Applied) Linguists in Language Policy'. In eds. Ryan, P. and R. Terborg. *Language: Issues of Inequality.* Mexico: CELE. 19–40.
Bell, J. 1999. *Doing your Research Project: A Guide for First Time Researchers in Education and Social Science.* Buckingham: Open University Press.
Berg, B.L. 2007. *Qualitative Research Methods for the Social Sciences.* Sixth Edition. New York: Pearson.
Blommaert, J. 1996. 'Language Planning as a Discourse on Language and Society: The Linguistic Ideology of a Scholarly Tradition'. *Language Problems and Language Planning* 20.3: 199–222.
Bratt Paulston, C. 1994. *Linguistic Minorities in Multilingual Settings: Implications for Language Policies.* Amsterdam: John Benjamins.
Bryman, A. 2004. *Social Research Methods.* Second Edition. Oxford: Oxford University Press.
Calvet, L.J. 1996. *Les Politiques Linguistiques.* Paris: Presses Universitaires de France.
Canagarajah, S. 2006. 'Ethnographic Methods in Language Policy'. In ed. Ricento.T. *An Introduction to Language Policy: Theory and Method.* Oxford: Blackwell. 153–70.

Cooper, R.L. 1989. *Language Planning and Social Change.* Cambridge: Cambridge University Press.
Crystal, D. 2000. *Language Death.* Cambridge: Cambridge University Press.
Dauenhauer, N.M. and R. Dauenhauer. 1998. 'Technical, Emotional, and Ideological Issues in Reversing Language Shift: Examples from Southeast Alaska'. In eds. Grenoble, L.A. and L.J. Whaley. *Endangered Languages: Current Issues and Future Prospects.* Cambridge: Cambridge University Press. 57–98.
Fishman, J.A. 1994. 'Critiques of Language Planning'. *Journal of Multilingual and Multicultural Development.* 15, 91–9.
Grene, M. 1969. *Knowing and Being: Essays by Michael Polanyi.* Chicago, IL: Northwestern University.
Grin, F. 2003. *Language Policy Evaluation and the European Charter for Regional or Minority Languages.* Houndmills: Palgrave Macmillan.
Grin, F. 2005. 'La gouvernance linguistique en Suisse'. In ed. Wallot, J.P. *La Gouvernance Linguistique: le Canada en Perspective.* Canada: Les Presses de l'Université d'Ottawa. 39–54.
Haugen, E. 1953. *The Norwegian Language in America.* Bloomington: Indiana University Press.
Hornberger, N. 2006. 'Frameworks and Models in Language Policy and Planning'. In ed. Ricento, T. *An Introduction to Language Policy: Theory and Method.* Malden: Blackwell. 24–42.
Jernudd, B.H. and J. Neustupný. 1987. 'Language Planning: For Whom?' In ed. La Forge, L. *Proceedings of the International colloquium on Language planning, Québec.* Québec: Presses de l'Universite Laval. 69–84.
Jernudd, B.H. 1993. 'Language Planning from a Management Perspective: An Interpretation of Findings'. In ed. Jahr, E.H. *Language Conflict and Language Planning.* Berlin: Mouton. 133–42.
Kaplan, R. and R. Baldauf. 1997. *Language Planning: From Practice to Theory.* Clevedon: Multilingual Matters.
LeBlanc, M. 2003. 'L'Aménagement Linguistique au Nouveau-Brunswick: L'État des Lieux'. Centre de Recherche en Linguistique Appliquée de l'Université de Moncton: Université de Moncton.
Moal, S. 2007. 'Sustaining Minority Language Communities: The Case of Breton'. Paper presented at the 7th Language and Politics Symposium on the Gaeltacht and Scotstacht, Queen's University, Belfast, 7–9 November.
Maykut, P. and R. Morehouse, 1994. *Beginning Qualitative Research: A Philosophic and Practical Guide.* London: Routledge.
Nekvapil, J. 2006. 'From Language Planning to Language Management'. *Sociolingiustica* 20: 92–104.
Nelde, P. 2003. 'Prerequisites for a European Language Policy'. In ed. Ahrens, R. *Europäische Sprachenpolitik / European Language Policy.* Heidelberg: Universitätsverlag. 415–31.
Nic Eoin, M. 2005. *Trén bhFearann Breac: An Díláithriú Cultúir agus Nualitríocht na Gaeilge.* Dublin: Cois Life.
Ó Flatharta, P. 2006. 'Gluaiseacht na teanga fós ar strae'. *The Irish Times,* 22 November, 15.
Ó hIfearnáin, T. 2006. *Beartas Teanga.* Dublin: Coiscéim.
Ó Laoire, L. 2003. 'Fieldwork in Common Places: An Ethnographer's Experiences in Tory Island'. *British Journal of Ethnomusicology* 12: 113–36.

Ó Riain, S. 1994. *Pleanáil Teanga in Éirinn 1919–1985*. Dublin: Carbad.
Ó Torna, C. 2005. *Cruthú na Gaeltachta 1893–1922: Samhlú agus buanú chonstráid na Gaeltachta i rith na hAthbheochana*. Dublin: Cois Life.
Ricento, T. 2000. 'Historical and Theoretical Perspectives in Language Policy and Planning'. *Journal of Sociolinguistics* 4: 196–213.
Ricento, T. ed. 2006. *An Introduction to Language Policy: Theory and Method*. Oxford: Blackwell.
Romaine, S. 2007. 'Preserving Endangered Languages'. *Language and Linguistic Compass*, 1.1/2: 115–32.
Romaine, S. 2006. 'Planning for the Survival of Linguistic Diversity'. *Language Policy* 5: 441–73.
Schiffman, H. 1996. *Linguistic Culture and Language Policy*. London: Routledge.
Shohamy, E. 2006. *Language Policy: Hidden Agendas and New Approaches*. London: Routledge.
Spolsky, B. 2004. *Language Policy*. Cambridge: Cambridge University Press.
Spolsky, B. 2006a. 'Language Policy and Language Planning in a Global World'. Paper presented at Royal Irish Academy Conference on Language Policy and Language Policy, Dublin Castle, 1–2 February.
Spolsky, B. 2006b. 'Language Policy Failures'. In eds. Pütz, M., Fishman, J.A. and J. Neff-van Aertselaer. *Along the Routes to Power Explorations of Empowerment through Language*. Contributions to the Sociology of Language 92. Berlin: Mouton de Gruyter. 87–106.
Spolsky, B. 2007. 'Towards a Theory of Language Policy'. *Working Papers in Educational Linguistics* 22.1: 1–14.
Spolsky, B. and E. Shohamy. 1999. *The Languages of Israel: Policy, Ideology and Practice*. Clevedon: Multilingual Matters.
Swann, J., Deumert, A., Lillis, T. and R. Mesthrie. 2004. *A Dictionary of Sociolinguistics*. Edinburgh: Edinburgh University Press.
Wates, N. 2000. *The Community Planning Handbook*. London: Earthscan Books.
Williams, C. ed. 2000. *Language Revitalisation: Policy and Planning in Wales*. Cardiff: University of Wales Press.

# The Breacbhaile Gaeltacht Community: A Sociolinguistic and Ethnographic Case Study in Language Policy

*Laoise Ní Dhúda*

## Foreword

The researcher greatly welcomes the opportunity to investigate the way in which minority language communities are nurtured. She hopes to shed light on one particular type of research in order to demonstrate the preliminary work that is to be carried out.

The title of the paper is 'The Breacbhaile Gaeltacht Community:[1] A Sociolinguistic and Ethnographic Case Study in Language Policy'.[2] It was decided not to reveal the name nor geographical location of the town in which the research was carried out and to use a pseudonym (Breacbhaile, situated in a Gaeltacht in Ireland) in order to ensure a high level of confidentiality and anonymity. The point of this research is not to report and dissipate details of Breacbhaile, rather to investigate aspects of language practice, language beliefs and language management.

This paper gives an insight into research that is currently being carried out as part of a PhD thesis that is still in progress and the researcher has spent one year to date working on it. Therefore, this is not the final word on the matter, rather some opinions and an example of the preliminary investigation that has been carried out. Suggestions that will enhance the research are warmly welcomed.

## Aim of the Paper

Firstly, the research will be summarised. The aims of the thesis, research questions and methodology used will also be discussed. The academic context for the research project will then be established and the discourse surrounding language planning, policy and management will be considered. It is essential to give this background information in order to establish a context for the theoretical framework of the study. Reference will be made to the basic ideas that underpin language planning. The concept of language policy will be closely examined and special attention will be paid to language management as part of this examination. In spite of the lack of clarity evident in literature in regard to the terms language planning and language management, differentiation will be made between the two as accurately as possible.

---

[1] The area in question is rural and not urban. Therefore, the adjective 'breac' ('speckled' or 'midway') is appropriate and sophisticated in this particular context because it encompasses the cultural and linguistic uncertainty described so comprehensibly by Nic Eoin in *Trén bhFearann Breac* (2005).

[2] The researcher spoke personally with Fidelma Ní Ghallchobhair from the Terminology Committee to discuss the terms 'polasaí teanga' and 'beartas teanga', meaning 'language policy'. The researcher wished to confirm with the Committee which term they use for 'language policy' and which term she should use in the context of the study she plans to carry out. Is there a difference between 'beartas teanga' and 'polasaí teanga'? The Committee has no definite answer to this question. According to Ní Ghallchobhair, 'beartas' is usually specific to legislation and 'polasaí' is used in everyday speech and in the media. In literature, the version used depends on the author. Ó hIfearnáin (2006), Ó Flatharta (2006) and Ó Torna (2005) use 'beartas teanga'. The researcher was advised to choose whichever version she preferred for 'language policy' and to state the reasons for her choice. 'Beartas teanga' was chosen in this case since Ó hIfearnáin (2006) has recently published on the subject. Language policy is an academic field in its own right (Fidelma Ní Ghallchobhair, personal correspondence, 05/06/07).

Spolsky's[3] tripartite classification will then be examined in relation to language policy and its suitability as a theoretical foundation for the purposes of this project will be evaluated. The three basic elements of this classification will be discussed both separately and as a unit: language practice, language beliefs[4] and language management. It is hoped that the paper will give an account of the main theoretical points rather than a comprehensive description of the subject, which is substantial.

To finish, the theory of language management will be discussed and afterwards, conclusions drawn.

**A Short Description of the Project**

An indepth ethnographic and sociolinguistic examination will be carried out of the way in which language policy operates in a Gaeltacht area. A conceptual and eimpirical insight will be given into Spolsky's tripartite classification of language policy (i.e. language practice, beliefs and management) in Breacbhaile. In other words, this doctoral thesis seeks to carry out a specific sociolinguistic and ethnographic study of the language policy in a contemporary Gaeltacht community.

It will seek to examine language dynamics or the implicit language policy at community level in Breacbhaile. Through close examination of Spolsky's tripartite classification, the sociolinguistic circumstances in the area will be investigated and baseline research will be provided accordingly. Specifically, an account will be given of the language practices of the Gaeltacht community in Breacbhaile using ethnographical tools and language beliefs in the community will be examined. Issues of power and their connection with language management, both overt and covert, will be investigated (Shohamy, 2006). The intrinsic link between simple management and organised management will be discussed as part of the examination of the theory of language management (Jernudd and Neustupný 1987; Nekvapil 2006).

A detailed sociolinguistic study will be carried out of the way in which language policy operates in a Gaeltacht area, using research notes and interviews. The aim of the thesis is to highlight the most notable aspects of the liveliness and vulnerability of language in a contemporary Gaeltacht community. The primary research question will be: how does language policy operate in Breacbhaile according to Spolsky's tripartite classification? In this way, a unique insight will be given into the process of examining and designing language policy at local micro level. We will see the role of the community as well as the responsibilities of the researcher in that process. The question will be raised: what is the function of language policy in a contemporary Gaeltacht area in Ireland?

According to Crystal, three major tasks must be carried out in order to maintain measures that work in favour of the future of a language: (i) diagnosis and evaluation (ii) description and analysis (iii) intervention and re-evaluation (2000: 145). This thesis seeks to give an insight into the first and second points in particular, in accordance with Spolsky's advice (2004: 218). On the same topic, Ó hIfearnáin says that no sensible intervention nor 'effective language planning' that would yield worthwhile results can begin unless correct and suitable research is carried out beforehand (2006: 3).

The differences between language planning, language policy and language management, if indeed they exist, will be discussed as part of this thesis. For now, it is

---

[3] Professor Bernard Spolsky is a famous sociolinguist (more information on http: //www.biu.ac.il/faculty/spolsb).

[4] 'Ideology' could be used in this case as well; however, Spolsky prefers 'language beliefs' because it avoids the political echoes associated with the word 'ideology' (2007: 3).

sufficient to mention that language planning usually refers to language-centred efforts carried out during a particular period in time from the top down, or, stemming from government. Jernudd and Neustupný use the term language planning to refer to the type of activity carried out during a specific period of time (controlled, unilateral, homogenous regulation). In their opinion, the term 'language management' refers to a wider field which emerged in parallel with developments in Canadian French literature:

> The use of this term, language management, in lieu of the currently widely used language planning *will leave the latter term free to refer to the particular phase of the 'linguistics of language problems' which developed in the 1970s*. This usage coincides with the Canadian French use of the term *aménagement linguistique* […] (1987: 71, italics are mine).

On the other hand, language management encompasses a wider field which includes macro aspects (legislation, rights) and micro aspects (the community's opinion) (Nekvapil, 2006: 99). As part of the investigation, the theory of language management will be considered (Jernudd and Neustupný 1987; Nekvapil 2006). Special attention will be given to the concept of language managers. Questions such as these will be raised: What is a language manager? Who are the language managers? Who is responsible for language management?

In very simple terms, language policy refers to the general language aims adopted in order to steer intervention. However, general national policy and specific community policy are not the same thing. Differentiation will be made between these concepts in as accurate a way as possible, even though there is widespread leakage within the relevant literature.

The results of the research and the recommendations emerging from it will be made available to the research community so that they may use it in order to consolidate their own language management process. The current literature will be built upon through an examination of language management efforts at local micro level. An analysis will also be carried out of the function of language policy in a contemporary Gaeltacht area. A conceptual and eimpirical insight will be given from a different point of view into language policy solutions for a Gaeltacht community, an aspect of the discourse which has not yet been discussed in Ireland.

**Methodology**

**Benefit of Ethnography**

This study seeks to examine in detail the community's implicit language policy according to Spolsky's (2004) tripartite classification, based on qualitative field work. In this regard, it was decided to use research and interview notes as ethnographical tools to build up a profile of the sociolinguistic situation of the community. As Wates said:

> Community profiling involves building up a picture of the nature, needs and resources of a community with the active participation of that community. It is a useful first stage in any community planning process to establish a context which is widely agreed (2000: 42).

Canagarajah adds to this. He supposes that the ethnographer has access to valuable inside information regarding the language network that is not available to every researcher. One must gain an understanding of the community in which the language is used in order to analyse, and even modify, language policy within that community. The ethnographer could make recommendations for solutions or review of language policy:

> Whatever the type or level of policy-making addressed, ethnography can bring out surprising findings about language relationships that elude those acting from outside the community. On the basis of their findings, ethnographers may offer recommendations that can make an important contribution to the formation or revision of language policies (2006: 159).

Ricento says that ethnography gives us an insight into the life of the ordinary person in order to gain a better understanding of the role of language in their life and the influence of overt and covert[5] policies on them:

> Ethnography can provide insights about life at the grass-roots level and lead to better understanding of the role of language(s) in the lives of people directly affected by overt or covert language policies or regimes (Ricento, 2006: 130).

A continuous description of research carried out and a research diary are of utmost value because it is through these notes that the researcher turns aspects of the research and information that are implicit into something more tangible that can be reported (Maykut and Morehouse, 1994: 33). '(A)ll understanding is tacit knowing, all understanding is achieved by indwelling' according to Polanyi (cited by Grene 1969: 160).

**Possible Weaknesses in the Methodology**

On the other hand, however, it is widely believed that qualitative research and ethnography are particularly subjective. Critical ethnography teaches that the ethnographer should move from passive listening to reflexive consideration (Canagarajah, 2006: 164). In this way, the researcher makes every effort to handle any observations critically and to find balance between the scholarly academic aspect of the work, the desires of the community and personal wishes (Ó Laoire, 2003: 127).

It is often said in criticism of the case study model being used that the results cannot be generalised. When there is only one area or small place in question, the case study could be said to be parochial or unique to that particular place (Bryman 2004: 51). This researcher does not intend to generalise the results of this case study. There is every chance that these results will be of use to other local language groups and committees (Bell, 1999: 13), but every community needs to examine its own circumstances before taking action. Romaine (2007: 122) reminds us that 'There is no one-size-fits-all solution for revitalisation and preservation'.

Keeping this context in mind, the methods used in the investigation are presented below, followed by the theoretic framework of the study.

---

[5] Overt policy refers to a general national policy, usually in written form. Covert policy is society's implicit policy or what happens at community level in everyday life (Schiffman 1996; Shohamy 2006). These terms will be discussed in the section on language policy.

## Methods of Investigation

At present, coincidental observations are regularly collated at the actual location where the research takes place i.e. any time the researcher goes to a public place (e.g. a shop, a garage, a pub, a chapel) reports are written in a research diary according to Berg's criteria (2007: 197–104). The date, time, subject, location and length of the event are noted. A description is given of what happened and the written account focuses particularly on questions and behaviour in relation to language.

Often handwritten notes are first written in the researcher's note book. The account is written as soon after the event as possible so details are not forgotten. Having said that, the researcher relies heavily on memory as well as her ability to perceive and notice. Reference is made to what happened, the number of people present, main details / speakers in the conversation, extracts of speech / words that stood out and so forth. The researcher keeps regular daily records and each event is allocated a reference number. A detailed description of the physical location is not given for the purposes of confidentiality. The researcher's writings in the research diary are based on Spolsky's tripartite classification i.e. the main focus of the research are matters and behaviour in relation to language. The main questions the researcher focuses on when writing in the research diary are: Who is/are the speaker(s) in the conversation? Who spoke first? Which language / version did he/she use? Did the language being used change during the conversation? What prompted the change? What language do these speakers normally use with each other? What language does the researcher use with that person normally? How did the researcher get to know the speaker? When did the researcher get to know the speaker? Where does he/she live? What is his/her occupation? Does the speaker work with a Irish language business / institution?

Differentiation is made between the observation itself and the consideration or opinions of the researcher, as recommended by Berg, Maykut and Morehouse. The main events of the diary entries are reconsidered in order to gain an understanding of what is happening in the area at present and to trace any pattern in language use. The researcher uses Spolsky's tripartite classification as a guide when reflecting on the events described in the research diary. The influence of the presence of the researcher on the language spoken is questioned: Why was one language chosen over another? What influence did the location have on the language chosen? What implication did the topic of conversation have for the language chosen? What implication did the participants in the conversation have for the language chosen? What language is normally spoken in this place? Why did these people start talking to each other in the first place? What are the different kinds of conversations to be noted? Are there subgroups within the people of the area? This kind of research involves a continuous reflexive process.

This information will be complemented by semi-structured interviews. At least sixty interviews will be carried out with people in the area. There is every chance that more interviews will be done, depending on time constraints and how the work progresses.

Open coding and focused coding will be applied to the details gathered (according to Spolsky's classification). It is not yet clear, however, how much of this analysis will be included in the final report. Various extracts from the research diary will be added to the thesis as support for the interviews done within the community (i.e. supplemented information). Every effort will be made to give a fair insight into the place where the research is being carried out. The two research tools (diary, interviews) will be of great help to the researcher in achieving this aim. The same questions and themes will be scrutinised (i.e. based on language practice, beliefs and management within the community) using different tools in order to re-affirm and confirm the research results i.e. two research tools will be used in order to strengthen the integrity of the results.

When the research is done, the results of the work will be presented to the public at a feedback session. The community in the area will be given an opportunity to give their opinions and suggestions regarding the current sociolinguistic situation and future policies. This information session will function as a kind of validity test.

After discussion of qualitative research based on the language habits of the people in the area, a comprehensive approach for a new language policy, applied through partnership, will be recommended. Each and every linguistic situation and research community is unique. Is it only right that the process be based on an individual basis, according to this researcher.

**The Literature of Language Planning, Policy and Management**

**Introduction**

This part of the paper looks at the academic discourse surrounding language planning, policy and management. It is within the context of this literature that the thesis will be developed.

In recent times, the academic fields of language planning, language policy and language management have blossomed and flourished. According to Hornberger (2006: 24) the reason for the renewed interest in the themes of language planning and policy is the domination of English (and other global languages) and the death of native languages throughout the world. She refers to the field of language planning and policy in such a way that means the two concepts cannot be separated (2006: 24). A rich and wide debate is taking place between two schools of thought regarding the differences, if indeed there are any, between language planning and language policy (Spolsky 2004; Ó hIfearnáin 2006). Are language planning and language policy enmeshed with each other? Or, are they two different schools of thought? If they are, must one consider a mixture of the two theories? Or, can a project of this kind benefit from considering the theme of *l'aménagement linguistique*? *L'aménagement linguistique* is the same as language management.[6]

Nekvapil places emphasis on the change in terminology evident in literature, from language planning to language management (2006: 94). Jernudd and Neustupný explain that the term 'language management' corresponds to the Canadian French concept *l'aménagement linguistique* (1987: 71). Grin writes about *gouvernance linguistique* and *gestion linguistique* (2005). It appears that Nekvapil has noticed more than simply a change in vocabulary and that it is worth attaching greater significance to the theory of language management. The intention is to examine these questions in the context of the thesis and differentiate between the concepts of language planning and language management. Opinions in this regard will be given in this paper, but for now, the focus will be on language planning.

---

[6] It is worthwhile examining literature in languages apart from English in order to gain a more comprehensive perspective. Often writing is done from the perspective of Euramerican English.

## Language Planning

Language planning is the activity which seeks to influence the community's language practice based on fixed aims (Swann *et al*, 2004: 173). Language and extra-language aims must be clarified and ideas regarding the process must be structured before carrying out the activity of language planning. Therefore, language planning is a mechanism. Usually, the government or some other authoritative organisation carries out this proces (Kaplan and Baldauf 1997: xi).

The area of language planning has its roots in a unilateral government agency and until now the majority of study carried out was done at this macro level. Scholars of language planning regularly only consider efforts on a larger scale or from a national perspective, the kind of planning that takes place at state level (Baldauf, 2006: 148). This is the classic approach to language planning where the authorities are envisaged as having all the power. This thesis, however, seeks to illustrate language activities at the micro level of the community.

Ó Riain also gives priority to the national context of language planning: 'an organised activity to solve language problems, usually on a national level ...' (Ó Riain, 1994: 1). This corresponds with Fishman's views:

> Most scholars limit the term language planning to 'the organised pursuit of solutions to language problems, typically at the national level' (Fishman, 1973: 23/4 cited by Bratt Paulston, 1994: 5).

Is this confirmation of the fact that language planning activities happen only on the macro level? Is language planning at national level only sufficient in today's society? Is there a place for community movements in language planning? These, and different kinds of questions regarding language planning (as well as various kinds of activities) will now be discussed.

## Different Kinds of Language Planning

### Introduction

Baldauf says that it is commonly accepted nowadays that language planning and planning of language happen at many levels i.e. micro level (local committees, individuals, parents, businesses), macrolevel (national and multinational government) and mesolevel (local government, media) (Baldauf, 2006: 147). In the same way, language planning is often divided in two parts; micro language planning (which usually happens at the micro level) and macro language planning (which usually occurs at the macro level).

One must question is it right to separate the different kinds of language planning so simply? In the ideal world, wouldn't it be right to design an all-encompassing language planning process that would include the micro level and the macro level?

### From the Top Down / Macro Planning

Usually, macro language planning occurs in a wider context, and this kind of planning happens at the macro level only (i.e. government / state level). Here is the classic approach to language planning mentioned earlier:

Most general frameworks (...) and much of the exemplary literature cited to support them suggest that language planning is a large scale activity, i.e. it occurs mainly at the macro level (Kaplan and Baldauf 1997: 52).

This kind of planning awakens questions regarding action, according to Baldauf (2006). He asks, who exactly has the power to influence language practices within the community or suggest changes (from the top down) in language planning at the micro level? Planning for language does happen, but it is normally a person, organisation or those in power who steer this process. Language planning does not happen without a planner. Ó hIfearnáin argues that the term language planning is used to indicate control and authority when arrangements are being put in place, a system that he criticises (2006: 7). According to Kaplan, this is language planning from the top down (1997: 55) (or, the classic approach to language planning). In this particular case, groups with power often make choices on behalf of the community with little regard for people's opinions. The role of the community is secondary. Is the top down approach prone to a lack of continuity and even one-sidedness?

In this approach to language planning the authorities have a very important part to play. Is it correct, however, to say that the scales are weighted completely in their favour? Is it actually a linear, negative, authoritarian concept because of the lack of attention paid to the community that speaks the language? Is there an inherent inconsistency between the macro and the micro in this traditional approach to language planning?

**From the Bottom Up / Micro Planning**

There has been a recent surge in English language literature about language planning in local contexts at micro level (Baldauf, 2006: 147). Micro language planning focuses on limited aims on a small scale (often at micro level). The kind of planning which encompasses the community's participation as part of the planning process is called language planning from the bottom up (Kaplan and Baldauf, 1997: 52).

Micro planning normally is envisaged with another type of activity carried out by businesses, institutions, local committees and the like. In this case, the agent (or the language manager) smooths the path for the language planning process at micro level so that a language/languages can develop at that level and language resources can become a commodity. It is desirable that the language manager understands the conventions and tacit rules of society in order to design a suitable policy for the community. This approach is very flexible. Priority is given to the will and participation of the community. This kind of planning responds to the unique needs and problems of the particular situation, and to the specific needs around language activities in the particular place (Baldauf, 2006: 155).

**Conclusion**

In the opinion of Baldauf macro planning and activities at micro level are complementary. He believes that micro planinng or macro planning are not sufficient in themselves (Baldauf, 2006: 165). From another perspective, it seems that the type of planning depends on the project aims and the context of the study. Romaine (2007: 122) suggests, 'Every group must decide what can best be done realistically for a particular language at a particular time'. Therefore, the success of language planning depends on participation and support of the community in particular (Kaplan and Baldauf, 2003: 201).

Overall, it is the view of this researcher that language planning is a comprehensive process. It would be erroneous to focus on one aspect of language planning (i.e. micro planning, for example) without having an understanding of the wider picture. The actions associated with language planning must have effect at the micro level on a coherent basis. At the same time, it is not sufficient for the two types of language planning to operate alongside each other – it is the opinion of this researcher that they must be relative to each other and interdependent. There is no certainty, however, that this will happen based on any given approach to language planning.

Blommaert argues that the scope of language planning is limited to a particular kind of actions and interventions which are usually influenced by politics and steered by government:

> The scope of the term 'language planning' is often intuitively confined to a particular type of activities: consciously planned, politically inspired but rationally implemented forms of language treatment in a multilingual context in third world or emergent states (Blommaert, 1996: 206).

This kind of planning is unilateral and is, therefore, weighted in favour of the administrators and is power-centred. It is possible, therefore, that there is a risk that control and the danger of bullying are intrinsic to actions based on this kind of language planning, where authorities implement rules in the community from the top down. This kind of planning is criticised:

> [...] governed by their (i.e. governments or leading elites) self-interests and reproducing rather than overcoming sociocultural and econo-technical inequalities (Fishman, 1994: 94).

Blommaert focuses repeatedly on the politics of language planning and it appears to him that there is no escape from this traditional approach to language planning. He refers to the prevention of certain language customs due to language planning, to the role of the state as the main agent in the process or the balance of power being in the hands of the authorities, and to the danger of bias and lack of democracy, all of which are intrinsic aspects in language planning (Blommaert, 1996: 206). These opinions clarify the position that language planning carries with it an ideological burden, that the language planning process encompasses certain understandings that usually are not for the benefit of the community:

> [...] language planning itself appears to be ideologically burdened. It carries implicit assumptions about what a 'good' society is, about what is best for the people, about the way in which language and communication fit into that picture, and about how language planning can contribute to a social and political progress (Blommaert, 1996: 215).

The main conclusion to be made based on this examination of language planning is that certain authors mention the lack of democracy intrinsic to it, an obstacle which creates serious doubt in regard the language planning approach in the context of this project. It appears that language planning is not a fair system because, until now, the balance of power has been with those who make the decisions. Is language policy (and/or the language management approach) more inclusive and democratic as a concept or approach? The concept of language policy will now be examined.

**Language Policy: Introduction**

To give a very simple explanation, language policy encompasses the general language aims laid out by governement, sometimes in written form, in order to steer intervention (i.e. general national policy). From another perspective, the heart of a language policy normally illustrates the beliefs and practices of the community in regard to the languages they use (i.e. specific community policy).

The advancement of language policy is connected with the changes that have occurred in civil society. Of course, the behaviour of the state in democratic societies in regard to the community has changed over the last generation. Authorities are moving away from intervening between citizens and their personal choices, including in regard to language (Ó hIfearnáin, 2006: 7). It appears that the state hopes to put an end to its meddling in people's lives (Ó hIfearnáin, 2006: 7). If indeed this is the case, and in accordance with it, language planning is giving way to the new concept of language policy, according to Shohamy (2006: 49). Has the concept of language planning run its course?

The definition of language policy in the Dictionary of Sociolinguistics illustrates that language policy and language planning are often referred to as meaning the same thing (Swann *et al*. 2004: 173). According to Kaplan and Baldauf, they are related, but different, concepts. They believe that even though there are many likenesses between them, the two processes are not the same (1997: 14). Baldauf says that language planning agents or language managers must explore this difference (2006: 149). There is a firm link between language planning and knowledge of the characteristics of language policy, according to Ó hIfearnáin. He explicitly says that one must understand the nature of language policy in order to carry out worthwhile language planning (2006: 5). Is there, therefore, a need for the two elements?

Language planning and language policy are referred to in literature, both academic and non-academic, in a way that is interchangeable. This type of obscurity and uncertainty is widespread. Here are some examples of the uncertainity, or the authors' convention of mentioning planning and policy in the same sentence without making any clear distinction between them: 'language policy and planning (LPP)' (Hornberger, 2006: 24); 'micro policy and planning' (Kaplan and Baldauf, 1997: 52); 'language planning policy' (Moal, 2007); 'Welsh planning and policy' (Williams, 2000: 1); 'language policy and planning (Ricento, 2000: 196); 'policy and planning' (Spolsky and Shohamy, 1999: 46); 'Language policy, or language planning' (Grin, 2003: 27). Language planning and language policy are almost interchangeable in today's literature. We will now focus on different types of language policy.

**What is the Difference between Written Policy and Implicit Policy?**

Swann *et al.* say that there are two types of language policy: overt policy and covert policy (2004: 173). Spolsky agrees with this argument and he refers to clear written policy as well as implicit non-written policy (2004: 11). He says that it is easy to recognise the clear written policy (2004: 11). This kind of policy can be seen in the formulaic statements found in official documents.

On the other hand, unwritten policy that is, nontheless, implicit within the community, can be seen in their behaviour and outlook in regard to the languages spoken in society (Ó hIfearnáin, 2006: 6). Schiffman says that covert aspects of language policy (or what happens at home/in a town on an everyday basis) are often disregarded. According to him, this method of working is faulty because this kind of policy policy is strongly connected with the community (1996: 13).

As well as that, language policy exists even if no clear written statement is available. It is not often that a community writes its policy down as if in a policy document (Ó hIfearnáin, 2006: 1). Even when a clear written language policy is available, one cannot always confirm its effect on public practice (Spolsky, 2004: 8). Where there is no public reference to language in official documentation, the policy can be ascertained from the community's practices or from the practices of the authorities in regard to the language, according to Ó hIfearnáin (2006: 6). This implicit policy is transmitted and maintained without question, in Schiffman's opinion (1996: 13). It is not easy to ascertain the implicit policy because it is rooted deeply in the mind of the community and because of that, it is often hidden (Ó hIfearnáin, 2006: 6). On the other hand, various policies can often be noticed among the community. The nature of language policy is complex and more subtle (Ó hIfearnáin, 2006: 6).

Spolsky's understanding is that language policy relates to the commuity's use of language and the way in which the behaviour related to language is managed. What he calls 'language policy' encompasses all the beliefs and practices of a language community or state and the management arrangements made in relation to those practices and beliefs. Ó hIfearnáin admits that the term 'management' is better than 'planning' in this context because it gives priority to the behaviour of the language community rather than to the will of the planning authorities (2006: 7).

If one wishes to assess the state's language policy, or that of any other entity, Spolsky advises focusing firstly on the complex linguistic state of affairs (Spolsky, 2004: 218). He argues that the community's language policy can be understood and that sense can be made of different kinds of details regarding language by focusing on the three constituent components, namely, language practice, language beliefs and language management.

Spolsky recommends deep consideration of old established practices, beliefs and pressures in the research location in order to enhance a general language policy and take specific steps in the direction of language management:

> To go from a general language policy to specific plans for language management, one must respect established practices and beliefs and pressures within the constituent social groups that make up the nation (…) (2006: 17).

We will now see if Spolsky's tripartite classification is a good starting point in the examination of language policy at the level of community in Breacbhaile or in diagnosing their sociolinguistic case, as Crystal recommends (2000: 145). We will now look at the connection between each component and field work.

**Language Practice**

Language practice encompasses the conscious and subconscious choices made in society in regard to different languages, the kind of language used or the normal pattern of choosing between the different versions contained in the sociolinguistic repertoire (for example; Irish v. English, high register v. low register, local dialect v. standardised language). The practices of the individual person, the community and the authorities must be taken into account. As well as that, classification of contemporary Gaeltacht speakers is necessary in order to illustrate the multiaspects of contemporary speakers in the Gaeltacht and to assess the composition of that particular Gaeltacht community. One must then work out what the various versions of language used in the area are (i.e. English of the locality, the local Irish dialect, school language and other internal versions).

The types of language spoken or the versions from the sociolinguistic repertoire used must be classified. This information gives a valuable insight into language in the locailty. For example, is there a trace or evidence of changing from one language to another (e.g. code-mixing) in the language versions? It is yet to be decided what the best way to classify language versions is.

From another standpoint, different communities at different stages sociolinguistically in the case of changing from one language to another (Haugen, 1953: 370; Baker and Prys Jones, 1998: 151). The sociolinguistic context influences the versions available in the linguistic bank, the types of speakers, opportunities to use language, and the level of language delivery and language practices within the community. Subject to the results of the research, a description will be given of the linguistic stage of the community of Breacbhaile and their position on the language change continuum.

Spolsky's ecological approach demands that non-linguistic variables and their connection with linguistic variables be taken into account (i.e. social, political, ethnic, religious, economic, cultural and other variables) (2004: 218). Through this analysis an account will be given of the communicative value of the language versions and the suitability of languages depending on the context.

**Language Beliefs**

Language beliefs of the community encompass the prevailing attitudes and opinions among people in relation to language and use of language. Although language beliefs have a direct influence on language policy, people don't always practice according to their beliefs (Ó hIfearnáin, 2006: 11). It is useful, therefore, to assess the community's beliefs in regard to the values attached to versions of language. One must gain an understanding of the ideological debates and comparisons among the community or seek to gain ideological clarity if the point of the research is to have a positive influence on language practice within the community (Ó hIfearnáin, 2006: 12). Dauenhauer and Dauenhauer explain simply what this means and they recommend an honest examination of the state of the language:

> This calls for an open, honest assessment of the state of the language and how people really feel about using and preserving it, replacing wishful thinking and denial of reality with an honest evaluation leading to realistic recommendations (1998: 63).

From the point of view of language beliefs, however, the commitment, motivation and esteem connected with the various language versions will be examined. As part of the investigation, the aim is to sift through the symbolic value attached to the national language and the values around identity attached to the minority language.

## Language Management

Language management is language intervention, or specific efforts to influence language practices and language beliefs. Usually, a person or group of people are behind these efforts and Spolsky calls this kind of intervention 'language management'. This component is effected by issues of power because both overt management (laws, rights) and covert management (road signs, school entry exams, government documentation) are involved (Shohamy, 2006). The role of the person, community, authorities and that of the researcher must be examined accordingly as part of the analysis. The influence of the individual's decision in regard to the language chosen in conversations and the implications of these decisions on the linguistic state of the community will be illustrated. Questions such as the following will be raised: Who are the language managers? What role do these language managers have in the advancement and shaping of Irish (English) within the community? For whom is language management being carried out? Who is responsible for language management?

Another complication is the possibility that various parties in society may have different policies that don't complement each other. The desirable linguistic situation and the actual situation are not the same and the language manager or the researcher has to investigate the inconsistency between the two.

There now follows an attempt to give a clear, conceptual description of language management, although it is merely an outline. There will be particular focus on the theory of language management (Jernudd and Neustupný 1987; Nekvapil 2006).

## The Roots of Language Management

Spolsky was not the first to use the term language management. Cooper includes it in the list of possible terms in his classic work on language planning (1989: 29). Kaplan and Baldauf give a longer account of the terminology they have chosen (1997: 27, 207–109):

> In this book we use 'language planning' as the generic term for the discipline and use it to encompass everything from government macrolevel national planning to group or individual micro-level planning. While language planning initially referred to government planning for national situations (e.g. Fishman *et al.*, 1968), the term has been used for many years to reflect a much broader range of issues and approaches to language planning, as we believe this volume demonstrates.
> However, Jernudd (1993: 133) among others, has argued that as 'language planning... takes decision makers, for example governments, specification of language problems as their axiomatic point of departure' and therefore a new term, language management, is needed to describe 'bottom-up' and discourse based planning. Reflecting this argument, language management or aménagement linguistique has begun to appear to a limited extent in the literature (Jernudd and Neustupn , 1987) (Kaplan and Baldauf, 1997: 27).

Therefore, Kaplan and Baldauf maintain that language management and the French term 'l'aménagement linguistique' are the same[7] (Kaplan and Baldauf, 1997: 207). At

---

[7] Due to time constraints it will not be possible to examine 'l'aménagement linguistique' in detail as part of this paper.

this point, it is worth mentioning that Nelde (2003) chose the French term 'l'aménagement linguistique' when dealing with questions of language policy in the European Union. He is of the opinion that the French term is the most suitable, modern and European (Nekvapil, 2006: 94). Nekvapil reminds us that Jernudd and Neustupn (1987) introduced the term 'language management' into sociolinguistic literature when giving a paper at a conference in Québec, Canada (2006: 94).

Calvet (1996) prioritises the gap in French literature. He refers to the lack of mention of other kinds of language or group-centred activities. Le Blanc divides *l'aménagement linguistique* into three parts: status planning, corpus planning and community-centred initiativies or *les initiatives émanant des communautés* (LeBlanc, 2003: 8).[8] This means that in recent times recognition is being given to another aspect of language planning in Canadian literature, community-based movements or initiatives (LeBlanc, 2003: 7/8). This marks a change in focus from traditional language planning to include other kinds of community action. Community actions are credited and acknowledged. It is accepted that a group can set up and run its own language movement. The government does not always have to be behind it.

In the language management approach, analysis is first carried out the way in which a person interacts with others and the way in which this person uses language in everyday speech is examined. This approach establishes a context or basis for language management within the community. This researcher wishes to take advantage of this approach to language management for the purposes of the project, especially since it involves the interaction of the individual person. In the next section there will be more discussion of language management theory in order to develop this point (Jernudd and Neustupný 1987; Nekvapil 2006).

**Language Management Theory**

This theory is strongly connected with differentiating between the two processes which govern language use, namely:

(i) production and reception of discourse (Nekvapil, 2006: 95).
(ii) the actions that influence production and reception of discourse i.e. metalinguistic activities (Nekvapil, 2006: 95). 'Metalinguistic' refers to clear language awareness, according to Swann *et al* (2004: 204/5).

The second point is called 'language management', a particular behaviour focusing on language (Nekvapil, 2006: 95). Language management happens on two levels (which are different but connected) according to this theory: simple management and organised management. These concepts will now be considered.

**Simple Management**

A speaker can manage different aspects of his/her own speech during a conversation (or interaction), for example, replacing (or correcting, according to himself/herself) a local version with a standardised version of the language. This type of management takes place in the moment and only the individual is involved (Nekvapil, 2006: 96). He/She contemplates reflexively his/her piece of speech, for example, and corrects

---

[8] Spolsky's breakdown of language management is different. He mentions planning for the status, corpus and acquisition (2006: 8). What about planning for the esteem of language cited by Baldauf? (2006: 147).

himself/herself accordingly. This involves a certain implicit awareness of language or noticing.

As well as this, a speaker can manage characteristics of the person he/she is speaking with during conversation, for example, replacing Irish with English, or vice versa. The language manager, thus, has a positive direct influence on the language choices the co-speaker makes. This means that the decision (as well as the authority and the power that goes with it) regarding the language chosen lies with the manager. This is the real transitive activity of language management, according to this researcher, because a manager and co-speaker, at least, are needed. Of course, language management doesn't exist without a manager. One must be able to either name or work out who the manager is, according to Spolsky:

> The third component is language management, the *explicit* and *observable* effort by someone or some group that has or claims to have authority over the participants in the domain to modify their practices or beliefs (Spolsky, 2007: 4, italics are mine).

Is it a conscious decision that drives the language manager? In the case of this project, I will investigate if the people (or managers) in Breacbhaile make a conscious decision to speak Irish or English, why they make that decision and if it is necessary. (Language beliefs are also intrinsic to this component). How does only one English speaker normally cause a group of Irish speakers to turn to English? Does English somehow dominate language management? If so, why? How can this convention be changed? (depending on the wishes of the community, of course).

This kind of management, which happens during discourse or live speech, is called 'simple management' (Nekvapil 2006: 96). Based on this, any person can take on the role of language manager, depending on the context and the incident. Therefore, the importance of simple management or individual interactions is clear (Nekvapil 2006: 98). The role of the person and the events within the community have a place in this process.

**Organised Management**

Organised management is not restricted to interaction only (Nekvapil 2006: 96). This kind of management, which is systematic, is directed to some degree. Some kind of organisation must be carried out because many different levels of management are involved, for example, at community level, at governement level, at school level and so on. Organised management must rely on simple management as much as possible, according to language management theory (Nekvapil 2006: 96). This theory demands relative contact between organised and simple management.

As part of the study into organised management, this researcher intends to interview the authorities in Breacbhaile i.e. the primary school principal, Údarás na Gaeltachta officers, committee members of the co-operative society and so on.

**Macro and Micro Effects in Language Management Theory**

Those involved in language management emphasise the capacity of language management theory to include both aspects on the micro level and macro level (Nekvapil, 2006: 99). Kuo and Jernudd enhance this point as they remind us that analysts and language activists should deal equally with the micro perspective and the macro perspective (Nekvapil, 2006: 99/100) i.e. by giving equal weight to the wishes of the community and the opinions of the authorities.

Basically, there should be a dialectical relation (or relative contact) between both *macro* and *micro* because they enhance each other, according to language management theory (Nekvapil, 2006: 100). Micro planning is attributed to simple management (based on ordinary interactions / speech), and micro language planning is recognised along with organised management (Nekvapil, 2006: 101). Normally (idealistically), these two types of language management are dialectically entwined i.e. organised management influences simple management but in another sense organised management is a result of simple management (Nekvapil, 2006: 101).

It is the aim of this researcher to find out if this is the case in the Breacbhaile Gaeltacht, and if not, what is the best way to implement it. It remains to be seen if it is realistic or practical to envisage such a thing.

**Conclusion**

It can be argued that language management is democratic because the voice of the individual and events within the community are central to the process. For that reason, it is a comprehensive approach because both *macro* (authority) and *micro* (community) are included.

This research seeks to manipulate Spolsky's tripartite classification theory of management in order to steer the project. It will seek to design a model for the community based on qualitative field work. The theory and the classification will be developed according to the research results.

**References**

Baker, C. and S.P. Jones, 1998. *Encyclopedia of Bilingualism and Bilingual Education*. Clevedon: Avon.
Baldauf, R.B. 2006. 'Rearticulating the Case for Micro Language Planning in a Language Ecology Context'. *Current Issues in Language Planning* 7.2/3: 147–70.
Baldauf, R.B. Jr. and R.B. Kaplan. 2003. 'Who are the Actors? The Role of (Applied) Linguists in Language Policy'. In eds. Ryan, P. and R. Terborg. *Language: Issues of Inequality*. Mexico: CELE. 19–40.
Bell, J. 1999. *Doing your Research Project: A Guide for First Time Researchers in Education and Social Science*. Buckingham: Open University Press.
Berg, B.L. 2007. *Qualitative Research Methods for the Social Sciences*. Sixth Edition. New York: Pearson.
Blommaert, J. 1996. 'Language Planning as a Discourse on Language and Society: The Linguistic Ideology of a Scholarly Tradition'. *Language Problems and Language Planning* 20.3: 199–222.
Bratt Paulston, C. 1994. *Linguistic Minorities in Multilingual Settings: Implications for Language Policies*. Amsterdam: John Benjamins.
Bryman, A. 2004. *Social Research Methods*. Second Edition. Oxford: Oxford University Press.
Calvet, L.J. 1996. *Les Politiques Linguistiques*. Paris: Presses Universitaires de France.

Canagarajah, S. 2006. 'Ethnographic Methods in Language Policy'. In ed. Ricento. T. *An Introduction to Language Policy: Theory and Method.* Oxford: Blackwell. 153–70.
Cooper, R.L. 1989. *Language Planning and Social Change.* Cambridge: Cambridge University Press.
Crystal, D. 2000. *Language Death.* Cambridge: Cambridge University Press.
Dauenhauer, N.M. and R. Dauenhauer. 1998. 'Technical, Emotional, and Ideological Issues in Reversing Language Shift: Examples from Southeast Alaska'. In eds. Grenoble, L.A. and L.J. Whaley. *Endangered Languages: Current Issues and Future Prospects.* Cambridge: Cambridge University Press. 57–98.
Fishman, J.A. 1994. 'Critiques of Language Planning'. *Journal of Multilingual and Multicultural Development.* 15, 91–9.
Grene, M. 1969. *Knowing and Being: Essays by Michael Polanyi.* Chicago, IL: Northwestern University.
Grin, F. 2003. *Language Policy Evaluation and the European Charter for Regional or Minority Languages.* Houndmills: Palgrave Macmillan.
Grin, F. 2005. 'La gouvernance linguistique en Suisse'. In ed. Wallot, J.P. *La Gouvernance Linguistique: le Canada en Perspective.* Canada: Les Presses de l'Université d'Ottawa. 39–54.
Haugen, E. 1953. *The Norwegian Language in America.* Bloomington: Indiana University Press.
Hornberger, N. 2006. 'Frameworks and Models in Language Policy and Planning'. In ed. Ricento, T. *An Introduction to Language Policy: Theory and Method.* Malden: Blackwell. 24–42.
Jernudd, B.H. and J. Neustupný. 1987. 'Language Planning: For Whom?' In ed. La Forge, L. *Proceedings of the International colloquium on Language planning, Québec.* Québec: Presses de l'Universite Laval. 69–84.
Jernudd, B.H. 1993. 'Language Planning from a Management Perspective: An Interpretation of Findings'. In ed. Jahr, E.H. *Language Conflict and Language Planning.* Berlin: Mouton. 133–42.
Kaplan, R. and R. Baldauf. 1997. *Language Planning: From Practice to Theory.* Clevedon: Multilingual Matters.
LeBlanc, M. 2003. 'L'Aménagement Linguistique au Nouveau-Brunswick: L'État des Lieux'. Centre de Recherche en Linguistique Appliquée de l'Université de Moncton: Université de Moncton.
Moal, S. 2007. 'Sustaining Minority Language Communities: The Case of Breton'. Paper presented at the 7th Language and Politics Symposium on the Gaeltacht and Scotstacht, Queen's University, Belfast, 7–9 November.
Maykut, P. and R. Morehouse, 1994. *Beginning Qualitative Research: A Philosophic and Practical Guide.* London: Routledge.
Nekvapil, J. 2006. 'From Language Planning to Language Management'. *Sociolingiustica* 20: 92–104.
Nelde, P. 2003. 'Prerequisites for a European Language Policy'. In ed. Ahrens, R. *Europäische Sprachenpolitik / European Language Policy.* Heidelberg: Universitätsverlag. 415–31.
Nic Eoin, M. 2005. *Trén bhFearann Breac: An Díláithriú Cultúir agus Nualitríocht na Gaeilge.* Dublin: Cois Life.
Ó Flatharta, P. 2006. 'Gluaiseacht na teanga fós ar strae'. *The Irish Times,* 22 November, 15.

Ó hIfearnáin, T. 2006. *Beartas Teanga.* Dublin: Coiscéim.
Ó Laoire, L. 2003. 'Fieldwork in Common Places: An Ethnographer's Experiences in Tory Island'. *British Journal of Ethnomusicology* 12: 113–36.
Ó Riain, S. 1994. *Pleanáil Teanga in Éirinn 1919–1985.* Dublin: Carbad.
Ó Torna, C. 2005. *Cruthú na Gaeltachta 1893–1922: Samhlú agus buanú chonstráid na Gaeltachta i rith na hAthbheochana.* Dublin: Cois Life.
Ricento, T. 2000. 'Historical and Theoretical Perspectives in Language Policy and Planning'. *Journal of Sociolinguistics* 4: 196–213.
Ricento, T. ed. 2006. *An Introduction to Language Policy: Theory and Method.* Oxford: Blackwell.
Romaine, S. 2007. 'Preserving Endangered Languages'. *Language and Linguistic Compass,* 1.1/2: 115–32.
Romaine, S. 2006. 'Planning for the Survival of Linguistic Diversity'. *Language Policy* 5: 441–73.
Schiffman, H. 1996. *Linguistic Culture and Language Policy.* London: Routledge.
Shohamy, E. 2006. *Language Policy: Hidden Agendas and New Approaches.* London: Routledge.
Spolsky, B. 2004. *Language Policy.* Cambridge: Cambridge University Press.
Spolsky, B. 2006a. 'Language Policy and Language Planning in a Global World'. Paper presented at Royal Irish Academy Conference on Language Policy and Language Policy, Dublin Castle, 1–2 February.
Spolsky, B. 2006b. 'Language Policy Failures'. In eds. Pütz, M., Fishman, J.A. and J. Neff-van Aertselaer. *Along the Routes to Power Explorations of Empowerment through Language.* Contributions to the Sociology of Language 92. Berlin: Mouton de Gruyter. 87–106.
Spolsky, B. 2007. 'Towards a Theory of Language Policy'. *Working Papers in Educational Linguistics* 22.1: 1–14.
Spolsky, B. and E. Shohamy. 1999. *The Languages of Israel: Policy, Ideology and Practice.* Clevedon: Multilingual Matters.
Swann, J., Deumert, A., Lillis, T. and R. Mesthrie. 2004. *A Dictionary of Sociolinguistics.* Edinburgh: Edinburgh University Press.
Wates, N. 2000. *The Community Planning Handbook.* London: Earthscan Books.
Williams, C. ed. 2000. *Language Revitalisation: Policy and Planning in Wales.* Cardiff: University of Wales Press.

## *Ón Bhun Aníos:* Resisting and Regenerating through Language in the North of Ireland

*Feargal Mac Ionnrachtaigh*

**Abstract**

In its introduction, this paper will briefly explore Ireland's cultural colonisation, which ultimately led to the demise of the Irish language as Ireland's spoken language in the late nineteenth century, as the defining structural context that shapes our understanding of the six county Irish language revival movement. The consequences of colonial*isation* will be seen to have inspired an ideology of decolonialisation and resistance which has been a central motivating factor in the contemporary Irish language revival movement in the North of Ireland.

It will view the survival and subsequent development of this movement in the North in spite of the often recalcitrant policies of a hostile six-county unionist regime as an example of resistance based language activism in practice. The paper, however, will also specifically focus on the transformational impact of the republican prison struggle in Long Kesh on the language revival in the North during the 1980s and it's continuing legacy of cultural resistance.

Concomitantly, the Irish language community's current struggle for language rights in the six counties and its many regenerative projects will be viewed as bottom-up decolonising, activist initiatives that have the potential to radically alter power relations in Irish society while simultaneously challenging the Global linguistic hegemony.

**Language and Power: The Cultural Colonisation of Ireland**

> 'It hath ever been the use of the conquerors to despise the language of the conquered, and to force him by all means to learn his.' (Edmund Spenser, quoted in Ó Fiaich 1969: 104)
> 'For Cultural invasion to succeed, it is essential that those invaded become convinced of their intrinsic inferiority. Since everything has its opposite, if those who are invaded consider themselves inferior, they must necessarily recognise the superiority of the invaders. The more the invasion is accentuated and those invaded are alienated from the spirit of their own culture and from themselves, the more the latter want to be like the invaders: to walk like them, dress like them, talk like them.' Paulo Friere (1989: 151)

Ambitions of empire would not only direct the English colonial project in Ireland and subsequently throughout the globe for centuries to come but also define an ideology of expansionism among 'technologically superior' western powers that shaped an often brutal 'scrabble for territories' which would leave unparalleled poverty, death and destruction in its wake.[1] Although the imperial approach in Ireland was multi-faceted,

---

[1] As Said (1993: 8) lucidly states, '"Colonialism', which is almost always a consequence of imperialism' is usually a merciless process which forges a relationship 'in which one state controls the effective political sovereignty of another political society. It can be achieved by force, by political collaboration, by economic, social, or cultural dependence' (*ibid.*)

utilising all means at its disposal, this paper will focus on cultural colonisation[2] and its legacy as a motivating factor in the ideology of resistance that often set out to overturn it.

The linguistic shift in Ireland from Irish to English during Ireland's protracted cultural colonialisation is ineluctably bound with more general questions of language and power. Thus, English and later British state policy arguably necessitated the tactical removal of the Irish language as a bulwark to its long-term colonial, imperial, and political ambitions which were ultimately defined by its desire for greater wealth and power. Therefore, in this context, the rise of the Tudor monarchy and the beginning of the colonial era in the sixteenth century envisaged the construction of a vast Empire in the future motivated partially by the flowering of capitalism with its insistence on the private ownership of property. (Crotty 1986)

Consequently, the task of colonial conquest in Ireland saw 'an outpouring of justifications for colonisation and conquest' (Canny 1973: 581) which explained strategic and tactical imperatives, as a moral crusade to civilise the culturally inferior Irish. Canny successfully uncovers striking parallels between the English descriptions and characterisation of Irish and Native American peoples in an all-encompassing ideology that both explained and justified conquest.[3] Inevitably, the process of colonialisation, whereby indigenous peoples throughout the world have, in May's (2002: 17) words, 'been consistently, often violently, dispossessed of their cultures, languages and lands, not to mention their very lives', resulted in a determined tradition of Irish resistance.

This extensive colonial practice served as a validation for the wholesale process of land confiscations and plantations which would culminate in the fateful Battle of Kinsale of 1601 which became a watershed in modern Irish history which would leave a bloody legacy and yield a reversal of fortunes for the Irish language[4] which would rapidly become the language of the dispossessed thus seemingly ensuring the success of the Elizabethan conquest. Resolute native opposition and violent reaction to the processes of plantation and dispossession, most notably in 1641,[5] necessitated a merciless colonial response in the guise of the post–1649 Cromwellian campaign and settlement ushered in an unparalleled campaign of death, destruction and land confiscation as

---

[2] The centrality of this aspect of the imperial project was similarly relevant throughout the world as attested to by Kenyan anti-colonial writer and activist Ngugi wa Thiong'o, 'The repression of the imperial power has many facets, physical subjugation is achieved by means of the bullet but language is the means of cultural and spiritual subjugation' (1997: 9)

[3] An illuminating description of this ideology was cited by Liam O'Dowd (1992: 27) as he quoted French commissaire-general Jules Harmond when referring to the British colonial project in Ireland, "*The basic legitimation of conquest over native peoples is the conviction of our superiority, not merely our mechanical, economic and military superiority, but our moral superiority. Our dignity rests on that quality, and it underlies our right to direct the rest of humanity.*" Many contemporary commentators like Chomsky (1999) and Curtis (2003) take the view that little has in fact changed and that colonialism has merely developed into 'neo-liberal', corporate Globalisation. They cite the current Anglo/American Government led 'War-on-terror' in the middle-East as a 'neo-colonial' manifestation of this age-old ideology which, in their view, uses the disguise of modernization to 'civilise the natives' according to language which assumes the superiority of so-called Western values of 'democracy'.

[4] Gearóid Ó Tuathaigh (2005: 42) succinctly sums up the centrality of the language to this violent transformation in Ireland in this period, 'Language and, even more crucially, religion, were the key elements of cultural discrimination in the great convulsion of the sixteenth and seventeenth centuries, the outcome of which was the establishment of a Protestant, overwhelmingly planter, new ruling class in Ireland, together with the triumph of the English language, law and politico-administrative institutions throughout Ireland, and the defeat of the whole institutional edifice of the Gaelic political and social order which had been sustained and mediated through the Irish language.'

[5] Interestingly, Ó Fiaich (*ibid.*: 106), contends that the native rebellion of 1641, 'must have been in its early stages almost exclusively an insurrection of Irish speakers'.

evidenced by the massive reduction in Irish population.[6]

By the end of the century, the Penal Laws, had forged the emergence of an English-speaking Protestant hegemony that enjoyed complete dominance of Irish cultural, political and economic institutions, while also viewing the language disdainfully as one of backwardness and poverty. Against this backdrop, a process of language shift to 'English, the language of power and of all the avenues to advancement, soon gathered momentum among those who aspired to improve their condition or to progress and participate fully in the life of the country under the new order' (Ó Tuathaigh 2005: 42).

The increased demand for literacy-in English- and the growing commercialisation of the rural economy contributed to the construction of the myth that traditional customs were the antithesis of modernity. Naturally, many native Irish speakers who faced stark poverty were influenced more by such necessity than personal choice as the process of cultural colonisation in Ireland intensified as explained in Memmi's *The Colonizer and the Colonised* (1965: 151):

> 'The colonized's mother tongue ... is precisely the one which is least valued ... If he wants to obtain a job, make a place for himself, exist in the community and the world, he must first bow to the language of his masters. In the linguistic conflict within the colonised, his mother tongue is that which is crushed. He himself sets about discarding this infirm language, hiding it from the sight of strangers.'

As fittingly described by one Irishman, loyalties were divided between his national language: 'the language of his heart' and English: 'the language of his commerce' (Crowley 2000: 34).

In addition, it is important to recall that the Catholic Church in this period essentially facilitated colonial assimilation in the interests of its own survival and increased status. For example, English became the language of choice at Maynooth, the national training college for Catholic priests, from its opening in 1795 (Crowley 2000: 84), despite the fact the overwhelming majority of its parishioners were monoglot Irish speakers, while constitutional nationalist, political leaders preached similarly assimilative tendencies.[7]

The National School system's imposition of 'civility' in 1831 saw Irish become a non-language and the Irish a non-people in a formal education process that Pádraig Mac Piarais would alter describe as '*The Murder Machine*'. This is illustrated by the notorious mandatory morning assembly recitation in state classrooms:

> I thank the goodness and the grace
> Which on my birth have smiled;
> And made me in these Christian days,
> A happy English child. (Kiberd 1993: 29)

Irish children were thus taught that learning Irish damaged the acquisition of English and that their parents' lack of English represented a lack of intelligence and civilisation,

---

[6] Cromwell's campaign of genocidal devastation had left Ireland in ruins and by 1653 the population had halved from 1.5 million people with over 616,000 dead, 40,000 conscripted to serve in European armies and a further 100,000 rounded up and transported to the new colonies of the Caribbean and America as slaves (Curtis 1984: 28).

[7] This is evident in the early nineteenth century campaign for Catholic emancipation with leaders like Daniel O'Connell, a native speaker from county Kerry, passively accepting the demise of the language; 'the superior utility of the English tongue, as the medium of all modern communication, is so great, that I can witness without a sigh the gradual disuse of Irish' (Curtis 1994: 26).

thereby internalising a sense of shame about their indigenous culture and non-literate parents (Nic Craith 2001: 103).

The imposition of this worldview was invariably bolstered by violent punishment for children caught speaking Irish both in the classroom and the home.[8] Despite the untold damage done by the national education system, more than half the population remained Irish speaking according to the census of 1841 (Hindley 1990: 15). However, this was rapidly overturned by the catastrophic demographic impact of the Great Hunger, which 'decimated Irish-speaking Ireland through death and emigration' (Ó Tuathaigh 2005: 43). This Irish assimilative experience mirrored wider British colonial strategy, which entailed the destruction and/or assimilation of indigenous languages and cultures as a means of facilitating the increase of economic power and wealth of the expanding empire.

In assessing the 'remarkable event in Irish cultural history', which 'the massive abandonment of Irish as vernacular language during the nineteenth century' represented (Ó Tuathaigh (2005: 43), many commentators separate language 'choice' from the all-pervasive reality of cultural colonisation in Ireland.[9] However, to underplay the historical significance of colonialism effectively obscures the fact that language loss rarely if ever occurs in communities of power, wealth and privilege, but rather to the dispossessed and disempowered. Moreover, as has been evident from the Irish example, as well as in countless other colonial situations, linguistic dislocation doesn't occur in isolation from socio-cultural and socio-economic dislocation but always forms part of a wider process of socio-economic, cultural and political displacement often involving overt discrimination, suppression and subordination. (May 2002: 4)

**Decolonisation and Resistance**

'To live, the colonised must ... do away with the colonised he has become. The most urgent claim of a group about to revive is certainly the liberation and restoration of its language.' (Alberto Memmi)

The processes of colonialism in Ireland, as in other situations throughout the world would inspire anti-colonial sentiments often posited in an ideology of decolonisation which first appeared in an Irish context in the guise of the romantic nationalism of the Young Irelanders' and the decolonizing narrative of its leader Thomas Davis, which cited the Irish language as the key to national revival. This would become a source of inspiration for a future generation of cultural and political activists.

Amongst those influenced by Davis was a young Douglas Hyde's whose inspirational decolonizing manifesto calling for widespread cultural revival provided

---

[8] While in Ireland the notorious tally-stick or 'bata scoir' was used to record and thus prevent children from speaking Irish with summary punishment being inflicted by the schoolmaster based on the amount of notches on the stick (Ó Giolláin 2000: 66), similar approaches were being used by the British regime in Kenya as late as the 1950s. According to Ngugi wa Thiong'o (1997: 11), children caught speaking Gikúyú in school were 'given corporal punishment- three to five strokes of the cane on bare buttocks- or was made to carry a metal plate around the neck with the inscriptions such as I AM STUPID or I AM A DONKEY.' A button was initially given to one pupil who was supposed to hand it over to whoever was caught speaking his mother tongue. Whoever had the button at the end of the day would sing who had given it to him and the ensuing process would bring out all the culprits of the day. Thus children were turned into witch-hunters and in the process were being taught the lucrative value of being a traitor to one's one community.'

[9] According to Edwards (1985: 62–3) for example, language shift in Ireland had less to do with socio-political factors Irish people becoming 'linguistically pragmatic', thus becoming 'more or less active contributors to the spread of English'. This view is echoed by Comerford (2003: 146) who believes 'parental pressure' on Irish children reflected a widespread 'societal enthusiasm' to adapt to the modern world.

the template for the formation of the Gaelic League in 1893. The League itself, when it was formed, differed radically in its objectives from all other previous societies in that it pro-actively aimed to eradicate the sense of inferiority generated by years of Anglicisation and colonialism by advocating the revival of the language as a spoken tongue. In this sense, the 'deliberate project of 'decolonisation...formulated and adopted by a group of intellectuals and artists' was designed to prevent a 'rupture in cultural continuity' and ultimately undo 'the shame of defeat, dispossession, humiliation and impoverishment- the classic colonial condition.'[10] (Ó Tuathaigh 2005: 47)

Thus against the backdrop of this decolonising framework, the League's radical educational policies emphasised instructional classes as well as more overt political campaigning aimed at increasing the language's status. The result was that by 1900 the Irish language had been accepted as a mainstream optional subject within the British National School System, to be taught during school hours. In 1904, the League's bilingual policy for primary schools in Irish speaking areas was accepted[11] (Ó Croidheáin 2006: 99). Arguably, the largest achievement was when Irish became a compulsory matriculation subject in the National University of Ireland after Gaelic league activists utilised its network of supporters in lobbying the university authorities (Comerford 2003: 141).

However, in reality, governmental policy in the early century era of 'killing Home Rule with Kindness' (Jackson 1999: 148) demonstrated that antagonistic British policy towards the language had merely become more veiled and sophisticated:

> An Conradh (the Gaelic League) continued to play a sort of game with the education authorities and the British treasury. The game went like this: An Conradh made certain demands for teaching of Irish. The British Government refused them. All shades of public opinion (were) brought to bear by An Conradh and the authorities gave in. However a short time later the Government introduced some new rule or measure which hit the teaching of Irish. An Conradh mobilised its forces again. There was another submission and a little later another wriggle by the government and Irish suffered again. (Ó Fearaíl 1975: 30)

Invariably, the British authorities only acceded to the League's demands due to political expediency. In the aftermath of any notable concession, the authorities typically pursued every available avenue to neutralise the validity or implementation of the reforms. Future British Governments would use a similar strategic template when subsequently dealing with the 'controversial' issue of the Irish language.

In this period, the Irish language movement naturally converged, as happened in numerous anti-colonial struggles throughout the world, with the growing forces of nationalism[12] which ultimately led to a dramatic increase in support which saw the

---

[10] In this 'condition', the colonised's revival or reinvention of indigenous culture and conscious claims to continuity with the historic past form part of a process, Algerian Revolutionary Theorist, Frantz Fanon (1961) describes as 'hegemonic mirroring' which amounts to a necessary strategy for survival in the face of the colonising power's determined objective to reduce the colonised to abject material and psychological poverty. As seen with the Davisian trend, this involves elevating the 'national culture' and reclaiming the native past in a 'counter-continuum that mirrors the dominant ideology in its liberal mix of myth and truth' (Ó Croidheáin 2006: 113). Since the narrative of the coloniser 'distorts, disfigures and destroys' (*ibid.*: 169) the natives' history, any attempt to survive and decolonise involved the initiation of a contrary construct.

[11] By 1916, over half the schools in the Gaeltachtaí were teaching through the medium of Irish. (Hindley 1990: 14).

[12] Again it could be argued that the Irish experience corresponds with Fanon's (1961: 193) three-stages of

number of Gaelic League branches rise from 120 in 1900 to 985 in 1906, with membership peaking at 75,000 members. (Hutchinson 1987: 178–9) During this period, radical revivalists such as Patrick Pearse resolved to take innovative measures to combat the 'mental enslavement' of the imposed national school system, which he named 'the Murder Machine', by becoming the first exponent of Irish medium education.

By forming *Scoil Éanna* and *Scoil Íde*, Pearse became one of the world's first advocates of the 'decolonizing of the mind' thus precipitating similar Latin American and African activists and writers in later years.[13] The Gaelic league project itself would become the catalyst for the Irish political independence struggle and accordingly, the Irish revolution,[14] with few commentators disagreeing with F.X. Martin's summation that 'the Gaelic resurgence was the revivifying force which made possible the Easter Rising of 1916.' (Rees 1998: 211) The practical extent of the linkage between the Rising and the Gaelic league is illustrated by the fact that six of the seven signatories of the Proclamation[15] were members and all but two of the officers of the *Coiste Gnótha* of the League were implicated in the Rising with 16 of its members being shot, wounded, taken prisoner or disappeared. (Ó Huallacháin 1994: 72)

In this aftermath, hundreds of Gaelic league activists were subsequently interned amongst over two thousand others in Frongoch internment camp in Wales and other English prisons in the aftermath of the Rising and thus began a pattern of armed resistance and political imprisonment. The key role of cultural revival as a central tenet of the independence struggle inspired imprisoned nationalists/republicans in the post-Easter Rising period to utilise the Irish Language as both an educational expression of their identity and as a political weapon of struggle that could challenge 'the colonial ideology of the British empire' (Ó Croidheáin 2006: 156–7) during their imprisonment. Their decision to learn and view the language in this manner, which will be looked in greater detail later, had set an historical precedent that continually re-emerged in various prisons with new generations in future phases of history.

The British Government responded to the emergence of radical republicanism by reverting to measures of repression and imposing Martial Law which saw many democratically elected representatives being imprisoned without trial or being forced underground. All expressions of Irishness were subject to these draconian measures including the Gaelic League was 'made illegal including its meetings and persons organising them or attending were liable to prosecution by a court under Army jurisdiction'. (Ó Huallacháin 1994: 75) Paradoxically, such persecutive measures actually strengthened the resolve of language revivalists and at the first public meeting

---

Decolonisation – the first phase recognising assimilation into the culture of the occupying power; the second phase involves returning to their roots and recalling their historic past; the final phase, the intellectuals aim to revive and awaken their people and realign themselves with their cause while producing a relevant yet revolutionary national literature (*ibid*.). Thus the cultural revival of colonised peoples couldn't be separated from the wider struggle for 'national liberation' which 'makes the building of a culture possible'. (*ibid*.: 187)

[13] For example, Kenyan activist Ngugi wa Thiong'o (1997: 3) argues that the colonised can 'decolonise the mind' by speaking 'the united language of struggle contained in their languages' while the Brazilian educationalist Paulo Friere concurs and states 'The more the alienated culture is uncovered, the more the oppressive reality in which it originates is exposed ... knowledge of the alienated culture leads to transforming action resulting in a culture which is being freed from alienation.' (1972: 162)

[14] Pearse himself wrote; 'if one thing has become plainer than another it is that when the seven men met in O'Connell street to found the Gaelic League, they were commencing ... not a revolt, but a revolution.' (Crowley 2000: 216)

[15] The Proclamation of the Republic was read out outside the GPO (General Post office) in Dublin on Easter Monday, April 24 1916, by the President of the declared provisional Government of the Irish Republic, Pádraig Pearse and had seven signatories including Pearse himself, Thomas Clarke, James Connolly, Eamonn Ceannt, Seán Mac Diarmada, Thomas Mac Donagh and Joseph Plunkett.

of Dáil Éireann, held at the Mansion House in Dublin in January 1919, the order of business was published bilingually and the proceedings were conducted primarily in Irish. (Ó Gadhra 1989: 57)

However, circumstances were completely transformed when the republican movement was split down the middle, and when the British government negotiated the Treaty with the Irish independence movement in 1921 copper fastening the partitioning of the six North-Eastern counties of Ulster into Unionist control. These would also irrevocably divide the language movement[16] with the Gaelic League itself going into sharp decline after 1922, partly because it was believed that the state would takeover the revival, but primarily due to nadir of the split and brutal Civil War which tore many branches apart. (Lyons 1973: 636) Ideological and political divisions nullified the League's drive and impetus causing membership to drop dramatically from 700 braches in 1920 to 565 in 1922. (Ó Fearaíl 1975: 45)

Ireland, according to Ó hÉallaithe (2004: 165), 'became a disturbing retreat into a conservative type of cultural protectionism' which subsequently alienated a whole generation of radical activists and intellectuals who might well have backed a more progressive cultural program. Concomitantly, the decolonising project which had inspired the Irish revolution 'lost an important ally when the intellectuals turned their backs'. Ó Croidheáin's (2006) viewpoint that a fearful and reactionary free-state administration[17] failed to promote the liberating aspirations of revival as a means of decolonialisation is echoed by cultural critics like Smyth (1999: 37) who sums up its legacy thus:

> Despite the best efforts of its liberal and left wings, radical decolonisation was commandeered by a nationalist bourgeois elite[18] which tried to arrest the process at the point where it assumed control of the state apparatus left vacant by an offshore power. The drive towards an essential national identity in the years after 1922 actually reinforced social and political hierarchies even as it claimed to be an agent of liberation from such hierarchies.

**'Promoting Sedition': The Irish Language and 'The Orange State'**

> 'What use is it here in this busy part of the Empire to teach our children the Irish language? What use would it have to them? Is it not leading them along a road which has not practical value? We have not stopped

---

[16] The Irish language becoming a source of competition between both Pro-treaty and Anti-Treaty camps as to who was most genuinely wedded to the revival project (Mac Poilín 1997: 43)

[17] This argument is comprehensively developed and put into context by Lee (1985: 673) who posits, 'Irish, battered, bruised and humiliated, recovered some dignity through the revival efforts of the Gaelic league, and the idealism and intellect of many of the early enthusiasts. It then fell into bad company again with the founding of the state. The ethos of the official revival, despite the commitment of genuine revivalists, fostered precisely those qualities of national character that were accentuated by colonial experience, ambiguousness, furtiveness, mendacity. The manner of the revival thus contributed more to reinforcing the inherited flaws in the national personality than to adopting, however gradually, the national character to the new dignity of independence.'

[18] Although a more detailed account of the ultimate failure of Irish Free State governments' after 1922 to rise to the challenge of reviving the language is the beyond the scope of this paper, it would be my contention, as the quote above indicates, that Fanon's (*ibid.*: 163) analysis of how a 'nationalist bourgeoisie' can appropriate the decolonising aspirations of a liberation struggle unless it becomes imbued with a radical political and social consciousness is wholly applicable to the Irish case.

the teaching; we have stopped the grants, which I think amounted to £1,500 a year. We have stopped the grants simply because we do not see that these boys being taught Irish would be any better citizens.' (Stormont Prime Minister, James Craig, 1933, quoted in Andrews 1997: 83)

The fate of the Irish language differed considerably, however, in the newly formed six-county, one-party state in the North-East of Ireland which was designed to cement a permanent unionist majority that prevented Irish nationalists' access to political power, employment and housing thereby relegating them to a subordinate status. (Farrell 1976) This tight repressive framework instituted a 'British 'effective dominant culture' through physical coercion' that left no room for any political or cultural expression of Irish nationalism or Irishness which was viewed as a 'threat to British cultural hegemony'. (Kachuk 1994: 176)

Moreover, this hostile 'settler-colonial' (Clayton 1998: 50–1) ideology, which undoubtedly had its roots in Ireland's protracted cultural colonisation,[19] didn't auger well for the Irish language, which was considered a threat and by association its main promulgators, the Gaelic league who were viewed by Unionists as 'an anti-British counter-culture dominated by republican separatists' whose promotion of the Irish language was nothing than 'the promotion of sedition and disloyalty under another name' (Andrews 1997: 56).

Meanwhile, state policy and state repression had a crippling effect voluntary effort on behalf of the language in the area under the jurisdiction of the Belfast Government. Before the end of 1922 all branches of the Gaelic League in the South of Ulster had ceased to function while the province organizer had to flee from the six counties, under threat of arrest and imprisonment, in 1923 and resign later that year (Ó Huallacháin 1994: 108).[20]

The unionist government seised the opportunity to implement its opposition to the Irish language with its 1923 Education Act which substantially negated the achievements of the Gaelic league over the previous twenty years, (Kachuk 1994: 155) in what effectively was the beginning of a policy of systematic neglect and legislative exclusion. Despite the fact that all special grants for the teaching of Irish in the new Northern state were terminated and its status downgraded to as low as grade 7, the Stormont regime came under increasing pressure from hard-line loyalists[21] to stop

---

[19] It is worth noting that there is considerable debate about whether Ireland can be viewed to actually constitute a colony following 1800 with commentators such as Aughey (1989) arguing that the Plantation was a long time ago and Irelands' colonial status effectively ended with the Act of Union of 1801.This view is challenged by Whyte (1990: 178) when he points out that 'settlers from England and Scotland did come over in 17th Century and settle in much the same manner as their compatriots were settling in America. No one has thought to call the American settlements anything other than colonies. Some of the same individuals were involved in the Irish and the American schemes of colonization. The result in Ireland at least, was to produce an enduring division of the population, as in other settler colonies such as South Africa and Algeria. The fact that Northern Ireland is legally not a colony, but part of the United Kingdom, does not destroy the analogy; Algeria was legally part of France, and Angola and Mozambique were legally part of Portugal, but that did not stop the French and Portuguese from eventually treating them as expendable , non-metropolitan parts of the state territory, and pulling out.'

[20] The leagues' 1926 report indicates the extent to which they had been eradicated; 'Little of the body of the Gaelic League remains after the destruction of the last 3 or 4 years. Most of the people are apathetic…older people fight shy of Irish in case it would draw the suspicion of the Government on them.' (Ó Huallacháin 1994: 108)

[21] One such MP named William Grant vehemently attacked the language in Parliament in an exchange with the Parliamentary education secretary; 'the only people interested in this language are the people who are the avowed enemies of Northern Ireland- and does he not think the time has now arrived when this grant should be cut off?' (Andrews 1997: 77)

paying fees for the Language as an extra subject. While these extreme loyalist attitudes were motivated by an objective which was shared by the Prime Minister and his government,[22] they resisted calls for a complete prohibition of Irish teaching in schools in favour of a less overt and more pragmatic and gradualist form of legislative repression which involved allowing it to continue as an optional subject while constantly limiting opportunities and finances for its teaching.[23]

Moreover, Craigavon's response to the Loyalist League demands in which he stated his Government felt it 'better to keep a control by means of regulations over activities of this character than to drive them underground where they will undoubtedly tend to germinate and exert a baneful influence' (Andrews 1997) is arguably concurrent with the strategically expedient position taken up by the British Government in its more veiled early twentieth century dealings with the Gaelic league, a position, no less, which characterised the attitude of the Northern Ireland state towards the language thereafter.

Therefore any attempts to gain legitimacy for the Irish language was viewed by the Unionist state as an attack on British cultural hegemony,[24] thus igniting further attempts to diminish or eradicate it. One of countless examples of this was in 1948, when discriminatory legislation was passed in the form of an amendment to the Public Health and Local Council Act which prohibited the erection of Irish street signs. This came as a direct response to the erection of Irish street signs by nationalist councils in Omagh and Newry which caused outrage in Unionist circles who, in the words of future Stormont Prime Minister Brian Faulkner, couldn't 'tolerate the naming of our streets in a language which is not our language' (Maguire 1991: 11).

Furthermore, this set the scene for a barrage of draconian legislation to be introduced throughout the 1950s to add specificity to the increasingly widespread application of the Special powers act. The Public Order Legislation (1951) and the Flags and Emblems Act (1954) amounted to drastic emergency measures that enabled the Stormont government to physically subdue any cultural or political expressions of Irish nationalism by the excluded Catholic minority. (Kachuk 1993)

---

[22] In a response by Craigavon to the Loyalist league signed by one of his officials, it stated that; 'he (the PM) is by no means convinced that repressive measures would affect the object which both you and he desire. A prohibition of Irish teaching in the schools might have a result the very opposite to that intended.' (Andrews 1997: 76) This quite clearly shows a correlation of interests between both pragmatic and extreme loyalists with regard the Irish language, namely, its elimination.

[23] When the opportune moment arrived in the end of 1933 the Government voted unanimously, in a parliament that nationalists had been boycotting for the previous year in frustration, to stop payment of fees for the teaching of Irish as an extra subject, for reasons summarised by Craigavon a few years later; 'We have stopped the grants simply because we do not see that these boys being taught Irish would be any better citizens' (Andrews 1997: 83)

[24] Under the settler-colonial rationale, according to Clayton (1998: 53–1), those who fail to appreciate or conform to the rigours of colonial cultural hegemony or worse still, those who actively opposed it were not only unworthy of its so-called benefits but regarded as disloyal, sub-human and dangerous. Thus she argues that loyalist portrayals of nationalists as 'both inferior and dangerous' could subsequently be used justify their cultural, political and socio-economic exclusion. According to this analysis, which conforms to the classic colonial stereotypes found in other settler colonies, the coloniser as articulated by Memmi will utilise 'mythical portraits' to define how the colonised were to be viewed. In the six counties, these 'mythical portraits' were manifested in institutionalised discrimination towards Catholics in employment and housing as notoriously articulated by future Prime-minister Basil Brooke MP when denouncing those who employed Catholics in a speech on July 12 1933, 'I would not have a Roman Catholic about my own place…and I would appeal to Loyalists to employ good protestant lads and lassies.' (Farrell 1976: 90)

## 'A Hidden Ulster': Survival, Decolonisation and Resistance

'Ná habair é, dean é / don't say it, do it' (famous Cumann Chluain Ard dictum)

Despite the official hostility and disregard towards the language displayed by the dominant unionist state following partition in 1920, voluntary language activists did their utmost to fill the void and take responsibility for providing Irish classes and promoting cultural revival thereby compensating for the dearth of Irish language instruction in the education system. Their various projects created independent bastions of cultural activity which according to De Brún (2006: 11) amounted to 'a hidden Ulster of revivalism which enjoyed hardly any relations with statutory authorities and which was entirely alienated from the culture of the state'. This provided an effective form of cultural expression that cultivated an established social, educational and recreational movement that was only tolerated because it neither openly undermined nor challenged the legitimacy of the unionist state.

The focal point for much of this activism was the Ardscoil[25] Gaelic league's headquarters, which was rebuilt in Belfast in 1928 becoming a mainstay for cultural revivalist activity in the decades that followed.[26] The language movement in this era, as it had done previously, acted as an ideological umbrella for nationalists, republicans and socialists with many deriving from working-class backgrounds. It was from this subtext in 1936, during a period of mass unemployment and endemic poverty that 'two unemployed young men Seamus Maxwell and Liam Rooney, set up Cumann Chluain Ard in an old covered gateway in Kane Street beside Clonard Monastery in West Belfast.' (Mac Seáin 2006: 4)

When the club eventually took the radical decision to become an 'Irish only' club in 1953 its new philosophy had according to Mac Seáin (2006: 4) effectively 'set up an alternative Irish language movement, more outspoken than the mainstream Gaelic league, which many of them looked upon as being too mild and bourgeois.' A core of idealistic young activists who first came to the fore in the club in the late fifties with the extraordinary idea of creating an urban Gaeltacht in West Belfast, which according to Andrews (1991: 98) was motivated by the hope that they could:

'[ ... ] construct a set of values and an institutional framework that could bring a modern independent Irish-speaking society into existence, using what remained intact and worthwhile of pre-colonial Gaelic Ireland. Preservation and development of the Gaeltacht and on the establishment locally of a variety of Irish-speaking institutions in the belief that they may coalesce, creating the nucleus of this new society [...]'

That this audacious decolonising project was conjured up by working-class people against an unfavourable socio-political and socio-economic backdrop in an area

---

[25] The Ardscoil was founded in 1911 as headquarters of Belfast Gaelic League where it resided in Queens Street at the centre of language revival activity in the city before moving to Divis street in 1928 where it continued in the same vein until being accidentally burned down in 1985. (Foras na Gaeilge 2007)

[26] This was described by republican ex-prisoner of that era Eddie Keenan, 'A new world revealed itself to me when I first saw the 'Gaelic' atmosphere of the Ardscoil in the late thirties. There were hundreds of young people attending classes, céilís and dances of every kind almost every night. There were Gaelic League branches from throughout the city in attendance and I found out that these branches were full of my fellow IRA members! My attitude towards the language changed from that point on.' (Mac Ionnrachtaigh, 2008)

crippled by political discrimination made their task as daunting as it did admirable. (Nig Uidhir 2006: 138) Although the planning and delivery of this initiative took nine years in all eventually reaching fruition in 1969, the core group who spearheaded it 'never wavered in their determination to realise their goal' and succeeded 'without one penny of grant aid or government subvention'. (*ibid.*)

In addition, the Shaws Road activists had succeeded in setting up the North's first Irish medium nursery school for their children in 1965 before subsequently following this up by meeting with the Stormont authorities to explore the possibility of setting up the an Irish primary school. (Mac Seáin 2006: 4) In its aftermath, they received a threatening letter saying 'that teaching through the medium of the Irish language would not be deemed to be proper instruction for young children' and that if the school was formed then 'the law would be allowed to take its course'. (*ibid.*)

This threat, which according to Mac Seáin (*ibid.*) effectively translated as 'set up a school and you go to jail', was duly ignored and the North of Ireland's first Irish medium primary school, Scoil Ghaeilge Bhéal Feirste and later Bunscoil Phobal Feirste, was established on the Shaws Road in with nine children in 1971 with the six counties in the throes of the political/military conflict. The formation of the North's first Irish medium school in 1971 against all the odds, which 'would propel the Irish language onto a dynamic and exciting course that would contribute to a language shift in Ireland during the reminder of the millennium' (Nig Uidhir 2006: 140) and beyond, was the defining aspect of the highly original Shaws Road decolonisation project that planted a seed that would flourish in the 1980s under the transformational influence of the republican prison struggle in Long Kesh.

**Republican Prisoners and the 'Long Kesh Prison Struggle'**

> Gaeilge más féidir, Béarla más gá ('Irish if possible, English when necessary') (Motto of Gaeltacht hut in Cage 11)

Irish republican prisoners have always taken an active interest in learning the Irish language while incarcerated. This tradition stemmed originally from the post–1916 period in Frongoch, through to prison ships like the Argenta; the Curragh in the 1940s and Crumlin Road Jail in the 1940s and 50s; and beyond to the latter decades of the twentieth century in prisons like Mountjoy, Armagh, Portlaoise and Long Kesh where the language became a mainstay of republican prisoner development and resistance. (Mac Ionnrachtaigh 2008)

In the cages of Long Kesh prison camp, where 'a group of dedicated language activists came through inspired by the writings of Pearse, Friere and Fanon'[27] (Interview with Jake Mac Siacais in Mac Ionnrachtaigh 2008), and during the Blanket protest,[28] the Irish language, as it had done previously, became a practical form of power that successfully challenged the prison authorities and, by historical implication, the validity of British rule in Ireland.

---

[27] This same group of activists according to Mac Siacais would be re-arrested and re-incarcerated in the H-Blocks during the Blanket protest (see below) and spearhead the Gaelicisation process amongst the prisoners.
[28] The Blanket protest was stage by republican prisoners in Long Kesh prison, in the new high security HMP Maze H-Blocks, between 1976–81 in opposition to the British governments' criminalization policy which removed political status from republican prisoners. Prisoners who refused to wear prison uniforms and do prison work lost all privileges and subsequently found they locked naked in their cells, 24 hours a day with only blankets as clothing. The protest culminated in the death of ten prisoners on hunger strike in 1981. (see Beresford 1986)

According to the accounts of sentenced republican prisoners in Long Kesh and especially in Cages 10 and 11 where Gaeltacht huts were formed; the Irish language was a focal point of prisoner life.[29] In addition, a highly politicised enthusiasm for the Irish language developed in conjunction with and was integral to the individual ideological advancement of activists who drew political inspiration from African and Latin American anti-colonial struggles.[30] This idealistic interest in the Irish language as a component of their overall political vision is attested by such prisoners like Jim McCann whose simple observation; 'we recognised the lengths the imperialists went to destroy the language and from this reasoned that it must be important' (Mac Ionnrachtaigh, 2008) perfectly illustrates the aforementioned Fanonian decolonising ideological construct. These prisoners began to benefit from reflective and liberating educational processes where, as McCann posited, 'not only did I learn the language but I learned why I had went [sic] to jail and what was keeping me in jail and more importantly we learned how to begin breaking all these things down' (*ibid.*). This educational process treated them as 'knowing subjects' and not 'as recipients' and helped them achieve 'a deepening awareness both of the sociocultural reality which shapes their lives and the capacity to transform that reality' (Freire 1972b: 51). Prisoners underwent an increase in confidence and self-esteem in accordance with an increase in fluency levels and/or general interest in Irish language development.

The central importance of educational and ideological development amongst republican prisoners in the Cages to the role of the language in the prison protests of the H-Blocks is clearly articulated by a wide range of narrators. These activists attest to the key organisational and educational role played by fluent Irish speakers and ex-cages prisoners like Mac Siacais, Bobby Sands and Séanna Breathnach *et al*. (Mac Ionnrachtaigh, 2008) By consciously ideologising the Irish language as both a critical practical and political means of resistance, and simultaneously replicating the Cages' language-learning model of informal education, which saw the 'pupil' become the 'teacher' after arriving at a particular level of fluency, these activists inspired truly phenomenal educational development in exceptional and often unbearable conditions.[31]

---

[29] According to republican ex-prisoner Jim McCann for example, 'one of the things we set down in Cage 11 was as soon as you got the green fáinne which was knowledge of the 11 irregular verbs you then became a teacher to someone who didn't have this much ... gradually, you move up the ladder ... silver fáinne was next and you had to have a degree of conversation skills and it was difficult, and the gold fáinne was at a very high standard, almost at the same level as the examiners were at and the pressure was unbelievable – the gold fáinne meant you were fluent. But once you reached a certain standard you became a teacher and you had to be prepared to teach as well as learn, and you had to be prepared to help other prisoners at any time…this summed up our approach in Cage 11, it was about helping each other and learning together…it moved away from the heavy compulsory, anti-English language mentality … our motto in the Gaeltacht was inclusive and simple, Gaeilge más féidir, béarla más gá (Irish if possible, English when necessary) … At this stage with all the classes you were taking yourself and with helping others we were doing up to 13 hours a day learning the language … towards the end of my time in prison, our Gaeltacht had developed amazingly I mean, between 1977 and '79, I really never spoke English at all except when I had to..' (Mac Ionnrachtaigh, 2008)

[30] This point is emphasised by Séanna Breathnach, who stated,'we read everything going about anti-colonial revolutions all around the world ... we read about Vietnam, Algeria Angola, Latin America, and all this shaped our political philosophies and also added to our interest in the language in that we really began linking it all together with our own struggle ...' (Mac Ionnrachtaigh, 2008)

[31] During the Blanket and 'No Wash' protests, prisoners lived 24 hours a day in cells covered with their own excrement. Cardinal Tomás Ó Fiaich famously described these conditions, 'Having spent the whole of Sunday in the prison I was shocked at the inhuman conditions prevailing in H Blocks 3, 4, and 5 where over 300 prisoners are incarcerated. One would hardly allow an animal to remain in such conditions, let alone a human being. The nearest approach to it that I have seen was the spectacle of hundreds of homeless people living in the sewer pipes in the slums of Calcutta. (Coogan 1980: 158) According to Mac Siacais (Mac Ionnrachtaigh 2008) over 300 prisoners reached Irish language fluency in these conditions over a two year period.

During the Blanket protest of 1976–81, prisoners who had nothing but their bodies to use as a weapon of protest, utilised the Irish language as a symbolic means of resistance and a practical form of salvation from psychological decay. It legitimised their sense of cultural distinctiveness and gave them strength to continue their protest. While their primary resistance may have been a refusal to wear a uniform and accept the label of criminalisation, they also demonstrated an extraordinary capacity to transform their sacrificial circumstances into an innovative and transformative arena that educated them and politicised their defiant acts of resistance.

The language represented a highly liberating power that transformed the prison and the prisoners, both for themselves and the outside world while also building bonds of comradeship that the authorities could not penetrate because it was incomprehensible to the English-speaking warders as a method of communication. This widespread use of the Irish language actually increased and yielded a yet more powerful political resonance during the most enduring periods of the protest when there was an intensification of prison warder brutality, As republican ex-prisoner Peadar Whelan (Whelan in O'Hagan 1991: 4) articulated:

> Learning and speaking Irish became a crucial part of our struggle against criminality and helped form our identity. We had to fight to learn and speaking it was a form of resistance. Every time we spoke Irish, we were telling our enemy that we were Irish republicans, protesting and struggling. We weren't going to let them silence us ... Irish was a weapon we used against the screws leaving them feeling totally frustrated and excluded. Our expression of identity left them feeling totally powerless. Knowledge is power and ignorance diminished their sense of power and control.

As a method of developing political consciousness and a sense of community amongst republican prisoners in Long Kesh during this period, the Irish language can also be conceptualised within Buntman's (2003: 236) reference to 'emancipation' as the following stage of development which follows the initial formative phase of resistance where it is 'not simply about saying no, reacting, refusing, resisting, but also and primarily about social creativity, introducing new values and aims, new forms of co-operation and action'. It is worth noting that these processes came about organically during the Blanket protest and not as the result of any grandiose political strategy; as Máirtín Ó Maolmhuaidh (Mac Ionnrachtaigh 2008) points out:

> There is a misconception out there that the Republican movement took a strategic decision to instruct the Blanket prisoners to learn the language as a secret weapon of war while incarcerated ... in my case, I understood that I was not English and because I happened to be Irish, I tried to learn my native language...what inspired me with the language was my identity and pride in my own area, and the community in that area ... I grasped the chance on the Blanket that I had not previously had on the outside ..but there is no doubt that in the difficult times on the blanket, that the language functioned as a weapon against the system ... as an inspirational tool to oppose the state from inside prison as we had opposed it on the outside.

The Long Kesh example is wholly in keeping with Buntman's (2003: 8) description of Robben Island in South Africa as the 'paradox of a site of repression being used to undo the material and symbolic origin of the power of the repressive apparatus' while simultaneously proving that 'events and patterns within prisons can and do shape political dynamics beyond the prison walls'. Therefore, the more general relevance of this cultural revivalism as a form of prisoner resistance would surpass the confines of the prison cell and the immediacy of the protest itself by having a wide-ranging impact outside the prison gates in the North of Ireland.

**'Bringing the Language to the People': Revival**

> 'In the H-Blocks with no books, no paper, no pens, no professional teacher, young Irish men living in filthy conditions, frequently beaten, stripped naked ... but unbowed, taught each other Irish by shouting the lessons from cell to cell. And as one hunger strike was followed by the other, the people outside heard those lessons too and they determined to carry on the cultural struggle – each one from where he/she was'. Pádraig Ó Maolchraoibhe (1986: 9)

The Long Kesh Prison struggle would transform the Irish language revival in the six counties, forging a dramatic increase on the amount of children attending the first Irish medium school in the North[32]. People outside of prison were inspired by these developments and felt that if prisoners could suffer in unbearable conditions, without pen or paper, to learn the language, then nothing should stop them from doing it with teachers and proper facilities. (Ó hAdhmaill 1984: 9) In addition there was arguably a subsequent radicalisation of the Irish language movement through the pro-active creation of widespread additional language classes, the formation of additional Irish language nursery schools, an Irish language newspaper, and pro-active campaigning on language rights issues such as Irish language street names.[33]

In the case of the blanket protest and the hunger strikes, the use of the Irish language, written and spoken, by republican prisoners such as Bobby Sands considerably enhanced its appeal for republicans and nationalists on the outside. The hunger strikes had a hugely politicising effect both North and South of Ireland and the Bilingual writings of Bobby Sand inspired widespread interest in the Irish Language and forged a strong link between cultural struggle and the wider political aspirations for national self-determination. (Sands 1998) As Irish prominent Irish language activist, Eoghán Ó Néill posits:

> The hunger strike changed everything….before this, there was a section of the nationalist community that was always in favour of the language

---

[32] Ó hAdhmaill's (1984: *ibid.*) study provides statistical evidence for this increase which would be precipitated by the formation of more schools throughout wider Belfast and the North of Ireland.

[33] Sinn Féin's Roinn an Chultúir (Cultural Department) which was formed in 1982, would oversee the organisation of scores of additional language classes throughout Belfast and a controversial campaign to create bilingual street signs, which remained illegal from the 1948 (it was finally prorogued in 1992) Stormont Public Health and Local Council Act (Ó hAdhmaill 1985). The Irish language street name project developed successfully across Belfast in accordance with the willingness of working-class communities to give generously to the fundraising activities that paid for them. For example, in one particular area, Twinbrook, where the unemployment rate was over 70%, local Irish language activists made and erected over 160 Irish street signs, raising in the region of £1,500 in the area itself to pay for them. (*ibid.*)

but there was another fairly big section that was not interested in it at all ... stories about the Kesh began coming out and spreading through people going up on visits about the way the prisoners learned Irish and the hostility they received from the screws because of this, people were sympathetic to them anyway but if you were interested in the language, this inevitably increased your sympathy for them ... I was involved along with a lot of other young Irish speakers in the Gaels against the H-Blocks and Armagh, we were visible at hundreds of marches in the campaign against Long Kesh, we would have Irish banners and posters and shout Irish slogans aloud ... this raised the feeling of identity created by the blanket protest and the hunger strike...the prisoners who died were known as fluent Irish speakers...this transformed the views of people who had never thought of the Irish language as a means of struggle before ... there was always sympathy for the language but now people wanted to do something about that sympathy. (Mac Ionnrachtaigh 2008)

This point echoes the analysis of Seamás Mac Seáin, founding father of the Shaws Road Gaeltacht community, who explained the additional activists and community support that the revival was receiving in the context of the 'climate of independence' following the Hunger Strike:

... not everyone wants to be part of violence or warfare but that does not mean that they were not conscious of the causes of the struggle that was going on ... people realised that we were pushing another worthwhile means to play a role in a non-violent way yet progress the same objectives ... that was why a lot of people connected with the revival and Irish medium education in general. (Mac Ionnrachtaigh 2008)

During this era of immense politicisation and popular mobilisation in nationalist/republican areas in the six counties, the Irish language would take on an added relevance amongst many ordinary working-class people who had not been previously associated with it.

British policy during this period, which involved denying official recognition to Irish-medium schools,[34] had the additional and implicit implications that both aspirations of Irishness and the nationalist community in general were somehow subversive and illegitimate. The alienation of nationalist working class areas from the British state became total, and one of the places where this anger came to be channelled was the Irish language. (Ó hAdhmaill 1984)

The development and growth of the language movement in the North also saw a corresponding growth in pride and self-confidence on both a group and individual level which effectively imbued the wider Nationalist community with a greater sense of self-reliance and self-respect. There was also a powerful social dimension to these new structures which created an alternative sense of identity thus leading to personal and collective empowerment amongst those involved. The Irish language educational movement came to represent a counter-hegemonic 'education for emancipation', which established itself as a popular alternative education system where power lay with the

---

[34] The North's first Irish-medium school, Bunscoil Phobal Feirste, was denied funding for 13 years, eventually receiving recognition in 1984 following considerable political lobbying. (Mac Ionnrachtaigh 2008)

community,[35] and where a cultural and linguistic alternative to that offered by the dominant society was promoted.

During this period in the early to mid 1980s and beyond, recently released republican prisoners, working in conjunction with others, played a role in the growth of alternative education system all over Belfast and throughout the North in Derry, Tyrone, Newry, Armagh, Fermanagh. One such ex-prisoner, Pilib Ó Ruanaí, the current CEO of Iontaobhas na Gaelscolaíochta (Irish Medium Trust Fund) and key founder of *An Droichead* Irish medium school and Cultural centre in South Belfast, stated 'The vision of Irish medium education had completely inspired me as a vision during that period. It was almost like an awakening of consciousness that made me realise the importance of other ways to take forward the struggle.' (Mac Ionnrachtaigh, 2008)

The fact that the British government reaction to this was overtly obstructive and antagonistic further fostered a sense of alienation from the British state and cemented the impression that the Irish language and Irishness remained wholly illegitimate. However, this overt British Goverment hostility and discrimination, that was directed towards language revivalist activities in nationalist and republican areas, was tempered by their attempt to strategically divide the language movement by providing financial assitance to a cross-community Irish language initiative.

This came in the form of the ULTACH Trust, set up in 1989 after the groundwork had been laid by the Cultural Traditions Group (O'Reilly 1998). As the first time in the history of the North of Ireland that the British Government had given financial assistance to Irish language development, Sinn Féin activist Bairbre de Brún, described it as 'a cynical tactic to give money to 'respectable Irish speakers' rather than revivalist organisations'.[36] (Mac Ionnrachtaigh 2008) Concurrently, the community-led, post-hunger strike language revival in the six counties, had effectively re-ignited the classic British colonial perception that the Irish language represented a threat to its cultural hegemony in the North and by extension its own strategic political objectives.[37]

---

[35] This empowering process is well depicted by republican ex-prisoner Scán Mag Uidhir from Ardoyne in North Belfast, 'I was released in 84 and had a totally different view of the Irish language in that I knew it was a living language and central to my politics ... a short while after this, I attended a meeting along with several other ex-prisoners organised by Martín Ó Muilleoir about forming a nursery school in Ardoyne. We organised a meeting with parents to give us a chance to share information with them about Irish medium Education. The area was extremely sympathetic to the language, particularly after the hunger strike. We put a committee together and most of those on it were ex-prisoners. We collected money, we organised youth discos and they all understood that all the money was going towards the nursery school and this helped us get people on board and to spread the word ... we also started Irish classes as well as the street name campaign, and we formed branches of the Gaelic League to carry out this work and we were happy to work with everyone, regardless of their political opinions, as long as they were sympathetic to the language. We got fifteen toddlers to start in the Nursery school and got a porter cabin on the Bone area to locate the nursery school. We painted it and were very enthusiastic as was the entire area at time regarding Irish language developments. (Mac Ionnrachtaigh 2008)

[36] Thus many language activists accused the government of deliberately designing a policy to portray the Irish revival movement as sectarian and, by association, blame state discriminatory practices against it as a consequence of its own links with nationalism and republicanism (O'Reilly 1998: 108–9). Under the auspices of 1985 Douglas Hurd principles, it was stated that groups that 'have the effect of improving the standing and furthering the aims of a paramilitary organisation, whether directly or indirectly' would be denied funding (*ibid.*: 115). West Belfast Irish language orgaisation, Glór na nGael, subsequently had its funding removed in August 1990.This decision would not only impact on community development but also remove funding from seven of the eight Irish nursery schools in Belfast. The Irish language community immediately began campaigning nationally and internationally to have the decision overturned. (*ibid.*)

## Legacy, Decolonisation and the Future

For the colonised just as for the coloniser, there is no way out other than a complete end to colonisation. The refusal of the colonised cannot be anything but absolute, that is, not only revolt, but a revolution. Albert Memmi (1965: 194)

These processes inevitably created a pattern of intransigence and resistance which according to another ex-prisoner who was active in the revival in this period, Jake Mac Siacais, who is current director of Belfast Irish language development agency *Forbairt Feirste*, would provide the impetus for radical Irish language activism right up to the present:

> The results of the 80s revival are to be found in a new and radical generation of language activists between the age of 24 and 32. These revolutionary activists are working in a number of different vehicles throughout the country. This network of activists understands that the Irish language struggle is part of a process of decolonisation that gives proper mental emancipation to the people of Ireland.' (Mac Ionnrachtaigh, 2008)

One of these younger activists, Ciarán Mac Giolla Bhéin, a leading member of Irish language campaigning group ACHT, describes how his attendance at Meánscoil Feirste[38] in the early 1990s, the North of Ireland's first Irish medium secondary school, and its subsequent high-profile campaign for state recognition had a hugely radicalising impact on him personally:

> There was something exceptional about the Meánscoil. We, as pupils, cleaned the school and our parents went out at nights collecting money in the local clubs on the road. Everyone was totally committed to the project and organising sponsored cycles and sponsored mountain walks etc on our behalf and for the sake of our education. Although we knew that we were involved in a struggle, this help gave us the confidence that we would succeed and that's exactly what happened in the end. Therefore, when I eventually left school, I felt it my duty to put something back in to the struggle.' (Mac Ionnrachtaigh, 2008)

The funding campaign for Meánscoil Feirste eventually succeeded in 1996 following a national and international campaign where it became an issue of 'parity of esteem' for the nationalist community in the North during the Peace process. (O'Reilly 1999: 132–3) However, it is worth noting that the British Government, similar to the beginning of the twentieth century, arguably only ever acceded to the demands of the Irish language community when the pressure became so great that do to otherwise would appear overtly intransigent.

A more recent example of this methodology in the North of Ireland has been evident in their approach to the Irish language community's long-standing demand

---

[37] A fuller discussion of divisive British Government funding strategy in this period and the consequent fostering of divisions within the North's Irish language community is beyond the scope of this paper. For a detailed account, see Mac Ionnrachtaigh (2008)

[38] Meánscoil Feirste was renamed Coláiste Feirste in 2005 and is the second largest Irish-Medium post-primary school on the island of Ireland. (Mac Ionnrachtaigh 2008)

for an Irish Language Act for the six counties which would grant Irish speakers similar legal protection to that enshrined for Irish speakers in the Irish Free State, and speakers of Welsh and Scottish Gaelic. Having agreed in November 2006 to enact an Irish Language Act through Westminster, following the ratification of the St Andrews Agreement, the British Government proceeded to delay the public consultation on the Act before announcing a second public consultation process until after the date for the restoration of devolution to the North of Ireland thereby granting intransigent Ulster unionism an effective veto over any future Irish Language Act.[39]

This intransigence continually manifests itself in an openly hostile attitude towards the Irish language that is defined by the age-old settler-colonial psyche as articulated in the DUP's (Democratic Unionist Party), the foremost unionist party in the North of Ireland, submission to the language act consultation process, which stated, 'The Irish language serves no communicative purpose in Northern Ireland, but simply the promotion of a political cause. An Irish language Act is divisive, would alienate the majority population in Northern Ireland and would be a complete waste of money'. (DUP Party submission, see http//www.dcalni.gov.uk) The habitual oscillation between pragmatic and extremist strands of recalcitrant unionism in relation to the Irish language was again evident in submissions from more hard-line elements in the Orange Order whose submission differed merely in tone but not in content.[40]

The obstructionist basis for these unfounded, and 'culturally racist' arguments are countered by the Irish speaking community with rights-based arguments like those presented by Language legislation experts like Fernand de Varennes (May 2002: 312).[41] The compelling logic of these arguments in favour of an Irish language act, however, are constantly rejected by the British government whose ambivalent discourse often accentuates and lends credence to flagrantly inequitable unionist attitudes.

A concise example of this discourse was illustrated in the introduction to the British government DCAL (Department for Culture, Arts and Leisure) document on the proposed Irish language Act in which they comprehensively revised the role of planned cultural colonisation in the decline of the Irish language which occurred in their view, 'due to the dominant growth of English in the fields of industry and trade' (http//www.dcalni.gov.uk, accessed March 2007). Additionally, the introduction stated that the Irish language in the North was 'controversial' because unionists held 'genuine fears and concerns' about 'the erosion of their British identity'. (*ibid.*) Thus in emphatic

---

[39] This much was made clear in the game of brinkmanship between the British Government and the main unionist party the DUP in the lead-up to 26 March deadline for restoring devolution in the North. A few days before, British Secretary of State for Northern Ireland, Peter Hain, effectively threatened the DUP by warning them that failure to agree to devolution at the end of March would mean the enactment of an Irish Language Act and the scrapping of academic selection whereas an agreement to share power with republicans would grant them a veto in both cases. (*Irish News*, 24 March 2007)[40] 'It is plain silly and wrong to give precedence to a minority language that nobody really speaks as part of a political concession to Sinn Féin/IRA. We would earnestly ask the government to reconsider this unwanted legislation which is discriminatory and not applicable to over 90% of the population.' (For Armagh Orange Lodge submission, see http//www.dcalni.gov.uk – last accessed March 2007)

[41] In de Varennes' submission to DCAL on Irish language legislation for the North, he explicitly stated that, 'It is time to end the legacy of almost 650 years of Laws restricting the use of the Irish language with legislation which promotes and protects it as part of Europe's heritage and cultural diversity'. He argued De Varennes argues that speakers of minority languages should have the right and opportunity to use their languages as part of the exercise of their individuals rights as citizens if they choose to; 'the respect of the language principles of individuals ... flows from a fundamental right and is not some special concession or privileged treatment. Simply put, it is the right to be treated equally without discrimination, to which everyone is entitled.' (http//www.dcalni.gov.uk, accessed March 2007)

terms, the classic British imperial/colonial rationale can be seen here to have clearly endorsed fundamentally discriminatory views by describing them as 'genuine fears' as a means of justifying the denial of rights to Irish speakers.[42]

When we extrapolate these obstructionist views of the Irish language in a global context they can be easily understood as a clear manifestation of a highly politicised global agenda which acts as a continuum and modern extension of imperialism and neo-colonisation.[43] Concomitantly, in arriving at an critical perspective of how Ireland's historical cultural colonisation has manifested itself in the modern world, it is imperative that we understand to quote Alexander (2004: 6) that 'colonial conquest, imperialism and globalisation have established a hierarchy of standard languages, which mirrors the power relations on the planet' which aim deliberately to hasten 'the extinction of innumerable language varieties and to stigmatise and marginalise all but the most *powerful languages*'.[44]

It is my contention that Ulster unionist and British government intransigence in relation to the Irish language fits adequately into this wider rationalisation practice that assert 'English Linguistic Imperialism' or 'Linguicism' as termed by Phillipson (1992) and undoubtedly aim to maintain and perpetuate social, economic, political and cultural inequalities between English and other languages and their respective speakers. Statistical credence is given to these views by the findings of leading linguist Michael Krauss (1992) which state that at the current rate of language shift, the $21^{st}$ century will see 90% of the world's languages or more precisely 5,400 out of six thousand languages either lost or forced into the final stages of decline.[45]

That this linguacide continues to occur an unprecedented scale is shaped by unequal socio-political and socio-economic power processes of neo-liberal globalisation is

---

[42] This analogy also illuminates the key oppositional argument presented by monolinguals and stakeholders for the world's most 'powerful languages' which derives from the wholly ignorant assertion that the granting or demand of minority rights somehow impinges on the rights of the majority. This is strongly and succinctly refuted by May (*ibid.*: 312) who argues that it isn't the demand for rights that renders minoritised languages 'controversial' but their continued denial.

[43] The Ghanaian revolutionary leader, Nkrumah Kwame (1965: ix) describes neo-colonialism in economic terms, 'The neo-colonialism of today represents imperialism in its final and perhaps most dangerous phase and is also the worst form of imperialism. For those who practice it, it means power without responsibility and for those who suffer from it, it means exploitation without redress ... the result of neo-colonialism is that foreign capital is used for the exploitation rather than for the development of the less developed parts of the world.' In addition an analysis of the cultural ramifications of Neo-colonialism can be found in the work of Edward Said (1993).

[44] In addition, Phillipson (1992) argues that this linguistic hegemony is channelled through an ideology of modernisation which is far from neutral but actually politically motivated. According to Phillipson, it buttresses the dominant economic and political position of Britain and the USA in the modern world by elevating the English language as the language of International/Global capitalism. his scathing critique of the international English linguistic hegemony, that its financially motivated monopoly of film/media, science, technology and the information/Internet age allows it to create a 'rationalisation process whereby the unequal power relations between English and other languages are explained and legitimated...in favour of the dominant language'.

[45] The commonality in each case is usually its contact with more a powerful majority language whose power is usually defined by its superior political, cultural or socio-economic power. According to Krauss, this inevitably leads to the marginalisation of both minority and minoritised languages that occurs in various different ways; 'the circumstances which have led to the present language mortality known to us range from outright genocide, social or economic or habitat destruction, displacement, demographic submersion, language suppression, enforced assimilation or assimilatory education to electronic media bombardment especially television, an incalculably lethal new weapon, which I have called 'cultural nerve gas'. (Krauss 1992: 8)

attested to by May (2002: 316) who warns that the ongoing disavowal of equality for minoritised cultures and languages means that they will 'continue so patently to play a significant (even central) part in many of the political disputes in the world today'. Moreover, the damaging consequences of neo-liberal globalisation according to acclaimed sociologist Manuel Castells (1997: 69) is being met with opposition by people all over the world, who 'with the exception of a small elite of wealthy *Globapolitans*' completely 'resent the erosion of their cultural identities, the loss of control over their lives, over their governments, over their countries, and ultimately, over the fate of the earth.'

Despite the all-prevalent nature of the hegemonic globalisation project, many contemporary Irish language activists echo the views of Castells and defined themselves within an ideology of decolonialisation and resistance which not only played a pivotal role in inspiring the Irish revolution in the early twentieth century but also continues to motivate Irish language activists to the present day. This determination to resist and overturn the impact of colonisation can be seen to have inspired a transformational activism by an increasingly organised and vibrant Irish language speaking community in the North of Ireland. This commitment is best exemplified by the tremendous growth of *Gaelscoileanna* which proves that emancipatory voluntary endeavour, has continued to provide the impetus for people-centred decolonialisation.

Nevertheless, with the rapid growth and success of the language movement in the North of Ireland come the dangers of institutionalisation whereby activist groups can often be assimilated, diverted or manipulated by the state or by conservative elites intent on maintaining the status quo. (Ó Croidheáin 2006: 315) Fears amongst activists that such a process is a dangerous possibility were posited by Ó Maolchluiche:

> Notwithstanding the considerable progress that has been made, there are still dangers in terms of the cultural revival. Because a lot of employment was created I suppose its inevitable that we are getting some people working in the Irish language sector to promote their own careers ... this lowers the standard of the activism. (Mac Ionnrachtaigh 2008)

Many of these realities outlined by Ó Maolchluiche were perhaps inevitable following the financial mainstreaming of the Irish language sector in the North of Ireland with the formation of cross-border funding institution, Fóras na Gaeilge, in the aftermath of the Good Friday Agreement. Theorists of institutionalisation, according to Hourigan (2006: 127), argue that it results 'in a loss of radical impetus within a social movement without the achievement of real gains'. This usually occurs when 'political elites' use 'social capital to divide and conquer a movement network and marginalise dissent within the public sphere.' (*ibid.*: 138)

McCoy (2002: 213) believes that the Irish language movement in the North has already 'undergone a rapid transformation from counter-culture to officialdom' during the peace process where state subsidies meant 'the rhetoric of resistance was discarded' and 'replaced by discourses of language rights, economic regeneration and consumerism.' McCoy credits these changes to a 'radical transformation' in the attitudes of the British Government towards the Irish language which he feels has shifted from 'reactive to a pro-active'. (*ibid.*: 216)

In the first instance, McCoy's conclusions on the 'pro-active' shift in British government polices in relation to the language can arguably be deemed grossly naïve and ahistorical considering the aforementioned patterns in colonial and neo-colonial methodology[46] whereby overtly discriminatory practices merely become more veiled and sophisticated in conjunction with the political expediencies of the particular era, as recently demonstrable in the Irish language Act campaign. Secondly, while McCoy is undoubtedly correct to point out the changes in discourse post-peace process and the huge potential pitfalls of over-reliance on state subsidies he's arguably inaccurate in assuming that campaigns for 'language rights and economic regeneration' cannot constitute forms of resistance[47].

Although there is an undoubted merit in arguments regarding the dangers of institutionalisation, the current status of the Irish language in the North of Ireland, would suggest that is somewhat premature to over-emphasise them. Whether it is the sustained close links between the language movement and grassroots communities or the continued structural manifestations of neo-colonialism within the Northern Ireland state, the language issue still retains a potent resonance for heightened socio-cultural and socio-political awareness in younger activists as evident in Mac Giolla Bhéin's comments,

> I feel that I'm continuing with the radical decolonising ideology that was promoted by Pearse, Ó Cadhain and Sands. Of course, the battleground and the context of struggle continually evolves and adopts to changing circumstances; ten years ago, for example, all our attention on Irish medium education while at the present time, we have moved on the to the campaign of human rights for Irish speakers. This battleground will continually change and develop…After 30 years of struggle, there are many things that we are not prepared to accept; we have a bottom line now regarding the Irish language that we will continue to raise in the future to ensure that our Irish language revolution goes from strength to strength.' (Mac Ionnrachtaigh, 2008)

While it would be exaggerative and presumptive to assume that this analysis is the prevailing view amongst the North's Irish speakers, it nevertheless conveys a prominent rationale, that indicates that Irish language activism in the North can still be defined in Freire's terms as a transformative expression of 'cultural resistance' and a form of 'counter-consciousness'. (Freire 1972: 68–9)

This can facilitate a radical perspective through which individuals and activists can critically examine the nature of their culture and politics in a national and global context. Thus grassroots Irish language activism can create 'a critical theory of knowledge' (*ibid*.) which provides opportunities for active participation, empowerment and purposeful action. One topical example of this participatory activism can be found in the current campaign in the North of Ireland for an Irish language Act, which has seen thousands of people, of all ages, marching for their rights, writing and collecting

[46] According to Rahman (2001: 65) 'moves by powerful states to appear more liberal and fair towards minority languages are merely symbolic moves in the power game.'

[47] As Mac Siacais illuminates, 'We have the same mentality now despite all the progress we have made. We are resisting be it in a different phase and in a different way. As a language activist, I'm resisting everyday of my life. The strength of this community is that it works in a continuum refusing to ever lie or be satisfied with what we've achieved. We'll keep coming back again with a new demand following the one that just been exceeded to.' (Mac Ionnrachtaigh, 2008)

submissions for the public consultation processes. These forms of activism from below can continue to imbue the language movement with that radical edge that provides succour from the dangers of complacency and institutionalisation.

Furthermore, they represent, as Ó Croidheáin (2006: 18) emphasizes; 'individuals and communities' playing a 'transformational....part in the revolutionary process of changing the general relations of power in Irish society' while simultaneously possessing the potential to challenge the current global Anglo-American cultural hegemony. The key to this potential, however, lies in the ideological continuum of emancipatory resistance-based activism where a 'thoroughgoing decolonisation envisaged by Memmi or Ó Cadhain' (Mac Síomóin 1994: 69) is embedded in communities. Therefore, it's as an inspirational bottom-up contribution to the wider global project of decolonisation that the Irish language revival in the North of Ireland should be viewed. A contribution that fits neatly with Maori academic, Tuhiwai Smith's (1999: 4) definition of the subtext and potential of such revivalist methodology: 'the past, our stories local and global, the present, our communities, cultures, languages and social practices – all may be spaces of marginalisation, but they have also become spaces of resistance and hope'.

References

Alexander, N. 1999. 'English Unassailable but Unattainable: The Dilemma of Language Policy in South African Education'. (downloadable from web.uct.ac.za/depts/praesa/OccPap3.pdf )
Alexander, N. 2003. 'The African Renaissance and the use of African Languages in Tertiary Education'. (downloadable from www.africavenir.org)
Andrews, L.S. 1991. 'The Irish language in the Education system of Northern Ireland: Some political and Cultural perspectives'. In ed. Pritchard, R.M.O. *Motivating the Majority: Modern Languages in Northern Ireland*. London: CILT Publications. 89–106.
Andrews, L.S. 1997. 'The very dogs in Belfast will bark in Irish: The Unionist Government and the Irish Language, 1921–13'. In ed. Mac Póilin, A. *The Irish Language in Northern Ireland*. Belfast: ULTACH Trust. 49–-94.
Beresford, T. 1987. *Ten Men Dead: The Story of the 1981 Irish Hunger Strike*. London: HarperCollins.
Canny, N.P. 1973. 'The Ideology of English Colonisation from Ireland to America'. *William and Mary Quarterly* 30: 575–98.
Castells, M. 1994. *The Power of Identity*. Oxford: Blackwell.
Chomsky, N. 1999. *Latin America: From Colonisation to Globalisation, in Conversation with Heinz Dieterich*. New York: Ocean Press.
Clayton, P. 1998. 'Religion, Ethnicity and Colonialism as Explanations of the Northern Ireland Conflict'. In ed. Miller, D. *Rethinking Northern Ireland*. London: Longman. 40–54.
Comerford, R.V. 2003. *Inventing the Nation: Ireland*. London: Arnold.
Crotty, R. 1986. *Ireland in Crisis: A Study in Capitalist Colonial Underdevelopment*. Dingle: Brandon Books.
Crowley, T. 2000. *The Politics of Language in Ireland 1366–1922: A Sourcebook*. London: Routledge.
Curtis, E. 1937. *A History of Ireland*. London: Methuen.

Curtis, L. 1984. *Nothing but the Same Old Story: The Roots of Anti-Irish Racism*. London: Information on Ireland.
Curtis, L. 1994. *The Cause of Ireland: From the United Irishmen to Partition*. Belfast: Beyond the Pale Publications.
Curtis, M. 2003. *Web of Deceit: Britain's Real Role in the World*. London: Vintage.
DCAL website. http//www.dcalni.gov.uk (March 2007)
De Brún, F. ed. 2006. *Belfast and the Irish language*. Dublin: Four Courts Press.
Edwards, J. 1985. *Language, Society and Identity*. Oxford: Blackwell.
Fanon, F. 1967. *The Wretched of the Earth*. Harmondsworth: Penguin.
Farrell, M. 1976. *The Orange State*. London: The Pluto Press.
Foras na Gaeilge, 2007. *Oidhreacht Feirste: An Ghaeilge i mBéal Feirste*
Friere, P. 1972. *Pedagogy of the Oppressed*. Harmondsworth: Penguin.
Hindley, R. 1990. *The Death of the Irish Language: A Qualified Obituary*. London: Routledge.
Hourigan, N. 2006. 'Movement Outcomes and Irish Language Protest'. In eds. Connolly, L. and N. Hourigan. *Social Movements and Ireland*. Manchester: Manchester University Press. 124–44.
Hughes, A.J. 2006a. 'Robert MacAdam and the Nineteenth-century Revival'. In ed. De Brún, F. 43–64.
Hughes, A.J. 2006b. 'The Ulster Gaelic Society and the Work of MacAdam's Irish Scribes'. In ed. De Brún, F. 65–100.
Hutchinson, J. 1987. *The Dynamics of Irish Cultural Nationalism: The Gaelic Revival and the Creation of the Irish Free State*. London: Routledge.
Jackson, A. 1999. *Ireland 1798–1998*. Oxford: Blackwell.
Kachuk, P. 1993. *Irish Language Activism in West Belfast: A Resistence to British Cultural Hegemony*. Unpublished PhD Thesis, University of British Columbia.
Kiberd, D. 1993. *Idir Dhá Chultúr*. Dublin: Coiscéim.
Krauss, M. 'The World's Languages in Crisis'. *Language* 68.1: 4–10.
Lee, J. 1989. *Ireland 1912–1985: Politics and Society*. Cambridge: Cambridge University Press.
Lyons. F.S.L. 1982. *Culture and Anarchy in Ireland, 1890–1939*. Oxford: Oxford University Press.
Lyons. F.S.L. 1973. *Ireland since the Famine*. London: Fontana.
Maguire, G. 1990. *Our Own Language: An Irish Initiative*. Clevedon: Multilingual Matters.
Maguire, G. 2006. 'The Shaws Road Urban Gaeltacht: Role and Impact'. In ed. De Brún, F. 136–47.
Mac Ionnrachtaigh, F. 2008. *'An Ghaeilge Faoi Ghlas': Republican Prisoners and the Irish Language in the North of Ireland, Power, Resistance and Revival*. Unpublished PhD Thesis, Queens University Belfast.
Mac Piarais, P. 1913. *The Murder Machine*. (downloadable at http://publish.ucc.ie/celt/docs/E900007-001)
Mac Póilin, A. 1997. 'Plus ca change: The Irish Language and Politics'. In ed. Mac Póilin, A. *The Irish Language in Northern Ireland*. Belfast: ULTACH Trust. 31–48.
Mac Seáin, S. 2006. 'Century of Irish Language Growth'. *Andersonstown News*. 9 October 2006.
Mac Síomóin, T. 1994. 'The Colonised Mind: Irish Language and Society in Daltúin'. In ed. Ó Ceallaigh, D. *Reconsiderations of Irish History and Culture: Selected Papers from the Desmond Greaves Summer School, 1989–93*. Dublin: Léirmheas. 42–71.

May, S. 2002. *Language and Minority Rights. Ethnicity, Nationalism and the Politics of Language*. Harlow: Longman.

Memmi, A. 1965. *The Colonizer and the Colonized*. New York: Orion Press.

McCoy, G. 2001. 'From Cause to Quango? The Peace Process and the Transformation of the Irish language Movement'. In eds. Kirk, J. and D.P. Ó Baoill. *Linguistic Politics: Language Policies for Northern Ireland, the Republic of Ireland, and Scotland*. Belfast: Cló Ollscoil na Banríona. 205–19.

Nic Craith, M. 2003. *Culture and Identity Politics in Northern Ireland*. Houndmills: Palgrave Macmillan.

Ó Croidheáin, C. 2006. *Language from Below: The Irish language, Ideology and Power in 20th-Century Ireland*. Frankfurt: Peter Lang.

O'Dowd, L. 1992. 'Colonial Dimensions: Settler-Native Mentalities'. In eds. Caherty, C., Storey, A., Gavin, M., Molloy, M. and C. Ruane. *Is Ireland a Third World Country?* Belfast: Beyond the Pale Publications.

O'Fearaíl, P. 1975. *The Story of Conradh na Gaeilge*. Dublin: Clódhanna Teo.

Ó Fiaich, T. 1969. 'The Language and Political History'. In ed. Ó Cúiv, B. *A View of the Irish Language*. Dublin: Institute for Advanced Studies. 101–11.

Ó Gadhra, N. 1989. *An Chéad Dáil Éireann (1919–1921)*. Baile Átha Cliath: Coiscéim.

Ó hÉallaithe, D. 2004. 'From Language Revival to Language Survival'. In ed. Mac Murchaidh, C. *'Who Needs Irish?': Reflections on the Importance of the Irish Language Today*. Dublin: Veritas Publications. 159–85.

Ó Huallacháin, C. 1994. *The Irish and Irish: A Sociolinguistic Analysis of the Relationship between a People and their Language*. Dublin: Irish Franciscan Provincial Office.

Ó hAdhmaill, F. 1985. *Report of a Survey Carried out on the Irish Language in West Belfast in the Winter of 1984/5*. Béal Feirste : Glór na nGael, Coiste Bhéal Feirste Thiar.

O'Reilly, C. 1999. *The Irish Language in Northern Ireland: The Politics of Culture and Identity*. Houndmills: Palgrave Macmillan.

Ó Tuathaigh, G. 2005. 'Language, ideology and national identity'. In eds. Cleary, J. and C. Connolly. *The Cambridge Companion to Modern Irish Culture*. Cambridge: Cambridge University Press. 43–58.

Phillipson, R. 1992. *Linguistic Imperialism*. Oxford: Oxford University Press.

Rahman, T. 2000. 'Language Learning and Power: A Theoretical Approach'. *International Journal of the Sociology of Language* 152: 53–74.

Rees, R. 1998. *Ireland 1905–25*. Newtownards: Colourpoint Press.

Said, E.W. *Culture and Imperialism*. London: Vintage.

Sands, B. 1998. Bobby Sands: Writings from Prison. Cork: Mercier Press.

Smyth, G. 1998. 'Decolonialisation and Criticism: Towards a Theory of Irish Critical Discourse'. In eds. Graham, C. and R. Kirkland. *Ireland and Cultural Theory: The Mechanics of Authenticity*. Houndmills: Palgrave Macmillan. 29–19

Tuhiwai Smith, L. 1999. *Decolonizing Methodologies: Research and Indigenous Peoples*. London: Zed Books.

Wa Thiong'o, N. 1986. *Decolonising the Mind: The Politics of Language in African Literature*. London: Heinemann.

Whelan, P. 1991. 'Irish on the Blanket'. In ed. O'Hagan F. *Éirí na Geal: Reflections of the Culture of Resistance in Long Kesh*. Roinn Cultúir Sinn Féin. 2–6.

Whyte, J. 1990. *Interpreting Northern Ireland*. Oxford: Oxford University Press.

# The Implementation of Language Legislation in Dublin and Glasgow

*John Walsh and Wilson McLeod*

## Introduction

This article examines the implementation of Irish and Scottish Gaelic language legislation in the cities of Dublin and Glasgow. The main mechanisms for implementation are the language schemes under Ireland's *Official Languages Act* (2003) and the Gaelic language plans under the *Gaelic Language (Scotland) Act 2005*. Both Acts aim, among other things, to increase incrementally the provision of public services in Irish and Scottish Gaelic. The article begins by assessing the symbolic and practical importance for Irish and Gaelic language development of revitalisation in an urban setting. It outlines briefly the Irish and Scottish legislation before analysing the contents of the language schemes for the four local authorities in the Greater Dublin area and the language plan for Glasgow City Council. It concludes by considering the appropriateness of the suggested measures for revitalisation of minoritised languages in urban settings.

## Methodology

This article focuses on textual analysis of the legislation itself, the statutory guidelines for both the Irish and Scottish acts, and the relevant language schemes or plans; it does not encompass fieldwork on their implementation, which would be premature in the Glasgow context. Because the Irish legislation was enacted two years earlier than the Scottish Act and is being implemented more quickly, four local authorities in Ireland are examined in contrast to just one in Scotland. Dublin city spreads into four administrative areas, whose combined population (1.13 million) is roughly twice that of the City of Glasgow (580,000) but comparable to that of the Greater Glasgow Settlement Area (1.2 million), which encompasses parts of six other local authorities as well as Glasgow itself. Of these, only Glasgow City Council itself has agreed a Gaelic language plan to date. Although Dublin could have been compared with Edinburgh as the capital city of Scotland, Glasgow was chosen as it is the largest city in the country and the principal centre of Gaelic development in urban Scotland. A further point of comparison is that both Dublin and Glasgow contain relatively high concentrations of Irish and Gaelic speakers (notwithstanding fundamental differences between the broader sociolinguistic contexts of Ireland and Scotland, discussed below), due to the historical pull of the largest city.

## Current Demographics of Irish and Gaelic

Although recognised an official language of the Republic of Ireland and widely accepted as an important symbol of Irish national identity, Irish is now a minoritised language, following sweeping language shift in favour of English, particularly in the eighteenth and nineteenth centuries. The situation of Irish is somewhat anomalous compared with other threatened languages because there are now far more L2 speakers than native speakers, a consequence of the fact that Irish is a core subject at all levels of obligatory education in the Republic (McCloskey 2001: 46). Thus, although a relatively high proportion of the population of the Republic, 1.67 million people or 41.9%, claimed competence in Irish in the 2006 census, the number of fluent speakers and the level of actual use of the language are much lower. For the first time in 2006, a question was asked about daily use of Irish within and outside the education system. 484,812 people (12% of the total population, or 29.2% of Irish speakers) reported that they spoke Irish daily either within the education system only or both within and outside the education system. Only 72,148 people (1.8% of the total population) spoke Irish daily outside the education system. The density of speakers, and of active users of the language, is often significantly higher in the Gaeltacht (the officially demarcated Irish-speaking area), where in some districts more than 75% of the population report using Irish on a daily basis (CSO, 2007). Conversely, the largest absolute numbers of speakers are concentrated in the urban areas, including Dublin, although in considerably lower density than in the Gaeltacht.

The position of Gaelic in Scotland is distinctly more marginal than that of Irish in Ireland. Where Irish was the language of the majority of the national population until approximately two hundred years ago, the minoritisation of Gaelic took root much earlier, beginning in the twelfth century. For present purposes, the most striking difference between the Irish and Gaelic situations relates to the divergence in language policy in the middle of the twentieth century, from the early 1920s to the mid–1960s. While the Irish government adopted a range of measures to promote Irish during this period, most notably in connection with the state education system, there was very little state intervention in Scotland, even though Gaelic continued to decline steadily. Crucially, Gaelic was kept to the margins of the Scottish education system, and although there have been significant advances since the 1970s, it remains the case that only a tiny minority of Scots study Gaelic at school or acquire any competence in the language. For the great majority of the Scottish population, Gaelic is an entirely unknown tongue. The most recent census, conducted in 2001, showed a total of 58,969 Gaelic speakers aged 3 and over in Scotland, a mere 1.2% of the national population. A further 34,632 persons could read, write or understand Gaelic but not speak it. As in Ireland, the proportion of Gaelic speakers is highest in certain outlying rural areas (rising to over 80% in some parts of the Western Isles), but the raw number of speakers in urban areas, including Glasgow, is also significant. Unlike in Ireland, however, there is no census data on language usage (General Record Office for Scotland, 2005; Walsh and McLeod, 2008: 34–5).

**Background to Language Revitalisation in Urban Areas in Ireland and Scotland**

There has been a strong historical association between urbanisation and anglicisation in both Ireland and Scotland. Even in the medieval period, towns and cities in both Ireland and Scotland developed as primarily English-speaking environments, and in recent centuries Irish and Gaelic have mostly been spoken in rural areas, and increasingly, as language shift progressed, in remote rural areas. At the same time, both Ireland and Scotland have become increasingly urbanised, with national institutions, economic development and, perhaps most of important of all, cultural hegemony all concentrated in the urban areas. Within this context, urban Gaelic communities have, since at least the eighteenth century, played a disproportionate role in Gaelic language revitalisation movements and cultural activity more generally (Wmffre, 2002).

Given the increasing economic and social dominance of urban areas, especially the largest cities, successful strategies for language maintenance and revitalisation in

Ireland and Scotland may well depend on building a stable foundation for the language in the urban environment, even though this task presents immense challenges and there is a risk of becoming embroiled in often unproductive debates about the arguably greater importance of securing the rural language 'heartland' (McLeod, 2007). One key factor in determining strategy and tactics is the question of the ultimate goal and what might reasonably be achieved. When (as is the case with Irish in Dublin and Gaelic in Glasgow) a language is used by only a very small minority of a city's population, and the majority language is invested with much greater cultural capital as well as socio-economic power, it is clearly not realistic to think in terms of displacing the majority language and systematically replacing it with the hitherto minoritised language. The task might be better conceived in terms of building community institutions and facilitating social interaction in the minority language for the benefit of minority language speakers, connected by only relatively loose social networks, who wish to use the language in their daily lives. Yet even this limited vision of making it possible to 'live one's life' in the city through Irish or Gaelic has been characterised as 'naïve, to say the least' by one prominent commentator (Edwards, 2010: 143).

Although neither the Irish or Scottish Acts or any of the language schemes/plans considered in this article address these issues directly, local government in urban areas can clearly play an important role in helping Irish and Gaelic speakers achieve objectives of this kind. Along with building educational and cultural institutions to serve the minority language community, making it possible to receive public services and to engage public authorities through the medium of Irish/Gaelic can make an important contribution to the strengthening of urban Gaelic communities.

Towns and cities were never strong points for the Irish language: following the Anglo-Norman invasion in 1169, attempts were made to make Norman French and later English the dominant language in place of Irish, particularly in urban centres (several of which, including Dublin, had actually been founded by Scandinavian settlers rather than the indigenous Irish). From the fourteenth century onwards, bilingualism and diglossia emerged in the towns as Irish speakers from areas where it was the principal language moved into the urban environment. English became dominant in urban areas and Irish was used for certain purposes only (Ó Murchú and Ó Murchú, 1999: 10). As argued by Gabrielle Maguire, in this dominance of English in towns and cities lie the roots of a deeply held belief that Irish is unsuitable for anything other than a rural, isolated environment:

> [T]he process of urbanisation has proved to be a powerful anglicising agent. It has reinforced the position of English as an outward sign of social advancement and undermined the value of Irish in that context. Those who left their rural homes for employment in the fast growing industrial cities of the nineteenth century found it necessary to acquire and use English. As economic circumstances uprooted large numbers of people from their rural environment so also did cultural and political necessity dictate that these people should change their language. The association of urbanisation with anglicisation hinges upon the relative economic prosperity of urban centres wherein the English language was totally dominant. In the nineteenth century English became most firmly established as the language of political and economic power and the process of linguistic assimilation became as inevitable in Ireland as it was in the countless other instances of language extinction (Maguire, 1991: 13).

Even so, Irish was still spoken in parts of Dublin City and County into the nineteenth century. The Irish language revival began in Dublin too, with the establishment of the Society for the Preservation of the Irish Language in 1876 and most notably the Gaelic League in 1893. The League first expanded in Dublin and remained an overwhelmingly urban phenomenon, organising large marches in favour of Irish in the capital at the turn of the twentieth century. Liam Mac Mathúna has described Dublin as 'céadionad ceaptha beartas agus céadláthair agóidíochta na Gaeilge' (the first place where Irish language policy was devised and the first site for Irish language protest) (1987: 62). It was in Dublin, too, that the first Irish-medium school was opened, in 1908.

Dublin's leading role in the formulation of language policy was cemented in 1922 following the establishment of the Irish Free State. New measures in support of Irish and the Gaeltacht were announced in Dublin and implemented from there. However, in the twentieth century, the failure to create contiguous Irish-speaking communities in towns and cities reinforced the popular perception that Irish was a rural phenomenon. From 2002 until 2010, for example, the name of the government department responsible for Irish was the 'Department of Community, Rural and Gaeltacht Affairs', doing little to dispel that belief. Therefore, any attempts to reverse this perception, and to re-establish Irish as a living language of a community in the heart of the very towns which were said to have destroyed it, can be characterised to a counter-cultural struggle, an attempt to reverse a potent symbol of cultural dislocation stretching back to the Norman invasion.

The most significant urban Irish language revitalisation initiative has been the 'Pobal Feirste' or 'Gaeltacht Bhóthar Seoighe' (Shaw's Road) project in Belfast, which was launched in 1969 with the aim of building a housing estate for Irish speakers (Maguire, 1991; Nig Uidhir, 2006). Ten couples were involved in the early stages, and nine houses were built. In 2005, Aodán Mac Póilín – himself a resident of the Shaw's Road – wrote that there were sixteen houses with an additional six being built (2005: 43). The Shaw's Road project has inspired other language revitalisation campaigns throughout Northern Ireland and in the Republic (for a recent study, see Armstrong, 2009). Notwithstanding challenges related to the tiny size of the community and the questionable replicability of the initiative, it is nonetheless significant in language policy terms because a reasonable percentage of first-generation children have themselves remained or returned and have transmitted Irish to their own children (Mac Póilín, 2007: 55). No other urban Irish language initiative can point to such obvious success.

In what is now the Republic of Ireland, there have been various efforts to gaelicise urban communities, although none has been as successful as the Shaw's Road. For example, an effort to establish an Irish-speaking housing estate was made in Dublin in the 1920s and 1930s. In 1924, a group of Irish speakers established a public utility company calling itself 'Nua-Ghaedhealtacht Átha Cliath Teo.' and sought two acres from Dublin Corporation to build ten houses for their members in the suburb of Whitehall on Dublin's northside. According to Ruth McManus: 'The rules of the society set out its objects to "establish and maintain a community of Irish speakers at places to be selected by the society", while eligibility for membership was based on being a native speaker of the Irish language or having passed the first exam for the Fáinne [ring worn on lapel to indicate ability to speak Irish]' (2002: 273–4). Unfortunately, the terms of the lease required the construction of roads which the Nua-Ghaeltacht group could not afford. In 1929, the Corporation surrendered the original lease and granted ten leases to the individuals who had built houses in the area. Despite appeals from them that the land be used exclusively for the Nua-Ghaeltacht project, the area was developed for other housing. Although the estate had been named 'Páirc na Gaeltachta' by 1932, and contained roads named after Gaeltacht areas (Falcarragh, Tourmakeady, Iveragh etc.), it would appear that the Nua-Ghaeltacht project failed to create a sustainable Irish-speaking community there (McManus, 1996 and 2002).

In an essay on efforts to revitalise Irish in urban areas of the Republic, Ó Murchú describes several past and contemporary projects. Most notable among these are the 'Scéimeanna Pobail' (community schemes) supported by the former Irish state language planning board, Bord na Gaeilge, between 1976 and 1983, two of which were based in suburbs of Dublin; the Gaillimh le Gaeilge ('Galway with Irish') project to promote the use of Irish by private businesses in Galway city; the Port Láirge le Gaoluinn ('Waterford with Irish') Irish language centre and services in Waterford city (since discontinued); the ongoing Glór na nGael language competition which operates in both urban and rural areas throughout Ireland; the Pobal Chrónáin and Pobal Naithí local community projects in Dublin and a feasibility study on the promotion of Irish in Dublin city centre (Ó Murchú, 2007; see also Mac Aongusa, 2006 and Ó hAilín, 2006). The 'Baile' project, which aims to build a new Irish-speaking community (it deliberately avoids the label 'Gaeltacht') somewhere in Leinster, refers to another 'micro-Gaeltacht' in the 'Ard Barra' housing estate in Glanmire, Co. Cork (Baile, 2007; see also Ó Liatháin, 2010).

Ó Murchú also considers the potential relationships between new urban Irish-speaking communities and Irish-medium schools (gaelscoileanna) (2007: 7–9). In 2010, there were 31 primary and 8 secondary Irish-medium schools in the Dublin area, serving just over 10,000 pupils (Walsh, C., 2010, p.c.). Another indication of engagement with Irish in Dublin is the data gathered by the office of the language commissioner (An Coimisinéir Teanga), the office responsible for monitoring compliance with the Official Languages Act. In 2008 and 2009, the largest percentage of complaints received by the commissioner (38%) came from the Dublin area, an increase from 32% in 2007, indicating the existence of a politically aware Irish language community in the city. This was higher than the percentage of complaints received from Co. Galway, which contains the country's largest Gaeltacht area and highest concentration of daily speakers of Irish outside the education system (An Coimisinéir Teanga, 2010: 36). Dublin is also the headquarters of most of the national voluntary and community Irish language organisations and is where the all-Ireland language promotion body, Foras na Gaeilge, has its principal office.

The role of Gaelic in Scotland's towns and cities has been even more limited than that of Irish in Ireland. The development of trading burghs from the twelfth century onwards coincided with the language shift in southern and eastern Scotland that brought about the displacement of Gaelic and its replacement by Scots/English. Indeed, the development of these new trading communities, with their reliance on English, Flemish, German and Scandinavian merchants and commercial links to the south and east, played a key role in triggering this language shift. Not one of the burghs established in the late Middle Ages was within the residual Gaelic area to the west of the new linguistic border, the so-called 'Highland Line' (McLeod, 2004: 15–18; Withers, 1984).

While Gaelic was for perhaps two centuries the dominant language in the Clyde Valley area, including Glasgow, which had been Cumbric (or British) speaking in the early medieval period, Scots became dominant by the thirteenth century at the latest. The modern history of Gaelic in Glasgow can be said to begin with the rapid expansion of the city in the later eighteenth century due first to trade and then to industrialisation. Gaelic-speaking migrants from the Highlands and Islands poured into the city during this era, creating the largest of Scotland's urban Gaelic communities and earning the city a reputation as 'Baile Mòr nan Gàidheal' or 'city of the Gaels'. In relative terms, however, the Gaels were always heavily outnumbered, not only by Lowland Scots but also by immigrants from Ireland (overwhelmingly English-speaking either at the time of their arrival or, by virtue of language shift, soon thereafter). Although successive waves of in-migration from the Gaelic areas helped sustain the Gaelic community in Glasgow until the late twentieth century, there has been a strong trend towards assimilation and language shift since the nineteenth century, and in recent decades out-migration to suburban areas (an important demographic shift affecting Glasgow more generally) has led to the further dissipation of the Gaelic community (Withers, 1998; Kidd, 2007).

In contrast to Ireland, there have never been any attempts to establish 'intentional' Gaelic communities in Scotland's towns or cities along the lines of that established in the Shaw's Road, although proposals are sometimes suggested, most recently in the context of Inverness (*The Scotsman*, 2008). This absence is easily explainable in terms of the relatively much smaller size of the Gaelic community in Scotland, and the extent of its marginalisation over the course of centuries.

In recent decades, Glasgow has consolidated its status as the leading urban Gaelic community in Scotland by emerging as a centre of Gaelic education, broadcasting and cultural activity, a Gaelic 'power centre' of sorts. Scotland's first Gaelic-medium primary school unit was opened in Glasgow in 1985 (the same year as the unit in Inverness), and the first dedicated Gaelic primary school and first dedicated Gaelic secondary school followed in 1999 and 2006 respectively. As the BBC has its Scottish headquarters in Glasgow, Glasgow became a centre for Gaelic television following the creation of the Gaelic Television Fund in 1990. There is also an especially lively Gaelic arts scene in Glasgow, in part because Glasgow City Council has implemented a Gaelic Arts Strategy and (since 2004) employed a Gaelic Arts Officer, in partnership with Pròiseact nan Ealan, the National Gaelic Arts Agency (GCC, 2010: 23–7). As is typical in Gaelic development discourse in Scotland (McLeod, 2002), these activities are often presented in terms of their economic benefit for the city. Research suggests that in total 'Gaelic arts and cultural activities bring £3.55 million to £4 million into the Glasgow economy and support almost 200 workers in professional and associated employment' (GCC, 2010: 29, citing Chalmers and Danson, 2009; see also Chalmers and Danson, this volume).

**Background to the Irish and Scottish Language Legislation**

Although Irish had been recognised as the first official language in Ireland's current constitution, which was adopted in 1937, and indeed in the previous constitution of 1922, the main impetus for language legislation in Ireland stemmed from the abolition in 1974 of the requirement for proficiency in Irish in order to obtain employment in the public service. The removal of this condition reduced considerably the ability of the service to deal with Irish-speaking customers. From the end of the 1970s, Irish language organisations began to agitate for a Bill of Rights, or Language Act for Irish speakers. In 1993, the state board for Irish, Bord na Gaeilge, produced guidelines for the public service on Irish language services. However, as they were not statutory, the guidelines were largely ignored. In 2002, the government published the first draft of a Bill which aimed to provide more Irish language services of a higher standard to the public (*Official Languages (Equality) Bill, 2002*). In 2003 – 66 years after the 1937 Constitution and 88 years after the 1922 Constitution – the Official Languages Act came into effect. Based on the Canadian model of language legislation, a language commissioner was appointed in February 2004. About 650 public bodies are covered by the legislation, whose obligations can be divided into three categories: obligations imposed by the statute itself (covering mainly written material, for instance annual reports, correspondence with the public, information distributed to the public), obligations based on regulations announced by the then Minister for Community, Rural and Gaeltacht Affairs (relating to signage, stationery, advertisements and oral announcements), and obligations based on language schemes, which public bodies are required to adopt if formally requested to do so. This language schemes are the mechanism by which most public services are to be provided in Irish (Section 11), in addition to the statutory obligations relating to written communication (section 9 (2) and (3) and section 10) and regulations (section 9 (1)). Each scheme lasts for three years and is then replaced by another. To date, 100 schemes have been published, covering 181 public bodies (An Coimisinéir Teanga, 2010: 27).

Although there had been earlier proposals for legislative protection for Gaelic in Scotland, notably an unsuccessful private member's bill in the Westminster Parliament in 1981, the push for a Gaelic act began in the mid–1990s, as Gaelic organisations and activists became concerned that the improved provision for the language that had been put in place from the 1980s onwards lacked a secure legal foundation. Although the government resisted these demands for several years, eventually in 2003 a Gaelic language bill was introduced in the Scottish Parliament (itself established only in 1999). Following significant amendment, the bill was enacted as the *Gaelic Language (Scotland) Act 2005* and took effect in 2006. As with Ireland's Official Languages Act, the cornerstone of the Gaelic Language Act is a language scheme system (although the operative term in the legislation is 'Gaelic language plan'). In other respects, the acts diverge significantly: under the Gaelic Language Act, an official language agency, Bòrd na Gàidhlig, plays a central role in administering the legislation; there is no precise counterpart to this agency in Ireland, while there is no Scottish counterpart to Ireland's language commissioner. The Bòrd may require any public body in Scotland to prepare a Gaelic language plan, but it is recognised both in the Act itself (section 3(5)) and in the Bòrd's guidance on the development of these plans (Bòrd na Gàidhlig, 2007) that they may vary considerably according to the extent to which those served by the body in question use the Gaelic language. This guidance identifies four principal 'corporate functions' which should be represented 'in some way' in every Gaelic language plan: 'identity', 'communications', 'publications', and 'staffing' (Bòrd na Gàidhlig, 2007: 19–27). As of 31 May 2010 only eight plans had been published, but a further 44 are expected by the end of 2013. (For more information on the background and the workings of the two Acts, see Walsh and McLeod, 2008).

A significant difference between Ireland and Scotland that bears on the language schemes/plans of local authorities (including those of Dublin and Glasgow) is the structure and mechanism of education provision. In Ireland, primary and secondary schools are controlled by the central government's Department of Education and Science, usually in partnership with the Catholic Church, while individual local authorities, such as those in County Dublin, have no involvement in running schools or organising teaching. In Scotland, in contrast, the role of central government is more circumscribed and each of the 32 local authorities has principal responsible for funding and running the public schools within their areas (Rogers and McLeod, 2006: 361–2). As such, the Gaelic language plans developed by Scottish local authorities, including Glasgow City Council, have education provision at their centre and make numerous commitments in this area, while the Irish authorities' language schemes do not address this field. As such, this article does not consider the education-related aspects of Glasgow's plan in detail, important as they are.

Although education is thus largely beyond the scope of this article, it is nevertheless important for an understanding of the wider context of the two contexts that education provision for Irish in Dublin is much greater than provision for Gaelic in Glasgow, even if Glasgow is generally recognised as the most innovative local authority in Scotland in relation to Gaelic education. With an anticipated enrolment of 345 pupils in 2010–11, Glasgow has the largest dedicated Gaelic primary school in Scotland (one of only two such dedicated schools, most Gaelic-medium provision being offered in units within English-medium schools); but there are no fewer than 31 Irish-medium primary schools in the four Dublin authority areas, with a combined enrolment of over 7,000. Similarly, the only dedicated Gaelic secondary in Scotland is located in Glasgow, with an anticipated enrolment of 200 in 2010–11, but there are eight Irish-medium secondary schools in the four Dublin authority areas, with a combined enrolment of almost 3,000. Finally, as is the norm throughout the Republic of Ireland, all 'mainstream' English-medium primary and secondary schools in the Dublin area teach Irish, and almost all pupils study it, while in the City of Glasgow Gaelic is not taught at any schools or to any pupils other than those at the dedicated Gaelic school. (There is limited learners' provision in some of the primary and secondary schools run by other local authorities in Greater Glasgow, however).

**Knowledge and Use of Irish in the Greater Dublin Area**

Due to the rapid expansion of Dublin in recent years, the 'Greater Dublin Area' is a fluid concept which may refer to the large commuter belt in the neighbouring counties of Kildare, Meath, Wicklow and even Louth and Westmeath. For the purposes of this article, the Greater Dublin Area is taken to refer to the four local authority areas which are coterminous with the area of County Dublin, with a total population at the 2006 census of 1,139,427: Dublin City Council (490,133), South Dublin (235,109), Fingal (227,012) and Dún Laoghaire-Rathdown (187,173). There are 410,669 Irish 'speakers' in the four areas, 37.2% of the population (slightly below the national average of 40.8%). The highest proportion of Irish speakers, 43.1% (79,251 people), is found in Dún Laoghaire-Rathdown while the lowest proportion, 33.8% (158,762 people) is in the Dublin City Council area . 39.4% of the population of Fingal (86,800 people), returned themselves as Irish speakers while 37.5% of the population of South Dublin (85,856 people) did so (CSO, 2007: 14). Figures for daily speakers of Irish outside the education system are considerably lower: 14,841 (1.3%) for all four authorities. Dún Laoghaire-Rathdown scores marginally higher than the rest at 1.5% (2,843 people), followed by South Dublin at 1.4% (3,204), Dublin City Council at 1.3% (6,459) and Fingal at 1% (2,335). The national average is 1.8% (CSO, 2007: 63 and 66).

**Language Schemes for Greater Dublin Area**

Presumably because of the relatively large absolute number of Irish speakers in Dublin – more than a quarter of the national total – the four Dublin authorities were among the first public bodies requested by the government to prepare draft language schemes. The schemes of Fingal, South Dublin and Dublin City Council were ratified in 2006, and Dún Laoghaire-Rathdown followed in 2007. All four authorities have been requested by the Department to prepare a second draft scheme, but at the time of writing no new schemes had yet been ratified. Although the schemes are based clearly on the Department's statutory guidelines (DCRGA, 2004), there are considerable differences between the specific commitments to enhancing service provision in Irish and in the structure of the published schemes. For instance, while the schemes of Dún Laoghaire-Rathdown, South Dublin and Fingal contain sections outlining proposed service enhancements, the commitments of Dublin City Council are more difficult to identify as they are spread throughout the text of the scheme. These structural issues make analysis difficult. Rather than describing each individual commitment, significant points of difference and similarity will be described in this section.

Two of the schemes contain introductory 'messages' of interest, apparently indicating engagement by senior management with the aims of the legislation. This is the exception rather than the norm in the Irish language schemes agreed to date. The scheme of South Dublin County Council begins with messages from the Mayor and County Manager outlining the importance accorded by the Council to the promotion of Irish. The then Mayor of South Dublin refers to the broader context of the use of Irish in the area: 'In a County which supports a vibrant Irish speaking public the Irish language Scheme should be very welcome and a means to develop and support Irish further in the County' (SDCC, 2006: 2). According to the County Manager: 'We have a significant number of naíonraí, Irish speaking pre schools, and also both primary and secondary schools ... South Dublin County Council see this Language Scheme as an opportunity to support all the ground work which has been done and to strengthen the growth of the language in this County' (SDCC, 2006: 3). Another illustration of greater engagement with the spirit of the legislation is the decision of South Dublin Council to include photographs of recent local Irish-language events (including a seminar on the implications of the legislation) in the scheme itself. The County Manager of Dún Laoghaire-Rathdown County Council, himself an Irish speaker, also refers to the broader context in his introduction: 'I hope the measures the Council are proposing to implement the Scheme will directly benefit the County's Irish language speaking community, students of Irish, and the growing number being educated through Irish in the County. I also hope the measures will raise the awareness of Irish, help create and sustain a positive attitude towards the language generally and contribute to its development and promotion in Dún Laoghaire-Rathdown' (DLRCC, 2007: 4). In contrast, there is no such introductory message in the schemes of Fingal Local Authorities and Dublin City Council, although the latter had adopted a non-statutory 'Action Plan for the Irish Language 1999/2003' (DCC, 2006: 4), which could be interpreted as an indication of a certain level of engagement with Irish before there was a statutory requirement to do so.

There are considerable differences between the commitments made in the schemes to enhancing written communication in Irish. Fingal Local Authorities commit to making all application forms, information leaflets and booklets available bilingually, inside the one cover, by the end of the scheme. It will ensure, somewhat vaguely, that the 'website layout will be bilingual, both in terms of navigation and content' (FLA, 2006: 13) and that all press releases will be released bilingually. Dublin City Council makes the same commitments about forms and leaflets, but is much more limited in its pledges regarding press releases (25% to be bilingual) and its websites (the content of six dedicated Irish language 'hub' pages to be increased by 100%) (DCC, 2006: 10). Dún Laoghaire-Rathdown Council makes similar commitments regarding forms and leaflets. It also commits to producing 25% of press releases bilingually and undertakes to develop an Irish-language version of 'all static content' of its website. It makes an additional commitment not made by other authorities: all invoices, bills and parking tickets are to be issued in Irish and English and at least 15% of the content of its two free newspapers is to be published in Irish (DLRCC, 2007: 10–11). South Dublin Council makes more limited commitments to written communication in Irish: while all application forms are to be made available bilingually, only an Irish summary will be provided of other new publications, information leaflets and posters and only press releases directly relating to Irish will be translated. The commitments to a bilingual website are similarly limited: a webpage of Irish language links will be developed and the homepage and description of each department will be provided bilingually (SDCC, 2006: 21).

As identified in an analysis of schemes from 2004 to 2006 (Walsh and McLeod, 2008), commitments to enhancing oral communication are weak in all four Dublin schemes. Another difficulty is that such already weak commitments are based entirely on staff training rather than on recruitment of Irish speakers. The issue of recruitment versus training is discussed below. Each scheme contains a commitment that receptionists and telephonists will be able to give the name of the Council in Irish (not that they will actively do so as a general practice) and in the case of Dún Laoghaire, South Dublin and Fingal, that such staff will be familiar with basic Irish greetings (again, not that they will routinely use them when greeting members of the public). Dublin City Council cannot commit to more than '50% of administrative reception staff/call centre staff' becoming familiar with the basic greetings in Irish (DCC, 2006: 11). Indeed, the commitments of Dublin City Council to oral communication are arguably the weakest of any of the four schemes. Given their high levels of interaction with the public, the Council says that it will prioritise its Customer Service Centre, the Motor Tax Offices and Dublin City Public Libraries for improvement of oral communication in Irish. However, the commitments in these departments are limited to offering staff language training and language awareness courses and there are no targets for achieving a basic threshold of staff who could provide a fully bilingual service by 2009, the expiry date of the scheme (DCC, 2006: 22). The other Councils also prioritise certain specific departments and make more concrete commitments to bilingual oral communication. For instance, over the course of two schemes (i.e. by 2013), Dún Laoghaire-Rathdown Council commits to provide all counter services bilingually. By the end of the first scheme, it commits to a 'fully bilingual counter service' in five departments (DLRCC, 2007: 12). South Dublin Council pledges that 'at least one member of the Customer Care staff and one person in each library' will be able to offer a bilingual service (SDCC, 2006: 23) while Fingal Local Authorities commit to ensuring that at least one staff member in each department as well as in each library will be capable of providing an Irish language service (FLA, 2006: 11). Despite these significant pledges, others are vague and arguably unattainable. For instance, Dún Laoghaire-Rathdown Council's scheme states that 'Council staff will be encouraged to use Irish' (DLRCC, 2007: 12). It is not stated how such encouragement would be given or with whom staff would be expected to use Irish.

All four schemes place a strong emphasis on additional training for staff, but are largely silent on the question of recruitment. South Dublin Council pledges to offer Irish language training and to include language awareness as part of induction and customer service training courses (SDCC, 2007: 25). A similar commitment is made by Dublin City Council (DCC, 2006: 22–3). South Dublin Council also promises to have regard for proficiency in Irish in the context of its 'staff mobility policies' (SDCC, 2006: 23). Fingal County Council will ascertain which staff have reasonable or good Irish language skills and offer them further language training during office hours (FLA, 2006: 11). Dún Laoghaire-Rathdown Council will provide '[i]ntensive Irish language training … to interested Council staff and councillors' (DLRCC, 2007: 11), a measure which will 'improve the provision of services through Irish' (12). Conversely, Dún Laoghaire-Rathdown Council is the sole public body in Dublin, and one of the few anywhere in Ireland, to mention the possibility of recruiting bilingual staff, although in qualified terms: 'If necessary consideration will be given to recruiting suitably qualified staff who are competent to conduct business through the medium of Irish' (12). As argued previously (Walsh and McLeod, 2008), international experience indicates that language training for non-Irish speakers is a costly and inefficient way of providing services in Irish, compared to a policy of recruiting bilingual staff to certain key jobs. Research indicates that fluent and native speakers of Irish are unlikely to choose to conduct their business in Irish with a public official if they sense language anxiety on the official's part (Ó Riagáin, 1992; Ó Cinnéide and Ní Chonghaile, 1996).

There are strong similarities in the sections of the schemes dedicated to implementation, monitoring and publicity. All four schemes nominate a senior staff member, usually in Corporate Services, as being responsible for overall implementation. Day-to-day implementation is the responsibility of the Irish Language Officer. Both Dublin City Council (DCC, 2006: 24) and Fingal County Council (FLA, 2006: 16) will monitor use of Irish language services. All four authorities will inform 'appropriate agencies' (for instance DCC, 2006: 24) that the scheme has been agreed, as well as undertaking other limited publicity measures.

Some other aspects of the schemes are also worthy of comment:

- All four local authorities have employed Irish Language Officers to co-ordinate Irish language services.
- Parts of the Irish version of the Fingal scheme are difficult to understand and bear the hallmarks of a poor translation. This could be an additional barrier to update of services in Irish.
- Dún Laoghaire-Rathdown Council has pledged to correct all incorrect Irish road names and street signage during the period of its scheme (DLRCC, 2007: 13). South Dublin Council makes the same commitment (SDCC, 2007: 25). It also pledges that 'appropriate translations' are to be provided for the names of all new housing developments in South Dublin and that both English and Irish versions are to be displayed on road nameplates (SDCC, 2007: 17, 19). No such commitments are made by the other two Dublin authorities. A steady stream of complaints about incorrect Irish on road signs is received by the language commissioner each year (e.g. An Coimisinéir Teanga, 2009 and 2010). Although initially dealt with on an informal basis, recent changes to interpretation provisions have empowered the commissioner's office to deal with such complaints in a more formal, statutory manner and, as a result to ensure that local authorities comply with the correct versions of Irish place names on road signs (Ó Cuirreáin, 2010, p.c.).

- Dún Laoghaire-Rathdown Council is the only Dublin local authority to make commitments in relation to the use of Irish in meetings of the council itself. It pledges that a 'simultaneous Irish / English translation service will continue to be provided at the monthly Council meeting' (DLRCC, 2007: 13). However no Dublin authority makes commitments in relation to the use of Irish in meetings with the public.

### Knowledge and Use of Gaelic in Glasgow

The 2001 census revealed a total of 5,730 Gaelic speakers in Glasgow out of a total population of 578,000, or almost exactly 1% (GCC, 2010: 21). In no ward within the city did even 5% of the population have even 'some' knowledge of Gaelic (GCC, 2010: 36–7). A further 3,414 people could understand spoken Gaelic but not speak, read or write it, 859 people could read and/or write Gaelic but not speak it, and 31 had other combinations of skills, for a total of 10,034, 1.7% of the overall population (GCC, 2010: 21). These figures for speaking and other Gaelic abilities are slightly below the corresponding national figures of 1.2% and 1.8%. As in Dublin, though, the total number of speakers is important in absolute terms. The 5,730 Gaelic speakers in Glasgow constitute almost 10% of the national total.

As noted above, Glasgow city is part of a wider metropolitan area, classified more narrowly as the Greater Glasgow Settlement Area, which encompasses 40 towns surrounding the city, and the larger Glasgow City Region, which comprises the local authorities of East Dunbartonshire, East Renfrewshire, Glasgow, Inverclyde, North Lanarkshire, Renfrewshire, South Lanarkshire and West Dunbartonshire. This region has a combined population of 1.75 million, 11,209 of whom could speak Gaelic and 9,308 of whom had other Gaelic skills, for a total of 20,527 (22% of the national population). North Lanarkshire and South Lanarkshire (the two largest authorities in the region, other than Glasgow itself) are currently preparing Gaelic language plans and the other authorities can be expected to follow suit in the coming years. When these other schemes are in place, it will be possible to conduct a broader 'regional' evaluation comparable to that done for Dublin here.

Unlike the Irish census, the Scottish census does not ask any questions concerning language use, as opposed to (declared) language ability. Nor is there other sociolinguistic data available concerning the level of Gaelic use within Glasgow. In the absent of robust data, the prevailing hypothesis, which is backed up by a small-scale study of Gaelic speakers in Edinburgh (McLeod, 2005), is that compared to speakers in 'traditional' Gaelic communities with a high density of speakers, Gaelic speakers in urban Scotland tend to use the language relatively infrequently, with a relatively small number of interlocutors and within very loose social networks. Even so, given that so few Scots acquire any Gaelic via the Scottish school system, the gap between the overall number of speakers indicated by the Census and the number of active speakers is unlikely to be as great as in Ireland.

### Gaelic Language Plan for Glasgow

Glasgow's Gaelic Language Plan was published in April 2010 and is thus still in its earliest stage of implementation. The presentation here tracks the analysis of the Dublin plans above, but it should always be borne in mind how much more marginal Gaelic is in Scotland (and Glasgow) compared to Irish in Ireland (and Dublin). Thus, a commitment on the part of Glasgow Council that is formally comparable to an undertaking by one of the Dublin authorities arguably is much more difficult to achieve and represents a relatively more radical step. In addition, while public bodies in Ireland have paid at least some attention to Irish for decades (even if a culture of tokenism has developed), Scottish bodies outside the 'traditional' Gaelic areas have had almost no engagement with Gaelic up to now in relation to their corporate functions or their provision of public services, so that Glasgow's new language plan takes the organisation into previously uncharted territory.

Even considering this context, Glasgow's plan is clearly unambitious in some important respects. Even more than is the case with the Dublin plans, almost nothing is said about providing oral services of any kind through the medium of Gaelic, although oral communication is arguably more important than written communication in terms of language revitalisation (Walsh and McLeod, 2008: 31–2). The plan provides that a Gaelic speaker will be recruited for the council's Shared Service Centre (GCC, 2010: 45), and presumably members of the public wishing to use Gaelic are to be directed to this staff member, but nothing is said about oral service provision beyond this initial point of contact. Administrative staff in the Education Services section whose work involves supporting Gaelic-medium Education are to 'learn key phrases and appropriate use' (GCC, 2010: 45), but this is much less than a commitment to facilitating substantive interaction with the public through the medium of Gaelic, even in this Gaelic-specific area of the council's operations.

In relation to written material, the plan's commitments are tightly circumscribed, and generally address only the small range of topics relating specifically to Gaelic language and culture rather than the Council's wider functions. Rather than making all its forms available in bilingual format, the council commits itself only to 'consider introducing Gaelic in selected forms' and to 'consider whether to introduce' 'translations of general forms [that may] become available through Bòrd na Gàidhlig or other councils' (GCC, 2010: 47). In relation to publications, the council promises simply to 'develop guidelines for publications in Gaelic where the subject matter relates to Gaelic issues, including language, education or culture and [to] produce a leaflet in Gaelic on the Council's services' (GCC, 2010: 49). The council's public magazine and staff magazine will also be used 'to promote Gaelic related information through bi-lingual articles' (GCC, 2010: 49). Media releases will be issued bilingually only 'when the subject matter relates to Gaelic language, education or culture' (GCC, 2010: 49).

Commitments in relation to the website are also distinctly limited. The council states that it 'will continue to expand Gaelic-related information on our website, making it accessible from one location' and to 'identify key corporate information which could be made available in Gaelic eg guidelines on access to information, Freedom of Information; Data Protection; Council Tax payment, refuse collection etc' (GCC, 2010: 51). This second commitment is much more limited than Dún Laoghaire-Rathdown Council's proposal to make all static content on its website available bilingually.

In relation to training, the Council plans both Gaelic-awareness classes and language classes. In terms of language training, the council plans to 'pilot two courses for staff to learn Gaelic mainly using work time … initially targeting those with some involvement with Gaelic' (GCC, 2010: 53), although it does not specify to what extent such courses might be 'rolled out' more widely following the pilot. It also makes more general commitments, both of them somewhat vague, although clearly indicating goodwill towards the language: to 'enable staff who already speak Gaelic to develop their competencies, including literacy' and to 'encourage staff to use Gaelic in the workplace and make this clear in staff publicity on the Plan' (GCC, 2010: 53).

In contrast, Glasgow's plan addresses the issue of recruitment more directly than any of the Dublin plans. The plan states that '[w]e will formalise Council policy that where a certain level of Gaelic skills is necessary for a post, this will be specified during the recruitment process and that such job interviews will be conducted in English and Gaelic', and that 'guidelines will be drafted for the designation of Gaelic posts' (GCC, 2010: 55). The number and range of these Gaelic posts is not made clear, however. The plan also makes a specific commitment to recruit a Gaelic speaker for the Council's 'Shared Service Centre' and 'a Gaelic Development Officer with responsibility for promoting, implementing and monitoring the Gaelic Language Plan' (GCC, 2010: 45, 55).

Other useful commitments in Glasgow's plan involve the use of Gaelic in public meetings and the careful monitoring of the plan's implementation. The plan states that 'we will formalise our procedures for the use of Gaelic in public meetings where there is reasonable demand or where the subject matter is of particular interest to Gaelic speakers' (GCC, 2010: 47). While this is much narrower than a systematic offer of interpretation services at all public meetings organised by the Council, it seems a reasonable approach bearing in mind that only 1% of Glasgow residents can speak Gaelic. In contrast, none of the Dublin authorities' schemes address the issue of Irish in the context of public meetings, though arguably the exclusion of education from their remit removes one of the principal contexts that might be 'of particular interest' to Irish speakers.

In terms of monitoring, the council commits itself to setting up a 'Gaelic Officers' Group within the Council which will meet quarterly to co-ordinate actions and oversee and evaluate progress on' the plan, with monitoring carried out through discussions at this Gaelic Officers' Group; liaison with the Executive Committee Member with responsibility for Gaelic; reports to the Corporate Management Team; reports to each meeting of the Gaelic Community Forum; annual reports to Bòrd na Gàidhlig; surveys, questionnaires, course evaluations, as appropriate; external evaluations, if appropriate; and an overall progress report for Plan period to the Gaelic Community Forum (GCC, 2010: 89). As is the norm with Gaelic language plans, a named senior official (in the Chief Executive's Office) is designated as having 'operational responsibility for overseeing the preparation, delivery and monitoring' of the Plan, and a second officer (a Corporate Policy Manager) is designated as having responsibility for the 'day-to-day operation of the Plan' (GCC, 2010: 91).

The scope of Gaelic language plans is somewhat wider than that of Irish language schemes because they also address certain matters which are directly regulated by the Official Languages Act 2003 and so do not fall within the scope of language schemes. As such, none of the Dublin plans deals with oral announcements, stationery, signage or advertisements (which are controlled by section 9(1) of the Act and the regulations issued thereunder) or with correspondence with the public in Irish (which is controlled by sections 9(2) and (3) of the Act), while these matters are addressed to some extent in Glasgow's plan, which tracks the guidance issued by Bòrd na Gàidhlig for the development of Gaelic language plans (Bòrd na Gàidhlig, 2007). For example, Glasgow states that it 'will increase the use of Gaelic in external and entrance signage ...

in city centre offices and introduce it as we upgrade or replace signs in other building[s]'; it also promises that 'when correspondence is received in Gaelic, a reply will be sent in Gaelic', but does not include the conventional guarantee that this will be done in the same time frame applicable to correspondence in English (GCC, 2010: 43, 45). The Dublin authorities also have an express statutory obligation (under section 10 of the Official Languages Act) to publish certain key documents in both Irish and English, including their annual reports, financial statements and, importantly, 'any document setting out public policy proposals'. Given that it proposes to produce bilingual publications only 'where the subject matter relates to Gaelic issues', as explained above, it is very unlikely that Glasgow will produce any of these important documents bilingually.

As noted above, Glasgow's plan also makes a number of undertakings beyond its core commitments in relation to service provision. Tracking Bòrd na Gàidhlig's guidance on the development of plans, these include measures relating to language acquisition, language use and language status. While clearly important in terms of the broader issue of language revitalisation in Glasgow, these aspects of the plan are not considered in detail here as the counterpart Dublin schemes do not address these issues in the same way. (The Dublin schemes are thus much shorter than Glasgow's plan, averaging 26 pages in length as against Glasgow's 98 pages).

Although its commitments in terms of service provision are, for the most part, limited and qualified, the introductory sections to Glasgow's plan are rhetorically much more forceful than any of the Dublin plans. This enthusiastic language, and the considerable media attention that the plan attracted when it was launched in March 2010, reflect the fact that Glasgow was the first local authority outside the Highlands and Islands to produce a Gaelic plan, and that the council is widely perceived as having been proactive and innovative in promoting the language in recent years.

The summary of the plan states that:

> Glasgow City Council recognises that Gaelic is an integral part of Scotland's heritage, national identity and cultural life. We are committed to the objectives set out in the National Plan for Gaelic and are ready to play our part in helping ensure that Gaelic has a sustainable future in Scotland (GCC, 2010: 13).

The introduction then sets out the Council's 'vision for Gaelic':

> We have a vision for Gaelic in our city. By 2020, the place of Gaelic in a thriving, multicultural Glasgow will be obvious to all. We'll see it around us – in our buildings, on our streets, in our shops; we'll hear it in conversations, in our schools and in the media; we'll enjoy it in all the arts, especially music, dance and theatre.

> By 2020, we'll hear Gaelic being spoken by our young people in Buchanan Street, without them feeling self-conscious about it, and people will recognise the language as Gaelic (GCC, 2010: 7).

Despite these rhetorical and practical expressions of support on the part of the council, the development of the Gaelic language plan has encountered a certain amount of resistance in the city. In the course of the public consultation on the draft plan, 'one in five respondents disagreed with the Council supporting Gaelic, with 15% strongly disagreeing that it is important for the Council to promote Gaelic. Some people found nothing at all useful in the Plan. Indeed, they were totally opposed to any effort or money being spent on promoting Gaelic, maintaining that it is of little relevance to most Glaswegians' (GCC, 2010: 33; GCC, 2009, paragraphs 17 and 19). The launch of the plan in April 2010 also attracted a fair amount of hostile comment in the media. Perhaps the most aggressive comment came from Ian Black, author of several popular humour books, including several on 'The Patter', or Glasgow dialect. Purporting to quote a play, Black said that:

> 'Gaelic is shite.' ... I don't mean the language or the culture, all 58,000 (last census) of its speakers are welcome to it, but what I object to is Glasgow City Council deciding, without asking me, to make me speak and read it. ... What precisely is the point of this exercise? Anybody who wants to learn Gaelic is free to do so. There are books, radio and television programmes (paid for with our money), night classes and even schools. (ditto)
>
> Arthur Cormack [chair of Bòrd na Gàidhlig] says Glasgow is 'often known as Baile Mòr nan Gàidheal – the Big City of the Gaels'. Precisely where is it known as this? I've been on this planet for quite a lot of years and I have never heard or read this phrase before last week. And I won't be using it again. ('Gaelic? Tapadh leat, but no thanks'. *Sunday Herald*, 11 April 2010).

Such expressions of hostility make clear the marginal and contested status of Gaelic in Glasgow, and the extent of the challenge that language revitalisation involves in such a context.

**Conclusion**

There are considerable differences, both in structure and content, between the Dublin schemes, although all four were prepared around the same time. These differences make it difficult to assess which scheme is the strongest in terms of Irish-language service provision. Although Dún Laoghaire-Rathdown and South Dublin Councils include personal statements from the Mayor or County Managers (possibly indicating a superior awareness of aims of the legislation), their commitments to improving written communication, in terms of press releases and websites, are much more limited than those of Fingal Local Authorities. Although Fingal Local Authorities commit to translating all press releases and maintaining a fully bilingual website, there are problems with the standard of some of the written Irish both in their scheme and (at the time of writing) on their website. Dún Laoghaire-Rathdown goes further than any of the other councils in pledging a fully bilingual oral service in five departments by the end of its second scheme. Given the importance of oral communication in the case of a language such as Irish where literacy levels are low, this is a significant commitment. Therefore, on balance, the scheme of Dún Laoghaire-Rathdown County Council makes the strongest commitments to enhancing service provision in Irish. Dublin City Council's scheme is arguably the weakest, as the commitments are vague and concrete targets largely absent.

The uneven service provision in four schemes serving different parts of the same metropolitan area raises questions about the approach adopted by the Department of Community, Rural and Gaeltacht Affairs when the schemes were being evaluated and approved between 2005 and 2007. In the interest of consistency, there is a strong case for similar targets across the domains of oral communication, written communication, training and recruitment being requested of local authorities operating in the same large urban areas. Given that none of the four public bodies employs a large number of Irish speakers, it is unclear why the Department should sign off on a commitment to providing fully bilingual counter service in five departments in Dún Laoghaire-Rathdown while accepting vastly inferior commitments from other, neighbouring local authorities (in particular those of Dublin City Council). The same principle applies to the varying percentages of website and press releases to be provided in Irish. Given that the schemes were prepared around the same time, there is also a strong case for co-ordination between the four public bodies. Had the four Dublin authorities been requested by the Department to pool their efforts in preparing draft schemes, a more consistent Irish language service could have been achieved for the public. The very uneven service commitments again highlight a key weakness of the system of language schemes. It is impossible for an Irish speaker seeking a service in Irish to know what to expect from a public body without studying its scheme in advance, a cumbersome and unattractive additional requirement for someone coping with the normal demands of life.

Although there are many parallels between Glasgow's plan and the four Dublin schemes in terms of the authorities' specific plans and commitments, it is difficult to make direct comparisons between the two cases, for several reasons. Glasgow City Council is the only one of the eight local authorities in the Glasgow region to have agreed a plan so far, and it will be a number of years before the process is complete and a systematic evaluation becomes possible. More importantly, it is not easy to determine the applicable criteria for comparison, given that Gaelic is so much more marginalised in Scotland than Irish is in Ireland and that the proportion of Scots having any knowledge of Gaelic is so much lower. It is obvious that there is significant support, indeed enthusiasm, for Gaelic on the part of Glasgow City Council, and this creates the potential for significant growth and development, even if, in some objective sense, the formal commitments in its first Gaelic plan are fairly minimal. It is important to remember that in both Ireland and Scotland it is intended that there will be incremental improvement and expansion from one language scheme/plan to the next. The extent to which progress is apparent in the second round of the Dublin-area schemes will be an important indicator for the future.

Finally, in methodological terms, a comprehensive investigation of the two cases would require systematic fieldwork and not merely a textual analysis of the plans themselves. Such fieldwork would involve assessing both the views and experiences of the Irish/Gaelic communities served by the bodies in question (what might be labelled the 'consumer' perspective) and of the bodies themselves, looking at the dynamics of the actual implementation of the schemes/plans and the challenges and obstacles encountered. This research could tease out often-conflicting ideologies in relation to Irish and Gaelic and assess how such beliefs may influence the provision and use of services in the minoritised languages. As Glasgow's plan was approved only in February 2010, implementation is still only in its initial phase and fieldwork would clearly be premature. In the Dublin case, the transition from the first to the second plans represents an important juncture and an excellent opportunity for taking stock.

## Acknowledgements

The authors would like to thank Marion Beaton and Domhnall Uilleam MacIlleMhoire of Bòrd na Gàidhlig, Thomas Owen Clancy (University of Glasgow) and Seán Ó Cuirréain, An Coimisinéir Teanga, for their help in connection with the preparation of this article.

## References

An Coimisinéir Teanga. 2009. *Tuarascáil Bhliantúil/Annual Report 2008*. An Spidéal: Oifig an Choimisinéara Teanga.
An Coimisinéir Teanga. 2010. *Tuarascáil Bhliantúil/Annual Report 2009*. An Spidéal: Oifig an Choimisinéara Teanga.
Armstrong, T. 2009. *Stèidheachadh Ghnàthan-Cànain Ùra: Cuairteachadh Ideòlais-Chànain ann an Trì Gaeltachtaí Nua*. Unpublished PhD thesis, Sabhal Mòr Ostaig, UHI Millennium Institute.
Baile, 2007. 'Gaeltachtaí Úra' [online]. Available at: http://www.bailegaelach.com/gaeltachtai/gaeltachtai.html (read 28 May 2010).
Bòrd na Gàidhlig. 2007. *Stiùireadh air Deasachadh Phlanaichean Gàidhlig/Guidance on the Development of Gaelic Language Plans*. Inverness: Bòrd na Gàidhlig.
Census Statistics Office. 2007. *Census 2006, Volume 9: The Irish Language* [Online]. Available at: http://www.cso.ie/census/census2006results/volume_9/volume_9_irish_language_entire_volume.pdf (read 14 April 2010).
Chalmers, D. and Danson, M. 2009. *The Economic Impact of Gaelic Arts and Culture Within Glasgow*. Glasgow: Glasgow Caledonian University.
de Brun, F. ed., 2006. *Belfast and the Irish Language*. Dublin: Four Courts Press.
Department of Community, Rural and Gaeltacht Affairs 2004. *Treoirlínte faoi Alt 12 d'Acht na dTeangacha Oifigiúla 2003/Guidelines under Section 12 of the Official Languages Act 2003*. Dublin: DCRGA.
Dublin City Council. 2006. *Scheme 2006–2009 under Section 11, Official Languages Act 2003*. Dublin: Dublin City Council.
Dún Laoghaire-Rathdown County Council. 2007. *Irish Scheme 2007–2010 under Section 11 of the Official Languages Act, 2003*. Dún Laoghaire: Dún Laoghaire-Rathdown County Council.
Edwards, J. 2010. *Minority Languages and Group Identity: Cases and Categories*. Amsterdam: John Benjamins.
Fingal Local Authorities. 2006. *Fingal Local Authorities Scheme 2006–2009 under Section 11 of the Official Languages Act 2003*. Swords: Fingal County Council.
General Record Office for Scotland. 2005. *Scotland's Census 2001: Gaelic Report*. Edinburgh. General Record Office for Scotland.
Glasgow City Council. 2009. *Draft Gaelic Language Plan 2009 to 2012: Public Consultation exercise September to December 2008*. Glasgow: Glasgow City Council.
Glasgow City Council. 2010. *Gaelic Language Plan 2009 to 2012*. Glasgow: Glasgow City Council.
Kidd, S. ed. 2007. *Glasgow: Baile Mòr nan Gàidheal / City of the Gaels*. Glasgow: Department of Celtic, University of Glasgow.

Mac Aongusa, B. 2006. 'Pobal Gaeilge Dheisceart Chontae Átha Cliath'. In: Ó Murchú 2006, 71–80.
Mac Mathúna, L. 1987. 'Pobal Gaeilge Bhaile Átha Cliath: Oidhrí agus ceannródaithe'. *Oidhrí agus Ceannródaithe: Pobal na Gaeilge*. Dublin: Coiscéim, 52–71.
McCloskey, J. 2001. *Guthanna in Éag: An Mairfidh an Ghaeilge Beo? / Voices Silenced: Has Irish a Future?* Dublin: Cois Life.
McLeod, W. 2002. 'Language Planning as Regional Development? The Growth of the Gaelic Economy', *Scottish Affairs* 38: 51–72.
McLeod, W. 2004. *Divided Gaels: Gaelic Cultural Identities in Scotland and Ireland c. 1200–c.1650*. Oxford: Oxford University Press.
McLeod, W. ed. 2005. *Gàidhlig ann an Dùn Èideann: Cleachdadh agus Beachdan / Gaelic in Edinburgh: Usage and Attitudes*. Edinburgh: Celtic and Scottish Studies, University of Edinburgh.
McLeod, W. 2007. *Gàidhealtachdan Ùra: Leasachadh na Gàidhlig agus na Gaeilge sa Bhaile Mhòr/Nua-Ghaeltachtaí: Cur Chun Cinn na Gàidhlig agus na Gaeilge sa Chathair*. Edinburgh: Celtic and Scottish Studies, University of Edinburgh.
McManus, R. 1996. 'Public Utility Societies, Dublin Corporation and the Development of Dublin, 1920–1940'. *Irish Geography* 29.1: 27–37.
McManus, R. 2002. *Dublin, 1910–1940: Shaping the City and Suburbs*. Dublin: Four Courts Press.
Mac Póilín, A. 2007. 'Nua-Ghaeltacht Phobal Feirste: ceachtanna le foghlaim?' In: McLeod 2007, 31–60.
Maguire. G. 1991. *Our Own Language: An Irish Initiative*. Clevedon: Multilingual Matters.
Nig Uidhir, G. [Maguire], 2006. 'The Shaw's Road Urban Gaeltacht: Role and Impact'. In: de Brún 2006, 136–46.
Ó hAilín, P. 2006. 'Muintir Chrónáin'. In: Ó Murchú 2006, 59–70.
Ó Cuirreáin, S. 2010. Personal communication with Seán Ó Cuirreáin, An Coimisinéir Teanga, 5 July.
Ó Liatháin, C. 2010. 'An Irishman's Diary'. *The Irish Times*. 8 March. Available at: http://www.irishtimes.com/newspaper/opinion/2010/0308/1224265794110.html
Ó Murchú, H. and H. Ó Murchú. 1999. *An Ghaeilge: a hAghaidh Roimpi/Irish: Facing the Future*. Dublin: EBLUL.
Ó Murchú, H. ed. 2006. *Léargais: Pobail na Gaeilge 2006*. Dublin: Glór na nGael.
Ó Murchú, H. 2007. 'Cur chun cinn na Gàidhlig agus na Gaeilge sa Chathair'. In: McLeod 2007, 5–8.
Rogers, V. and W. McLeod. 2006. 'Autochthonous Minority Languages in Public-Sector Primary Education: Bilingual Policies and Politics in Brittany and Scotland'. *Linguistics and Education* 17: 347–73.
*The Scotsman*, 2008. 'Plan for all-Gaelic-speaking communities'. 1 November.
South Dublin County Council, 2006. *Irish Language Scheme*. Tallaght: South Dublin County Council.
*Sunday Herald*, 2010. 'Argument of the week: Should the Patter city become the home of the Gaels?' 11 April.
Walsh, C. 2010. Personal communication with Clare Walsh, officer, Gaelscoileanna, 28 May.
Walsh, J. and McLeod, W. 2008. 'An overcoat wrapped around an invisible man? Language Legislation and Language Revitalisation in Ireland and Scotland'. *Language Policy* 7: 21–46.

Withers, C.W.J. 1984. *Gaelic in Scotland, 1698–1981: The Geographical History of a Language*. Edinburgh: John Donald.

Withers, C.W.J. 1998. *Urban Highlanders: Highland-Lowland Migration and Urban Gaelic Culture, 1700–1900*. East Linton: Tuckwell.

Wmffre, I. 2002. 'Urban Celtic subcultures 1700–1850'. In eds. Esser R. and T. Fuchs. *Kulturmetropolen – Metropolenkultur: Die Stadt als Kommunikationsraum in 18. Jahrhundert*, 29–58. Berlin: BWV.

# The Economic Impact of Gaelic Arts and Culture in Glasgow

*Douglas Chalmers and Mike Danson*

### The Continuing Story of Glasgow: City of the Gàidheal

> Historically, Glasgow and the Gaels are inextricably linked and if anywhere there is a potential to grow audiences for Gaelic art and culture it is here.
>
> *Glasgow Grows Audiences* (2007)

> Gaelic is Scotland's oldest living indigenous culture and a definitive part of Scotland's cultural identity ... The SAC believes that the Gaelic arts play an essential roll in developing the Gaelic language and culture as part of the mainstream arts and cultural diversity of Scotland and have an important international dimension.
>
> *Scottish Arts Council Gaelic Arts Policy* (2003)

### Introduction

The quote from the *Scottish Arts Council Gaelic Arts Policy* above demonstrates that, in the twenty-first century, Gaelic has been accepted as a critical and essential element of the Scottish nation: how it sees and portrays itself and how it is perceived by the wider world.

In recent years, the importance of Gaelic arts and culture has been recognised more explicitly in terms of identity and society but also as a significant part of the economy. More generally, jobs, incomes and economic impacts of the cultural and creative industries have been promoted as instruments for regeneration across old industrial areas and traditional industries alike, but such promotions have always been rooted in and have built upon pre-existing community legacies and attachments.

This chapter explores the contribution of Scottish Gaelic to the economy of Glasgow in the modern world. It embeds this examination within the historical context of a Gaelic city which, increasingly over the last two decades, has been rediscovering its origins and associations.

The early introduction of both a Gaelic Language Plan and a Gaelic Arts Strategy for Glasgow is described to confirm the city's new commitment to Gaelic. By recognising its Gaelic heritage and the contemporary and dynamic role for Gaelic arts and culture, Glasgow has attracted a significant share of the national activity evolving around the language. It is the generation of quality employment and education in the city which is outlined here.

The economic impacts of the sector are discussed and analysed in the penultimate section, based on interviews and questionnaires across the key players in Gaelic arts and culture in Glasgow. The conclusion pulls together the argument that, by giving an appropriate role to the cultural industries and heritage of Glasgow as the City of the Gàidheal, there are important and wide positive impacts across communities within the locality and beyond.

## Towards Understanding the Impact

Much of the literature, and indeed chapters in this and similar volumes, would not consider as a priority the economic impacts of the retention of language or the promotion of cultural activities in terms of their employment or income effects; in fact many would deem them unnecessary if not unworthy concerns. However, as well as adding to the richness and diversity of the cultural and artistic environment, most cities and regions now have an explicit recognition of the wider economic and social benefits to communities of investment and support for such activities. Importantly for this chapter, there has been increasing interest in the whole question of language, culture and diversity *as a motor for economic change* through its impact on 'human capital'.[1] This links to a growing prominence given to the importance of 'intangibles' in economic development by local development agencies.[2] Cities at the heart of old industrial areas which have suffered closures and redundancies have often pursued strategic attempts to regenerate and revive through the service sectors, including tourism, leisure and other creative and cultural industries. A significant driver in such developments has been a perceived need to re-imagineer the city or region, changing the external perception of the locality from what was to a new vision. This is captured in the title of a forthcoming volume 'Cultural Political Economy of Small Cities' (Lorentzen and van Heur, 2011), highlighting the strategic interest amongst regeneration policymakers and practitioners in the role of the cultural and creative industries in the economic development of twenty-first century societies. Typically, though, much of the attention in the literature has been on towns, villages and rural areas, with their cultural proximity to unique national and regional heritage and traditions privileged over metropolitan claims (Burnett and Danson, 2004), and that edited volume similarly focuses on smaller towns and communities. Now, consistent with this approach although previous work has explored the importance of Gaelic arts and culture to particular economies in the north and west of Scotland (Chalmers, 2003), there has been an increasing realisation in the field of evaluation that there is a need to describe and analyse the impact of the moves within the Central Belt of Scotland, and Glasgow in particular, to promote the language and its derivatives. Further, as we have argued previously (Chalmers and Danson, 2006), the tools for analysis and examination in both sets of environments can be common and so this chapter reports on Gaelic arts and culture in the context of the city of Glasgow applying techniques and models that have been successfully used in the Gàidhealtachd.

In particular, this study initially reviewed census and other data regarding the current situation of Gaelic speakers and learners within the Glasgow market area. All known Gaelic organisations within Glasgow then were surveyed to ascertain the extent of their activities, expenditures and employment numbers associated with Gaelic, including the cultural and artistic aspects of their activities. Complementing this, a review was undertaken of the existing secondary research on the impacts of the arts in Glasgow. All these data on direct employment and monetary effects were analysed and multiplier and other dynamic effects identified to allow a robust estimation of the overall economic impacts within the Glasgow area.

---

[1] "People and ideas are increasingly the source of competitive advantage", Scottish Office (1997).
[2] For instance, Scottish Enterprise has based its current strategy on the 'emerging knowledge economy', where economic value is found more in the intangibles, like new ideas, software, services and relationships, and less in the tangibles like physical products, tonnes of steel or acres of land', Scottish Enterprise (1999).

## Glasgow – City of the Gàidheal: A Short Historical Perspective

To understand the current interplay between Glasgow and today's Gaelic community, a short historical perspective may be useful.

Although it is likely that Glasgow and its surrounding areas were predominantly Gaelic speaking up to the late eleventh and early twelfth centuries, Gaelic was superseded as the everyday speech in central Scotland between 1157 and 1400 (MacKinnon, 1991: 30). General political developments, changes in the Scottish crown, the last Gaelic speaking monarch being James IV (1488–1513), and later hostility towards the perceived Catholicism of the highland Gaels led to a redefinition of the language and lifestyle of rural Gaelic society as alien, particularly in the period following the Scottish reformation of 1560.

An early encapsulation of the problem can be seen in James VI's well known aphorism differentiating between 'mainland' Gaels and those in the Islands when he referred to his Gaelic speaking subjects as being of two types of people:

> the ones that dwelleth in our mainland and are barbarous for the most part, and yet mixed with some show of civility; the others that dwelleth in the Isles and are utterly barbarians without any show of civility. (Dorgan and Maclean, 2002: 4)

This enmity towards Gaelic and the portraying of the Gael as 'the other' – was to have long lasting detrimental effects on the community and the language, which it might be argued may still exist in some low level prejudice.

In 1609, the statutes of Iona set out in official formulation how the traditions of the Gaels were to be discouraged, an act that followed a general trend of isolating the culture and language – it had only been from two generations back that common Lowland speech was now overwhelmingly referred to as *Scots*, with Gaelic now increasingly been portrayed as *Irish* – thus the speakers becoming regarded as in some way alien within their own nation (MacKinnon, 1991: 39)

Nevertheless Gaels continued to be prominent in Scottish society outwith the Islands and rural areas as study of medieval Glasgow at the time can show.

According to Gaelic scholar Ronald Black (Black, 2007: 20) early references to Glasgow in Gaelic verse can be found as early as the 1580s and in the early seventeenth century in traditional waulking songs – one of which already mentions the city as a trading centre, with another outlining Glasgow as a place of wonder for the Gael *Glaschu nam buadh*. Yet another reference in 1792, talks of *Glaschu nan aoigh* ('the welcoming or nurturing Glasgow'). It is known that by the early 1700s an inn, the Black Bull, was opened on Argyle Street to cater for the needs of arriving Highlanders and, in 1727, the Glasgow Highland Society was founded to raise funds for the educating of sons of Highlanders in Glasgow. In 1767, a church was opened on Queen Street in which the services were conducted in Gaelic, evidencing a stable community (Edward, 2008: 15).

With the industrialisation of Glasgow however, this idyllic vision was not to last, the great Gaelic singer Mairi Mhòr nan Òrain later referring to Glasgow as a place where one was more likely to be *chacadh leis an stùr's ga mo mhùchadh leis a'cheò* ('choked by the stoor and suffocated by the smoke').

The industrialisation and increasing commerce in Glasgow of the time undoubtedly impacted on the large Gaelic population in the city, estimated at 39,000 by 1831 (Edward, 2008: 24), the damp climate of Glasgow proving ideal for cotton production, and the constant stream of Highland and Irish immigration providing the huge labour force necessary. According to the 1851 census enumeration books, evidence exists that Glasgow had the highest highland migrant population of any Scottish city in the mid-nineteenth century, drawing most of its Highland born from Argyll.

By the end of the nineteenth century, however, following the Irish famine and mass Irish immigration, the Glasgow Gael was no longer to be the largest of the immigrant groups in the community, that position now being occupied by the Irish. Nevertheless, such was the impact of the Gaelic speaking community that up to 1800, it is estimated that of the 190 or so books written in, or containing Scottish Gaelic between 1567 and 1800, 62 appear to have been published in Glasgow. Indeed, a 'dedicated' Gaelic publisher Archibald Sinclair was to set up in Argyle Street in 1852, and the following 50 years to 1900 were to see 138 Gaelic publications appearing in the city, with a weekly paper *An Gàidheal* appearing in nearby Paisley.

The equivocal attitude sometimes held by the Gaelic community towards cities such as Glasgow in the period up to industrialisation is also referred to by the Gaelic scholar John MacInnes. Quoting a verse by Gilleasbuig na Ceapaich, he finds evidence, on the one hand, of the city being regarded as akin to one of the seven wonders of the world: *Chunna mi Eaglais Ghlascho* ... ('I have seen the Church of Glasgow ...') but points out that references such as *àilaedh nan cladhan* ('the stench of the gutters') and *glagraich nan sràid* (the 'din of the streets') are more common references at that time (MacInnes, 2006: 47).

Although only 0.5 percent of the population in 2001could *speak, read and write* Gaelic, (Hecla, 2009) (although 1.7% had some ability in the language), numerous parts of the city have Gaelic names, or anglicised versions of those, hearkening back to when Gaelic in Glasgow was more predominant. Thus Simon Taylor tells us we find Blochairn *Blàr* ('field') plus *càrn* ('cairn', 'burial mound'); Garscube *Gart* ('field') plus *sguab* ('sheaf', 'field of sheaves of corn'); Gartnavel *Gart* plus *an ubhal* ('field of the apples'), and, possibly something less to celebrate, it is suggested that the main Prison Barlinnie or *Blairlenny* comes from *Blàr* plus *lèannuch* ('swampy') (Taylor, 2007: 14).

According to Withers, despite Gaelic in Glasgow growing weaker – as it has in Scotland overall – Glasgow, while 'Second City of the Empire' has always been the 'first city' of Gaelic Scotland (Withers, 1998: 131). Up till the late 1930s, parts of Glasgow were well known as meeting places of the Gael – firstly by the Clyde at the bottom of Jamaica Street, then from the mid-twentieth century under the Central Station Bridge in Argyle Street – well known in common Glasgow parlance as the 'Hielanman's Umbrella'. The city's Highlanders' Institute was a flourishing centre throughout the mid-twentieth century till the early 70s.

Given this continuing, if somewhat lessened, importance, it is perhaps fitting that Glasgow was amongst the first to draw up a Gaelic Language Plan – which, as will be seen below, places stress on the role of arts and culture.

**Glasgow's Gaelic Language Plan and the City's Gaelic Arts Strategy**

One of the welcome achievements of Scotland's new Parliament was the passing of the Gaelic Language Act, and establishment of the Bòrd na Gàidhlig (BnG), in early 2006. The Board published its National Plan for Gaelic in 2007, one aspect of which was the requirement put on relevant public bodies, including local authorities, to prepare a language plan for their organisation.

Glasgow City Council elected to prepare a draft language plan (2009) – earlier than it would have been compelled to – and, throughout 2008, discussions took place with Gaelic organisations, individuals and interested bodies with the aim of establishing a plan that could be rolled out within three years, commencing in 2009. The four areas within the language plan are comprised of the themes:

> *Language acquisition* – Gaelic in the home and education;
> *Language use* – in the community, Council Services and the media;
> *Language status* – raising the image of Gaelic;
> *Language corpus* – support for its usage and research.

Much of the actions in Glasgow's plan will be targeted towards those with some knowledge of Gaelic already, whether native speakers, or already in Gaelic education, or those who would wish (with help) to improve their Gaelic. While in the view of the City Council, Education will remain key for the success of the language, of interest for those interested in a sustainable Gaelic cultural sector is the Council's specific pledge to 'raise the profile and visibility of Gaelic more generally among Glaswegians through publicity, promotions and art and cultural activities'. This echoes the findings of *Glasgow Grows Audiences* whose major survey in 2007 found that the city's potential to grow Gaelic audiences was unparalleled relative to other Scottish cities (GGA, 2007: 5).

Examining the *Language Plan Arts and Cultural Strategy* from 2009–12, in terms of the heritage left by the previous Gaelic Arts strategy operated in Glasgow and promoted by *An Lòchran* ('the Lantern') between 2006–09, is also of some interest. *An Lòchran* was formed in 1999 to promote and develop Gaelic arts and culture in Glasgow, with the aim of establishing a *permanent and visible presence* for Gaelic arts in the city (*An Lòchran*, 2005: 1).

Amongst the aims of the organisation, which worked closely with Glasgow City Council's part-time Gaelic Arts officer, were to '*Establish and develop an infrastructure for Gaelic arts in Glasgow including a Gaelic arts centre; Extend and enhance the range of Gaelic arts; Increase access and participation, develop audiences; Raise the profile and visibility of Gaelic arts and culture.*'

The *An Lòchran* strategy had been developed following consultations with representatives of Gaelic and arts communities in the previous five years.

In the *An Lòchran* strategy, 25 Gaelic and Highland associations in the city were identified, including four adult Gaelic choirs; an annual city Mod and Fèis Òigridh, Gaelic religious services held throughout the city on a regular basis and finally several pubs with a Gaelic or Highland focus, providing Gaelic entertainment.

In the three years of the plan, they initiated a successful Gaelic monthly music and culture club, Ceòl 's Craic (see below), and substantially boosted the profile of Gaelic arts and culture in the city

It was the view of *An Lochran* that '*creating a physical and cultural home for Gaelic arts in the city will be one of the main ways to ensure connection with current, emerging and future generations of Gaelic speakers and Gaelic communities – Scottish and Irish – in the city*' (*An Lòchran*, 2005: 3). The creation of a permanent physical Gaelic arts and cultural space has not, to date, been achieved, but another of their aims seems to have had more success: that of placing creativity and innovation at the heart of Gaelic artistic projects, rejecting any 'fossilisation' of Gaelic in the city and demonstrating the contemporary relevance and potential of Gaelic culture in Glasgow.

The Al Lochran document talks of *sustainability* – through a commitment to collaboration and development of partnerships and audiences, and also highlights *added* value – seeking to add value to all their projects by capitalising on their educational, media, tourism and economic potential thus looking for a 'joined up' long term strategy. In many ways, this is similar to the Pròseact nan Ealan's principles of innovation not conservation in relation to Gaelic arts and culture. (see http://www.gaelic-arts.com)

In attempting to integrate arts and culture with Gaelic language development, the Bòrd na Gàidhlig has drawn on the work of GASD (see http://www.gasd.org.uk/ga) whose stated objectives include a secure and sustainable infrastructure for the delivery of arts, cultural and heritage initiatives, professional development in the sector and a greater understanding of the role of the arts in educational community and economic development.

Within the 'outcome and activity targets' of the Glasgow Gaelic Language Plan, arts and cultural activities are seen as positive to help develop fluency amongst Gaelic Medium Education parents through involving them in the local Fèis and Mod. Partnerships are also envisaged between Gaelic Drama groups and GME secondary school pupils to help encourage language use. Overall, the city Gaelic arts strategy in its next phase to 2012 is seen as a way of helping get Gaelic used in informal settings, with the establishment of a Gaelic Arts Forum seen as a key element of this.

**The Experience of the Gaels in the City Labour Market**

As described in the historical perspective above, in many ways Glasgow has long had an ambivalent attitude towards the language. However, its role as the 'first city' of Gaelic Scotland (Withers, 1998, 131) has been strengthened in recent times as Glasgow has become one of the globe's leading post-industrial cities (Mooney, 2004; Danson and Mooney, 1998), actively pursuing an economic strategy with a significant arts and culture component, and as Scotland's national institutions in arts and culture have concentrated their operations in the city.

The details of the prime organisations and actors in the arts and culture sector locally will be presented in the next section, but first the dimensions of the 'Gaelic Labour Market' and labour force will be covered. Many of the jobs in this labour market demand higher level skills and qualifications, so that higher education becomes an important if not essential requirement for entry. As with the experience in many other peripheral nations, of increasing importance to the demographic development of their communities and regions is the location of Universities in attracting young people to the four Scottish cities (Aberdeen, Dundee, Edinburgh and Glasgow) plus St Andrews and Stirling, and correspondingly away from all the communities in the rest of Scotland (Hecla, 2009). With especially high rates of participation in Higher Education, the Gàidhealtachd areas are some of the biggest losers in these migration flows. Compounding this, across the country, there are relatively few jobs which can use graduate level skills back in these communities so that many who are able to speak, read or write (SRW) Gaelic are unable to return home on graduation. Further, the need to maintain part-time employment and accommodation throughout the year tends to present a barrier to Gaelic SRW students even seeking vacation work back home. This exaggerates the increasing dependence of tourism, hospitality, cultural and food processing sectors in rural Scotland on migrant labour which undermines attempts to raise the visibility of Gaelic.

All the indicators are that this growth of professional and management and of associated jobs will be related to economic growth in the Central Belt, with centralisation and concentration of careers which use graduate qualifications in

Glasgow and Edinburgh and their metropolitan areas (Hecla, 2009). Training and development, promotion and career development therefore are being focused in this region, attracting and retaining graduates. In contradistinction to the advantages of being in this escalator region – where advancement is more rapid than in smaller more peripheral labour markets, staff in these occupations outwith the geographical centre face slower progression and fewer opportunities. Evidence from the UK (where Greater London is the prime escalator region – see Fielding, 1991) and Scotland in particular (with Scots reluctant to return unless incomes are commensurate with city regions elsewhere and career opportunities protected – see Harrison et al., 2004, in research for Scottish Enterprise) confirms the strength of such factors in influencing job location decisions. For Gaelic SRW, there is no reason to believe that the same attributes and behaviours do not apply.

Associated with such choices, it appears that most Gaelic SRW are attached to a professional, managerial or other specific occupation first, whilst retaining the capacity to speak, read and write in the language. If so, then their prime motivation is to progress in a dedicated career which may or may not have a language content but – from the discussion on where the opportunities are located, including the role of escalator regions, there may be costs involved in pursuing employment outwith the Central Belt. Thus, for most they are in an occupational labour market rather than some generic 'Gaelic Labour Market'. For this reason, it would be expected that attempts to attract graduates to such jobs with a Gaelic requirement would create a wage premium to overcome the supply side barriers.

So, in the primary sector of a dual labour market there will be a tendency for Gaelic speakers to command higher wages especially in rural North and West Scotland at least until such time as sufficient jobs, career progression and pathways are established across the country. Without budgets reflecting this, there will barriers to dispersing Gaelic essential or desirable jobs away from Glasgow and Edinburgh. In the rest of the labour market, those positions which do not require degree qualifications will be less affected by the outward movement of young people to the cities and so subsequent reluctance to return. In recent years and, without significant changes in the labour process, into the future a high proportion of such employment will go to migrant workers with little or no knowledge of Gaelic language or heritage and with limited desire to learn the language.

Normalising the use of the language within the community again will naturally tend to raise the demand for – and use of – the language in everyday life. The decline and ageing of the populations of the traditional Gaelic areas of the North and West do not form the most productive environment for such growth. Conversely, for the cities an expanding Gaelic SRW community should lead to opportunities not only in the sectors formally supported by organizations promoting the language, cultural and heritage but also in consumer-based activities driven by a growing market.

**A Sustainable Gaelic Arts and Cultural Sector?**

The importance of Arts and Culture to Scotland's government was outlined in the First Minister's St Andrew's Day Address in 2003, when he said:

> 'Culture cuts across all these portfolios of government, and it can make a difference to our success in each. [...] 'This is about how Ministers use

arts and culture to achieve more effectively their policy objectives. [...] 'I want to see imaginative and new proposals coming forward from all Ministers that help create access to cultural activity.' (Scottish Government, 2003)

This has been echoed in Glasgow's existing cultural strategy where the claim is made that cultural thinking needs to be embedded across all departmental concerns, requiring an integrated response from local authorities embracing all council services (Scottish Government, 2003: 3)

Interestingly however, Gaelic does not seem to be 'mainstreamed' in terms of prominence in general Glasgow City Council documents regarding Arts and Culture – it is not specifically mentioned in the strategic key priorities document nor the general Cultural Strategy document except in a passing reference to the Gaelic School.

However one of the strategic priorities outlined is the right to explore, express and extend cultural identity (Glasgow City Council, 2006: 7). This is echoed in the Executive Summary which outlines the entitlement of Glasgow citizens to 'Develop a sense of belonging for all communities (community cohesion), by celebrating the varied culture and traditions of Glasgow population (2006: 2).

However it would seem that Gaelic (like other Glasgow minority languages and cultures) is envisaged as being dealt with by specific strands of activity – such as the Glasgow Gaelic Arts Strategy (mentioned above), rather than by being encompassed within a wider statement of arts and cultural remit. Whether this leads to more or less attention being paid to the sector and thus supports or hinders the emergence of sustainable practice is possibly arguable.

A vibrant and sustainable arts and cultural sector does not, of course, rely solely on size of workforce and questions of turnover. Questions of how 'embedded' the sector is, how creative it is seen, are also crucial, together with questions such as the extent to which the sector relies on the public purse, or is free standing.

Where a culture is linked to a language, further questions might include the extent to which cultural and artistic health impacts positively on linguistic health.

Research carried out and reported elsewhere (Chalmers and Danson, 2009) outlines in detail the main actors in this sector. However the summary below illustrates some of the key factors underlying present developments

*The Media Sector*

The key player within this has been and continues to be the BBC, whose Glasgow based Gaelic related operations at Pacific Quay at the time of this research employed 63 staff – almost all full time. Of this the majority was educated to degree level. Employee turnover in the Gaelic Unit is relatively small – being estimated at perhaps 3–4 staff per year suggesting a major contribution to high level Gaelic related jobs in the creative sector.

In 2006–7, the period under study (before the current expansion towards the BBC Alba joint service with MG Alba), BBC Gaelic spend in the Greater Glasgow area was approximately £2.1m, mostly relating to TV and on-line with, in addition, MG Alba contributing approximately £2.7m to the BBC for production in the Glasgow area; educationally related Gaelic provision also added £0.75m.

When the work of independent media companies is taken into consideration it can be shown that overall the Gaelic media sector in Glasgow employs some 120–140 people, most of whom have degrees, with total expenditure about £2.5 million. This sector in the city is, therefore, nationally significant both with regard to employment for those graduates who can speak, read and write Gaelic and as an active participant in a leading creative industry cluster.

*Gaelic at Celtic Connections*

Glasgow hosts the annual Celtic Connections festival which continues to grow and is now of international importance. During the period of this research, approximately 120,000 tickets were sold at the 2008 event, bringing in an estimated income of £6m to the city. Within this, recent years have seen an increase in the visibility and involvement of Gaelic related artists.

Analysing the involvement of Gaelic artists in the event, it was possible to estimate that, in total, the minimal ticket sales which could be ascribed to a Gaelic input into Celtic Connections amounted to £119,860 with Gaelic related attendances 15,359 (approximately 12.7% ) – one eighth of the attendances at all events. If the estimated share of the income to the city, after multiplier effects, was similar, then Gaelic could be considered to have contributed approximately £750k to the Glasgow economy.

*Fèis Glaschu*

According to the RSAMD's 2005 report on the impact of the Fèis movement, 76% of Fèis participants reported that the Fèis had a positive or strong positive influence on their motivation to learn Gaelic.

In 2008, 97 children took part in the Glasgow Fèis – from pre-five, primary school, to teenage. Although the financial expenditure in this area is relatively minor compared with the media, the absence of this activity would clearly diminish the continuing development if not the continuing presence of wider language and related arts and cultural activities.

Ceòl 's Craic, 'Glasgow's Gaelic Night Club', meets monthly between September and May in the Centre for Contemporary Arts in Sauchiehall Street and was then in its fifth year. As well as music nights, recent activity broadened out to include film showings and language tuition linked to the monthly events. Collaborative work took place with partners across art forms such as Ceòlas, the Gaelic Books Council, Celtic Connections, the National Piping Centre, and Iomairt Colm Cille (the Columba Initiative) As with the Fèis, Ceòl 's Craic remains dependent on the public purse although clearly its recent expansion indicates potential to become more self-supporting.

The potential for the burgeoning Gaelic publishing sector can also be seen in the beginning of a book festival: Leabhar 's Craic, which took place in May 2008 and then again in February 2009. Similarly, with the support of the BBC and the Gaelic Media Sector, a successful Gaelic film festival was launched at the CCA in January 2009, showing more than 20 Gaelic films or features over three days, and hosting discussions on Europe seen through Gaelic eyes, and on the way forward for Gaelic Television.

*Summary of the Arts and Cultural Impacts*

There appear to be relatively limited linkage effects – backwards and forwards – for the consumption of Gaelic arts and cultural sectors in Glasgow. Overwhelmingly these are based on service delivery by highly skilled professionals. Most of these transactions are in the private market place, even where there is local or national state support to the ventures. Identifiable expenditure in the city was at least £300k, with almost all of this representing wage income to artists, musicians, tutors, technical and professional staff, etc. About 50 professionally trained Gaelic speakers gain significant supplements to their annual incomes through these activities, almost all securing a premium to the salary they could earn in parallel mainstream work in the city.

It can be argued strongly that the contribution of the Gaelic language and culture to Celtic Connections, and the life of the city more generally, should be more explicitly recognised as essentially greater than is suggested by these data: inevitably incorporating such an approach into the analyses would enhance these impacts appreciably. This is one of the challenges for those seeking to delineate the sustainability of the burgeoning Gaelic arts and cultural sector.

Similarly, it has not been possible to separate out the economic impacts of non-centrally organised activities in Glasgow. These include informal folk sessions in bars; ceilidhs and other events in independent venues, student unions and clubs; local Gaelic Associations and Mods. While some of these have no direct economic payments, there are necessarily associated expenditures and so incomes which may be additional to the city's economy, rather than simple displacement or diversionary activities from within the Glasgow.

## Discussion and Conclusions

Glasgow has had a long history as the City of the Gàidheal and, although it is not the main population centre for those with the language in Scotland, it does offer a significantly disproportionate share of the high quality jobs where a working knowledge of Gaelic is 'essential'. Higher education is likewise concentrated in the cities of Scotland and, with its historical links to the Highlands and Islands, there is a natural focus on Glasgow. Together these core functions and roles in serving the Gàidhealtachd have attracted the attention of the economic regeneration agenda for the city and region, embedded into the different plans and strategies for the arts, culture, language and economy. The synergies and developments generated by these different elements of Glasgow society have been important in boosting the aggregate impacts of Gaelic Arts and Cultural Activities on the city economy; including the media sector these have been shown to be in the region of £3.55–£4 million supporting approximately 200 workers in professional and associated employment (Chalmers and Danson, 2009).

As outlined in Glasgow's Cultural Strategy (Glasgow City Council, 2006), it is clear that the arts and cultural sector of the Glasgow economy will play an increasing role in the City's future, in coming years. There are tensions, undoubtedly, between focusing these developments on the city and the potential to have decentralised Gaelic arts and cultural activities to the traditional heartlands of the Gàidhealtachd. However, the analyses here – of the tendency for both labour markets to promote centralisation of highly paid occupations and workers in the metropolitan cores on the one hand, and of the consumer-driven Gaelic arts and culture sectors to be encouraged to co-locate in these same places on the other – is creating an inevitability about these movements.

There is an irony that twenty-first century footloose and mobility-enhancing technologies are providing a new impetus to Glasgow's claim to be City of the Gàidheal when they might have been expected to redress the centripetal forces of modern economies. How the creative and cultural sectors might be harnessed to overcome these new forms of peripherality remains on our agenda for future research and will be returned to over the coming period.

**References**

*An Lòchran*, 2005. *Gaelic Arts Strategy 2006–2009*. Glasgow City Council and An Lòchran.
Black, R. 2007. 'Some Notes from My Glasgow Scrapbook 1500–1800'. In ed. Kidd, S.M. 20–54.
Burnett, K. and Danson, M. 2004. 'Adding or Subtracting Value? Constructions of Rurality and Scottish Quality Food Promotion'. *International Journal of Entrepreneurial Behaviour Research* 10.6: 384–403.
Chalmers, D. 2003. *The Economic Impact of Gaelic Arts and Culture. Division of Economics and Enterprise*, Unpublished PhD Thesis, Glasgow Caledonian University.
Chalmers, D. and Danson, M. 2006. 'Sustainable Development? Building Social Capital in Gaelic Communities'. In ed. Macleod, W. *Revitalising Gaelic in Scotland: Policy, Planning and Public Discourse*. Edinburgh: Dunedin Academic Press. 239–56.
Chalmers, D. and Danson, M. 2009. *An Economic Impact Study of Gaelic Arts and Culture in Glasgow*. Report for City of Glasgow Council, March.
Danson, M. and Mooney, G. 1998. 'Glasgow: A Tale of Two Cities: Disadvantage and Exclusion on the European Periphery'. In eds. Lawless, P., Martin, R. and S. Hardy. *Unemployment and Social Exclusion*. London: Jessica Kinglsey. 217–34.
Edward, M. 2008. *Who Belongs to Glasgow?* Second Edition. Edinburgh: Luath Press.
Fielding, A. 1991. 'Migration and Social Mobility: South East England as an Escalator Region', *Regional Studies* 26.1: 1–15.
Glasgow City Council. 2006, *Glasgow: The Place, The People, The Potential: Glasgow's Cultural Strategy*. Glasgow City Council.
Glasgow City Council. 2009. Draft Gaelic Language Plan, available at http://www.glasgow.gov.uk/en/YourCouncil/PolicyPlanning_Strategy/Corporate/GaelicLanguagePlan/
Glasgow Grows Audiences. 2007. *Gaelic Arts and Culture Audience Development*, Glasgow: An Lòchran.
Harrison, R., Mason, C., Findlay, A. and Houston, D. 2004. *The Attraction and Retention of High Skilled Labour in Scotland: A Preliminary Analysis*. Edinburgh: Scottish Enterprise. [available at http://www.scottish-enterprise.com/sedotcom_home/about-us/se-whatwedo/public-sector-info/search-iar/search-iar-1.htm?ID=115002]
Hecla. 2009. *Measuring the Gaelic Labour Market: Current and Future Potential*. Inverness: Hecla Consulting for Highlands and Island Enterprise and Skills Development Scotland. March.
Kidd, S.M. ed. 2007. *Glasgow Baile Mòr nan Gàidheal*. Department of Celtic, University of Glasgow.
Lorentzen, A. and van Heur, B. eds. 2011. *Cultural Political Economy of Small Cities, London*: Routledge.
MacInness, J. 2006. *Dùthchas Nan Gàidheal*. Edinburgh: Birlinn.
MacKinnon, K. 1991. *Gaelic: A Past and Future Prospect*. Edinburgh: The Saltire Society.

Mooney, G. 2004. 'Cultural policy as Urban Transformation? Critical Reflections on Glasgow, European City of Culture 1990'. *Local Economy*, 19. 4: 327–40.

Dorgan, T. and Maclean M. 2002. 'Historical Background: Celtic Languages'. In eds. Dorgan T. and M. Maclean. *An Leabhar Mòr*. Edinburgh: Canongate. [also available at http://www.obrien.ie/resources/LeabharMor-CelticLanguages.pdf]

Scottish Enterprise. 1999. *The Network Strategy*. Glasgow: Scottish Enterprise Network.

Scottish Office. 1997. *Towards a Development Strategy for Rural Scotland*. Edinburgh: Scottish Office.

Scottish Government. 2003. First Minister Jack McConnell St Andrew's Day Speech, Royal Scottish Academy of Music and Drama Glasgow, Sunday, November 30. [available at http://www.scotland.gov.uk/News/News-Extras/176]

Taylor, S. 2007. 'Gaelic in Glasgow: The Onomastic Evidence'. In ed. Kidd, S.M. 1–19.

Withers, C. 1998. *Urban Highlanders: Highland-Lowland Migration and Urban Gaelic Culture, 1700–1900*. East Linton: Tuckwell Press.

# Sustaining Minority Languages

*Matthew M. MacIver*[1]

Let me make it clear at the beginning that I am not a Gaelic scholar, I do not work in the Gaelic world, I do not earn my living from Gaelic. But it is my first language despite the best efforts of the formal education system to ignore that fact. Although I have gone through the education system and collected a few degrees and some honorary awards, I have never once been taught in my own language let alone been taught about it. Like many others from minority cultures who are illiterate in their own language, I am one of these people who are domiciled on the margins of an educational world which dabbles with a language in an academic way but has little to offer the real demands and frustrations of a linguistic community.

This is a historic moment for Gaelic in Scotland. A National Language Board, Bòrd na Gàidhlig, has been set up with statutory powers.[2] A National Plan has been issued,[3] after a very positive consultation process, and six public bodies have been charged with bringing forward their language plans.[4] I welcome all of that and I took on the responsibility of Chair of Bòrd na Gàidhlig because I see that we have an opportunity now that we have never had before to save our language. I am tired of listening to people telling me and the world that the *Gaelic Language (Scotland) Act 2005* is the last chance for Gaelic. It is not the last chance for Gaelic – it is the first chance for Gaelic. Ever since the *Education Act* of 1872, our language has been systematically diminished. As a community, we have had our self-confidence taken away, and sometimes we have been led to believe that our language is an obstacle and a barrier to advancement and success. As a country, we did little about that, not because we did not care, but because we did not think about it.

We also have had a linguistic context in Scotland which has been pretty inhibiting. A few years ago, I attended a church service at the Edinburgh International Festival organised by Pròiseact nan Ealan to commemorate the 1400th anniversary of St Columba landing in Iona. I listened to Professor Donald Macleod, Principal of the Free Church College, describe our Celtic heritage as "domiciled on the margins of the world". Many of us, he argued, are "children of the periphery". I think many of us would understand exactly what he is saying. Yet there has been, I believe, no agenda against minority languages; it is simply that they were not high on the political agenda. Neither were they high on the educational agenda. That is why I believe the *Gaelic Language (Scotland) Act 2005* is so important. It is not just about Gaelic. It is saying something else. It is saying something to all of us who so often feel marginalised, isolated and peripheral because of our language and culture.

Given that context where do I see the challenges for a Gaelic Language Board? I think I see three basic challenges: the production of a National Plan that will be acceptable not just to the Gaelic community but to the Scottish public at large.; the restoration of self-confidence to the Gaelic community; and thirdly the use of a new political order to develop the language.

---

[1] Matthew MacIver resigned as Chairman of Bord na Gaidhlig in 2008 to take up an Honorary Professorship at the University of the Highlands and Islands Millennium Institute. He now chairs its Board of Governors.
[2] http://www.gaidhlig.org.uk/
[3] http://www.gaidhlig.org.uk/plananaiseantanagaidhlig/national-plan-for-gaelic.html
[4] http://www.gaidhlig.org.uk/planaichean-gaidhlig/gaelic-language-plans.html

Let me first address the issue of the National Plan. At Bòrd na Gàidhlig we believe that in a modern devolved Scotland the acceptance and the development of other cultures and languages are really quite important. I think we do accept that, in Scotland, Gaelic will operate on a number of levels. For those of us who are native speakers and those who are learning the language, it becomes almost an act of faith. There are others in Scotland who have a huge sympathy for the language and probably a little guilt complex as well. Then there are those who really do not think about it – not because of any sinister reason, but because it is simply not part of their being. We accept that there are also those who would see the public money which is being spent on less than 60,000 as a complete waste of money and a complete waste of time. We accept that as well. Overall, however, there is in the Gaelic community a growing awareness that our language and culture can contribute to a new and modern Scotland.

The role of Bòrd na Gàidhlig, as I see it, is to cultivate interest in and develop the Gaelic language and culture and, in so doing, will need to enter into relationships and partnerships with the public at large and specific public bodies. I do not see Bòrd na Gàidhlig's role as forcing anything on anybody. That, I think, would be suicidal. I want to see public bodies engaging with us to develop our language as best we can.

We have identified six public bodies as the very first bodies to develop that agenda. The first six bodies are:

- The Scottish Executive;
- Highlands and Islands Enterprise;
- Highland Council;
- Argyll and Bute Council;
- Comhairle nan Eilean Siar;
- The Scottish Parliament.

It is not surprising why these bodies have been chosen first. It is also quite clear why other public bodies have been chosen to follow them. They are quite integral to public life in Scotland and in their own different ways can help us.

The National Plan will set out a strategy designed to reverse the overall decline in the number of Gaelic speakers in Scotland, to increase the occasions and circumstances in which Gaelic can be used in Scotland with equality to English, and to promote acquisition of the language and thereby participation in its culture by all who wish it. The positive effect anticipated from this endeavour cannot be produced by a single agency, but relies on the co-operation and contribution of a wide range of organisations and individuals. I believe that support will be forthcoming not just from public bodies but from many private organisations as well.

Let me now turn to the Gaelic community itself.

This new world challenges the Gaelic community quite significantly. On one level, it is now up to us. We must work together in a way that we have never worked before. All the Gaelic organisations must stop ploughing individual furrows. We must now plough the same furrow. A National Plan will provide a National Strategy. No one organisation will save Gaelic but we can all do it if we have the resolve.

The Gaelic community is a broad church encompassing many skills and many talents. I want us to use these skills and talents. We all now have to accept that we can change the world. We have a very strong base from which to advance and from which to try to secure the survival of our language. We must go forward as a united community helping each other and supporting each other. We have to go forward as a community which recognises that an old world has gone and that a new world beckons. We have often looked back, and now we have to look forward. We need a language which can survive the rigours and the challenges of a new century. We need a language which is spoken by the young, but quite frankly we need a language which also must be spoken by the old. A National Plan will not save the language but it will help. Gaelic schools will not in the end keep our language alive but they will help. But what will keep a language alive is a community which wants it to be alive.

What, then, is my vision for the new Gaelic communities? Let me give you a taste of where I want us to go. I see working in the communities as fundamental to the survival of the language. I want to see Gaelic organisations developing strategies to support families so that Gaelic is spoken confidently in the home. I want to see Gaelic organisations trying to ensure that we create a culture where people are proud of their Gaelic language. I want to see Gaelic Language Plans from the Islands, the Highlands and Argyll and Bute which concentrate on building Gaelic in the traditional Gaelic communities.

If we can have Gaelic schools in Glasgow and Inverness, then we must have them in Skye and the Western Isles. I want to see a community education system which will not only support learners of the language but will also support the fluent speakers as well. We have to give fluent Gaelic speakers the opportunity to write, read and learn their own language. We must create an environment where fluent speakers can begin to read the books, novels and poems which are increasingly written by Gaelic writers. These writers need our support and are critical to our success. We need to look very sharply at the role which broadcasting is going to play. We need to welcome a new television channel but move towards other areas.

First, we need to embrace a new world of technology which will attract our young people. As well as a television channel, we need to develop a digital service which will involve the internet, podcasting and all other technologies in order to attract the young.

Secondly we need to develop in the traditional heartland a community radio service which will complement Radio nan Gaidheal. It is simply not good enough that the present community radio stations in the Gaelic heartlands are English-medium stations. We need to encourage local businesses not only to spnsor sports teams but to sponsor them with Gaelic signage. We also need to give support to local community groups like local history societies, and especially local community newspapers. We must encourage publishing in Gaelic. These are some of the kinds of things that I want to see happening. They are just a part of what I want to see happening. They will give you an idea of where I see the priorities.

As a community we must now look ahead with a confidence but with some strategic awareness. I am convinced, for example, that we need now to develop a leadership class in Gaelic. We really have come to a stage in our development where we need people to manage organisations, we need people to manage the development of the National Plan and we need people to manage the growth of Gaelic. We need people who are strategic thinkers, we need people who are qualified in leadership skills, and who are capable of using new methods and ideas to drive Gaelic forward into this new century.

My own view has always been that we now will have to set our sights on a Gaelic university. That should be our long-term aim. But, of course, it will not come overnight. In the interim we now need partnerships throughout Scotland and across the world. We must not just look to our traditional friends. We must now look to Europe in particular for role models and good examples. It is time to raise our vision and our sights and think of bigger things. It is time that we ask sharp questions of a Higher Education system where Gaelic is still on the periphery.

The Gaelic community can now be empowered. And this brings me to my third challenge. It can be empowered because we now have a political power and a political support we have never had before.

In a devolved Scotland Gaelic has become important politically. A new Gaelic body with statutory powers, Bòrd na Gàidhlig, is now firmly within the political fraternity. That certainly does not mean that political struggles are over. What it does mean is that devolution in general has changed the political map of Scotland; and it also means that we have a potential influence which we did not have before. We have seen a level of political support for the language which we have never seen before in our history.

This will demand a new strategic approach from the Gaelic world. It is now absolutely essential to engage with the political process at all levels – at community council level, at local government level, and at parliamentary level. We must move away from this corrosive idea that every civil servant in Edinburgh and London is by definition against Gaelic, that the political establishment is in the business of erecting barriers and that we have to fight for every inch of progress. I would like that culture changed, and I would like the Bòrd to change it. I would like the Gaelic community to understand that devolution has changed the political landscape, that politicians can and do listen, that the creation of the Bòrd itself is a testament to that, and that the future depends on an engagement with the political process.

That is why I firmly believe that this is the beginning of a process, not the end of one. A National Plan for Gaelic is a beginning – no more, no less. It is not an end in itself. We must now go on to fulfil some of our dreams. I want to see a Gaelic community confident enough to see its language as fundamental to its existence. I want to see Gaelic schools in the traditional Gaelic heartland. I want to see learners supported and catered for simply because the language will not survive without them. I want to see a sustained programme of Adult Education. I want to see the Churches engaged in this process. I want to see a vibrant publishing sector confident in the knowledge that there will be a healthy demand for books from it. I want to see a Gaelic University. I want to see a Gaelic broadcasting service where the Gaels feel a sense of ownership and not sub-service to the national broadcasters. I want to see Gaelic seen as essential for certain jobs. I want to see Gaelic being used unashamedly as a marketing tool. I want these and much more.

But above all I want this: I want no longer to be a child of the periphery. I want the Gaels no longer to be children of the periphery. We have been on the periphery long enough. It is time for us to move to the centre ground. It is time for us to proclaim our language and our culture. Let us not apologise for it.

My message, therefore, is quite clear. The Gaelic community is in a stronger position than it has been for some time. But it is only strong if we take advantage of the opportunities open to us. I have always maintained that the *Gaelic Language (Scotland) Act 2005* is the beginning of a process, not the end of one. I do believe that and that is why I look ahead with optimism. This is a new world for Gaelic. It will bring many challenges but I believe it will bring more opportunities. The Gaelic community must grasp these opportunities now.

# Part 4: Sustaining Scots

Introduction

The focus of the symposium out of which this volume of papers has arisen was not on Scots as such but on the ways and means whereby communities in which Scots is spoken are sustained. A central concern was the role of Scots in forming a stabilised community and the role in sustaining Scots which a community might have?

To the authors of the following papers, there was presented for addressing a series of questions not unlike those presented to speakers on Irish and Gaelic, and of which the following may be typical:

(A) What's wrong with current arrangements and practice? What research is needed to show what needs to be done?

(B) Is Scots self-sufficient to ensure its vibrancy and maintenance as a community language?

(C) How far is the sustaining of Scots communities in Scotland, Northern Ireland and the Republic of Ireland conditional on infrastructure, environment, society, employment, urban renewal, culture, or anything else?

(D) What is the role of education in the sustaining of a Scots-speaking community – e.g. developing social skills, cultural identity or linguistic confidence?

(E) How far is the integration of Scots and culture into the community an environmental issue?

(F) Is the approach to such questions top-down or bottom-up? Whose task or responsibility is it ultimately to sustain a Scots-speaking community?

(G) What role can universities and other institutions of higher education play?

(H) With the arrival in Scotland and Northern Ireland and the Republic of Ireland of significant numbers of speakers of Eastern European languages, how far has the future role and supporting mechanisms for Scots been undermined?

(I) Where are there communities where minority languages are being successfully sustained? What comparisons may be drawn with Scots, and what lessons are to be learned?

# Scotland and Northern Ireland as Scots-speaking Communities

*John M. Kirk*

When Dónall Ó Baoill and I devised the set of ten questions for the symposium prospectus, it was with Scottish Gaelic and Irish in mind. It became clear, however, that the same questions could be addressed to the present situation of Scots – in Scotland, Northern Ireland, and indeed in the Republic of Ireland. Before looking at the questions in turn, let me begin by considering six factors that might lie behind any possible answers.

## The Languageness Issue

Academically qualified descriptive linguists have shown that, as a language system, particularly at a syntactic level, where propositional meaning, speech-act and other pragmatic functions are encoded, Scots is bound up with English as a communicative system - or in Saussure's terms, each of the varieties which is spoken in Scotland and English are *paroles* (or manifestations) of the *langue* English (the underlying language).[1] With no system of its own, Scots is without structural uniqueness and, in Kloss's terms, without *Abstand* from English – even allowing for the acknowledged subjectivity in Kloss's terminology.[2] In such arguments, morphological variation is simply regarded simply as Scottish exponence of the shared underlying English system of part-of-speech categories and classes, which in any case readily accommodates variation, including in England itself. To the already extensive and richly varied vocabulary of English, a Scottish dimension is simply added through multiple domain extension – that Scottish dimension itself being huge, as testified to by the two historical dictionaries and their spin-offs,[3] and of the highest indexical importance to Scottishness.[4] Claims about languageness on the basis of syntax are dubious, perceiving variation among surface realisations as indexical of separate linguistic identity without regarding them as alternatives or variants of the same underlying system, or without telling the wood of a shared system for the distinctive exponence of a few individual trees. Finally, phonological variation is also explicable as local exponents within an overall English system – after all, the Survey of English Dialects found every vowel possible in pronunciations of the word *stone*.

For those linguists espousing a 'Scots-is-English' view, the arguments of Aitken's seminal 1980 paper have been definitive: Scots does not have a separate linguistic identity. As Falconer (2007) shows, Scots has not 'converged' with English, as Kirk (1997) once claimed, but has become 'asymmetrically converged' or 'dialectalised' with English. Görlach (1998) talks of a vicious circle, with the loss of users cyclically begetting the loss of functions; Falconer presents the situation as a dynamic 'gyre of dialectalisation', with the intimate functions at the centre the ones that survive. The language issue is, rightly, dialectalisation. Besides, in another location, despite efforts by Noah Webster and others, there is still no American language,

---

[1] See, for instance, Kirk 1986, 1987, 1998; Bergs, 2001, 2005; Miller 2004, and numerous histories of English.

[2] Kloss 1978. For discussion of Kloss, with regard to Scots, see also Falconer 2007, Millar 2005, 2006.

[3] *Dictionary of the Older Scottish Tongue*, *Scottish National Dictionary*, *Concise Scots Dictionary*, *Scots Thesaurus*, *A Dictionary of the Scots Language*, etc.

[4] 'A knowledge of Scots is necessary for a knowledge if Scotland.' (*Statement of Principles*, reproduced in this volume on p. 216)

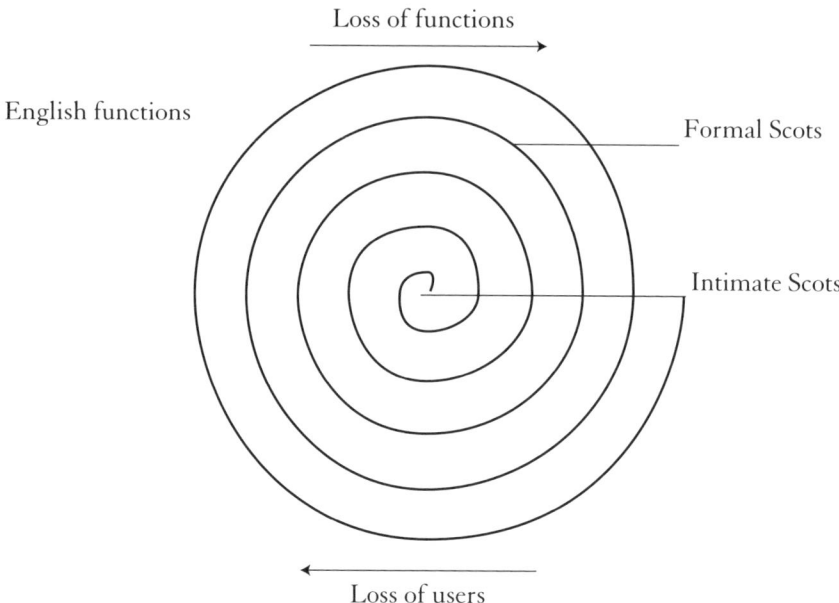

**Figure 5: The Gyre of Dialectalisation**[5]

American English being another standard dialect of the language, just like Scottish English, with various regional dialects within each.

Against this, other linguists, usually ignoring syntax and pragmatics, have simply asserted that the accumulation and combination of exponents or realisations – especially at the lexico-phonological level (*hame* for *home*; *hoose* for *house*, etc.) and at the morphological level (*-it* for *-ed* participles, *the bairns cries oot*, etc.) – amount to a system of their own. Add its massive vocabulary and Scots, therefore, is nothing other than its own language.[6] Because of those realisations, and their widespread prevalence, Falconer (2007) argues that Scots fulfils Kloss's *Mindestabstand* criterion – called 'borderline Abstand' by Millar (2006).[7]

The central language issue concerning Scots is without a doubt 'languageness' – for Scots to be a language (its own *langue* rather than *parole*), dialectal variation has to be codified to the level of that pertaining between languages, not dissimilar to Dutch and Deutsch.[8] If Scots meets Kloss's minimum criterion of *Mindestabstand*, it becomes qualified as a potential *Ausbau* language – or a language which is developable in terms of registers and function and domain. Examples of just such developments in the form of Civil Service Scots are provided by *Lallans* and more recently Corbett (2003) and Corbett and Douglas (2003).

---

[5] I am grateful to Gavin Falconer for permission to publish this figure and for comments on a draft of this paper.

[6] There is an abundance of such views in the literature, including McClure (e.g. 1995, 2009), Purves (2002).

[7] Falconer's (2007) suggestion that regional subvarieties of Scots such as Doric and Shetlandic are *Abstand* languages vis-à-vis Standard English need not concern us here.

[8] Falconer (2007) also contends that North-eastern Scots is *more different* from Standard English than Dutch is from German, even today, while traditional Central Scots is about *as different* from Standard English as Dutch is from German, or the Scandinavian languages from each other today.

In two articles by Jim Miller (2003, 2004), the same morphosyntactic material is presented with identical examples, which are described, in the one, as 'Modern Scots' and, in the other, as 'Scottish English'. No doubt the choice reflects their place of publication: the Modern Scots article appears in the *Edinburgh Companion to the Scots Language*, the purpose of which is to assert and describe Scots as 'a language continuum with Scottish Standard English'; the 'Scottish English' article occurs in a massive compendium of articles pertaining to English all over the world, entitled *A Handbook of Varieties of English: A Multimedia Reference Tool.* Volume 2: *Morphology and Syntax*,[9] where each 'variety of English' is treated in terms of a common set of morphosyntactic features, and where the Englishness of each variety is vindicated.[10] The variationist work throughout Britain and Ireland by Sali Tagliamonte and her collaborators[11] also shows the heteronomy of Scots with the rest of English in these islands and that variation amounts simply to different choices of realisation. There is insufficient *Abstand* with English. So at the core of any debate or tension around Scots is the inescapable descriptive issue around its languageness. *Scots simply ain't a language.*

A further descriptive issue is, however, perfectly clear – if the languageness of Scots *were* granted, there are not two Scotses: a Scotland Scots and an Ulster Scots. Ulster Scots is dialectalised Scots. Falconer (2007) provides an irrefutable deconstruction of the languageness of Ulster Scots claim. As Falconer (in this volume) also shows, following the *Scottish National Dictionary* and Caroline Macafee (2001), Ulster Scots is a contact variety of Central Scots, better to be labelled as Hiberno-Central.[12]

## The Apperceptional Issue

Claims about the languageness of Scots are also made on the basis of apperception. The apperceptional argument would contend that, in their minds, regardless of the descriptive facts, people *classify* Scots as a language, so that, for them, that is what Scots is or becomes. It is Humpty Dumpty's argument: 'a word means what I say it means'. Apperception is the usual basis for the languageness claim, particularly among activists.

Bound up with the language issue for some people is thus also the question of whether Scots actually exists. In a post-devolution age, Scotland may be becoming culturally more and more Scottish, with younger age groups increasingly inclined to think of themselves as only Scottish (and not Scottish and British or only British as their parents or grandparents may havedone). At the same time, what Scottish people regard as their language seems not to be 'Scots', and if they do not get as far as the label 'Scots', they are certainly not getting to the languageness classification. Unless and until there we know the results of the Census question, asking people whether they speak 'Scots', we may not know how many people share the apperceptional view.

## The Literary Language Issue

For some, Scots is an important and powerful functional literary register, expressing states of heart and mind which, for Scottish people, Scots alone can express. Burns's

---

[9] Kortmann and Szmrecsanyi 2004. Cf. also Kortmann, 2008; Szmrecsanyi and Kortmann 2009.

[10] Incidentally, that volume has a fine chapter on Irish English where the common set of features are treated for both the North and South of Ireland by Markku Filppula.

[11] See, for instance, Tagliamonte, Smith and Lawrence. 2005a, 2005b.

[12] Because the identification of the present four main regional dialects of Scots by the SND is largely on the basis of contact, Ulster Scots merits reclassification as the fifth regional dialect – also on the basis of contact.

Kilmarnock edition presented 'poems chiefly in the Scottish Dialect'. As a result of the inspiration from MacDiarmid's poems in *Penny Wheep*, writers in Scots came to form the Scots Language Society, whose main purpose was to encourage the writing of literature in Scots. At the society's meetings, I have observed how MacDiarmid's achievement is referred to as an example and inspiration in discussion after discussion.

However, despite the significant *oeuvre* in traditional literary Scots, much present-day Scottish literary output about the country's mores and characteristic traits of its contemporary people had come to be written in Scottish English. James Kelman, A.L. Kennedy, William McIlvanney, Andrew O'Hagan, Irvine Welsh, for instance, to name but a few, articulate the present-day Scottish condition to Scottish people and to the world, but it is through Scottish English. Roddy MacMillan's play *The Bevellers* was revived in the winter of 2006–7 by the Glasgow Citizens Theatre. After the performance on 6 February 2007, there occurred a discussion between the actors, the director and the audience, in which I participated. I asked whether the actors considered the language which they had just been uttering as Scots. Not one did. It was a Scottish cast, but for each and every one, in their view, the language of *The Bevellers* was 'English', although they were prepared to call it 'Glaswegian', i.e. 'Glaswegian English'. (Yet the text of the play had been published in *Scots Plays of the Seventies*, an anthology compiled by the late Bill Findlay, the title of which categorises the language of such plays as 'Scots'.) Would those novelists have had that success had they written in a 'dense', 'thick', literary Scots (McClure 1995) as used in *Scorn: My Inheritance,* a novel by William Graham? Or how would the Citizens actors have felt about a play by Robert McLellan written in a more traditional literary Scots?

On the other hand, Donald Dewar, one of the few politicians who could show that he had done his reading of Scottish literature, once remarked to the effect that 'as we all know what Scots is, there is no need to do anything for it'.[13] Whereas Dewar may almost certainly have considered Scots to be a literary language, he may also have realised that much literary output was nowadays in Scottish English. Therefore, for a literary language his (and presumably subsequent) Scottish Executive(s) felt that they did not need 'to do anything'.

**The Legislative Issue**

As far as I am aware, it was thanks to lobbying by the Scots Language Society and prime movers such as David Purves and the late John Law that Scots was recognised as a language under the *European Charter for Regional or Minority Languages*.[14] The argument seemed to be that, as Scots was a literary language, and a society existed to promote it as such, it was *tout court* a language. In this context, Scots is better considered as a regional rather than minority language, for demographically it is the tongue of the majority of Scottish people. The Charter is an international convention and thus has status under international law (even if not justiciable under the national laws within the UK). By ratifying it, the UK Government and its devolved institutions were committing themselves to courses of actions with regard to the languages named, to producing reports on those action every three years, and to receiving feedback on those reports by the Council of Europe's Committee of Experts. So the argument is made

---

[13] The remark occurred during a discussion on Scots at the ISAI Conference TCD, October 2000, a few days before his death.

[14] Available from http://conventions.coe.int/Treaty/EN/cadreprincipal.htm

that because the Charter recognises Scots as a language, that is what it is, and everyone should follow its example, as Macafee (2001) once urged. Politics precedes language, as it were. It is certainly this fact of inclusion in the Charter that, in Northern Ireland, Ulster Scots is apparently recognised by the authorities and talked up by the activists as a language. For some, no matter what the arguments of the linguistic case – or their merits – might be, the Charter has decided: Scots is a language, and Ulster Scots, it would seem, another.

### The Speech vs. Writing Issue

Literary language entails a further issue: how far is Scots a matter of speech or writing. No matter how mimetic of actual speech literary writing might be (e.g. James Kelman, Tom Leonard; cf. Kirk 1997, 1999), writers tend to regard their work as 'imaginative' … as an artistic creation crafted out of language. In a recent dissertation on the Belfast dramatist Martin Lynch, which I supervised, the candidate invoked numerous models in pragmatics to show how highly realistic of everyday speech Lynch's play *The Interrogation of Ambrose Fogarty* was.[15] Towards the end of her work, with her arm strengthened by the arguments she had mustered, the candidate interviewed Lynch. Of 'speech realism' he would hear nothing. His plays he regarded as 'pure imagination', as works 'out of his head'. Any overlap with everyday speech was pure coincidence.

When Scots is conceived of as a spoken language, however, it is rural dwellers or the urban working classes who come to mind, arousing mixed reactions. Rural speakers are admired for loyalty to their social origins, although that loyalty is breaking, with some traditional realisations being upheld while others are being abandoned in favour of English forms, as Jennifer Smith (2005) shows with regard to Buckie. And it was with regard to urban speakers that the notion of 'Bad Scots' arose, so labelled because to the language were being transferred associations with its speakers, social judgments masquerading as linguistic categorisation. Thus spoken Scots has tended to be associated with class judgments both favourable and otherwise, and also stigmatisation, and a ' cringe factor'.

A general belief is confirmed that the middle classes in Scotland know more Scots – and more about Scots – than the working classes because it is the middle classes who read literature in Scots; and that it is from literature that the knowledge particularly of vocabulary as well as attitudes of positive approval towards 'the guid Scots tongue' are derived.[16]

There is some convergence between the speech and writing arguments among a very small number of academics and activists, whereby non-literary, i.e. informational and transactional prose is coming to be written in Scots, and speeches made in Scots – albeit mostly speeches first scripted in Scots and then read aloud. Collectively, such Scots has been labelled 'Civil Service Scots' by John Corbett and Fiona Douglas (2003: 202), who provide a good overview and positive assessment of these developments. Also the examples by Ian Brown, Andy Eagle, Billy Kay and John Law in this volume, as well as numerous papers in previous Language and Politics proceedings volumes (e.g. Kirk and Ó Baoill 2000, 2001, 2003), and documets such as a *Statement of Principles* (see this volume p. 216).

---

[15] The play was coincidentally revived by Tinderbox during the summer at the Grand Opera House, Belfast.
[16] Karl-Inge Sandred, *Good or Bad Scots? Attitudes to Optional Lexical and Grammatical Usages in Edinburgh.* Studia Anglistica Upsaliensia 48. Uppsala: Acta Universitatis Upsaliensis. 1983.

The challenge thus rests with the expansion or *Ausbau* of the literary language to other domains not sounding too literary and yet at the same time not sounding too colloquial, vernacular or stigmatised, none of which seems likely to win approval.

**The Social Need Issue**

Experiments in formal prose in Scots are extremely few. As Falconer (2007) shows, Scots is entirely revivable – Scots could legitimately reclaim its languageness again, 'a once and future language'. Without experimentation, there can be no *Ausbau*, and the experimentation of 'Civil Service Scots' referred to two paragraphs ago are cases in point. But what holds back further experimentation is almost certainly the lack of will or desire, or the absence of a rationale or justification, on the greater part of both the population as well as Holyrood politicians, to take any action. Such, too, are the reactions to some of the striking experiments in Northern Ireland: Civil Service Ullans is not giving ordinary people their *braid Scotch* back again. There is a huge schism – 'dislocation', according to Millar (2009; also this volume) – between ordinary speakers and revivalist activists whose apparent aim was to increase *Abstand* rather than *Ausbau*. There is even less comprehension and a lot more incredulity about experimentation in the Republic of Ireland.

So the social questions of 'why bother?' and 'for what use?' bring us back to the central theme of the 2007 symposium. There appear to be two polar positions: If the twin premises of Scotsness and languageness (*langue*) are granted – that Scots exists as a language – then is the matter resolved? Has Scots arrived so that it needs no further pleading? Was Dewar right that there is nothing to be done? If the twin premises of Scotsness and languageness are not granted, is Scots merely *parole*? Does the commonality of the various dialects amount merely to a supra-regional dialect, a national tongue? If the national tongue is not a language, is it ultimately English? Even *'Northern and Insular Scots* (Millar 2007) appears subordinated under the general series title of *Dialects of English*. And for dialects of English, whither the provisions of the Charter? The fine line surrounding languageness is the source of much debate and a cause of much tension. As Johnson observes: "the attribution of 'languagehood' is as much of a socio-political judgement as a linguistic one' (207: 105).

Either way, as 'language' or 'dialect', Scotland can still be claimed as Scots-speaking. Or is Jim Miller's implicit point that 'Scots' and 'Scottish English' are two names for the one and the same socio-political reality? Perhaps it is an implicit rather than explicit language:[17] if anything is to be done, it is more a question of awareness-raising and attitude shift. Was there any need for Scots to recognised by the European Charter? Is the Executive thereby justified in its stance hitherto of effectively of 'doing nothing'?[18]

If one accepts that Scotland is not Scots-speaking, is the goal of all activism to make Scotland so and to provide for promotion and implementation? Or is writing Scots the goal – ultimately nothing short of full-scale revival? Fully-fledged Civil Service Scots?

Or is the goal to do neither? Is the goal rather more about changing underlying attitudes and values? Is the goal to get people like the Citizens Scottish actors to accept that plays such as *The Bevellers* are written in Scots (as Findlay claims) and that that is a good thing for Scottishness? Is it about adopting the label 'Scots'? Is it about

---

[17] Other metaphors have been used for such borderline cases. Ó Riagáin (2003: 301) talks of 'hidden' and 'eclipsed' languages; Montgomery (1997) talks of Ulster-Scots as a 'submerged' language.

[18] For further discussion of this point, see Kirk 2008.

encouragement 'where useful', 'where there is demand', as the Charter puts it? The papers on Scots on economic development in Kirk and Ó Baoill (2009) identify that what was exploiting Scots as a marketing tool was the commercial entrepreneurial world, without any legislation or government directive.

Perhaps, if left to market or consumer forces, less than full-scale revival is a worthy goal. If people find it beneficial to use Scots, or to refer to their way of speaking or writing as Scots, so be it. It might all come down to *laissez faire*, however *laissez faire* would not be justified in terms of the European Charter because it makes explicit reference actions rather than inactions.

Less than full-scale revival might amount to no more than symbolism – after all, Scots people have always used their knowledge of Scottish words and locutions to reinforce their Scottishness. The English of any Scottish speaker contains Scotticisms galore – Scottish people switch and drift in and out of Scotticisms willy-nilly, unconsciously, as circumstances require. The real difference is in written language – not just official prose, but public signage, newspapers, forms, packaging, menus, labels, and so on. Giftware from t-shirts, coffee mugs, coasters to mouse mats has come to display Scots words and sayings. (I have t-shirts with *braw* and *blether* and another with *It's a sair fecht* on it.) It strikes me that short texts with a symbolic value might well be the way forward, rather than texts with a functional or transactional value (such as instructions or minutes or the myriad of Civil Service documents), where the utilitarian or communicative value is doubtful. It is hard to justify transactional written Scots to secure co-operation or an intended communicative goal; but there is no end to symbolism, which is both easier to achieve and much harder to object to.

In speech, there is a fair deal of symbolism already in operation. Quite apart from distinct lexical items like *dreich* or *gollach*, or *scunner* or *tatties*, Scottish pronunciations of core vocabulary shared with English such as *hoose* or *hame*, *fae* or *tae*, *doon* or *oot* are shibboleths or markers of Scottishness, indices to a shared Scottish culture with a set of references and values inexpressible through any other exponents or realisations, as one would find in the rest of the English-speaking world. For many, it is simply those realisations which put the vitality into Scots and may be sufficient. Others, like my late father, who left school at 14 without much formal education, for all he uttered such Scottish realisations continually, never once considered himself speaking Scots – it was always English. For him, Scots was what I did when, as a boy, I would recite ballads or Burns.

### The Nine Symposium Questions

The crucial point is that answers to these questions hang on the stance adopted towards languageness, or status as an autonomous linguistic system, for every question depends crucially on the languageness issue.

**(A)** *What's wrong with current arrangements and practice? What research is needed to show what needs to be done?*
Regardless of whether the Scottish Executive thinks of Scotland as Scots-speaking, or whether it considers Scots simply to be English, if the Scottish Executive believes that nothing needs to be done, it probably thinks current arrangements and practice are fine. But if activism wishes Scots to be promoted either in terms of the European Charter Part II, or even Part III, then the arrangements and practice need to be spelled out. Events have progressed since the 2007 symposium. The Scottish Executive/ Government, elected in 2007, created a working group on Scots under the

chairmanship of Derrick McClure in 2009.[19] The group submitted its first report on 30 November 2010.[20] For a review of the group's work, see Robinson (2011).

**(B)** *Is Scots alone sufficient means to ensure its vibrancy and maintenance as a community language?*
If it is accepted that Scotland is Scots-speaking, Scots is being maintained as a community language and thereby its vibrancy is confirmed. It is beside the point what qualities the language itself has. Scots is no less sufficient than English or Gaelic or Irish. Where Scots is deficient is in its functionality owing to disuse. If it is not accepted that Scotland is Scots-speaking, the central questions concern its utilitarian value and people's desire to benefit from using Scots.

**(C)** *How far is the sustaining of Scots communities in Scotland and Northern Ireland and the Republic of Ireland conditional on infrastructure, environment, society, employment, urban renewal, culture, or anything else?*
If it is accepted that Scotland, Northern Ireland and the Republic of Ireland are Scots-speaking, then there is no dependency on such factors as listed, for its communities are being sustained. If it is granted that Scots needs to be promoted, it will take more than greater literary effort or new dictionaries to ensure community-wide adoption and communicative success. Activism will have to define its goals and its means to achieve them through the Executive and their agencies and through the local authorities, but if, crucially, public opinion could be swung in line, activism might come to be reinforced in its calls for support from such factors as infrastructure, environment, or employment.

**(D)** *What is the role of education in the sustaining of a Scots-speaking community – e.g. developing social skills, cultural identity or linguistic confidence?*
I had a good school education in literature in Scots, which was probably the source of my interest in Scots today. As a fresh graduate in the mid-seventies, I joined a group run by Joy Hendry called CASLS (Campaign for the Advancement of Scottish Literature in the Scottish School) for it seemed to me essential that Scottish Literature should be taught in the Scottish school. The success of the campaign may be doubtful – Scottish Literature is now mainstreamed among a set of other options within English, so that, whereas its presence on the curriculum no longer needs to be campaigned for, it may be easy to ignore it.

Education needs to take a broader approach to contemporary language – not as historical philology, but as sociolinguistics and pragmatics, showing and explaining how language is used in society, to help or occasionally hinder us, how it empowers or manipulates us, and so on, regardless of whether it is in Scots or not.

**(E)** *How far is the integration of Scots and culture into the community an environmental issue?*
If it is accepted that Scotland is Scots-speaking, the environmental issue is presumably solved. Just as public life is now smoke-free, with smoking zones part of the innovation, so everyone could be encouraged to speak Scots in situations of public exchanges or service transactions. Although people are probably speaking in Scots anyway, signs could be displayed informing customers or clients that the premises are 'Scots-speaking' or 'Scots-colloguin'. It might not change too many people's habits, but there would be the potential for a shift of attitude and perception.

[19] see http://www.scotland.gov.uk/News/Releases/2009/10/29151643
[20] see http://www.scotland.gov.uk/Publications/2010/11/25121454/0

(F) *Is the approach to such questions top-down or bottom-up? Whose task or responsibility is it ultimately to sustain a Scots-speaking community?*
In Scotland, since devolution, the former Executive moved slowly; the Dewar strategy of 'doing nothing' mentioned above exposed that almost all effort was bottom-up. *A Strategy for the Scotland's Languages,*[21] published in 2007 was anything but a language strategy (see Kirk 2008); since 2007, there has been some acceleration with an audit, a conference, a working group, and now a report. Meanwhile, a question about Scots in the 2011 Census in Scotland and Northern Ireland has also been agreed.[22]

The top-down approach in Scotland seems to be facilitation of bottom-up efforts through the Scots language organisations, especially Scottish Language Dictionaries and the Scots Language Centre, which have received direct funding from the Government since 2009, and others, such as the Scots Language Society, and also in a steady and unheralded way, by commercial enterprise producing words in Scots on giftware and business signage (see Hance 2009). In Northern Ireland, the Inter-departmental Charter Implementation Group signals some top-down responsibility and intent.[23]

(G) *What role can universities and other institutions of higher education play?*
Universities can provide leadership through research and dissemination, although there must first be suitably qualified subject expertise in place, sadly a dwindling resource. Much good would come from an Institute for the Languages of Scotland[24] where all questions pertaining to Scots, Gaelic and any other language could be addressed, especially if such an institute were based in a university, with access for research in a range of ways and facilities for dissemination.

(H) *With the arrival in Scotland and Northern Ireland and the Republic of Ireland of significant numbers of speakers of Eastern European languages, how far have the future role and supporting mechanisms for Scots been undermined?*
With recently arrived Eastern European languages in the Scottish and Irish communities, both the language question and that of need are immediately answered. At a recent church service in Belfast conducted in English, and which I attended, Polish speakers were encouraged to respond in Polish. If there is a case for Scots, that case should not be undermined by immigrants, as that case remains the same. The arrival of new languages has simply made the demand for provision bigger out of communicative need, whereas provision for Scots (and indeed Gelic and Irish) involves the need for creating demand through increasing ability, encouraging intergenerational transmission, raising status, etc.

(I) *Where are there communities where minority languages are being successfully sustained? What comparisons may be drawn with Scots, and what lessons are to be learned?*
The closest parallel may be with Low German, but the clearest success parallel is with Switzerland (see Fischer 2001 and Eagle in this volume).

(J)*In comparison with Gaelic, where does Scots stand with regard to its being a community language for much of the Scottish population, and what is being or should be done for it? And for Scots speakers in Northern Ireland and the Republic of Ireland?*

---

[21] See http://www.scotland.gov.uk/Publications/2007/01/24130746/0
[22] http://www.scotslanguage.com/articles/view/1307
[23] http://www.dcalni.gov.uk/index/language-cultural-diversity-r08.htm
[24] For the feasibility study into an institute, seehttp://www.arts.ed.ac.uk/celtscot/institutelanguagesscotland/

Happily, Scots is neither in conflict nor experiencing rivalry with Gaelic (except perhaps for funding). Gaelic wins on the languageness issue; Scots wins on numbers. The large Gaelic-speaking population in Glasgow makes Gaelic a national issue, as the almost country-wide distribution of place-names also shows.[25] Not to accept Gaelic as a national issue is tantamount to accepting it purely as a regional language. In Northern Ireland, Scots has become politically linked with Irish. Regardless of functional or utilitarian merits, equal rather than equitable treatment for Scots is urged by its activists. Because of this focus, arguments about Scots in Northern Ireland tend not to link with Scots in Scotland, to the detriment of both, despite their shared ancestry and common dialectal status. It is as if Scots in Northern Ireland matters more as a badge of identity mirroring and challenging Irish than as a kin-tongue shared with Scotland.

As Mari FitzDuff (2000) reminds us, language is always used in politics to sort something else out. Spolsky (2006) makes the same point by arguing that language policy functions in an ecological relationship between linguistic and non-linguistic factors ... i.e. it serves as a surrogate political issue of another ideological agenda, i.e. to sort something else out ... so language choice in the Scottish Civil Service may be considered as a question of Scottishness vs. Britishness. Categorising Scots as English and refusing support is no doubt connected to an all-British agenda; recasting Scots as a language and providing support goes hand in glove with a Scottish nationalist agenda. Paradoxically, providing support for Scots in Northern Ireland and building on the European Charter's designation as a language under its own name lets unionists feel more secure within a regionalist discourse; at the same time, 'Ulster' nationalists may feel that bit closer to repartition and their own brand of nationalism within an independent Ulster state. Whatever one's view of Scotland and Northern Ireland as Scots-speaking communities, there are serious costs and implications.

Because of these conflicting views, it is hardly surprising that there is no language policy for Scots. For there to be a language policy, according to Bernard Spolsky, three factors have to be operating coherently and cohesively: practice, management, and beliefs (or ideology). As I have indicated, beliefs and ideology thrive in abundance, but they are only operationalised in a limited way through literary writing[26] or experimentation in other written registers. Literary endeavours do not require a language policy, however, and, as Lo Bianco has argued, no policy is also a policy.

Any state management with regard to Scots has been conspicuous by its absence. With a nationalist Government now in power in Scotland, there appears rapidly to be a sea-change afoot, which might, at last, lead to some kind of policy. The preparation for such a policy can build on years of research, reflection and commentary by the likes of Derrick McClure, the working group's chairman. The Government can take forward initiatives such as the proposal for a Languages Institute, and it can continue to encourage literary expression and study. To be a general language policy, however, the preparation needs to connect with the changing attitudes towards Scottishness and nationalism, to convince the people of Scotland the fact that the strongest and most abiding sense of Scottish identity is not through its distinctive political, legal and religious institutions but through its native tongue – Scots – and to assess the appetite and demand for full-scale revival or for something less. If the way forward for Scotland

---

[25] MacCaluim (2007) shows just how widespread Gaelic is throughout Scotland.

[26] In, for instance, *Lallans*, the Scots Language Society's magazine, where successive style sheets have been adopted with the intention of managing the language and influencing practice, mostly at an orthographical level. By contrast, in an anthology of short stories such as *A Tongue in Yer Heid*, compiled by James Robertson, there is a wide variety of spellings, from the traditional literary to the urban demotic.

is as a Scots-speaking community, let us welcome the working group's report for it provides what is currently the best opportunity for a policy to be formulated and the implemented for the whole nation. With such a report, for once, Scots may be learning from Gaelic.

**References**

Aitken, A.J. 1980. 'The Good Old Scots Tongue: Does Scots have an Identity?. In eds. Haugen, E., McClure, J.D. and D. Thomson. *Minority Languages Today*. Edinburgh: Edinburgh University Press. 72–90.
Bergs, A. 2005. *Modern Scots*. Second Edition. Languages of the World/Materials 242. München: Lincom Europa.
Corbett, J. 2003. 'Language Planning and Modern Scots'. In eds. Corbett, J. *et al.* 251–72.
Corbett, J., McClure, J.D. and J. Stuart-Smith, 2003. *The Edinburgh Companion to Scots*, Edinburgh University Press.
Corbett, J. and F. Douglas. 2003. 'Scots in the Public Sphere'. In eds. Kirk, J.M. and D.P. Ó Baoill. 198–210.
Falconer, G. 2007. *Scots: Decline, Revival, Divergence*. Unpublished PhD Thesis, Queen's University of Belfast.
Filppula, M. 2004. 'Irish English: Morphology and Syntax'. In eds. Kortmann *et al.* 73–101
Filppula, M. 2008. 'Irish English: Morphology and Syntax'. In eds. Kortmann and Upton. 328–59
Findlay, B. ed. 2001. *Scots Plays of the Seventies: An Anthology*. Dalkeith: Scottish Cultural Press.
Fisher, A. 2001. 'Language and Politics in Switzerland'. In eds. Kirk, J.M. and D.P. Ó Baoill. 105–22.
FitzDuff, M. 2000. 'Language and Politics in a Global Perspective'. In eds. Kirk, J.M. and D.P. Ó Baoill. 75–80
Görlach, M. 1998 'Text Types and the History of Scots'. In his *Even More Englishes: Studies 1996–1997*. Varieties of English Around the World General Series, vol. 22. Amsterdam: John Benjamins. 55–77.
Graham, W. 1997. *Scorn: My Inheritance?* Glasgow: Scotsoun.
Hance, M. 2009. 'Scots and the Economy'. In eds. Kirk, J.M. and Ó Baoill, D.P. eds. 183–185.
Johnston, P.A., Jr. 2007. 'Scottish English and Scots'. In ed. Britain, D. *Language in the British Isles*. Cambridge: Cambridge University Press.
Jones, C. ed. 1997. *The Edinburgh History of the Scots Language*. Edinburgh: Edinburgh University Press.
Kirk, J.M. 1986. *Aspects of the Grammar in a Corpus of Dramatic Texts in Scots*. Unpublished PhD Thesis, University of Sheffield.
Kirk, J.M. 1987. 'The Heteronomy of Scots with Standard English'. In eds. Macafee, C. and I. Macleod. *The Nuttis Schell: Essays on the Scots Language*. Aberdeen: Aberdeen University Pres. 166–81.
Kirk, J.M. 1997. 'Irish English and Contemporary Literary Writing'. In ed. Kallen, J. *Focus on Ireland*. Varieties of English Around the World General Series, vol. 21. Amsterdam:: John Benjamins. 189–205.
Kirk, J.M. 1998. 'Ulster Scots: Realities and Myths'. *Ulster Folklife* 44: 69–93.

Kirk, J.M. 1999. 'Contemporary Irish Writing and a Model of Speech Realism'. In eds. Taavitsainen, I., Melchers, G. and P. Pahta. *Writing in Nonstandard English*. Pragmatics and Beyond New Series 67. Amsterdam: John Benjamins. 45–61.

Kirk, J.M. 2008. 'Does the UK Have a Language Policy?' *Journal of Irish and Scottish Studies* 1.2: 205–22.

Kirk, J.M. and D.P. Ó Baoill. eds. 2000. *Language and Politics: Northern Ireland, the Republic of Ireland, and Scotland*. Belfast Studies in Language, Culture and Politics 1. Belfast: Cló Ollscoil na Banríona.

Kirk, J.M. and D.P. Ó Baoill. eds. 2001. *Linguistic Politics: Language Policies for Northern Ireland, the Republic of Ireland, and Scotland*. Belfast Studies in Language, Culture and Politics 3. Belfast: Cló Ollscoil na Banríona.

Kirk, J.M. and D.P. Ó Baoill. eds. 2003. *Towards our Goals in Broadcasting, the Press, the Performing Arts and the Economy: Northern Ireland, the Republic of Ireland, and Scotland*. Belfast Studies in Language, Culture and Politics 10. Belfast: Cló Ollscoil na Banríona.

Kirk, J.M. and D.P. Ó Baoill. eds. 2005. *Legislation, Literature and Sociolinguistics: Northern Ireland, the Republic of Ireland, and Scotland*. Belfast Studies in Language, Culture and Politics 13. Belfast: Cló Ollscoil na Banríona.

Kirk, J.M. and D.P. Ó Baoill. eds. 2009. *Language and Economic Development: Northern Ireland, the Republic of Ireland, and Scotland*. Belfast Studies in Language, Culture and Politics 19. Belfast: Cló Ollscoil na Banríona.

Kirk, J.M. and D.P. Ó Baoill. eds. 2011. *Strategies for Minority Languages. Northern Ireland, the Republic of Ireland, and Scotland*. Belfast Studies in Language, Culture and Politics 22. Belfast: Cló Ollscoil na Banríona.

Kloss, H. 1967. '"Abstand Languages" and "Ausbau Languages"'. *Anthropological Linguistics* 9: 29–41.

Kloss, H. 1978. *Die Entwicklung neuer germanischer Kultursprachen seit 1800*. Second Edition. Düsseldorf: Schwann.

Kortmann, B. 2008. 'Synopsis: Morphological and Syntactic Variation in the British Isles'. In eds. Kortmann and Upton. 478–95.

Kortmann, B., Burridge, K., Mesthrie, R., Schneider, E.W. and C. Upton. *A Handbook of Varieties of English*. Vol. 2: *Morphology and Syntax*. Berlin: Mouton de Gruyter.

Kortmann, B. and B. Szmrecsanyi. 2004. 'Global Synopsis: Morphological and Syntactic Variation in English'. In eds. Kortmann *et al.* 1142–202.

Kortmann, B. and C. Upton. 2008. *Varieties of English: The British Isles*. Berlin: Mouton de Gruyter.

Macafee, Caroline, 1980. 'Characteristics of Non-standard Grammar in Scotland'. Unpublished typescript.

Macafee, C. 2001a. 'Scots: Hauf Empty or Hauf Fu?' In eds. Kirk, J.M. and D.P Ó Baoill. 159–68.

Macafee, C. 2001b. 'Lowland Sources of Ulster Scots: Some Comparisons between Robert Gregg's Data and *The Linguistic Atlas of Scotland* (Volume 3). In eds.Kirk, J.M. and D.P. Ó Baoill. *Language Links: The Languages of Scotland and Ireland*. Belfast: Cló Ollscoil na Banríona. 119–132.

McClure, J.D. 2009. *Why Scots Matters*. Third Edition. Edinburgh: The Saltire Society.

McClure, J.D. 1995. *Scots and its Literature*. Amsterdam: John Benjamins.

McMillan, R. 1974. *The Bevellers*. Edinburgh: Southside.

Millar, R.McC. 2005. *Language, Nation and Power: An Introduction*. Houndmills: Palgrave.

Millar, R.McC. 2006. '"Burying alive": Unfocussed Governmental Language Policy and Scots'. *Language Policy* 5: 63–86

Miller R.McC. 2007. *Dialects of English: Northern and Insular Scots*. Edinburgh: Edinburgh University Press.

Millar, R.McC. 2009. 'Dislocation: Is It Presently Possible to Envisage an Economically Based Language Policy for Scots in Scotland?'. In eds. Kirk, J.M. and D.P. Ó Baoill. 75-80

Miller, J. 1993. 'The Grammar of Scottish English'. In eds. Milroy J. and L. Milroy, *The Grammar of English Dialects in the British Isles*. Harlow: Longman. 99–138.

Miller, Jim. 2003. 'Syntax and Discourse in Modern Scots'. In eds. Corbett, J. *et al*. 72–109.

Miller, J. 2004. 'Scottish English'. In eds. Kortmann *et al.* 54–72.

Miller, J. 2008. 'Scottish English: Morphology and Syntax'. In eds. Kortmann and Upton. 299–327.

Montgomery, M. 2004. 'Ulster-Scots: Lost or Submerged?' In eds. Kelly, W. and J.R. Young. *Ulster and Scotland, 1600–2000: History, Language and Identity*. Dublin: Four Courts Press. 121–32.

Ó Riagáin, D. 2003. 'Walloon and Scots: A Response to Jean-Luc Fauconnier'. In eds. Kirk, J.M. and D.P. Ó Baoill. 301–2.

Purves, David, 2002. *A Scots Grammar: Scots Grammar and Usage*. Second Edition. Edinburgh: The Saltire Society.

Robinson, C. 2011. 'The Ministerial Working Group on the Scots Language'. In eds. Kirk, J.M. and D.P. Ó Baoill. *Strategies for Minority Languages: Northern Ireland, the Republic of Ireland, and Scotland*. Belfast Studies in Language, Culture and Politics 22. Belfast: Cló Ollscoil na Banríona.

Smith, J. 2005. 'The Sociolinguistics of Contemporary Scots: Insights from one Community'. In eds. Kirk, J.M. and D.P. Ó Baoill. 112–25.

Spolsky, B. 2006. *Language Policy*. Cambridge: Cambridge University Press.

Spolsky, B. 2010. *Language Management*. Cambridge. Cambridge University Press.

*Statement of Principles*. 2003. Edinburgh: The Scots Parliament Cross Party Group on the Scots Language.

Szmrecsanyi, B. and B. Kortmann. 2009. 'Vernacular Universals and Angloversals in a Typological Perspective'. In eds. Filppula, M., Klemola J. and H. Paulasto, *Vernacular Universals and Language Contacts: Evidence from Varieties of English and Beyond*. London: Routledge. 33–53.

Tagliamonte, S., Smith, J. and H. Lawrence. 2005a. 'No Taming the Vernacular: Insights from the Relatives in Northern Britain'. *Language Variation and Change* 17.2: 75–112.

Tagliamonte, S., Smith, J. and H. Lawrence. 2005b. 'English Dialects in the British Isles in Cross-variety Perspective: A Base-line for Future Research'. In eds. Filppula, M. Klemola, J., Palkander, M. and E. Pentilla. *Dialects Across Borders: Selected Papers from the 11th International Conference on Methods in Dialectology*. Amsterdam: John Benjamins. 87–117.

# Lowsin Time, Yokin Time: The Scots Leid in Twa Thoosan an Seiven

*Billy Kay*

Back in ma hame toun in Ayrshire a pickle year syne, a local bodie that wrocht as an electreician an hed duin gey weel for himsel in the wark wi his ain companie an a wheen sparkies unner him, cam up tae me in the pub, eident tae recoont for me an incident that had happened the efternuin afore ... says he. 'It wes gey nearhaun fower o clock, Billy, sae I says, "Richt boys, redd up and gaither aw yer graith thegither, its lowsin time".' Just then a bit cam on the wireless aboot the daith o the Scots language, wi an 'expert' lamentin the fack that 'once common words like *graith* and *redd up* and *lowsin time* were no longer in currency'. Me an the boays juist luikit at ane anither, dumbfoonert, an speirin whit kinna planet we wes leivin on!

I aften think o sic 'expertise' when I see anti-Scots harangues by the likes o kenspeckle feigures like the richt wing historian Michael Fry scrievin in *The Sunday Times* or slightly less richt wing politeicians o the Labour Pairty like Paisley's MSP Hugh Henry scrievin in the *Paisley Daily Express*, an they gie wersh vent tae scunnersome levels o ignorance anent Scots. Mr Fry, conteinually threips that Scots doesnae exist, an in ae parteicularly ugsome airticle whaur he wes on an election campaign trail in the Howe o the Mearns aince described the fowk o the Mearns as speakin Gibbon ... an echo o the brilliant Scots makar Lewis Grassic Gibbon author o the Seminal triliogy, *A Scots Quair*, ... but also perhaps a reference tae the species o monkey cried gibbon? Mr Henry, on the ither haund, spelt his opposeition oot thus:

> There are some who believe that what is described as 'Scots language', should be given the same status as Gaelic ... In support of this I received an e-mail from, and I quote the 'Secretair o Scots tung' My computer went into overdrive trying to spell check the e – mail. My brain went numb trying to understand it .... I would rather ask questions which produce information on whether our society is tackling inequality, poor health, bad housing, low incomes than confuse people with strange words which few would understand.

The toun o Paisley aff coorse, like a wheen toonships here in Ulster is hame tae a great tradeition o Scots poetry and sang wrocht by the rhymin wabsters, a tradeition celebratit throughout Scotland in the sangs o Robert Tannahill and raxin as faur as the United States in the wark o Alexander Wilson ... naebody but the dowf ignorant cuid be 'confused' by their 'strange words which few would understand.' Whit a dowie indictment o a society whan a prominent chiel like Henry can be that fremmit an faur fae the cultural history o his ain airt that he can miscry an disparage the language at its hert. Like Henry and Fry, ma experience is that monie o thaim that threaps on aboot Scots wuidnae ken a Scots word gin it lowped up an skelped thaim on the puss! An that is the problem for uphauders an upsteerers for Scots whan we discuss themes like sustainabeility – there ar fowk in poseitions o pouer, fowk in poseitions o influence that wad raither maintain an sustain the divine richt o kings, than gie succour tae the language o ower a million and a hauf o their fella countrymen, women an weans.

Luikin at the Prospectus for the symposium, the follaein thochts struck me anent Scots – factors that gar it hae a gey different status fae Gaelic for example, in fack the best parallels wi Scots are mebbe tae be seen in the like o Galicia or tae a lesser extent Catalonia, in the days afore the dramatic revival that haes taen place in the hinner enn o the twentieth centurie since the daith o Franco.

Altho maist o thaim wadnae welcome the comparison, monie o the fowk that hae wieldit pouer in cultural maitters ower the last wheen years hae been the Scottish equeivalent o the Guarda Civil, that yist tae tell Catalans in Barcelona tae stop barkin like dugs, an speak the language o the empire when they yaised their mither tongue in public places when fascism bore the gree.

In the new edeition o *Scots: The Mither Tongue*,[1] I describe ma personal experience o tryin tae mak linguistic democracy wark through bein a memmer o the Cross Pairty Group for Scots. Whit I feel is that until recently, maist o the fowk we've had tae deal wi come fae a nerra spectrum o Scottish life, fowk that conteinue the auld, unionist focus of baith left an richt in the auld districk cooncils maist were thirled tae afore makin the step up tae whit they should regaird as their National Pairliament. Haein seen our politeicans frae a closer perspective, I feel that the hosteility an ignorance o ethnic Scottish culture displayed by possibly the majority in the mak up o the previous pairliament means that the hard chave tae gie Scots ony status whitsoever wad hae been resisitit wi virr. In fack, afore the raicent chynge o goverment, I wes o the opeinion that we micht hae needit tae mak an appeal tae Europe tae gar the Scottish Executive fulfil its responsibeilities towards Scots. For while whit they cried the "slave mentality" existed in Catalonia and certain elites identified wi Spanish culture, maist Catalans still had a regaird for Catalan culture. Monie Scottish politeicians houever see Scottish culture as something tae be duin doun because it is an uncannie harbinger o nationalist sentiment. Exaggeration? Here are twa examples, quotations by Labour meinisters related tae me fae traistworthy sources . In the first an education meinister is spiered why there isnae mair duin tae forder Scottish studies in the Schuils' curriculum. The repone; "I do not see my role as educating a generation of young nationalists." In the saicont, a member o the CPG asks the meinister for culture whether he hes receivit the invitation sent oot in English an Scots tae come tae the neist gatherin o the group? The repone; "Oh, that thing, written in the funny writing – I threw it in the bin." Noo thon is the level o ceinicism that bore the gree within the last admeinistration. On the Conservative side, the attitude tae Scots wesnae much better. In Februar 2000, there wes a debate as to whether a question on Scots should be includit in the 2001 Census. Here are extracts fae twa o the Tory contributions.

> Jamie McGrigor
> I am a firm advocate of the protection of the Scots language. Like Gaelic, its history is timeless and is surrounded by romance. I love the poetry of Burns and MacDiarmid and never go anywhere without my nickie-tams

> Brian Monteith
> In concluding my speech in the debate on a census question on Scots language, I feel that it is only right that we say that we are gaunae no dae that.

Ane quotin fae a comedian, the ither being a comedian, hard tae say whit ane wes the

---

[1] Billy Kay, *Scots: The Mither Tongue*. Third Edition. (Edinburgh: Mainstream, 2006)

biggest scunner, but baith certainly gart me grue at the time! Haein spent years chavin an fechtin for a Scottish pairliament, it was a salutory experience tae thole the fack that at the first opportunity tae discuss Scots, ye hae electit members and fellae Scots makin a fuil o the issue. On siccan occasiouns whan I feel nocht but alienation fae ma brither an sister Scots, in ma lugs I hear Hugh McDiarmid's humorous repone tae the same conundrum:

> "Mercy o' Gode, I canna thole
> wi sic an orra mob to roll"
> *"Wheesht! It's for the guid o your soul."*
> (from 'A Drunk Man Looks at the Thistle')

It micht be for the guid o my soul, but I dinnae like whit it duis tae ma heid!

Thirs examples o the kinna fowk wi pouer in our societie in raicent years, sae it will tak a muckle shift o sensibeilitie tae chynge things for the better. Until nou they haenae thocht it pairt o their remit tae dae ocht aboot hainin the culture an language o the community that electit thaim.

Sae ti turn tae the prospectus for the Symposium, (see Innin tae Part 4 o this buikie).

### Pynt A
Ae major source o sustainabeility – support fae the government – haes rarely been available ti the Scots speakin community. It hes aye been the screivers o buiks, an poetry, and the singers o sangs, an maist o aw the fowk that hae a guid Scots tongue in their heid that hes sustainit the leid against the odds. Whit we hae hed is sporadic tokenism, gestures for the language tae schaw that they cannae ignore it aw thegither, but as faur as helpin sustain or cherish it as a leivin entity, forget it. The refusal tae pit in a question in the last census kythes that there wes never an eident desire tae finn oot ocht aboot the leid an dae ocht for its survival. As faur as thon census then, an the neist ane's concerned, the auld Scots saw hains a lot o wisdom …'ye cannae dae ocht gin ye've nocht tae dae ocht wi'.

### Pynt B
Can leids like Scots survive on their ain resources. In the past aye, in the praisent, Naw.

### Pynt C
Hou faur is the sustainin o sic languages dependent on infrastructure? A wheen European examples can be citit tae kythe hou crucial this is whaur the same leid drees gey different weirds because the poleitical will tae provide an infrastructure is that different in different airts whaur the leid is the historic leid o the area. Contrast the muckle an successful normalisation programme for Catalan in Catalonia, the varied resistance tae that concept in neebourin Valencia an the Balearics and even waur, the near daith o the leid ower the border in France whaur it bides an tholes as the leid o a stigmatised minoritie, the traivellers an gypsies.

Regairdin employment, rural Aiberdeenshire wes ane o the hertlands o spoken Scots afore the ile rush o the later 20th centurie, but the inrush o ootsiders efter the ile rush, haes resultit in erosion o the native Doric dialect. I wad jalouse the day that the richest dialects o spoken Scots amang younger fowk will be funnd in unemployment bleck spots in former minin communities in the like o Wast Fife an Sooth Ayrshire. In the latter, remoteness, an the leivin Burns tradeition are baith factors as weel – in the late Eichties when I wes makin a televeision programme on the history o the Scottish miners, I mind tellin ma ain faither that I haed been doon filmin at miners raws in the muirs abuin Patna, an he said 'By, ye've been oot amang the whaups the day, son!!' Gin Scotland ever duis hae the poleitical will tae re-vitalise Scots, thae banks an braes o bonnie Doon cuid be a grand airt tae hae simmer schuils an residencies alang the lines o whit's been tried in Ireland in the *Gaeltachti*. We jist need tae lowse the reigns o the Cannae Dae mentality o the pit powney, an get yokit tae the muckle Can Dae mentality of the Clydesdale!

We hae tak tent tae o the importance o sic tradeitional industries lik minin, biggin hooses, weavin, fermin, fishin etc in hainin leivin Scots words in the mooth o the populace an makin shuir whaur possible, gin the industry gaes doon an disappears, then the relevant vocabulary is kept – yokin an lowsin are fine for stertin an feinishin ony darg for example.

### Pynt D
Whit is the role o Education in developin social skills, identity an confidence? Ma frien Matthew Fitt haes gien vivid examples o hou gien status tae a bairns language hes dramatically affected their wey o behavin in the cless. I'm shuir his Cuddy Brae experiment wull lang be citit an spiered at, as regairds this maitter. Closer tae hame, I'm gey shuir that the abeilitie I hae tae speak ither leids cam fae belangin a bilingual faimily environment whaur the native Scots wes encouraged – thaim wi a guid Scots tongue in their heid are fit tae gang ower the world – wes ma faither's favourite saw, an I follaet it an preived it richt. In turn, ma ain confidence tae promote ma mither tongue cam fae ma success in learnin French, German, Russian an Portuguese. An I've seen it in my ain bairns – whaur hearin Scots, English an Portuguese in the hoose gied thaim a confident facility wi language.

### Pynt E
How faur is the integration o language an culture an environmental issue. Aw leivin things need tae be cherished an looed, an nurtured – languages are nae different – Scots needs the same kinna educational an cultural support as ither languages in normal societies. Tae be at ane wi the environment that wrocht us, we hae tae ken the words fowk hae yaised ower the years tae descrive it – the hichts an howes, burns an firths, drookin rain an lowin heat etc etc.

### Pynt F
Wha's responsible? The government or the masses – in a normal societie, baith are intertwined – sae baith ar responsible.

### Pynt G
The Universities? They hae a muckle role – I wes aye impressed bi the fact that a lot o the guid wark on early Scots cam oot o the German universities wi their great tradeition o philology. In fack it struck me whan I wes scrivein this paper at I've gien mair talks on and in Scots in German- speaking airts than I've duin in Scotland itsel – Stuttgart, Heidelberg an Freiburg in Germany, Basel in Switzerland, and Poznan formerly Posen in Poland. There wes tae, a sair danger in the Scottish universities in my days there in the early 1970's o Scots whiles bein treatit lik a deid language, an scholars pickin ower the banes o a corp raither than celebratin its abeility tae endure an bide vibrantly alive.

## Pynt H

Cuid the arrival o foreigners, speakers o gey different leids affect Scots. Nae need for thon ti be the case if the native leid is thrawn an alive. I mind aince in Logan in Ayrshir stertin an interview wi an auld gentleman that haed been born nearhaun Seville, but haed wrocht aw his days in the iron warks at Lugar. Bairh o us wes speakin Ayrshire Scots. Jist intae the interview, houever, Maister Esquierdo gradually did whit the schuil haed tellt him tae dae, an switched ti English. Insteid o gowden Scots, I wes gettin fankled English an wesnae shuir whether tae stop an stert again, when fortunately his wife intervened an said "Hey, you, stoap pittin it oan, talk Scoatch like the rest o us ". Like her man, she wes born in Spain, but lik the fowk roun aboot her haed absorbed Scots as the language o her adoptit community a soorce o identity for her and her family.

## Pynt I

The former sae cried minoritie leids o Iberia are, as I glisked at earlier, guid an diverse examples o hou language can bes sustainit or dwyne dependin on the poleitical will. Fae the Scots pynt o view, there's the encouragin fack that the leids at ar sib wi Spanish – Catalan an Galego are percievit as haein mair success in this maitter than Basque which is gey different fae Spanish – in ither words, the reason for Scots bein whiles perceived as a mere dialeck o English – because o the similarities an shared vocabulary – cuid turn oot tae be the savin o the leid. In this an this anely, at the praissent time, Scots hes an advantage ower Gaelic.

## Pynt J

Cairryin on fae the statement abuin, Scots is that sib tae English, that monie fowk hae it an dinnae realise it. Ane o ma favourite scenes fae French Leiterature is whan the eejit Bourgeois Gentilhomme in Moliere's play is gien a language lesson an gets learit the difference atween poetry an prose: The follaein dialogue ensues:

> MAÎTRE DE PHILOSOPHIE.- Non, Monsieur: tout ce qui n'est point prose, est vers; et tout ce qui n'est point vers, est prose.
> MONSIEUR JOURDAIN.- Et comme l'on parle, qu'est-ce que c'est donc que cela?
> MAÎTRE DE PHILOSOPHIE.- De la prose.
> MONSIEUR JOURDAIN.- Quoi? Quand je dis: "Nicole, apportez-moi mes pantoufles, et me donnez mon bonnet de nuit" c'est de la prose?
> MAÎTRE DE PHILOSOPHIE.- Oui, Monsieur.
> MONSIEUR JOURDAIN.- Par ma foi, il y a plus de quarante ans que je dis de la prose, sans que j'en susse rien; et je vous suis le plus obligé du monde, de m'avoir appris cela.

> Naw, Sir, everythin that's no prose is verse, an awthing that's no verse, is prose.
> An, when we're jist talkin, whit's that.?
> That's prose.
> Awa wi ye! Sae when I say "Nicole, bring me my baffies and rax me ower my nicht cap", I'm talkin prose?
> Exactly
> Faith, that's mair nor 40 year I've been talkin prose withoot kennin a

haet aboot it – I'm muckle obleeged tae ye, Sir, for haein taught me that. Maister Jourdain realises wi the force o revelation that he's been been speakin prose aw his days withoot realisin whit a gleg clever chield he wes. For a wheen Scots, kennin they are heirs tae a glitterin leiterarie an linguistic heritage cuid hae the same life enhancin revelatory pouers, withoot the idiocy. Ane o the maist hert warmin sides o ma wark promotin Scots haes been the nummer o fowk that's come up tae me at gaitherins tae tell me whit a difference tae their ain self image they hed experienced readin *Scots: The Mither Tongue* – for maist it wes the first an onlie time they hed this crucial pairt o wha they were explained, and validated.

My hope for the future – an its ane that hes been gien a muckle heize up since the last Scottish Election – is that it is comin yet for aw that, that the Scots will eventually be governit by fowk that validate their culture, their language, their bein … mindin McDiarmid's words:

> Tae be yersel's – and tae mak that worth bein,
> Nae harder job tae mortals hes been gien

The lang, lang era o lowsin time is shuirly ower, let the real yokin time begin.

# The Scots Commonty

†*John Law*

### ill ti kill, an kittle ti cuiter

Gin ye turn til the letters o Robert Burns, it is a disappyntment ti finnd he didna write mair nor ae plain prose ane that we ken o in Scots. Howk at the Sent email faulders o hunners o fowk the day, tho, an ye'll finnd a haill new braird o epistolary Scots brocht forrit bi the oncome o new technology. Indaed, the haill maiter o writin letters this wey insteid o phonin the wey we did fifteen year syne is a camsteerie chynge o culture wi the haill human race sidie for sidie, but gie them a computer. Houiver, the ettle o daein it in Scots is new amang Scots fowk; a new uiss for a steerin vernacular, wi rael speak gettin uised in a new wrutten wey that suin biggs oot an ayont the wey o speak itsel.

O coorse, Scots wis deein oot in Burns's time. The pleywricht Sheridan haed been lairnin[1] the warthies o Embro guid Inglis sae thay needna affront thairsels wi Scotticisms, an Sir John Sinclair haed documentit this fashious leid in a wee beukie[2] that can gar ye smile the day, at aa whit things he threipit fowk shuidna say, but aye div. Aa throu the nineteenth century it wis deein oot. Three generation sinsyne, it wis deein oot in Aiberdeen, whan ma graundy's auld neibour an boss Charles Murray haed wan hame frae Sooth Africa, an in 1925 wis ruised at an event in the Airt Gallery hostit bi John Buchan.[3]

> I have seen the suggestion that we should dredge Jamieson and go back to the old writers, bring in a lot of the old words that have gone out of use, and build up our language afresh. I do not believe it will do any good, but it will be much if we can preserve for our children the language as we know or, perhaps, as we knew it. Nor do I think it will do any good to teach it in our schools as a language, but the teachers could do a great deal even if they occasionally used some of our sappy words and pithy phrases in their conversation with the children. I do not mean that they should teach the children the vernacular, but get them to feel that there is nothing to be ashamed of in having a good knowledge of their own home language. I can remember as a boy when talking to the teacher we always felt somewhat shamefaced if we could not express ourselves, or properly make our point, without falling back on the Scots. This should not be. The children should be taught that it is the best thing in every way for a nation to be efficiently bi-lingual.

Twa-three quaistens gaun beggin thare, nae dout; but aye the Scots language wis deein. It wis deein aff in the Fifties whan the ae beuk I can mynd on at the wee schuil wis the *Lanimer* beuk o verses,[4] and it wis deein in the Saxties whan the big schuil haed juist *Poet's Quair*[5] in the press.

---

[1] Or linin his pootch, onie roads
[2] Sir John Sinclair, *Observations on the Scots Dialect*. London and Edinburgh, 1782.
[3] Scott, A.R. *Ours the Harvest: A Life of Charles Murray*. Aberdeen: Charles Murray Memorial Fund, 2003. 159–63.
[4] *Lanimer Books of Verse: Infant, Junior, Senior*. Glasgow: Blackie and Son, 1956.
[5] *Poet's Quair*, eds. Rintoul D. and J.B. Skinner. Edinburgh: Oliver and Boyd, 1950, with numerous reprints.

# The Scots Commonty

It wis deein aff at Jordanhill teacher trainin college in the aerlie Seiventies whan an auld tutor whase nem it disna suit me ti mynd on, but I dout a contemporary o John Buchan, wauxit fell angrie wi ma young sel for pyntin oot til him that Scots wis the language o near aboot aa the fowk roun aboot whaur I cam frae, gin I gaed onie pynt o the compass the lenth o Ashgill, Netherburn, Rosebank, Stonehouse or een crossed the waa inti Larkie, an for drawin conclusions, contar til his likin, aboot whit ocht ti be in the curriculum.

"It is dying out! It is dying out!" he raired an threipit, reid in the face. Puir auld fella, I mynd he wis a cheil that cuid fairly pit ower a ballant, tae.

Scots wis deid but wadna lie doun later in the Seiventies, whan George Bruce gaed til its yirdin:

Urn Burial

It wis hardly worth pyin fur a casket,
the body wis that peelie-wallie,

nae bluid in't
luikit like a
scrap o broun paper

papyrus mebbe?
nae gran eneuch
for that,

but there wis some gran mourners, the
Editor o the Scottish National Dictionary,
Heid o the Depairtment o' Scot. Lit.,
President o the Burns Federation,
President o the Lallans Society,
President o the Saltire Society,
aa present in strict alphabetical order
an
ane/twa orra Scots. Nats.

Syne cam a fuff o win
an liftit it oot o the bowlie
an hine awa.

a wee bird sang.

Dew dreep't
on the beld heids
o' the auld men
stude gloweran
at the tuim tomb.

'She's jinkit again,
the bitch!'
said the auld man wi the spade.

Maugre aa the deein, it seems that juist as Adam Smith telt the mannie wha telt him on his daith bed, 'the country was ruined', that 'there was a deal of ruin in the country', the'r mair ruin in Scots nor maks for onie quaet dwyne an yirdin. Sae whan we think aboot the yokin o leid an commonty, the first thing we hae ti think aboot is whit haes been hainin the leid aa this whyle, afore we think aboot whit weys muckle mair siller micht best be brocht forrit til its better hainin.

1. Ye canna weel no lairn Scots gin ye speak Inglis. It's aye sypin in. Corollary: ye canna hinner yersel ti lairn mair as ye get aulder. Corollary: it's aesie lairned, aesie read: fowk the lenth awa o Kiev an Japan sends ye letters whyles in Scots that guid it fair astounds ye. It's *swack*. The dominies that disna waant ti lairn the bairns onie Scots, the dingers-oot an ignorers, haes haen less degree o success wi thae ploys nor thair umquhile ubiquity wad gart us fear.
2. The existence o an important pairt o the naitional heirskep o letters in Scots, aye growein, means ye canna weel be conseidert letterit or cultured gin ye'r no acquant wi it. This yokes on the haill educatit middle clesses o Scotland, eien whan anglophone university education haes booled them sairly in the mooth. The best dominies, thaim that aye keepit Scots that bittie til the fore in orra neuks o the curriculum, the readers an hainers, haes haen mair degree o success nor the smaa time gien wad gart us dout. Scots is itsel whit ye canna be, waantin Scots: it is *perjink*.
3. The workin cless o Scotland hains the leid in the bygaun, throu sang, tradeition, the Burns cult an ither sub-cultures o work, sport an entertainment. Is it in rejection o bourgeois, or capitalist culture? – it is, I dout. It is *subversively attractive*, an we cry that *gallus*.
4. It's a maiter o naitional pride, Scots, an whyles a meetin-grun for fowk that widna gree on independence politics. It's *leif*.
5. Can ye write ocht warth readin aboot Scotland the day, an miss it oot? It's *necessar*.

I cuid anecdote ye aa day wi whit lifesome Scots aye is – an o coorse the editor o *Lallans* aye sees the best o it that's wrutten doun – but here three instance: a neibour cooncillor a month syne wis peingin aboot the auld Scots Executive hunker-slidin bi no greein waste mainagement plans, a maiter o ongaun interest til Scots Cooncils the day, sen we'r aa awa ti get muckle euro-imposts gin we dinna cut back tonnage gaun til the polis-cowps, an dae mair raikin-on an firin-aff. Says he, "we were thrawed at every turn".

Syne here's me a year or twa back, mischeivious-myndit, in the wee veg shop in Auchterarder:

"I'll hae some o that okra."
"Hou much?" says the young wife.
"A gowpenfu," says I.

Fair taen wis I wi her, an she wi hersel that she neiver lat dab wi a smile, whan she bumbaized her frein that wis in by clashin, an juist pit ma dooble haunfu in the poke.
I dinna ken gin ye taen tent o thon poet ye neiver haerd o afore, yon Innes Dow that kythed furst in *Lallans* 70 wi a braw skelp o natur poems, nae implume cheepie o a bard him, but sen it is a *nom de plume* I maun tell ye nae mair nor this, that aa the

prentice flichts wi his Muse wis in Scots Gaelic, yit thare he is, able ti flie fine weel in Scots feddram an aa.

The truible is, I cuid anecdote ye aa the day efter wi ither sadder tales, like the wife in the neuk o a cooncil chaumer I wis chairin a by-meetin in this week past, no *sotto voce* eneuch ti jouk ma lugs, haein ti be telt bi her neibour whit *siller* is; or chairin a by-meetin o the Audit Comatee an haein anither wife sayin she wis pleased ti hear the word *pauchlin* sen it wis years frae iver she haerd it. In case thir words comes til the lugs o the wifes concerned, an thay micht faa affrontit ti be mintit as *wifes*, an clypes me til the Staundarts Commeission for sayin the like, I maun jot an avou here that *wifes* is juist a better non-sexist Scots word for *leddies*, wioot the unwaantit tash o cless ascription til it. Gin I haed sayed *wifies*, nou, that wad be a soo o anither gruntle ti diss.

Binna we get a puckle siller pauchelt oot this Scots government suin, an a richt system wrocht ti stell Scots, thare michtna be muckle pynt, fifty year frae nou, cryin it a *Scots* government avaa. Mairatowre, the Saltire, an the letters can come aff the face o Victoria Quay onie time, that spells oot 'Government'. Gin 'Executive' gangs back up, as it can and alas, will dae the onie time the Unionist majority sees it til thair benefit in the birl o events, we'll can whustle for it aye as melodious as Murray's wee hird, but oor maisters'll see that whustle brunt yit for aa that, nae maiter whit swack, perjink, gallus, leif or necessar we micht think it. Nae speakers, nae wal for the writers ti gang back til an renew the lang stend o the Vernacular Revival that caas Scots forrit as a leivin leid, an nae dout avaa, Census or nane, but whit the nummer o speakers is on the faa.

I come til the thirl-pin o this paper, an that is that thae processes an properties that haes made for the survival o Scots faas maistlins ootby the scowth o direct government action. Thay ar thrawart facts o oor cultural an poleitical condeition. Eien whit teachers dis or disna dae, is mediatit throu an education profession wi its ain thrawn threip on intellectual independence. Richtly sae: we'd haurdly waant ti bring forrit a chynge that wad allou a future government ti hae Scots strucken frae the curriculum expleicit, unlike tho sic a thing seems the day.

Siller for the airts is trokit at airms' lenth. The BBC isna run bi government, and eien its legal chairter isna ocht avaa adae wi the *Scots* government. The newspapers isna warth thinkin aboot: thay'r aathegither apairt frae government, an rin bi journalists that disna ken ocht aboot Scots, for a mercat that disna fash its thoum aboot it aither.

A government ettlin ti tak steps an stell Scots, tharefor, maun gie thocht til whitna agencies it will uise ti deleiver the policy, an will hae ti mak up its mynd hou ti owercome the fact that a puckle o its agencies isna weel-ordert ti dae whit's necessar. For example, the Airts Cooncil Depairtment o Leiterature is the ae condie evenou for siller til Scots organisations, but its staff an graith an skeel an siller isna answerable til the darg or demand, as I think thay wad gree thairsels – an this is no ti miscaa the guid strategic deceisions thay hiv made, like thair support for Itchy-Coo, SND, SLC.

We maunna haud forrit speirin for some o the kind o things I hae seen us gang leukin for, as a Scots language muvement, whaur we wad fast ootrin oor ain capacity ti mak onie fordel wi them: aspirations o principle wioot onie weel-wrocht wey o daein thocht oot. Ceivil servants (an eien cooncillors, lat alane MSPs) disna fail ti speir aboot this, whan thinkin gin thay'll gie ye siller or gie ye nane.

The *Statement of Principles* pitten forrit bi the CPG[6] is a braw eneuch philosophical statement, shuir. But it fair murls awa when ye speir at it for policy airtin:

---

[6] *Statement of Principles*, Embro: The Scots Pairliament Cross Pairty Group on the Scots Language. 2003.

1. Scots is a language
   *Ay, ay. (Sayed the Meinister.)*
2. Action maun be taen tae pit an end tae aw prejudice an discrimination agin the Scots language
   *Neist time we'r at a human richts bill, syne, we'll mynd o that.*
3. The Scots language is integral an essential tae cultural an personal identity in Scotland
   *I ken.*
4. A knowledge o Scots is vital tae a knowledge o Scotland
   *I ken that an aa.*
5. Action maun be taen tae gie the Scots language whitiver means is needit tae mak siccar its transmission an continuity
   *Whit actions ar ye wantin?*
6. Scots shuid be an essential pairt o the educational curriculum in Scotland at aw levels
   *In whit weys?*
7. Naebody shuid be penalised or pitten doun for speakin Scots
   *Gree'd.*
8. Scots proper names an place names shuid be valued an safegairdit
   *Ay, sae thay shuid.*
9. Speakers an writers o Scots shuid hae scowth tae develop an active role an presence for the Scots language in aw pairts o the communications media
   *Ye'll be speirin at the media, syne? Guid luck.*
10. Ongaun study an documentation o the language maun be gien ful resourcin
    *I'm telt the scholars' peys is aa on the same scale. The unions threip on it.*
11. Initiatives shuid be stertit tae mainteen an uphaud Scots terms an uisage specific tae sindry trades an occupations
    *Scottish National Dictionaries telt us thay hae duin that aareadies.*
12. The Scots language shuid be uised in adverts, in signs, in signpostin, an in the presentation o an accurate image o Scotland
    *Ye'll be speirin at the adverteisin agencies, Cooncils, an SDD syne? Ye'll can tell them the Meinister's aa in favour.*
13. The people o Scotland has the ability an responsibility tae uphaud the Scots language an gar Pairlament uise its pouer an authority tae realise thir foregaun principles an statements o intent
    *Ar ye sayin ye'll pit up Scots Language Pairty candidates? Ye ungratefu deivils, an I gree'd wi ilka word ye sayed.*

This is aa ti gie ye a smile, an fell unfair – the blad wis niever ettelt as a business plan. But we maun turn oor tent that airt, an offer rael policies that can be cairried oot.

The Cross-Pairty Group o the Scots Pairliament on the Scots Leid, syne, haes pitten forrit the propone that we'r leukin for a 'McPherson Report' anent Scots, (tho we howp it micht be a McClure Report) a sizin exerceise for Scots the like o whit wis duin successfu for Gaelic, thinkin oot whit shuid, micht an cuid be duin for the language, ti serve the Scots commonty and its letters an airts in future, an mak shuir the language disna dee oot. In speirin for that, we howp ti offer til whit we maun aye mynd is a minority government, a wey forrit for thaim, ti tak the gate in sic a wey thay'r no rebukit or hinnert bi the Pairlament, or kennlin opposeition.

Gin sic a report gets roadit, I think masel it maun tak a gey sceptical leuk at a puckle o the ploys fowk haes speired for afore nou, and a fair apen leuk at sindrie ither possible ontakkins less weel canvassed. And I waant ti suggest a nummer o quaistens that micht be pitten fornent onie ploys proposed, in the mainer I think thay wad be pitten:

1. Did this bigg up the capacity o Scots organisations ti gie guid service; an whit weys wad thay hae us think it proven?
2. Did this gie fowk the chance ti hear, speak, write or onie wey lairn an uise the language; an hou monie o them teuk the chance?
3. Did this schame cuiter the best Scots writers or performers; an did we get onie mair oot o them for the cuiterin?
4. Did this schame bring forrit onie new Scots writers or performers; an wha war thay an whit did thay dae?
5. Did this schame rewaird an set teachers on ti lairn (an teach) Scots; an did thay?

No ti haimer the pynt flet aathegither: targets the day is aa grundit in affcomes, an it winna be nae deiferent for Scots language ontakkins, gin better-fundit an no the wee atomies o taiken presence hingin rig-bare we hae the day.

Ae affcome, an that the heidmaist, disna lend itsel as faur as I can see, onie wey aesie til sic shawin: an that is: did mair bairns stert speakin Scots onie the mair, at mair times, in mair weys, as a result o whit we did? But whyles ye hae ti dae something that ye winna ken the affcome o it in yer ain generation, an whyles ye juist hae ti persuade the cheils wi the pouer an the siller ti mak the lowp o faith.

Kittlest o aa ti cuiter or kill, bydes the writers an singers an fowk-comics that aye adds thair chuckies til the cairn o Scots letters an braid culture. Letters in parteicular needs ti be brocht an keepit til the fore, an here government cuid dae muckle, gin it wad aim the siller weel. I dinna ken whit it is wi Ireland, that the haill o thair naitional letters aye fills lang shelfs in ilka Dublin beukshop, whan Scotland's writers, gin published, see thair beuks haled awa oot the door efter a towmond, an rowpit in bings for buttons in remainders shops. I dout it haes muckle ti dae wi the tax haunlin o publishers' stocks – aiblins the growthe o prent-on-demand can help.

But we hae ti leuk til oorsels, tae, an bring forrit readable edeitions o the Scots clessics, sairly waantin. Think on Gavin Douglas, whase *Eneados* canna be gotten onie place, an gin ye dae get it, can haurdlie be read but bi scholars gey weel-acquant wi the Scots an the spellin o the aerlie saxteent century. We dinna think o pittin Shakespeare's texts fornent weans the wey he set thaim doun in his time, dae we? A modren Scots readin edeition o thon wad be something ti work for; an I think it haes the pouer in a wyce walin o its rhymin pentameters some wey ti mak a stage version that wad staun along wi the *Satire o the Thrie Estates*.

# Linguistic Democracy?

*Robert McColl Millar*

## 1. Introduction

In a previous paper, (Millar 2009), I spoke about the *dislocation* from which the Scots language presently suffers: *dislocation* between government and activists; *dislocation* among activists; *dislocation* between speakers and writers. In a sense, I suggested, the language was itself *dislocated* from its speakers, many of whom did not even recognise what they were speaking as separate or even worthy of survival. We can recite the historical, social and political reasons for this sad state of affairs until we are blue in the face. This doesn't alter the problem, however. The elements necessary for language revitalisation and the development of a coherent policy for Scots are fragmented and misunderstood by both practitioners and end-users.

At a local grassroots level, where most sociolinguists would, of course, consider there to be the greatest chance for success in status and acquisition policy and planning success, the language is at the mercy of who happens to be there in a particular place at a particular time: teachers, activists, writers, speakers. In one place, for a while, interesting status planning activities take place in schools, for instance; ten kilometres down the road, however, nobody has even heard of Scots. Please don't misunderstand me: I'm not criticising anyone for this. I know that without this localised activity, we could forget about Scots entirely in a matter of years. But we have to recognise that it is patchy. There is nothing at all similar to the groundswell in favour of linguistic democracy found in analogous situations where political democracy was suddenly possible, such as nineteenth century Norway (Haugen 1966; Bucklen-Knapp 2003) or Catalonia in the late 1970s (Fishman 1991; Wright 1999).

What then can a language movement do; more importantly, what can native speakers do? François Grin (2003) reinforces the idea that for language policy to work, three factors must integrate successfully: *effectiveness, cost-effectiveness* and *democracy*. In this essay I will suggest how an *effective* language policy for Scots might be activated. Cost-effectiveness will also be considered along with this. As is common (although not necessarily useful) in such a framework, I will present a top-down approach, envisaging change being instigated by consideration by a Scottish government of implementation of Part III of the *European Charter for Regional or Minority Languages* for Scots (thus bringing it into line with provision for Gaelic: see Millar 2006). The local, grass root reaction will be given as we pass through the details, however. It is difficult to over-emphasise the centrality of native speakers if any activity is going to succeed.

## 2. A Democratic Language Policy for Scots?

So let's set a possible future in motion. The Scottish Government decides to implement Part III of the Charter for Scots, including a Scots Act to stand beside the 2005 Gaelic Act. What happens?

There's a serious problem even before we get to the 'upgrading' of Scots in *Charter* terms: I think it very unlikely that any Scottish government, of whatever political kidney, would willingly carry out this action. They would marshal all kinds of arguments about lack of clarity and distinction on the part of the Scots-speaking population, and about how much they are doing already for creative and academic use and study of the language, but in the end the bottom line is financial. I don't want to hazard a figure for how much it would cost to grant basic rights to Scots within Scotland, but it would be an impressive amount; an amount which I fear no government would be happy to bear. As a nationalist and as someone who is most comfortable towards the left end of Scotland's already rather left-oriented political spectrum, I would like to think that a progressive administration would be much more open to calls for linguistic democracy; somehow I doubt it, however.

But let's imagine what would happen if Scots *was* ratified under Article III with the government promising, say, that there would be a guaranteed position for Scots throughout a child's school life, with particular emphasis on the nursery school and early primary school years. Where, first of all, will the teachers of and in Scots come from? We have had centuries of the education system being, on the whole, the instrument of Anglicisation; how could we change that around? Would this education in Scots be obligatory for all children (with the exception, I suppose, of Gaelic-speaking children) or would there be a competing English-only system? If the latter was the case, is it not possible that even some Scots-speaking parents might opt for the latter, since it would be perceived as the norm – particularly after all these years where English was the default language of School? Would any government feel itself strong enough to face up to years of civil disobedience if they enforced compulsory Scots? The Norwegian government backed down against protests over a much less radical issue in the 1950s (Haugen 1966).

Even if all this went through without much fuss, what would the teachers teach? There are many excellent teaching aids for Scots and Scottish culture already available; the position of the subject within the curriculum is considerably more marginal than we are now envisaging, however. If Scots literacy was being taught, there would have to be a standard orthography and, at the very least, prescriptive grammars. There would have to be books designed not to entertain children who were essentially English-literate, but rather as the primary means of learning to read and write. Nothing of the sort exists. The funding implications would be immense. We would also have to have teachers equipped to teach in and about Scots, and enthusiastic to do so. There is probably already a cadre of such teachers around, but there are many more that at present would be unable to and might always be unwilling to teach Scots. How could these deficits and problems be overcome?

But the *Charter* is not merely about education: its intentions are holistic. Although what features a government signs up for may differ, the following at least would be likely. Government and bureaucracy at all levels would have to be available in the language on demand. All forms of employment would eventually be expected to conduct business in Scots, should the need be shown. The broadcast, print and online media would be expected to give up more than a token amount of space to material in the language; this would have to be more than entertainment programming. All of this would require a considerable cadre of adult speakers and writers. Few of these exist at present. Any Scottish government would therefore have to find a way to produce literacy among native speakers and active ability in the language for non-native speakers. These problems are not insurmountable; they are considerable nonetheless.

Many Scots language activists look towards Norway and Nynorsk to provide a potential solution to these problems. But while there is much we can learn from the Norwegian experience, there are glaring differences also. In the first place, the 'heroic age' of Norwegian language planning took place during a period when literacy was fairly low; moreover, although Danish had an almost exclusive presence as the language of literacy in Norway, almost everyone spoke their local dialect. The new language situation spread with literacy and, while never appearing natural to Norwegians, bears the mark of normality about it, particularly since the variety of Danish used has been progressively Norwegianised in the course of the last two centuries. I do not need to point out the many occasions in which the situation of Scots differs to its detriment from this situation.

The Catalan model is also appealed to. This is certainly similar to Scots from the point of view that there was limited literacy in Catalan at the end of the Franco dictatorship, and that this was accompanied by a fierce prejudice against the language among a small but vocal number of its speakers. But the democratisation which followed in Spain inevitably included within it special understanding of how the speakers of minority languages had suffered under the dictatorship, thereby guaranteeing sympathetic consideration in the Castilian centre. While the devolution settlement of 1999 was in its own way revolutionary, the Catalan process of democratisation was much smoother (and this is without entering into the debate over the difference between having one and having two national languages). Moreover, Catalonia is the wealthiest province of Spain. It can, to a significant extent, do what it likes and expect to be permitted to do so by the centre. Indeed, a delicate dance is ongoing over whether Catalonia will remain part of Spain or not; it is obviously in Spain's interest to remain tolerant of the use and spread of Catalan. Again, Scotland is not in such a happy situation. While there are only a few pockets of genuine poverty in the country, its economic output is inevitably smaller than that of, say, the South-East of England. This means, of course, that the central organs at Westminster would be less worried by Scotland leaving the Union than Madrid would be over the secession of Catalonia; it also implies that any Scottish government would not have anything like the financial and political clout of Catalonia for *any* policy, never mind language policies.

The problems Scots at present has are manifold, therefore, but they can be boiled down to a relatively limited number of issues: lack of recognition of the problem by most Scots speakers; lack of a literate adult population and lack of government support and understanding. I would suggest that there is no point in moving towards Part III status for the language without attempting to do something to address these issues: so let's rewind a bit. What do we need to get to Part III status? Other countries, such as the Netherlands, had consultations with language groups before they even approached Part II recognition for their *kin-tongues* (van der Goot 1999). Scotland has not, of course, been as well-served; certainly such consultation should now take place (and not just in a token way). But what we need is intervention, at an individual, and societal, level. These activities would, unfortunately, not be democratic as things stand at present; they certainly could be effective and cost-effective, however.

To carry them out, there would need to be meaningful government acceptance of the existence of a problem and a willingness to carry out remedial action. A two-pronged attack is probably best: education for educators and education for adults. In order to be effective, this cannot merely be window-dressing. Genuine and considerable investment must be made in the process. One possibility could be the institution of summer schools at all the universities and colleges for all educators involved, perhaps lasting two months, with a commensurate shortening of the school year. Although it would be difficult to compel teachers to attend these courses, an attractive 'carrot' might be preferred: taking part in the course would imply extra payment, which participants would receive on successful completion. An extra increment on the pay scale might also be established for proven Scots competence. Given the present state of technology, it would be quite possible to take part in at least most of the work involved in the course from home. The different arrangements for the school year would stand for two years at most; following this, the distance learning route would be the primary one for those already involved in education (the changes would by then have been embedded in all teacher training in the universities); no extra pay would be involved in studying for the qualification, but the pay 'step' would be maintained. Although teachers of 'English' and Primary School teachers would be particularly encouraged to take part in the programme, all teachers would have the same incentive offered them.

What would the educators be taught? This would depend on the linguistic competence of the individual. Many teachers speak their local dialect; course materials would encourage a reflective analysis of their own language use in relation to the children they teach, who may speak a different dialect. Much of this reflection will come from the compulsory units which are discussed below. Many other teachers may not speak their local dialect or the dialect of the area in which they live but may have an interest in the dialect stemming from their passive comprehension. Again, this comprehension will be enhanced by the inculcation of understanding of structure and history. The same process, although with more groundwork, would be carried out by those who do not come from a Scottish language background.

As well as the reflective modules within the course, all teachers would take modules on linguistic analysis, with particular thought being given to phonology, but not disregarding morphology, lexis or syntax. This would be coupled to modules on the history of language in Scotland and on contemporary dialectal diversity. Both of these would be taught from the same scientific perspective. Although literary study would be included in each unit, everyday language use of whatever type would be given priority.

But surely a programme of this type would produce a new set of passive comprehenders of the Scottish language situation, teaching *about* the language – albeit more accurately than was previously the case – rather than *in* it? This is certainly true, but ignores a further important element in the educational programme.

If all teachers, or those immediately associated with language, were expected to teach in Scots after this short course, there would be great stress, uproar and quite possibly a major revolt against the proposal. It would be much more useful for there to be (a) a small cadre of peripatetic Scots teachers who were employed to give the core teaching in Scots once a week in a range of about three high schools, and (b) a dedicated Scots teacher in every primary school (or, realistically, in a small group of schools). These teachers would be the 'front line' of the new movement for linguistic democracy: encouraging the oral skills and developing the written skills of Scots-speaking children; and introducing and teaching the language to those with little or no native competence. If full low-level coverage is not possible at first, then it would be better to have provision in every appropriate county, with these experts teaching the experts for the next stage in the process.

Unlike the present situation, where Scottish culture and language is given little more than marginal status in schools – particularly secondary schools – Scottish Studies would form a compulsory part of the school curriculum until a child reaches the age of sixteen. The curriculum would be flexible, incorporating assessment for those with native speaker abilities in Scots or Gaelic or non-native abilities in either language. All children who had lived for four or more consecutive years in Scotland would be expected to be assessed at some level in these matters. Naturally, Scottish Studies would include historical, economic, political, musical and geographical focuses as well as linguistic and literary; whenever possible, however, these would be taught in one of the national vernaculars. Every child who went through this programme would have considerable command of at least one of the national languages.

With adults, the problems are different, although they are analogous on occasion. Many Scots-speaking adults will have been educated (both at home and school) to consider Scots to be inferior to English; practically none of them will be able to read or write the language to any degree. Bearing this in mind, a roll-out of face-to-face night school classes and on-line interactive courses will be employed to encourage the oral use of the language in a wider range of domains than was previously the case. This would go hand in hand with initiatives towards public bodies in particular to encourage the use of local dialect in their relations to their customers. Literacy would come second under these circumstances, but would definitely be the intended goal of the outreach.

For those who had at best passive understanding of their local dialect, the move in the first place would be towards greater passive understanding of the language in its various varieties, interconnected to a greater feel for its history and structure. Many elements of such a course would be shared with the teachers' courses already envisaged. Scots as a second language courses would also be available to encourage greater spoken and eventually written abilities in the language.

But why would adults choose to take on an extra responsibility? Of course, we could be idealistic and suggest that people would want to do it because it is the right thing to do. More realistically, some people might feel compelled to take the study up because of the changes in the school curriculum. It has to be said, however, that financial incentives might also help. If those employed in the public or semi-public sector were guaranteed an extra increment for having passed one of these courses, attendance would rise. Outside the public sector, employers could be awarded for encouraging the use of Scots in their workplace by paying lower business rates than other businesses. This is in line with the language maintenance model put forward by Fishman (1991).

But while this programme is certainly possible, and could, if implemented intelligently, be quite effective, there is a remaining problem. As with the training of children in the new educational system, there would be a limited number of adult education experts who were also experts on Scots or even Scottish matters. Further investment would therefore have to be made into the education of the educators. Further redirection of finite public resources would be expected.

## 3. Discussion

Inevitably, questions will be raised about the cost-effectiveness of such a programme, particularly since its effectiveness would be extremely difficult to measure in the short-term. Bearing this in mind, it is likely that any future Scottish government embarking on language policy and planning for Scots would develop a scaled-down version of this initiative, concentrating in the main upon 'Scottish Studies' being an option for schoolchildren in their final examinations, as well as being compulsory in earlier years of school. Particular emphasis might be given to the publication of prose, particularly fiction, in the language both as a teaching aid and as an aim in and of itself. As can immediately be recognised, this is essentially a beefed-up version of what we now have.

This means that it will also suffer from the same failings. As we all know, the present sociolinguistic state of non-Gaelic Scotland is one of fundamental inequality between Scots and English. English, the High variety, is considered, at least under most circumstances, to be the more prestigious variety, the language which will 'get you places'. This view will be held by those who primarily only speak their local dialect as well as those who do not. I have my suspicions that if the language is made a voluntary school course, it will normally be given lip service in the early years and will rarely be taken higher up the school. We certainly have enough evidence of this happening now. The question would then be: to what extent is this more cost-effective than the larger programme promoted above? Is doing too little economically better than doing enough?

There is also, of course, a problem with the idea of *democracy* in this context, since a part of the Scottish population would be at best indifferent towards the new situation. Could such radical proposals then be termed democratic? I think here you have to distinguish between *grass-roots* and *majority*. Without a strong top-down approach any major policy initiative of this type would be highly unlikely to be effective; without support from below, any chance of effectiveness would be non-existent. Cost-effectiveness is another matter: I have already suggested that any effort for Scots would be likely to be 'shrunk' due to financial concerns by any government. But what does *cost-effective* actually mean? It need not be concerned with getting the lowest possible costs for activities; rather, it is about getting value for money, no matter the cost. This means that you get what you're willing to pay for. Many who would benefit from these alterations in language policy are probably unaware that there is much of a problem. For radical language policy measures such as I am suggesting, democracy may subsist in the activists and the conscious users, not in the majority.

## 4. Conclusion

The thing with change – any change, but particularly to do with a language situation within which most speakers of Scots are fairly comfortable – is that it is unlikely to be supported by the majority, at least to start off with. What any integrated language policy in Scotland for Scots would have to do is co-ordinate activity so that not just the activists, not just the civil servants, not just the educationalists, but the speakers at the centre would see the results as transparently and as promptly as possible. This would be genuine linguistic democracy.

Such an ambition is not easy; it is possible, however.

## References

Bucklen-Knapp, G. 2003. *Elites, Language, and the Politics of Identity: The Norwegian Case in Comparative Perspective*. Albany, NY: State University of New York Press.
Fishman, J. 1991. *Reversing Language Shift*. Clevedon: Multilingual Matters.
Grin, F. (with contributions by R. Jensdóttir and D. Ó Riagáin). 2003. *Language Policy Evaluation and the European Charter for Regional or Minority Languages*. Basingstoke: Palgrave Macmillan.
Haugen, E. 1966. *Language Conflict and Language Planning. The Case of Modern Norwegian*. Cambridge, Mass.: Harvard University Press.
Millar, R.McC. 2006. "'Burying alive": Unfocussed Governmental Language Policy

and Scots'. *Language Policy* 5: 63–86

Millar, R.McC. 2009. '*Dislocation*: Is It Presently Possible to Envisage an Economically Based Language Policy for Scots in Scotland?'. In eds. Kirk, J.M. and D.P. Ó Baóill. *Language and Economic Development: Northern Ireland, the Republic of Ireland, and Scotland.* Belfast: Cló Ollscoil na Banríona.

van der Goot, A. 1999. 'The Experience of the Netherlands in Implementing the Charter'. In ed. Council of Europe. *Implementation of the European Charter for Regional or Minority Languages*. Regional or Minority Languages 2. Strasbourg: Council of Europe Publishing. 30–7.

Wright, S. ed. 1999. *Language, Democracy, and Devolution in Catalonia*. Clevedon: Multilingual Matters.

# Using It or Losing It? Scots and Younger Speakers

*John Corbett and Wendy Anderson*

**Abstract**

This paper explores the potential role of the AHRC-funded Scottish Corpus of Texts and Speech (SCOTS) project in helping to sustain Scots language use. SCOTS is a multimedia corpus, containing 4 million words of written and spoken texts, ranging from Broad Scots to Standard Scottish English. Here we demonstrate how the integrated corpus search tools can be used to identify sub-corpora of texts, representing for example the language of parent-child interaction and the speech of university students. These sub-corpora can be investigated to reveal the typical features of particular text types and the respective roles of Scottish English and Scots in speaker interaction. The data can also be exploited in the creation of activities to encourage the production of Scots lexis, such as evaluative terms, by learners.

**Introduction**

This paper considers the potential role of a particular type of language resource, a *corpus*, in helping to sustain a language community. The term *corpus* (plural: *corpora*) has come to mean a collection of texts, normally in electronic form, which has been designed to represent a language, such as Scots or English, or a type of language, whether defined in terms of genre (e.g. correspondence, conversation, poem), mode (spoken or written), or perhaps geographical variety (e.g. Shetland Scots, north-east English). A corpus can be composed of raw, unanalysed, data, although analytical information, *annotation*, might be added to corpora to facilitate certain types of linguistic research. Corpora have many applications, including the linguistic analysis of lexical, grammatical, phonetic and discourse features, and as an aid to translation. Here, however, we focus on their role as a resource for developing educational materials and teaching tools.

We shall explore what corpora have to offer by looking at a particular resource which we, as part of a research team, have developed at the University of Glasgow. This is the Scottish Corpus of Texts and Speech (SCOTS).[1] The paper begins by introducing the resource and describing some of the different ways in which it can be exploited. We then turn to the implications of this for the development of teaching materials.

---

[1] The Scottish Corpus of Texts and Speech (SCOTS) project was carried out by the Department of English Language and STELLA project at the University of Glasgow. The first stage of the project was grant-funded by the Engineering and Physical Sciences Research Council (EPSRC Grant no. GR/R32772/01): the second, three-year, stage was funded by the Arts and Humanities Research Council (AHRC Grant no. B/RE/AN9984/APN17387). The project website can be found at www.scottishcorpus.ac.uk. A companion corpus project, the Corpus of Modern Scottish Writing (1700–1945), is now being developed. This is also grant-funded by the Arts and Humanities Research Council (AHRC Grant no. AH/E00184X/1).

## The Value of Corpora

To explain what a corpus is and what it can offer, it is useful to contrast it with another, more familiar, type of language resource which has a recognised role in sustaining a language community, a dictionary. Dictionaries of course contain lexical, grammatical and phonological information which is based on an analysis of data by professional lexicographers, and which is carefully presented with a user-group in mind (whether language learners or native speakers, adults or children). Corpora, unlike dictionaries, often consist of raw, that is, unanalysed, data, in the form of texts. While dictionaries present *information*, corpora present *data*, which remains to be turned into information by the user: this process is facilitated by software tools which allow the data to be manipulated and viewed in different ways. So a corpus is a body of text, or rather a collection of texts, which has been designed for a purpose, usually linguistic research. Most corpora seek to contain a balance of material, so that conclusions that are made on the basis of the data they contain can be generalised to a language or type of text as a whole.

Corpora are useful in linguistics because, if they are carefully analysed, they can enable new perspectives on language, by allowing researchers to see patterns that emerge from large quantities of data. This is a perspective that is not easily accessible to us as individuals; the pioneering corpus linguist John Sinclair summed it up by observing that "The language looks rather different when you look at a lot of it at once" (Sinclair 1991:100). While our knowledge of language as individuals is based on our past experience of it, our memory of all of the language we have ever encountered is not unbiased. Instead, we tend to remember what is salient, unusual, amusing, and interesting in language. Corpora offer a more reliable, less skewed, yet still nuanced picture of language.

As noted above, unlike dictionaries, corpora do not provide definitions of words: rather they show the word in its immediate context, and this in turn helps us to come to a fuller understanding of its meaning. Wittgenstein claimed in his *Philosophical Investigations* that "the meaning of a word is its use in the language." (Wittgenstein 1958, passage 43). For example, to apprehend the meaning of the Scots adjective

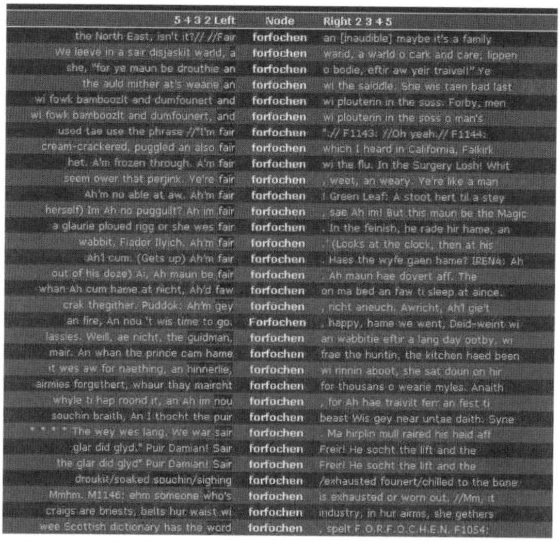

| 5 4 3 2 Left | Node | Right 2 3 4 5 |
|---|---|---|
| the North East, isn't it?// //Fair | forfochen | an [inaudible] maybe it's a family |
| We leeve in a sair disjaskit warld, a | forfochen | warld, a warld o cark and care; lippen |
| she, "for ye maun be drouthie an | forfochen | o bodie, eftir aw yeir traivell" Ye |
| the auld mither at's weane an | forfochen | wi the saiddle. She wis taen bad last |
| wi fowk bamboozlt and dumfounert and | forfochen | wi plouterin in the soss. Forby, men |
| wi fowk bamboozlt and dumfounert, and | forfochen | wi plouterin in the soss o man's |
| used tae use the phrase //"I'm fair | forfochen | ".// F1143: //Oh yeah.// F1144: |
| cream-crackered, puggled an also fair | forfochen | which I heard in California, Falkirk |
| het. A'm frozen through. A'm fair | forfochen | wi the flu. In the Surgery Losh! Whit |
| seem ower that perjink. Ye're fair | forfochen | , weet, an weary. Ye're like a man |
| Ah'm no able at aw. Ah'm fair | forfochen | ! Green Leaf: A stoot hert til a stey |
| herself) Im Ah no pugguilt? Ah im fair | forfochen | , sae Ah im! But this maun be the Magic |
| a glaurie ploued rigg or she wes fair | forfochen | . In the feinish, he rade hir hame, an |
| wabbit, Fiador Ilyich. Ah'm fair | forfochen | ." (Looks at the clock, then at his |
| Ah'l cum. (Gets up) Ah'm fair | forfochen | . Haes the wyfe gaen hame? IRENA: Ah |
| out of his doze) Ai, Ah maun be fair | forfochen | . Ah maun hae dovert aff. The |
| whan Ah cum hame at nicht, Ah'd faw | forfochen | on ma bed an faw ti sleep at aince. |
| crak thegither. Puddok: Ah'm gey | forfochen | , richt aneuch. Awricht, Ah'l gie't |
| an fire, An nou 't wis time to go. | Forfochen | , happy, hame we went, Deid-weirit wi |
| lassies. Weill, ae nicht, the guidman, | forfochen | an wabbitie eftir a lang day ootby, wi |
| mair. An whan the prince cam hame | forfochen | frae the huntin, the kitchen haed been |
| it wes aw for naething, an hinnerlie, | forfochen | wi rinnin aboot, she sat doun on hir |
| airmies forgethert, whaur thay maircht | forfochen | for thousans o wearie myles. Anaith |
| whyle ti hap roond it, an Ah im nou | forfochen | , for Ah hae traivilt ferr an fest ti |
| souchin braith, An I thocht the puir | forfochen | beast Wis gey near untae daith. Syne |
| * * * * The wey wes lang. We war sair | forfochen | . Ma hirplin mull raired his heid aff |
| glar did glyd." Puir Damian! Sair | forfochen | Freir! He socht the lift and the |
| the glar did glyd" Puir Damian! Sair | forfochen | Freir! He socht the lift and the |
| droukit/soaked souchin/sighing | forfochen | /exhausted founert/chilled to the bone |
| Mmhm. M1146: ehm someone who's | forfochen | is exhausted or worn out. //Mm, it |
| craigs are briests, belts hur waist wi | forfochen | industry, in hur airms, she gethers |
| wee Scottish dictionary has the word | forfochen | , spelt F.O.R.F.O.C.H.E.N. F1054: |

**Figure 1: Concordance of *forfochen* in the SCOTS Corpus**

*forfochen* (which the dictionary tells us means 'exhausted'), we need to know the contexts in which it is used: for instance the fact that it is often paired with the adverbs *fair* or *sair*, and the fact that it is often found in conjunction with other adjectives and adverbs denoting physical or emotional states. A concordance of the word, as used in the texts in the SCOTS corpus, illustrates this in Figure 1.

## The Scottish Corpus of Texts and Speech

The Scottish Corpus of Texts and Speech (SCOTS) project began in 2001, achieving its designated targets in 2007. The aim was to create a corpus for the languages of Scotland, focusing on Scottish English and varieties of Scots, including for example urban varieties from Glasgow and Edinburgh, the Doric of the North-East, Ayrshire Scots, and insular varieties from Shetland and Orkney. Following linguists such as Aitken (1979) and McArthur (1979) among others, the project takes the view that Scots and Scottish English exist on a continuum of variation: we did not therefore attempt to label texts as examples of particular varieties. Such labels should result from *post hoc* linguistic analysis rather than be *a priori* assumptions.

SCOTS contains just over 4 million words of text, and over 1100 individual texts, both spoken and written. The corpus is not perfectly balanced, but does contain a wide range of textual genres. The final design of SCOTS was influenced by various issues, most notably the difficulty of obtaining copyright permission to include certain types of texts, given the free availability of the resource on the internet. The written component of the corpus, which accounts for 80 per cent of the complete size, includes genres such as correspondence, diaries, essays, instructional texts, invoices, prose fiction, poetry, reviews, official documents from the Scottish Parliament, and the written record of speech. The remaining 20 per cent is the spoken component, made up of 84 hours of recordings, and comprises texts in such genres as conversation, interviews, lectures, speeches, poetry and prose readings. Spoken texts are made available as orthographic transcriptions accompanied by the original audio or video recording, which means that features such as intonation and accent can be studied. Relatively few freely-available linguistic corpora currently contain spoken material: fewer still are multimedia. However, for non-standard language varieties like Scots, a multimedia corpus presents a much fairer representation of the linguistic community: varieties of Scots after all are more commonly spoken than written.

The range of material in the SCOTS corpus means that even if the complete corpus does not suit certain research purposes, sub-parts of the corpus can be defined and used as smaller, more balanced corpora for specific purposes. For example, the spoken component can be easily selected if spoken language meets the criteria for a particular kind of research.

## SCOTS Search Facilities

To cater for different types of user, SCOTS offers three search systems: a straightforward *Quick Search*, which simply looks for a given word in the corpus as a whole; a *Standard Search*, which allows limited searching based on contextual features; and a powerful *Advanced Search* facility which offers access to the detailed demographic and textual metadata which accompanies every text. The metadata includes information such as the speaker's decade of birth, place of birth, occupation, parents' places of birth, other languages spoken; and contextual information such as whether a text has been published; whether it is a translation; the level of spontaneity of spoken

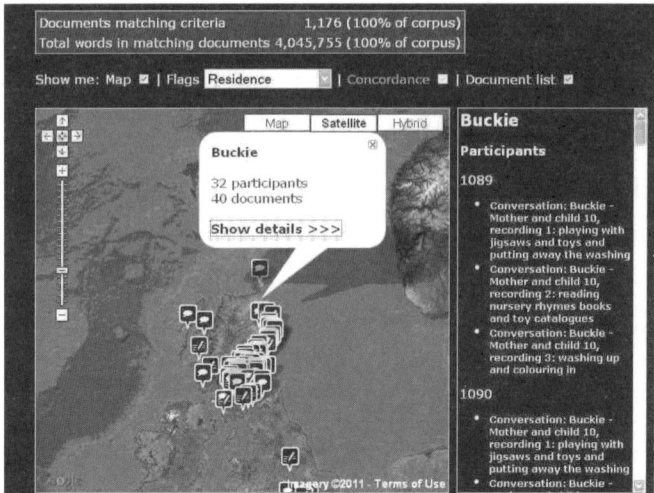

Figure 2: SCOTS Advanced Search, incorporating geographical visualisation

material, and so on. Such metadata is critical because it allows the user to make connections between the language data in the corpus and the community from which the language was drawn, and to recontextualise the text. The Advanced Search facility also offers geographical visualisation of the data, powered by Google Maps.

**Uses of Corpora in Teaching and Learning**

We turn now to the uses and applications of corpora, particularly the SCOTS corpus, in teaching. Corpora are quite a new resource in teaching, but are rapidly gaining in popularity. (see for example O'Keeffe, McCarthy and Carter 2007; Anderson and Corbett 2009). The use of corpora in the classroom presents opportunities and challenges, but in the first instance it presents a choice: should students or pupils be taught to exploit corpora for themselves to allow them to discover facts about language using raw data, or should teachers exploit the corpus in order to inform their own teaching?

The first approach is an inductive one, commonly known as data-driven learning, and involves situations in which students are given direct access to corpora, with the necessary training and guidance, and encouraged to make generalisations about patterning and tendencies in language from the evidence itself. The second approach on the other hand is typically deductive, and involves the teacher in a mediator role between the data and the students.

The level of engagement with the language in a corpus can take different forms too:
- A corpus as a repository for texts
- A corpus as a source of authentic examples
- A resource for the design of educational materials
- A representative body of data for linguistic research

We structure our illustrations in this paper around these ways of approaching a corpus, which offer an increasing level of engagement with the data.

**1. A Corpus as a Repository for Texts**

Used as a straightforward repository for texts, a corpus is akin to an archive. Like many archives too, most corpora have a search system, which enables the user to specify particular criteria for a text. SCOTS, for example, allows the researcher to locate texts fitting criteria recorded in the metadata. The screenshot of an extract from the search system in Figure 3, for example, demonstrates a query which will retrieve all texts which are conversational in genre, involve at least one participant born since 2000, contain the word *pink*, and involve at least one participant resident in Buckie at the time of the recording.

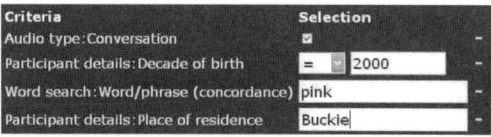

**Figure 3: SCOTS Advanced Search**

Looking at texts selected according to the age of participants allows us to investigate the respects in which the linguistic community is changing over time. SCOTS contains a good balance of material by speakers of different ages. This includes a number of recordings made with students originally from various parts of Scotland, and a large quantity of recordings of caregiver-child interaction from the North-East (generously donated to the project by Dr Jennifer Smith) which is complemented by additional recordings of parents speaking with their young children in the Glasgow area. This latter set of data is particularly valuable for the study of inter-generational transfer, as the recordings represent children young enough not yet to have felt the influence of the education system, recorded while going about daily businesses with their caregivers (in most cases their mother). Figure 4 gives an extract from a recording of a mother (F1131) and her young son (M1132) in the North-East.

| | |
|---|---|
| F1131: | Right, fitt are we gonna awa tae dae? |
| M1132: | Mum, mum mum! |
| F1131: | What, what, what? What? Ooh! |
| M1132: | Cat. |
| F1131: | Dinna scare it. |
| M1132: | [inaudible] Hello hello! |
| F1131: | Hello pussycat. |
| M1132: | [inaudible] |
| F1131: | Want to go doon and see it? Watch it doesna eat your carrot. |
| M1132: | [exhale] [inaudible]. //Go and see it.// |
| F1131: | //[inaudible]. Come on then, we'll go. Come on and I'll take your hand. //Hello pussycat. Hello. //[noise to entice the cat]// |
| M1132: | //Look.// |
| F1131: | Here's [CENSORED: forename] to see you. Hello! Here's [CENSORED: forename] to see you. Are you saying hello to the pussycat? //He's nae got a name, poor wee tat.// |
| M1132: | //Hello.// |
| F1131: | Eh? You're nameless. Will we name you? What will we call it? //Wha-?// |
| M1132: | //Mm.// [inaudible] |
| F1131: | What kind o name would you like to give her? |
| M1132: | I don't know. Ca- can I, will I give her some mu- some muck? |
| F1131: | No. |
| M1132: | No s- no some milk. |

**Figure 4: Extract from SCOTS Document 1566**

This second extract (Figure 5) is part of a conversation between two male students in their early twenties from the Glasgow area.

| | |
|---|---|
| M819: | Erm, anyway what have you, what have you been up to over the last few months? |
| M818: | Last few months? Er I've just been [exhale] been at uni and stuff and been goin out too much probably, spending a lot of money and stuff that I don't really have. [inhale] //Er I had to actually get an// |
| M819: | //[inaudible]// |
| M818: | overdraft extension which isn't very good //inaudible// |
| M819: | //Yes!// |
| M818: | [laugh] Are you all usin it to the //to the max?// |
| M819: | //God do you, do you no work?// Do you no work? |
| M818: | Whit? |
| M819: | Like at Direct Line and that? |
| M818: | Oh, do I work? //Oh,// |
| M819: | //Aye.// |
| M818: | right aye aye ehm, I do, I mean but the thing is, see I worked over the summer last year and erm I got erm like I got extra wages obviously for workin extra hours and em basically like I was getting paid like a good bit more every month like. But then after the summer they kept payin me the higher wages and then forgot to take it down again, so basically now what they're doing is kinda like, after I let //them know// |
| M819: | //They're dockin you// your wages aw! //Aw, that'// |
| M818: | //Aye, nightmare.// |

**Figure 5: Extract from SCOTS Document 811**

Both of these sets of data, students and caregiver-child, offer a picture of relatively unguarded language use. On occasion, it becomes clear that participants are aware of the presence of the microphone, but for the most part, they appear to forget about it. As a result, strongly colloquial speech, gossip and swearing are all evidenced in the corpus.[2]

There are many ways in which such data might feed into educational materials. From the point of view of studying the respective roles of Scots and English in the linguistic community, for example, it would be an interesting exercise to examine the circumstances in which participants, in the course of a single conversation, switch between variant forms, such as *fitt* and *what* in the extract in Figure 4, or, across a number of conversations, how these and other variants correlate with factors such as level of formality and how well participants know each other.

## 2. A Corpus as a Source of Authentic Examples

Exploiting a corpus in this way involves selecting examples to illustrate any given lexical or grammatical point under investigation. For example, a word or phrase such as *oxter, miss yersel* or *cairry-oot* can be searched for and its use examined in the corpus. Here, however, a cautionary note or two must be raised.

---

[2] SCOTS has adopted a system of Content Warnings, to mark texts which contain language which some may find offensive. This warning can be found alongside text titles.

*Using It or Losing It? Scots and Younger Speakers* 231

First, in terms of size, the SCOTS corpus is a relatively modest resource, its 4 million words a drop in the ocean beside the 100 million words of the British National Corpus and the TIME corpus, not to mention the 400 million words of the recently-launched Corpus of Contemporary American English. SCOTS therefore is good for investigating commonly used lexical terms and frequently recurring grammatical items such as prepositions and conjunctions. However, many words that people use less frequently but know intimately might not be represented in the SCOTS corpus.

Secondly, like other corpora that feature languages that are not fixed to a regular spelling system, SCOTS faces technical challenges when it comes to searching for variants. If you are interested in football, you might wish to search for *football, fitba, fitbaw, fitbaa* and so on. If you are interested in the Scots equivalent of *above*, you have to search separately for *abune, abuin, abinn, aboon*, etc. While research into automatic searching of spelling variants is proceeding apace, there is as yet no technical solution to this basic problem.

Even so, given its limitations, SCOTS still provides a wealth of examples for many features of Scots. Moreover, as well as presenting examples, corpus data can be used to encourage students to *produce* words, such as in an exercise shown in Figure 6, where the task is to find one word that can fill the gap in all of the concordance lines.

```
         It is lown in here. Nae crouds _____ me. Ah'm brichter in masell, an mair
    the ferm. For he wis tired wi mony a _____ an fyke Whan yowes had brakken
  PEGGY I'll get ye a cup. BESSIE Dinna _____ yoursel'. I'm a' richt (But Peggy
     sum fushionles excaise. Weill, dinna _____ yeirsell, ye mukkil sumph, ye; ar,
  Stein incam wi tay, an telt hir no ti _____ hirsell, bot Staun didna lyk sojers an
         shae isna," sechtit Mirren. "Dinna _____ ! We'l aw be heir the morn, sen we
        he speired "Thae sojers dinna _____ thainsells about gairdin the railwey,
        at the en o the cessioun. "Dinna _____ yeirsell, laddie, he wul deleiver
  ocht Ye're welcome tae it. But dinnae _____ yorocl for me - Gang yer ain gait and
      just at this moment when I want nae _____ in the toun or in the press? It'll be
     gane." "Ay, A ken pal, but dinnae _____ yersel aboot that the noo. The'r
  banes? At lang an last, we heard the _____ o the firth An won ti the mou o the
   live pretty rough. DEANA: I wouldny _____ about that JACK: You? DEANA: I can
       Dreich the day the craws cannae _____ thirsels croupin Dull today: the crows
  Cleared it like a swallow, wi naither _____ nor fyke. Sae I turned back tae the
```

**Figure 6: Concordance from SCOTS Corpus Data**[3]

This exercise involves pupils or students identifying a word that suits several different contexts at once, working out the appropriate part of speech, and considering issues such as language variety and level of formality of the text.

### 3. A Resource for the Design of Educational Materials

As the activity illustrated by Figure 6 suggests, one of the most exciting prospects for using SCOTS is as a source of information for teachers, parents and pupils on how the Scots language is actually used, in speech and writing. This information can then be

---
[3] The word missing in each line is *fash*, meaning *bother, worry, concern*.

used in the design and refinement of activities that can enrich Scots language usage at early levels of education. The recordings of caregiver-child interaction, for example, illustrate how a mother teaches her son vocabulary, including numbers (Figure 7A).

| | |
|---|---|
| F1127: | Oh, right, come and see this thing here. //How many// |
| M1128: | //No.// |
| F1127: | spiders can you see? Come here. |
| M1128: | Fitt? |
| F1127: | How many spiders can you see? You've to count them. Can you see any spiders? Eh? //How many can we see? Let's hae a look at them.// |
| M1128: | //One,// two, three, four, five, six! |
| F1127: | How about that ain? Another ain. |
| M1128: | Five. |
| F1127: | Seven. //Eight.// |
| M1128: | //Eight,// nine, ten, eleven, //twelve!// |
| F1127: | //Twelve.// //That's right.// here |

**Figure 7A: Extract from SCOTS Document 1653**

The extract illustrates part of the mother's interaction with the child, while they are both playing with Spiderman stickers. Some Scots is being used (e.g. *fitt, ain*) but the use of Scots lexis could be greater. A dialogue such as this could be used with parents and teachers of young children, in conjunction with books for bairns such as Itchy Coo's *A Moose in the Hoose: A Scots Counting Book* (Fitt and Robertson 2006) to raise awareness of how the dialogue in Figure 7A could be enriched. A 'Scotticised' version of the dialogue is given as Figure 7B.

| | |
|---|---|
| F1127: | Oh, **richt**, come and see this thing here. //How many// |
| M1128: | //No.// |
| F1127: | **wabsters** can you see? Come here. |
| M1128: | Fitt? |
| F1127: | How many **wabsters** can you see? You've to count them. Can you see any **wabsters**? Eh? //How many can we see? Let's hae a look at them.// |
| M1128: | //**Ane**,// twa, three, **fower**, five, **sax**! |
| F1127: | How about that ain? Another ain. |
| M1128: | Five. |
| F1127: | **Seeven**. //**Echt**.// |
| M1128: | //**Echt**,// nine, ten, **eleeven**, //**twal**!// |
| F1127: | //**Twal**.// //That's **richt**// here |

**Figure 7B: Extract from SCOTS Document 1653 adapted**

In short, the SCOTS corpus can be used alongside other current teaching resources to raise parents' and teachers' awareness of how cross-generational opportunities for transferring Scots might be grasped rather than lost. Awareness-raising would involve parents and teachers looking at such resources as the Itchy Coo *Wee Readers* in conjunction with caregiver-child interactions in the SCOTS corpus to think critically about how best to expose young learners to the lexical and grammatical features of the language.

When recording speakers for the SCOTS corpus, we often found that people like to talk *about* language, and as a result the corpus contains numerous overt discussions of attitudes to language, as well as the spontaneous use of Scots words. The SCOTS recordings are a particularly rich resource, therefore, for exploring evaluative Scots words. Their dictionary meanings can be compared to how people feel about them, and how people (especially younger people) continue to use them.

Take, for instance, the commonly used derogatory adjective *mingin,* formed from the present participle of the verb *ming.* The online *Dictionary of the Scots Language* (DSL) gives a definition of the Scots verb (Figure 8):

> DSL – SNDS MING, *n.*2, *v.*2 I. *n.* A smell (em.Sc., Lnk. 1975).
> II. *v.* To be smelly or noisome, to be malodorous, to stink, gen. in ppl.adj. *mingin*, smelly (Ags., Ayr. 1975), also in extended use, 'stinking' drunk, very inebriated, in a state of semi-stupor from liquor (Ags., Fif. 1975); bad of its kind, of no use or poor quality (*Id.*).
> *Sc. 1970 *Daily Express* (20 Aug.) 5:
> They were "Mingin" or "Pissed"—the state before complete drunkenness.

**Figure 8: Definition of *ming* in the *Dictionary of the Scots Language* (www.dsl.ac.uk)**

As we observed earlier, the dictionary definition is distilled by professional lexicographers from a range of raw data. Corpora can take us back to the data and provide users with a perspective on how other people use particular words and phrases, and how use may vary according to age, gender, region, and so on. Figures 9A and 9B show examples of the use of *mingin* in the SCOTS corpus.

| | |
|---|---|
| F1145: | Well if someone was very unattractive, they would be hackit. [laugh] |
| F1054: | That's a good word, yeah. |
| M1146: | **Mingin**? |
| F1144: | [laugh] I've got that as well, //[inaudible]// |
| M1146: | //[laugh] **Mingin**.// I can't think of any other re- repeatable words! [laugh] //[laugh]// |
| F1144: | //[laugh]// //You're allowed to say unrepeatable words. [laugh]// |
| F1054: | //Erm, if they're whit// you'd say naturally, then just |
| F1144: | Yeah, no, I've no got anything like that, but I've I've got ugly and **mingin** and gawkit, and as the kids say nowadays, "He's a dog", or "She's a dog". So I g- guess dogs are unattractive for some. |

**Figure 9A: Extract from SCOTS Document 1572**

| | |
|---|---|
| M941: | //You've never heard that story before [CENSORED: forename], so shut your mouth.// When are you gonna sand your feet, they're a state? |
| M942: | //Leave my feet alone.// |
| M939: | //[laugh]// |
| M941: | //For the, for the benefit of the tape [CENSORED: forename] has scabby feet.// |
| M942: | //they're not needin sanded [inaudible]// //I don't have scabby// |
| F940: | //[laugh]// |
| M942: | scab- scabby, **mingin**, crass or any kind of feet; they're proper feet ye get by workin //an you'll only get those feet by working hard in [CENSORED: company name].// |

**Figure 9B: Extract from SCOTS Document 1379**

The corpus evidence supports the definition given by the DSL of *mingin* as unattractive or smelly, and shows awareness among speakers of this meaning. The corpus also illustrates how young people use this – and other – Scots evaluative terms in more or less spontaneous contexts. A cursory examination of these contexts suggests that teenagers and young adults use Scots evaluative lexis in banter, often to form close-knit peer groups. Scots evaluative items often act as signals of peer-group membership. It follows, then, that exposing children and young teenagers to a rich, Scots evaluative lexis should give them resources for banter, and so would encourage cross-generational transfer of this kind of vocabulary. Educationalists can therefore devise activities to encourage the production of this lexis in appropriate situations.

Vocabulary enrichment activities are, of course, a staple of language courses more generally. Morgan and Rinvolucri (1986) is one of a number of resource books for teachers that provides a wealth of imaginative vocabulary-enhancing activities aimed at younger learners of English, and many of these can be adapted for Scots, often making use of other lexical resources such as the *Scots Thesaurus* (Scottish National Dictionary Association 1999). One such ('Fishy adjectives', pp. 60–1) shows an illustration of a single fish isolated from a shoal, and arising from its head is a thought-bubble containing an image of an eel. Learners are invited to choose appropriate vocabulary to describe the isolated fish. In Scots, possible expressions might include: *abuin itsel, mutton dressed as lamb, upsticken, high-bendit, crouse, in a dwam, habblit, doitered, bumbazed, peerie-heidit,* and so on.

Only a few of these expressions are currently attested in the SCOTS corpus. Once again, the relatively modest scale of the SCOTS resource may account for their absence, at least to some extent. However, unless younger learners are exposed to this kind of language and are encouraged to use it in contexts in which we know they are popular, the rich treasury of Scots lexis will continue to decline.

### 4. A Representative Body of Data for Research

A final consideration of the SCOTS corpus is its potential for shedding light on the use of Scots beyond the domains of lexis and grammar. Because the corpus includes recordings and transcriptions of spoken interaction, and written representations of speech (for example in drama and in the records of Scottish parliamentary debates and meetings), the SCOTS corpus provides raw data for research into the use of Scots in speech behaviour across a representative body of texts, from spontaneous casual interactions to formal discussions and lectures. This data allows us to develop activities to draw attention to aspects of everyday speech which are common but whose significance might not be obvious to language users, old and young. One very common feature of everyday speech in Scotland is the use of the term *wee*, whose function is discussed at some length in Douglas and Corbett (2006). Once more, research insights can be transformed into educational activities at school level, as in Figure 10.

#### Task: *wee* in Scots

The adjective *wee* functions in Scottish English and Scots to mean *small* and also to convey the level of formality in speech. Of the following concordance lines, which ones do you feel indicate *informality*?

> Did she have her **wee** alcoholic friend with her?
> you know that sonsie sorta face that **wee** babies have in their pram
> AGNES: (TO BETH) You huv a **wee** seat, hen.
> Juist you hae a **wee** rest or ye gether yeirsell!
> If you want to wait a **wee** second I'll take you to it
> You can help wi some o the **wee** particularities.
> [laugh] Make you look like a **wee** old fart.
>
> Replace *wee* with the more neutral adjective *small* in each example. Is it fair to say that *wee* is the Scots equivalent of the English (and Scottish English) *small*? If you feel it is not, why not? Is there an equivalent in English (or any other language known to you) of the effect of *wee* in Scots?
>
> Now perform an Advanced Search of the SCOTS corpus to find a document that is a recording of a conversation between family members. What other indicators of informality can you find in the transcriptions? How can you tell from the language used that the speakers know each other well?

**Figure 10: Task to Explore the Function of *wee* in Everyday Speech**

This particular task focuses on the fact that although we consider the word *wee* to be synonymous with *small*, it has different connotations and different types of usage. In some of the examples above, it does not indicate small size at all, but rather informality, friendliness, or triviality. That is, a *wee seat* is not a small chair, but a brief sit-down. A *wee second* is no shorter than a normal second, but the expression mitigates the imposition of the request. And in the final example the noun cannot be literally *wee* or *old*, but both adjectives lessen the force of the insult. In short, while the basic meaning of *wee* equates to that of *small* or *little*, it is preferred to either of those two adjectives in speech by Scots who wish to express informality, friendliness and even intimacy. It is also used as a 'downtoner', that is a part of speech (usually an adverb, but here an adjective) that weakens the meaning of the words that follow it (cf. Carter and McCarthy 2006: 901).

**Conclusion**

It is widely accepted that cross-generational transfer of Scots is a major challenge to the survival of the language. Given the status of Scots – or lack of it – in informal and formal education in the pre-school and school years, it is vital, if knowledge of the language is to survive, that children and young adults be exposed to the language in rich contexts, and that they develop a confident and sophisticated understanding of the range of ways in which it has been and can be used. On the positive side, a range of educational resources now exists to meet this challenge. The SCOTS corpus adds a major new asset to the inventory of educational resources available to teachers and parents. It can be used as a stand-alone resource or, as shown above, it can be used in conjunction with other educational materials such as early readers and the Scots dictionaries. In particular:

- The SCOTS corpus can be analysed to see how people interact using a range of Scots features
- SCOTS shows how Scots and English are distributed in child-caregiver interaction, and can provide models for parents and teachers who wish to enrich their Scots repertoire
- SCOTS shows how Scots evaluative terms are used in teenage/young adult banter, and suggests ways of enriching this aspect of Scots
- SCOTS demonstrates how Scots terms continue to be used in everyday speech and writing, often embedded into Scottish English texts, to convey particular meanings and attitudes that are not otherwise expressed through English.

Corpora present raw data that must be interpreted, and it is increasingly urgent that teacher training courses develop teachers' and pupils' skills in searching and understanding corpus data, in particular how corpora can be used to raise awareness of language in all its variety. Corpora offer teachers:

- A vast source of texts and textual examples
- A body of naturally-occurring documents for the analysis of words and grammatical structures
- A wealth of potential insights into how speakers use language in everyday interactions
- And – not least – an enhanced understanding of how language is used in the construction of personal and social identity.

**References**

Adolphs, S. 2006. *Introducing Electronic Text Analysis: A Practical Guide for Language and Literary Studies*. London and New York: Routledge.

Aitken, A.J. 1979. 'Scottish Speech: A Historical View with Special Reference to the Standard English of Scotland'. In eds. Aitken A.J. and T. McArthur. *Languages of Scotland*. Edinburgh: Chambers. 85–118.

Anderson, W. and Corbett, J. 2009. *Exploring English with Online Corpora*. Houndmills: Palgrave Macmillan.

Carter, R. and McCarthy, M. 2006. *Cambridge Grammar of English: A Comprehensive Guide to Spoken and Written English Grammar and Usage*. Cambridge: Cambridge University Press.

Douglas, F. and Corbett, J. 2006. '"Huv a wee seat, hen": Evaluative Terms in Scots'. In eds. Caie, G.D., Hough C. and I. Wotherspoon, *The Power of Words: Essays in Lexicography, Lexicology and Semantics. In Honour of Christian J. Kay*. Amsterdam and New York: Rodopi. 35–56.

Fitt, M. and J. Robertson. 2006. *A Moose in the Hoose: A Scots Counting Book*. Edinburgh: Black and White Publishing/Itchy Coo.

Kennedy, G. 1998. *An Introduction to Corpus Linguistics*. London: Longman.

Macleod, I. with Cairns, P., Macafee, C. and R. Martin, 1990. *The Scots Thesaurus*. Aberdeen: Aberdeen University Press.

McArthur, T. 1979. 'The Status of English in and furth of Scotland'. In eds. Aitken A.J. and T. McArthur. *Languages of Scotland*. Edinburgh: Chambers. 50–67.

Morgan, J. and Rinvolucri, M. 1986. *Vocabulary*. Oxford: Oxford University Press.

O'Keeffe, A., McCarthy, M., and R. Carter, 2007. *From Corpus to Classroom*. Cambridge: Cambridge University Press.
Sinclair, J.M. 1991. *Corpus, Concordance, Collocation*. Oxford: Oxford University Press.
Sinclair, J.M. 2003. *Reading Concordances: An Introduction*. London: Longman.
Wittgenstein, L. 1958. *Philosophical Investigations*. Trans. G.E.M. Anscombe. Oxford: Basil Blackwell.

**Online resources**

BYU-BNC: interface to British National Corpus (Mark Davies, Brigham Young University): http://corpus.byu.edu/bnc/
Corpus of Contemporary American English (Mark Davies, Brigham Young University): http://www.americancorpus.org/
Dictionary of the Scots Language: www.dsl.ac.uk
IViE Corpus: Intonational Variation in English: http://www.phon.ox.ac.uk/IViE/
SCOTS: Scottish Corpus of Texts and Speech: www.scottishcorpus.ac.uk
TIME Corpus (Mark Davies, Brigham Young University): http://corpus.byu.edu/time/

# The Role of Dictionaries in Sustaining a Language Community

*Christine Robinson*

This paper explores the role of dictionaries, in particular of Scottish Language Dictionaries (SLD), in supporting a language and how work related to lexicography fits into the greater language planning issues of codification and elaboration.

The dictionary and the grammar book are the essence of codification, but it might be argued that the influence of the lexicographer – for good or ill – goes beyond the restricted remit of lexical codification and has a potentially profound effect on attitudes to language within a language community, and beyond that language community, in a variety of ways.

Scotland has a long and distinguished tradition in lexicography. This has provided the Scots language with resources which are unequalled among minority languages. There is a high standard to be maintained and, as a lexicographical organisation working in Scotland today, we are daily reminded that, as a planning issue, making dictionaries is not a short-term affair.

Boswell, a Scot and the constant companion and biographer of Samuel Johnson, tells us that the father of lexicography had six amanuenses – and let it be remembered by the Natives of North Britain, to whom he is supposed to have been so hostile, that five of them were of that country. There were two Messieurs MacBean; Mr Shiels, who we shall see hereafter partly wrote The Lives of the Poets to which the name Cibber is affixed; Mr Stewart, son of Mr George Stewart bookseller at Edinburgh; and a Mr Maitland. The sixth of these humble assistants was Mr Peyton who, I believe, taught French and published some elementary tracts.

To all these painful labourers, Johnson shewed a never-ceasing kindness, so far as they stood in need of it. (Boswell p.47)

Johnson famously defined LEXICOGRAPHER as 'a harmless drudge' and indeed there is certainly a lot of drudgery as well as delight in the production of a dictionary. I'd like to go along with 'harmless' as well. Certainly no one at SLD would every knowingly do anybody an ill turn – but the uses to which dictionaries are sometimes put can indeed cause harm and perhaps lexicographers themselves should examine their motives at every step.

There is an early example of what can go wrong. Johnson provided the first real bench mark for dictionaries but his is a very personal view of English. The American lexicographer, Noah Webster, swayed by his own particular linguistic views and also by political anti-British feeling, in his own dictionary made a deliberate point of making his spelling as different as possible from Johnson's. The result is that the spelling divide between one side of the Atlantic and the other was at least in part the consequence of the idiosyncrasies of two very idiosyncratic and opinionated individuals. This reliance on a dictionary to produce a so-called 'right' spelling is something we will return to.

Johnson might have set the ball rolling but John Jamieson picked it up and ran with it, and comparing the scale of Johnson's Dictionary with Jamieson's really does show the immense dedication of Jamieson to his scholarly task. His groundbreaking *Etymogical Dictionary of the Scots Language*, with its wide range of illustrative quotations, was an inspiration for the figure who laid the foundation of modern lexicography. This was yet another Scot, James Murray, the original editor of the *Oxford English Dictionary* (OED). It is hard to imagine lexicographic life without the OED.

The concept of such a comprehensive dictionary, using reliable data to chart the meanings of words from the earliest time up to the present day, reflecting all the changes and subtleties of meaning in a structured manner and providing a scholarly etymology using and adding to the developing science of philology on such a scale was something that Jamieson could only dream about. Even to think of doing something like that was like starting to build a Rolls Royce when the wheel was newly invented. It was a dramatic, colossal vision, but Murray proved it could be done and it was not long until the idea of a Scots equivalent was proposed.

In 1907, following an address by William Craigie to the English Association in Dundee, on 'What steps should be taken to Secure the Co-operation of Members in Collecting Scottish Words, Ballads, Legends and Traditions still current', the unpromisingly-named Council of the SCOTTISH Branch of the English Association was formed with William Grant as convenor and he and 150 volunteers set to and began collecting. These two names – Grant and Craigie – were to become synonymous with the two great Scots Dictionary projects.

Craigie publicly announced in 1919 his intention to edit a dictionary of Older Scots. He and his sister-in-law Miss Hutchen began excerpting and editing began in 1925 on the Dictionary of the Older Scottish Tongue. His nose was put out of joint a little when the Scottish National Dictionary Association was formed in 1929 with view to producing a dictionary of Scots from 1700 onwards. Really, the appellation of 'National' should include the historical material. Grant edited the SND until 1946 when he died aged 83 having got as far as Cr – 842 pages. David Murison took over until the the tenth and final volume was completed in 1976.

In the production of DOST, Craigie was succeeded by the great Scots scholar AJA Aitken, and he in turn was succeeded by Marace Dareau, who drove the project on to completion in 2002 with the publication of volume XII.

Taking DOST and SND together, we have 22 large volumes of Scots words and all 22 volumes with supplements bringing them up to 2005 are now available free, online at the *Dictionary of the Scots Language* (DSL) website www.dsl.ac.uk.

This is of particular interest to scholars of Ulster Scots, since the DOST element of the DSL is also the first part of a historical dictionary of Ulster Scots.

Monumental scholarly dictionaries of this nature have the potential to make a very strong statement about a language. One might think that such a body of work would be very hard to ignore, but apart from academics and a small band of Scots language enthusiasts, most Scots seem not to know of its existence and the paper dictionaries have remained, by and large, the hunting ground of academics. Now, however, the searchable, online DSL is becoming increasingly widely used and the encyclopaedic nature of many of the entries makes it a rattling good read.

There are, however, some unresolved problems. The two dictionaries were compiled according to different editorial principles and the DSL, although it is a very useful tool, does not reconcile the two dictionaries. One major difference was the unfortunate policy of the Scottish National Dictionary Association to exclude from the SND any material shared with English. That could be remedied as part of a rolling programme to apply modern scholarship to some of the earlier parts of this dictionary, correct the inevitable errors, add new words as they appear and generally nurture the dictionary with the same assiduity that is accorded to the OED, but which requires the dedicated attention of more staff than we have available.

Right now, we urgently need a major investment to restructure the DSL and improve its search capabilities. With such a long distance travelled and such a goal within sight, it is to be hoped that the Scottish Parliament will recognise the value of having an online dictionary that, for a very small investment, could be a shining example, a benchmark, for other minority languages and a source of national pride to the Scottish people. However, that investment must be secure and long-term to ensure that the DSL is maintained as the national record of Scots lexis.

That is the output. What is the input? Word collection starts with our 30 or so volunteer readers. They read books and periodicals in which they are asked to underline Scots words and phrases. Informants monitor other media such as radio and even overheard conversation. Words are reported to us as known to or heard by our informants. Wherever possible a quotation and biographical metadata about the speaker are supplied. These written and aural examples go to an editor to be marked up for excerpting. Even common words can be important to build up as complete a picture as we can of all the regions, all levels of formality, all genres and variant spellings. We need to ensure, too, that continuity is maintained so that changes can be traced back by future scholars as well as ourselves.

This goes into the National Word Collection, which was launched during 2008. This database will provide raw data for our future activities. From it, we will be able to see where the gaps are in our evidence and measures can be taken to fill these gaps. The ultimate aim will be to build a picture of the words in use in any part of the country, at any time, by any age group in a variety of registers. In fact it will become a complete linguistic survey of Scots. That is the vision. The reality, as ever, is tempered by financial constraints. There is also the inevitable constraint of sampling. We cannot recover and record every written word, far less every spoken one and inevitably there will be unanswered questions such as when, where and how a new word made its way into Scots. Nevertheless, the National Word Collection will be a further resource to which researchers will eventually have access though a website. Meanwhile, we will be able to welcome visitors, by appointment, to consult the database. Any grammatical features are also noted, so the database is potentially able to provide a corpus to assist research into the grammar of Scots.

Dictionaries are great levellers. Among our earliest Patrons, we can number Ramsay MacDonald, Stanley Baldwin, John Buchan and the Sultana of Johore. But we must also acknowledge a great debt to the readers and the contributors of oral material. Like the OED who had a reader in Broadmoor, SLD has made its forays into Saughton Prison, Shotts Prison and Glenochil Prison. We have boxes of material from schools. Over-50s groups, Burns Clubs, Brownies and the Scottish Women's Rural Institute all take part in oral word collection. And this highlights an aspect of lexicography which is very important to SLD. Whose language is it anyway? Academics do not own the language. We see it as essential that we involve and consult with as wide a range of Scots speakers as possible, because they are the true owners of the language – and the tragedy is that they are too often unaware of their own language skills and of the value of their own linguistic heritage.

What we very often find is that people say 'A cannae speak Scots, hen, A jist speak slang', and when you ask what they mean they tell you that *ken* and *hoose* and *bairn* are all slang words. A quick run through the history of the Scots language dramatically raises their own self image, along with their new found pride in their own language.

Although the editors at SLD have a healthy awareness of their own limitations, people have a curious faith in dictionaries. This puts a great moral responsibility on lexicographers. They have to give an accurate reflection of the language. No longer do SLD's dictionaries exclude Urban Scots or regard it in any way as inferior to the speech of the auldest chiel on the Buchan ferm. Whatever is chosen for inclusion or rejected, these choices can skew the data. Integrity, impartiality and consistency are essential.

We have to reflect the changing meaning of words, which some purists may deplore. Trying to strike the right formality level in a definition can be a matter requiring great sensitivity to language. And it is not our role to say what is good Scots or bad Scots. We just report what is there.

Crucially, we have to balance our desire to be PC with giving a true meaning for some objectionable or judgemental words. No longer to can we countenance a definition such as that given in the SND for *hunnspoo*:

> HUNNSPOO, n. A contemptuous epithet for a worthless person or animal, a "useless specimen" (Cai. 1940 John o' Groat Jnl. (2 April), Cai. 1957). [Perhaps a corruption of Norw. *hundsvott*, a scamp, from Du. *hondsvot*, Ger. *hundsfott*, id., a term of coarse abuse. For second element, see FUD.]

Another word which is defined as a 'worthless person' is *wallidrag* but, even more than these rare or obsolete words, terms in current use require all our ingenuity and sensitivity, words such as *schemie* for example. It is difficult to define this in a way that does not lack proper respect for the many perfectly ordinary and respectable people who live in housing schemes and that does not trade on prejudices of dress or superficial appearances. Why is it so important to get this right? Because people trust dictionaries and we all understand the power not only of the word, but also of its definition.

Perhaps the most obvious effect of trust in dictionaries is the fond belief that herein you will find the 'correct' spelling. What DOST, the SND and therefore the DSL do is give a list of variant spellings. As a result of SNDA editorial policy, spellings shared with English were frequently excluded, although idiosyncratic or utterly bizarre spellings may appear. The topic of orthography is one which goes beyond the scope of this paper, but it is certain that the acceptance of any standardised spelling system by teachers, writers and the general public would be heavily influenced by the headword form used in dictionaries and, with the previously mentioned caveats, these are based on the most common usage. Again, the ownership of spelling is being given back to the language community who actually write in it.

As things stand, we have a proud heritage: 22 vast volumes of historical etymological dictionaries compiled to the highest academic standards and an energetic outreach programme providing a bridge as no other language activity can do, between academe and the real world. We have derivative works, bearing all the authority of the historical source dictionaries, from the scholarly, best-selling *Concise Scots Dictionary* to the *Pocket Scots Dictionary* and a *Scots Thesaurus* for the encouragement of writers. The *Essential Scots Dictionary* is particularly targeted at schools. The historical dictionaries are online – and a strong web presence is increasingly important as the predominant if not the only form of reading material for a growing number of the population.

Still more remains to be done. There is a case for including at least one type of dictionary in the elaboration category of language planning and that is a type of dictionary that Scots does not yet have. Germans have their *Duden* in German; the French have the *Grande Larousse* in French, even the English have the *OED* in English – but the Scots as yet do not have a monolingual dictionary. This may be seen as a staggering anomaly or sensible pragmatism given that all Scots speakers can understand definitions in English and many of them even speak it fluently. But that is just the point. By not having a Scots-Scots monolingual dictionary we are conniving at a restriction of the spread of Scots. It is not being allowed into every corner where language is used. It is being excluded from lexicography itself and that in language planning terms, is a very dangerous omission. It is actually quite hard to write good definitions in Scots when all your editors have spent their lives writing definitions of Scots in English, but it a challenge SLD would love to take up.

We also need to have a full dictionary of Scots covering all the lexemes shared with English. Without it, we are unable to have a useable spell-checker and automatic translation cannot even be contemplated. A related lexicographical omission is the absence of a dictionary of Scottish English. American, Canadian, Indian, Australian and South African Englishes all have their own dictionaries. The Chambers dictionaries were the nearest approach to this with their extensive coverage of Scottish English but they were intended to have a more UK wide appeal.

In spite of these shortcomings, Scots is fortunate in having the historical dictionaries. We need to improve and maintain them. The academic community at home and abroad are highly supportive of Scots language and of SLD as a provider of academic resources. The research basis of SLD's work, gives a privileged position and lends a kind of authority with which comes responsibility. This is why we are conscious of the importance of our role in actively working to promote Scots at all levels of education and in the community. We work closely and co-operatively with other language organisations. In fact, we are working far beyond the traditional definition of lexicography to give Scots speakers, beyond the already committed band of language activists, a deeper appreciation of their language and the will to make that language self-sustaining through extended use.

Since this paper was given, Scottish Language Dictionaries have been funded by the Scottish Government. This has enabled the organisation to take on additional staff. The re-editing of the *Concise Scots Dictionary* continues apace and work on improving the searchability of the DSL is now well advanced. The reorganisation of DSL's structure, currently being undertaken by our computing officer, will facilitate revision and correction and we have a full-time editor dedicated to this task. We also have a new education and outreach officer who is taking the work of the dictionaries into the heart of the community, working with nursery children upwards, assisting teachers in the planning and delivery of Scots in the classroom and forging links with a wide range of community organisations. The National Word Collection at the end of March 2010 contained almost 40,000 quotations and over 60,000 keywords and is growing rapidly.

**References**

*A Dictionary of the Older Scottish Tongue* (DOST) 1931–1002. eds. W. A. Craigie, A. J. Aitken, J. A. C. Stevenson, H. D. Watson, M. G. Dareau. 12 vols. Chicago: Chicago University Press (1931–77); Aberdeen: Aberdeen University Press (1983–91); Oxford: Oxford University Press (1994–2002).
Boswell J. 1791. *The Life of Samuel Johnson, LLD.*
*Dictionary of the Scots Language.* www.dsl.ac.uk (last updated 2005).
Robinson, M., *Concise Scots Dictionary*, Edinburgh: Edinburgh University Press. 1985.
*Scottish National Dictionary* (SND) 1929–76. Eds. W. Grant and D. Murison. 10 vols. Edinburgh: Scottish National Dictionary Association.

# Drama as a Means fir Uphaudin Leid Communities

*Ian Brown*

In a chapter in *Belfast Studies in Language, Culture and Politics 19: Language and Economic Development* (Brown, 2009),[1] A refer tae the apparent fact that the presentation o a pley in Scots wis likely in the professional view o mony theatre directors in Scotlan tae increase box office income bi near ten per cent owre a pley no in Scots. A arguit then that in economic terms this wis beneficial, bit firbye that it cam less fae economic reasons than through a virtuous circle that maintained the yiss o Scots in Scottish theatre an literature. This, A jaloosed, wis acause its yiss:

> develops stronger cultural consciousness, empowers and gives voice to Scots speakers on stage and listeners in the auditorium and beyond [...] It speaks to – and so generates – an additional, and effectively new, audience and readership sector. (Brown, 2009: 203).

This chapter complements thon yin in that it conseeders the role o Scots leid on stage as a means o uphaudin the status o Scots in its leid communities. It taks on the gate bi whilk makars micht yaize a leid wioot giein a conscious thocht tae leid-plannin.

Pairt o the thrust o this paper is that the yiss o Scots on the professional stage is a means o uphaudin the status o the leid in its communities an sae uphaudin the leid community itsel. In a kenspeckle newspaper interview in 1968 when he hid served twa year as Artistic Director o the Royal Lyceum Theatre, Edinburgh, Clive Perry gied opeenion furth that he thocht there wis nae future fir Scots on stage:

> [audiences werenae] willing to sit through a play whose vocabulary they don't understand. As regards the future of Scottish theatre, it may be that there is no such thing as a totally individual Scots language left. National drama with a tongue of its own is not for the future. Plays about contemporary Scotland will be in English with only a slight accent.[2]

This no entirely weelcome observation wis met wi some surprise an a wee bit collyshangles amang no anerly the public, bit the theatre profession in Scotlan. In a recent airticle,[3] A hae suggestit that this statement wisnae jist as gyte ir chauvinist in the late 1960s as micht at first sicht appear. In thon airticle, A discuss the weys in which bi then Scots on stage hid become in a sense constraint. Firstly, a wheen o pleyscrievin in Scots hid becam couthy, the sphere o amateur drama an slight pleytexts unner the itherwise admirable aegis o the Scottish Community Drama Association. Secondly, the grand tradeetion o radical poleetical theatre in the vernacular demotic – representit bi the 1920s phase o the wirk o Joe Corrie ir the post-war Glasgow Unity Theatre

---

[1] Ian Brown, 'Drama and Literature in Scots as an Economic Generator'. In eds. Kirk, J.M. and Ó Baoill, D.P. *Language and Economic Development: Northern Ireland, the Republic of Ireland, and Scotland*. Belfast: Cló Ollscoil na Banríona. 2009: 196–203.
[2] Quoted in Bill Findlay, ed. *Scots Plays of the Seventies*. Dalkeith: Scottish Cultural Press. 2003: p.xvi.
[3] Ian Brown, 'The Scots Leid in Modren Scots Drama: 'World Drama' an 'our National Peculiarities", *Lallans* 70. Ware 2007. pp. 33–44.

pleywrights, abune aw aiblins Ena Lamont Stewart – hid somewise fadit fae view. Thirdly, the remarkable pleys o Robert Kemp, Alexander Reid an Robert McLellan cid be seen tae be retrospective, een firbye retrogressive, in that they seemed concernt either wi a gey auld-fashioned historical drama ir wi owresettins o comic classics, mainly Molière, that brocht thair ain air o historicism. Katja Lenz his famously argued that sic wirk wis intendit tae provide a tradeetion that, fir historic reasons, wis missin in Scottish theatre, observin that a motivation fir this sort o historical drama "may lie in its usability as a vehicle for asserting the national culture, for marking it off from the English or the joint British one, by demonstrating the existence of a separate history" (Lenz 1996: 309).[4] Nanetheless, thae pleys wisnae, except bi indirection, aboot contemporary issues. In ither wirds, Perry's intervention arose fae a perception that the status o Scots leid on stage wis that o a leid suitable fir langsyne maitters ir unfashionable topics ir amateur drama, generally o a licht nature.

It wisnae ayewis yon wey, certes. Efter the Jacobean flittin tae London fir, *inter alia*, tae sponsor Shakespeare, drama in Scotlan wis occludit fir a century, save gey intermittently.[5] It began, nanetheless, tae develop again in the early eichteenth century. Then, some o the initiators cam fae London ir Dublin an wirked in English, bit we firbye fin important wirk sic as Allan Ramsay's Scots leid ballad opera *The Gentle Shepherd* (1725). Bi the middle o the eichteenth century, theatre hid become a centre fir intellectual an cultural debate an conflict, at least in the Scottish cities, aften as pairt o the war inby the Kirk atween the Moderates an the conservative Evangelicals.[6] Theatre wis again fashionable, bit the leid selectit fir pleyscrievin, as in Home's *Douglas* (1756), tendit aye tae be English. That wis the leid o the Enlightenment, in the age o Hume's lists o scotticisms an Blair's chair in Rhetoric an Belles Lettres. Yet theatre bidit an arena fir linguistic contention atween different leid ideologies an audiences drawn fae different leid communities. Bi the end o the century, there wis pleys drawin on aw the then leids o Scotlan tae be fund on popular Lowlan stages, includin, leastweys in pairt, Gaelic, as Barbara Bell his pinted oot. Bell cites the ensaumple o Airchibauld Maclaren's *The Highland Drover*, first published in Greenock in 1790. There the central character's exchynges 'with his fellow drover and with a maidservant are conducted entirely in Gaelic'.[7] Sic Anglo-Scoto-Gaelic pleys wis clearly intendit fir an audience that unnerstood Gaelic acause the nature o mony jokes dependit on bilinguality in the audience. Scenes micht depend, accordin to Bell, on the fun 'derived from the ability of the Highlander to frustrate the Lowlander by switching languages in mid-sentence', a technique yaized bi Maclaren in his 1789 *The Humours of Greenock Fair*.[8]

This wisnae a high airt ir literary movement, o coorse, bit yin intendit fir a popular audience. Sic an audience wis firbye served bi the National Drama: pleys on, aften,

---

[4] Katja Lenz, "Modern Scottish Drama: Snakes in Iceland – Drama in Scotland?". *Zeitschrift für Anglistik und Amerikanistik* XLIV.4. 1996. p. 309
[5] Though fir fuller discussion o the liveliness o Scottish theatre even in this occludit phase, see Ian Brown, 'Public and Private Performance 1650–1800', in ed. Ian Brown, *The Edinburgh Companion to Scottish Drama* Edinburgh: Edinburgh University Press. 2011: 22–40.
[6] Fir a brief discussion o this neglectit aspect o the history o Scottish theatre, see Ian Brown, 'Gateways from the past to the future' in Ian Brown, ed. *Journey's Beginning: The Gateway Theatre Building and Company, 1884–1965*. Bristol: Intellect Books. 2004. pp. 4–5.
[7] Barbara Bell, 'The Nineteenth Century'. In ed. Bill Findlay. *A History of Scottish Theatre*, Edinburgh: Polygon. 1998. 137–206. At p. 137.
[8] *ibid*.

patriotic Scottish themes presentit at first in W H Murray's Theatre Royal in Edinburgh an includin in large pairt adaptations o Walter Scott's novels. These wis highly popular across aw sectors o society and, acause they drew greatly on Scott's ain dialogue, mony serious pairts wis scrievd an pleyed in Scots. Efter aw, we get the term 'The Real Mackay' fae the guiser Charles Mackay, whase speciality wis guisin Baillie Nicol Jarvie wi his Scots dialogue. Bi the end o the nineteenth century, hooever that micht be, the rail revolution hid bitten: large sections o the legitimate theatre business throughoot the UK wis driven bi the economics o the West End o London an large-scale companies tourin UK-wide. Scots, meanwhiles, hid becam the leid o the popular penny geggie an appeared on the legitimate stage mainly as comic relief ir quaint detail. Corrie an the Unity Company pleywrights an Reid, Kemp an McLellan wis reactin against this degringolade, bit, as Perry seemed tae be suggestin in 1968, thairs wisnae an easy task.

Yet, wiin fowre year o Perry's diktat, the Royal Lyceum, his ain theatre unner his ain direction, wis presentin *Willie Rough* (1972) tae fu hooses, enthusiastic audiences an critical acclaim. Whit hid happened? While it wid be unfair tae minimise the role o companies like Unity an the serious pleywrights awready mentioned in uphaudin Scots as a stage leid alive, yin key consideration wis that Scots hid never disappeared fae theatre as a whole. Aw through the period o apparent serious degringolade on the legitimate stage, Scots continued as a fell versatile stage leid in the popular theatre. In the licht o the wirk o thinkers like Bertolt Brecht and, in Britain, Ewan McColl an Joan Littlewood, a number o Scots-scrievin practitioners cam tae recognise the value o Scots as a serious stage leid. Makar/directors like Bryden, comin fae the Royal Court back tae wirk wi Perry in 1970, an John McGrath, wi the development o 7:84 (Scotland) Theatre Company fae 1973 – baith wirkin deliberately wiin a popular an newly radicalised tradeetion – wis inclined tae respect the leid. This wis on pairtly theatrical, pairtly poleetical an pairtly social grunds, bit, whitever the motivation, it wis clearly a vital popular theatre leid, it wis the leid o 'the fowk' and, o coorse, fir Bryden an his contemporaries it wis the leid o thair upbringin. In 1971 Stewart Conn's *The Burning* began the flood followed in 1972 bi *Willie Rough* an the seminal *The Great Northern Welly Boot Show*, starrin Billy Connolly an addressin the then-current UCS sit-in. The last in pairticular showed that it wis possible tae deal wi important current poleetical issues in Scots an wis a substantial influence on John McGrath's iconic 1973 *The Cheviot, the Stag and the Black, Black Oil*. In the 1970s, a veritable corrievreckan o new scrievin on serious topics emerged bi siclike as Bryden, Conn, John McGrath, Tom McGrath, Donald Campbell an even masel. Fir this group o makars an fir thair audiences suddenly there wis nae question. Scots hid fine-weel eneuch status tae deal wi ony topic an theme an audiences cam in substantial additional numbers tae enjoy pleys in that leid. A virtuous circle o status wis establisht. The makars an audiences fed off yin the ither. Whit wey wis this achieved?

In yin sense the key wis motivation. If A may presume tae tak ma ain case, ma reaction tae Perry's remarks wis indignation. At the same time, A hid tae recognise that, as A hid been stertin tae scrieve fir the theatre – wi, certes, sair scant success – whit A hid scrieved, wi yin exception, wis aw in English. A hid jist no engaged wi ma ain leid community. In fact, in whit hid become the tradeetional wey fir an educatit Scot A hid been 'educatit' awaw fae the community in the midst o which A growed up an intae speakin an scrievin English. A suppose A hid scrieved aboot six pleys o yin kind ir anither – maistly no awfy gid – afore the time A left university in 1967 an nane wis in Scots. Jist efter A left, A began *Mary* which ten year later in 1977 wis tae be produced bi the Royal Lyceum in Scots. In ither wirds, the thocht o scrievin in Scots wisnae anerly no then at the front o ma mind, it wis bi a lang wey an efterthocht. Whit Perry did, aiblins even intentionally, wis tae challenge the drift awaw fae Scots-leid scrievin. On reflection, ye can see precisely whit wey he micht hae makit the stramash-provokin statement he did in 1968. An it wid be gey hard fir me tae deny that the weys he saw theatre in Scots wisnae actually the weys A saw it then. Serious drama wis thon o Arthur Miller, Harold Pinter, Samuel Beckett in English owresettin. As A hae awready said, Scots wis 'a leid suitable fir langsyne maitters ir unfashionable topics ir amateur drama, generally o a licht nature'. Perry gied the inner hert o thon assumption a gey fleg. Ye micht turn aroon his intervention an sey that its subtext wis 'yaise it ir loss it'. If serious dramatists didnae yaise the leid, it wid disappear as a valuable an viable stage leid. The anerly wey that cid be avoided wis fir thae interested in scrievin texts fir the stage tae scrieve them in Scots. Tae be honest, A doot Clive Perry was that intricate in his reasonin an jaloose that in 1968 he genuinely thocht Scots wis deid as a leid fir the professional stage. Nanetheless, the effect o his remark wis certainly pairt o a process o abreaction that led tae the revival o that leid that is pairt o the topic o this paper.

Whit is important aboot the generation o which A am noo speakin, Conn, Bryden, Tom McGrath, Campbell, even masel, is that while it micht be stimulated bi the Renaissance generation an Reid, McLellan an Kemp, they wisnae o thair age ir ideology. While in yin wey ir anither thae makars tendit tae wirk, if no in Lallans, at least in a Synthetic Scots tradeetion, this yinger generation tendit tae wirk in a demotic based aften on thair ain dialect area. This isnae tae sey that the wirk o the aulder generation wisnae important ir inspirational tae them, bit thair approach wisnae derived fae a synthesisin impulse. Tom McGrath, reflectin on the conflict when Hugh MacDiarmid attacked the wirk o sic makars as Edwin Morgan, Tom Leonard an hissel, his observed:

> I suppose at that time we were coming up with a different ideology. We were coming up with a different approach after all that work, work that had been done in Scots language. We were coming up with this street level sound of existentialist man in the street, "black man in the ghetto" type of writing. It just upset the applecart.[9]

Liz Lochhead his said o MacDiarmid's influence on her scrievin:

> I love the Scottish lyrical short poems of MacDiarmid. They're delightful, but I don't think he's been an influence, while Eddie Morgan has been a huge influence because of his humanism, and his Glasgowness too. [...] MacDiarmid's work I feel excluded from [...] because it is so male and bardic in the old priestly kind of didactic tradition.[10]

Indeed, there wis times when the yinger generation made fun o some o the possible extremes o the aulder. Scene 23 o ma ain *Mary* is a comic send-up o kailyard drama, whase openin lines hauds a near direct quotation fae the openin lines o McLellan's *Toom Byres* (1936), which is itsel shairly no kailyaird.

---

[9] Ian Brown, "Cultural Centrality and Dominance: The Creative Writer's View. Conversations between Scottish Poet/Playwrights and Ian Brown", *Interface* Issue 3. Summer 1984. p.48
[10] *ibid*. p. 21.

LENNOX IS SITTING IN A CHAIR, DRESSED AS AN OLD WOMAN. HE IS KNITTING. KNOX ENTERS, DRESSED ALSO AS AN OLD WOMAN. LENNOX PUTS DOWN HIS KNITTING.
LENNOX: Oh dearie me, is it yersel, Jeannie Knox?
KNOX: Aye, it's me, Aggie Lennox.
LENNOX: Sic a ding ye gied ma pair pulsin hert. Hirplin in there the like of an oossie puddock.
KNOX: Aye, hinnie. It's a dour lift aboon us baith and a queer eldritch nicht the nicht. The birdies and the beasties, Aggie, the birdies and the beasties is ower awfy restless. The hens're ill tae lay and the kye's kicked ower the mune. The hoonds're howlin, the hoolets hootin, and, hoots, it's gey eerie the nicht, a nicht for bogles and whigmaleeries.[11]

Tae be blunt, this generation wisnae drawn intae the specific linguistic battle o the Renaissance generation, fund some o whit they hid scrieved foosty an retrospective an wantit tae yaise a leid that wis in thair visions mair up-to-date an contemporary. Bit that leid wis Scots yaised fir non-nostalgic purposes an its anerly soorce fir us wis oor ain leid communities, inflected nae doot bi the experiments o the generation we thocht we, in oor then-youthfu arrogance, wis movin ayont. There is nae doot that this avoidance o a quasi-poleetical programme an the desire tae relate tae oor ain diurnal leid experience may explain whit wey some o this second generation is vague as tae jist whit leid they yaise. Liz Lochhead, fir ensaumple, his been kent tae sey, whiles, she isnae scrievin in Scots bit, at different times, in 'Glaswegian' ir 'Scottish English'. That, hooever, isnae jist a problem arisin fae the lack o a specific leid ideology. It is shairly a result o the failure o the Scottish education system fir generations tae teach unnerstaunin o Scots leid jist as it his aften failed tae teach Scottish literature ir history. A by-blow o this failure, certes, is the uncertainty an even distrust some makars feel aboot the concept an nature o the Scots leid. It may even be that pairt o this arises fae the programmatic nature o Scots leid campaigners an pairticularly ideologically driven creative scrievers o the first pairt o the twentieth century. When these are seen as layin claim tae Scots an whit they scrieve is seen as difficult bi some readers, even highly educated yins, an separate fae thair ain community leids, then thae community leids can be seen as no really Scots in some ideal ir essentialist sense supported bi an ideological leid programme. This micht weel be an explanation fir, fir ensaumple, Liz Lochhead's reluctance tae concede she scrieves in Scots when that is whit she evidently does.

Hooever this micht be, gied the failure o the Scottish education system fir generations tae teach unnerstaunin o Scots leid, a strikin aspect o the yiss o Scots on the professional stage owre the last fowre decades his been its range. Its yiss on stage hisnae been the result o an ideological programme fir yaizage, bit raither the appropriation tae the stage o a wide variety o registers an dialects o Scots wi which pleywrights hae felt at hame. Whether we observe Bryden's yiss o the dialect o his native Greenock, Lochhead's o her Glaswegian ir the present author's o Fife/Clackmannan dialect as a basis fir thair dialogue an dramaturgy, whit is clear is an absence o phonological ir dialectological rigour. Whit exists is much mair a series o attempts tae employ whit, tae the pleywright's ear, enshrines the leid o her/his community. When linguistic scientists

---

[11] Ian Brown. *Mary*. unpublished typescript. 1977. p. 74

hae looked at the results o this process, they hae aften fund inconsistency in linguistic terms in yaizage: John Corbett his, fir ensaumple, discussed this *passim* in conseederin the Bill Findlay an Martin Bowman owresettin o Michel Tremblay's *The House Among the Stars*. Here, the pley requires no jist the yiss o Scots, bit the representation o the chynges in its yiss owre three generations and Corbett highlights the shoogliness o some o Findlay an Bowman's yaizages.[12] Yet, the current yaizage bi pleywrights isnae diminished bi thon shoogliness, bit in fact reflects whit is aften a dynamic confusion in contemporary Scots yaizage that is airt an pairt o the dynamism o a livin an chyngin leid. In this sense, firbye, the pleywright speaks tae the leid community whase leid is drawn on fir the pley's dialogue.

Certes, the range o pleys scrieved an performed in Scots owre the last fowrty year covers a byordinair range o material: poleetical, social, philosophical, domestic an mony ither registers an discoorses. This range gies the lie tae the canard that contemporary registers o Scots are limited an can deal anerly wi sic specific registers as those of, sey, comedy ir wirkin class life. Indeed, yin area in which pleywrights hae socht, rather in the gate o fifteenth- an sixteenth-century Scottish makars, tae assert the competence o Scots is in owresettin. Nae sowel, o coorse, his producit onythin o the quality o Gavin Douglas's *Eneados*, bit Liz Lochhead an Edwin Morgan, tae name bit twa, hae showed the scope an flexibility o varieties o modern Scots as a target leid fir owresettin. This is evident in Lochhead's versions o Molière's *Tartuffe* (1985) an *The Misanthrope* (as *Miseryguts*, 2002) an her version o the *Medea* (2000) an in Morgan's verbally fantoosh an coruscatin *Cyrano de Bergerac* (1992). Sic creative acts assert the vibrancy, range an power o Scots.

This isnae tae argify that awthin is fine in the gairden. The maist widely owreset an internationally kent o the contemporary generation are nae doot David Greig an David Harrower, the baith o whilk are identified bi Paul Barnaby an Tom Hubbard as bein ' translated into of the order of twenty languages at the time of writing [2006]'.[13] An while thair yiss o English is weel inflectit bi rhythms o Scots, they dinnae scrieve muckle in Scots at aw. Bit thon is tae sey that there is nae single ideological line aboot the yiss o Scots ir ony ither leid on the contemporary Scottish stage. There is a variety o yisses o the leids o Scotlan on its stages an Scots hauds a central place in thon yisses in a wey aiblins no tae hae been predicted fowrty year syne when Clive Perry steered his stramash. An in thae fowrty year, there can be nae doot bit that the pleywrights hae contributit muckle tae the maintenance o Scots as a dynamic leid in its community an promotit it amang braider theatre audiences. The recent an continuin success o Gregory Burke's *Black Watch* (2006) is anerly yin ensaumple of jist hoo muckle the yiss o contemporary Scots can treat wi contemporary issues an in a wey that speaks no jist tae Scots, but across the warlt. Burke didnae plan the leid o his pley. Thon isnae his role. As a makar, he heard it an scrieved it. An aiblins the role o professional drama in uphaudin Scots isnae tae plan, but tae hear an speak it fir audiences – een warltwide. An in thon wey, it can aiblins uphaud its leid communities.

---

[12] See, fir ensaumple, John Corbett, 'COMET and the House Among the Stars: Scottish Texts via the Internet'. *Glasgow Review* 4. 1996. pp. 86–95. Available from http://www2.arts.gla.ac.uk/SESLL/STELLA/COMET/glasgrev/issue4/comet.htm#Title

[13] Paul Barnaby and Tom Hubbard, 'The International Reception and Literary Impact of Scottish Literature of the Period since 1918'. In eds. Ian Brown, Thomas Clancy, Murray Pittock and Susan Manning. *The Edinburgh History of Scottish Literature*. Vol. 3. Edinburgh: Edinburgh University Press. 2007: 31–41. At p. 40.

# Hiberno-Central as an Unroofed Dialect of Scots

*Gavin Falconer*

A brief passage in chapter 39 of Sir Walter Scott's novel *Waverley* sheds light on attitudes to Scots speech at a time when Anglicisation of the spoken language was only beginning.[1]

> 'A fine evening, sir,' was Edward's salutation.
> 'Ow, ay, sir! a bra' night,' replied the lieutenant, in broad Scotch of the most vulgar description.
> 'And a fine harvest, apparently,' continued Waverley, following up his first attack.
> 'Ay, the aits will be got bravely in: but the farmers, deil burst them, and the corn-mongers, will make the auld price gude against them as has horses till keep.'

The final sentence spoken by the character of the lieutenant includes two features common in Ulster – not only in the littoral Scots-speaking areas but in urban centres such as Belfast – the relative pronoun *as* and the use of the preposition *till* with the infinitive. Although Scott does not state explicitly that it is these features that render the lieutenant's speech 'Scotch of the most vulgar description', the latter is stigmatised among revivalist writers, while the former is so uncommon in mainland Scots literature that one is tempted to conclude that it may have been chosen for a purpose. Although one cannot be sure that the author is employing these devices to suggest a lack of education on the part of the character, it is interesting to note that infinitive *for till* is used in the same way today in BBC Northern Ireland's comedy programme *Give My Head Peace*. The character of Red Hand Luke, the least intelligent, also makes most use of the form, which may be doubly vulgar in that it is used as a generalised infinitive marker rather than with the meaning 'in order to'.

At this point it may be appropriate to raise two further points in which the grammar of literary Scots, in some of its manifestations at least, may differ from speech, the use of *wha* as a relative pronoun in preference to *that* or Ø, and the marking of finite verbs for number regardless of syntactical context. Neither suggestion is entirely uncontroversial. *Quha* was used as a relative form historically in Middle Scots, and while there was a clear development towards not marking verbs for number if they were not adjacent to a preposition,[2] the written record at least shows that the change was never entirely completed. The belief has been voiced often enough by activists that writers' choice to ally themselves with Standard English in preference to the strong tendency of spoken Scots may suggest a certain sensitivity in how the language was viewed, and the fact that, in the Modern Scots period, it happened in the context of orthographic practice that was not only English-based but in which Scots realisations were often left to the reader to interpolate can have done nothing to dispel such feelings.

---

[1] From a contemporary perspective, there may not have been much difference between the linguistic situation of 1745 and that of 60 years later when Scott wrote the novel, since the Lowland middle classes had begun to adopt Standard English pronunciation only at the end of the eighteenth century.
[2] See Montgomery (1994).

However, such spellings, while perhaps most strongly associated with Central Scots, were used everywhere from the north-east of Scotland to County Donegal, and it is also possible to see the existence of a nascent Standard Scots in the fact that grammatical and register issues were broached. The notion of such a standard literary variety is nothing new to scholars of the language. While the lack of a firm standard is a commonplace when discussing Scots, it is more correct to say that a standard existed but was not rigorously applied in the same way as that of English is today. Indeed, in previous centuries, Scots may have been in advance of English in standardisation.[3] After the First World War writing in the language became an increasingly intellectual pursuit, with no popular successor to the *kailyard*. Subsequent developments including mediaeval pastiche, increased diversity wrought by successive failed attempts at standardisation on the part of activists, and the advent of satirical Scots-influenced eye dialect may have partially obscured the only popular standard that has ever existed for Modern Scots. Another, more recent development, has been the revival of writing in the Ulster dialect of Scots in the context of a literary tradition that has not merely been weakened, but has broken down entirely.

The taxonomic position of Ulster Scots has attracted comment over recent years, and even academic articles on the subject have on occasion adopted a polemical slant. The first academic introduction to Lowland Scots approximating to modern standards of scholarship, J.A.H. Murray's *The Dialect of the Southern Counties of Scotland* (1873), is notable for dealing only with the vernacular language of mainland Scotland in any detail, with little attention paid to either Ulster or the Northern Isles. Murray distinguishes three main Scots dialect areas, the demographically largest Mid Scots variety – nowadays more commonly known as Central Scots – Northern Scots and Southern Scots. It is notable that the Southern dialect, of which he was a native user, was much less strongly differentiated from the main Central variety than was Northern Scots. It was also much weaker in speaker numbers, a consideration irrelevant to taxonomy but of some importance to debates regarding sustainability and the targeting of spending to promote linguistic diversity. The introduction to the *Scottish National Dictionary* (*SND*) distinguishes five main dialects, adding Ulster Scots and the Insular Scots of Orkney and Shetland to Murray's original three. More recently, Macafee (2005: 71) has suggested that Ulster Scots might more properly be viewed as a sub-dialect of Central Scots, being alone among the four peripheral dialects listed in the introduction to the *SND* in commonly being indistinguishable in written form from Central Scots and derived literary varieties.[4] Regardless of whether one accepts that reclassification, 'Hiberno-Central' is a useful tag, since it neatly summarises the variety's genesis.

Two developments relevant to the taxonomy of the Scots dialects in Scotland itself have occurred since Murray's time, the first and most important being that the diglossia that previously determined a speaker's choice of Scots or Scottish Standard English has now given way to style-drifting over much of the country, with almost complete loss of velar fricatives in vocabulary cognate with Standard English and 'free' alternation between diphthongised and undiphthongised forms of prepositions and other common words, whereby a speaker might say [ut] or [brun] one minute and [ʌut] or [brʌun] the next. A second change concerns loss of the velar fricative in a specific situation in the Southern dialect in particular, something at least reinforced by the influence of Standard English but easily conceivable as an autonomous development. The historical realisation of Scots *micht* in the Southern dialect, while retaining the velar fricative,

---

[3] See Quirk (1982: 54).
[4] This applies only to the poetic tradition, whose last major representative was David Herbison (1800–80).

had also included a diphthong similar to that in Standard English *might*. By the time Hugh MacDiarmid, a native speaker of Southern Scots, stepped in front of the microphone to record his poetry, that velar fricative had been lost, rendering the regional Lowland Scots form identical to the regional form in Scottish Standard English.

The effect has been to blur the dividing line between Central and Southern Scots. The contemporary Southern Scots realisation of *micht* could easily be mistaken for the result of Anglicisation, and the fact that it diphthongises open syllables in words such as *hou* ('how') but not in closed syllables such as that in *broun* ('brown') could similarly be understood as the sort of free variation heard from speakers of Scots or Scots-influenced English elsewhere in Scotland. As Scots as a whole grows closer to Standard English through asymmetrical convergence, the individual Scots dialects themselves will also grow closer to each other, and although the two features discussed above are not the only ones that distinguish Southern Scots from its much larger Central Scots neighbour, at some stage in the future it may be appropriate to speak of only two dialects in mainland Scotland, a Northern Scots occupying much the same area as it has always done, and a Central Scots extending to the south-eastern border with England.

The above discussion suggests a maximum of five main dialects, as suggested in the introduction to the *SND*, and a minimum of three. If the highly and irregularly differentiated Insular Scots dialects are considered separately, we are left with only two, Central Scots and Northern Scots. Given that the latter dialect, popularly known as 'Doric', as well as being relatively highly differentiated, is demographically and sociolinguistically strong, while Scots in the Central Belt is increasingly diluted by English or abandoned entirely, it is not implausible to suggest that we might at some point hear funding calls for a regional language called 'Doric' as talk of a Scots language fades into history.

Subsuming Lowland Scots dialects into Anglic taxonomic groups extending beyond the borders of Scotland and Ulster is of course also possible, and not only in the case of Berwick-upon-Tweed. Structural difference notwithstanding, treating Scots as a form of English, if need be with some qualification, is amply justified on functional grounds, but such an approach can be criticised for its lack of relevance to the maintenance or revival of an independent language, an aim now accorded Government backing, in word if not yet in deed. From a purely academic perspective, the classification might almost be thought so general as to be facile.

Another possibility, refreshingly separate from debates on constitutional issues, is to classify the Scots dialects as part of a larger Northumbrian group delimited in its most basic sense by the retention of historic monophthongs such as that in [dun], use of the negative clitic *-na* or *-nae*, particularly with modals, and a rich adstrate of Norse loan words and realisations (*bing*, *kirk* etc.). Treating Northumbrian as a half-language in Scotland and dialect in England provides a partial parallel with Low German, a fully codified and autonomous language in the Netherlands and Belgium and half-language in northern Germany.[5] Drawing on the example of the *langue d'oc* and *langue d'oïl* tags of French linguistics, and referring to commonly used interjections, it might be tempting to refer to an *aye*-group in contradistinction to a *yea-* or *yes*-group further south. However, *aye* is also common as a dialect feature and archaism – notably in parliamentary settings – south of the Humber. In any case, according to the *Oxford English Dictionary* it is unattested before 1575, long after the linguistic border had come

---

[5] The term 'Low German' can also be used to refer to Low Saxon varieties in particular, thus excluding the Low Franconian speech of all of Belgium and most of the Netherlands.

into existence, and when its downgrading or disappearance was already on the horizon.

In conventional linguistic terminology, a variety is 'unroofed' if formal functions are either not catered for or ceded to an unrelated language; if the high language is related, the relationship is dialectal. For example, in Germany, Alemannic functions as a dialect of Standard German, while in France, under the name of Alsatian, it is unroofed by any form of Germanic, with French used for formal communication. On the face of it, the case of Scots is simple, since, as suggested above, formal functions are very largely the province of Standard English. However, terming Scots a 'half-language' suggests the existence of a partially functional – moribund or nascent – alternative standard dialect. In the century prior to 1560, that alternative was Middle Scots, but over the next 100 years the Scots Reformation, the rise of printing, and the Union of the Crowns led to that written dialect's virtual disappearance, even if the spoken language probably remained relatively untouched until much later.

By the end of the eighteenth century, a time when the Anglicisation of upper-class speech meant that realising Standard English orthography as Scots was becoming problematic, the language had once again made an appearance in written form. This time around it was, on the whole, limited to literature,[6] where it was found mainly in poetry and as dialogue in novels. It did not, therefore, threaten the position of Standard English, which, despite its largely external origins, had taken on an air of neutrality. Given the limited field of use of such Scots, and the relative flexibility of the standard employed, it is perhaps unsurprising that some commentators might call its very existence into question. However, wide reading of Scots material from the time confirms a 'mezzanine' of pan-dialectal standard Scots between the regional dialects and Standard English. The written Scots dialect in question is copiously described in Eagle (2006).

Any claim that there is no standard, if made without qualification, is simply wrong. Modern Scots writing from the time of Allan Ramsay (1686–1758) until the end of the Second World War clearly exhibits a high degree of codification, even if it is flexible or even polycentric. In that codification, there are two key principles: first, diverging from the orthography of Modern Standard English, the first language of literacy of all Scots-speakers, must be justified by phonological relevance; second, where possible, diversity within Scots should be accommodated by the use of pan-dialectal forms capable of variant realisation. As Standard English was an etymologically spelt language, the two aims were mutually reinforcing.

The first attempt to codify Scots by committee, the Makars' Club style sheet of 1947, continued in the same vein with the modest suggestion that the digraph <aa> was a better pan-dialectal representation of [a], [ɑ] and [ɔ] than <aw>. However, since there was no state backing to reprint the canon of Scots literature taking the new reform into account, the result was to add to the heterogeneity of Scots spelling. That had already been seen in the introduction of <ü> in preference to the historic <ui> and <u_e> by Robert Louis Stevenson[7] and imitators for the set of realisations that A. J. Aitken would later term 'vowel 7'. With the Makars' Club suggestion, the centrifugal tendencies of dialectal diversity meant that writers who said [a] wrote <aa>, while those who said [ɔ] wrote <aw>.

---

[6] Scotland's Roman (not Common) Law and mainly Presbyterian (not Anglican) religion dispose over a large number of distinctive Scots terms, but the nuts and bolts of formal language are invariably Standard English.

[7] Robert Louis Stevenson *Underwoods*, London: Chatto and Windus. 1887.

By the 1970s, two further tendencies had emerged. First, for reasons of Nationalist ideology, Middle Scots orthographic elements not relevant to phonological difference were reintroduced. Although pastiche Middle Scots had been around from the time of the poet Lewis Spence (1874–1955),[8] use was clearly demarcated. Now, however, orthographic code-switching gave way to mixing, with the introduction of individual elements, mainly relevant to the vowels, on a more general basis in the work of writers such as Tom Scott and David Purves.[9] Second, while eye-dialect respelling for effect had been around since the advent of the nineteenth-century newspaper tradition, decline in spoken Scots meant that contemporary work by such writers as Tom Leonard[10] in which eye-dialect difference outweighed phonological difference was now more likely to be spoken of in the same breath as writing in traditional Scots, a development helped by the strong bias towards literary rather than transactional use in half-languages. The inconsistency of Anglic spelling itself, a difficulty born of hybridity and conservatism, now also came under attack, since the freedom enjoyed by writers of Scots was both an invitation and a challenge to reform. That reached its academic apotheosis in McClure (1981), a rigorously logical scheme that ultimately required too much of an intellectual *tabula rasa* on the part of its audience to have much influence. The piecemeal, sometimes unapprised reforms pursued by activists and writers, on the other hand, were having a noticeable effect.

Macafee (2000: 62–3) argues that:

> [...] insteid o defendin Scots agin the chairge at it 'has no standard form', activists haes acceptit this creiticism, an [...] haes set aboot creatin a new staundart fae the grund up – ower an ower again. Insteid o pittin doon variabeility, they've gien it a hyste, an haes endit up heels ower hurdies. [...] Spellin haes gotten tae be a free-for-aa, wi the tradeitional model bemeanit, an nae popular replacement.

However, although weakened, there is no doubt that the Modern Scots standard has survived in Scotland. In Ulster, however, very few books at all were published in Scots during the twentieth century, and even today the corpus of traditional Scots writing from the province remains largely unavailable to the general public.

The fact that Ulster speakers have been separated from Scotland for 400 years may provide a temptation to treat the local dialect as a separate entity. One might counter that argument by pointing out that the largest group of Scots arrived not as Planters at the beginning of the seventeenth century but as refugees from a famine in its final decade, that until the advent of the railways travel over water was generally easier, and that, in the absence of massive language shift or language planning, varieties do not speciate at the rate suggested. However, the separation argument, which is at its most basic level circumstantial – one is tempted to say 'emotional' – is in any case directly refuted by the linguistic evidence of identity between the Scots of Ulster and its parent dialects in central Scotland. With regard to the language status of Hiberno-Central, the relevant separation is ethnic and political, and attempts to impose independence on the local dialect spring directly from the 'narrow ground' occupied by Ulster Protestants.

Mac Póilin (1999: 116) states that it is difficult or impossible to justify classifying

---

[8] *The Collected Poems of Lewis Spence*, Edinburgh: Serif Books. 1953.
[9] This can seen in works such as Scott's *The Ship and Other Poems* (London: OUP, 1963) and in the revivalist magazine *Lallans*, which Purves edited from 1987 to 1995.
[10] Tom Leonard. *Intimate Voices, Selected Works 1965–83*. Newcastle-upon-Tyne: Galloping Dog Press. 1984.

Ulster Scots as an independent language using structural criteria:

> The case for Ulster-Scots being a distinct language, made at a time when the status of Scots itself was insecure, is so bizarre that it is unlikely to have been a linguistic argument.

A structural case can be made for the appropriateness of recognising Scots as a whole as a language: it is already partially codified; its degree of *Abstand* from Standard English is such that full codification would make it an *Ausbau* language; uncodified it might well die out; and according language status is the first step in such codification. It is difficult to make such a case with regard to an individual, relatively undifferentiated dialect such as that spoken in Ulster, however. Montgomery (2004: 131) has suggested recognising Ulster Scots as a language on apperceptional grounds, which although not of themselves structural are of relevance to demarcating the language community on whom the success of any revived variety will rest and harnessing the power of the identificational symbolism that a language might hold. However, even in Scotland and even with regard to Scots as a whole *vis-à-vis* English, it is doubtful whether a majority of ordinary users believes that they speak an independent language, and since no structural case can be made for the separate recognition of Hiberno-Central, one cannot speak of false consciousness either, as Tait (2002) has done with regard to Scots and Shetlandic.

Northern Ireland civil servants believe that the UK Government's declaration on the *European Charter for Regional or Minority Languages* furnishes a legal basis for treating Ulster Scots as separate. That case is weak even in its own terms, however,[11] and if structural study of Hiberno-Central suggests that advertising jobs and services as being for speakers of an 'Ulster-Scots language' is indirectly discriminatory against much more numerous and generally better qualified Scots-born speakers, an opt-out from equality legislation might be necessary if the practice is not to be declared illegal. Above all, from a linguistic diversity perspective, it is difficult to see what benefit Hiberno-Central might derive from separate treatment, so there is no overwhelming public-good argument.

Apart from civil servants, support for Ulster Scots as an independent language is generally limited to local activists and Unionist politicians. Todd (1987) suggests that emblematic differences between 'Ulster British' and 'Ulster Loyalist' identities do not apply to such elected representatives, who are often members of the loyal orders, even if they are liberals.[12] Terming Ulster Scots a language may provide a further example of their being required to adopt stances not representative of those who voted for them. The reason in the case of both the loyal orders and Hiberno-Central may be that Unionism's vertically integrated and corporatist (but schismatic) nature makes it important to keep disparate groups on board, with the result that the negotiated [13] Nelson McCausland's amendment of 9 October 2007 to David McNarry's motion in the Northern Ireland

---

[11] For example, the former Permanent Secretary of the Department of Culture, Arts and Leisure, Dr. Aideen McGinley, maintained in personal correspondence with the present writer dated 16 June 2005 that the non-justiciable European Charter made Ulster Scots a language, and that the same language was additionally defined, under the name 'Ullans', in cross-border legislation as a variety of Scots without any qualification of its language status.

[12] Another instance of such disjuncture that one might adduce is a consistency in using the long form of the name 'Londonderry' that is by no means universal among ordinary Protestants, although that may be connected with the relative formality of political discourse.

'Unionist view' may differ from the view held by most Unionists.[13]

Hiberno-Central does, of course, have some differences from Scots in Scotland. There are Irish loan words, and the influence of Irish can also be detected in the variety's phonology, although not at a level that altered its traditional written representation *vis-à-vis* Central Scots. Like all Scots varieties, Hiberno-Central can differ syntactically from Standard English, but many of the differences that demarcate it are either native to Scots elsewhere (Murray 1873: 222) or of Goidelic origin and also common in the west of Scotland. It is notable that Hiberno-English, much more heavily influenced by Irish, is not generally considered a language. Moreover, the most striking differences in contemporary Ulster-Scots writing are not in syntax but in orthography, despite the fact that, as suggested above, the phonological differences are rather modest. However, differences in spelling practices may provide evidence of Hiberno-Central lacking the 'roof' of the Modern Scots literary tradition; given the difficulty of accessing the authentic canon, that would be unsurprising. A morphological difference in contemporary Ulster-Scots writing is that the tendency towards verbal syncretism common to all varieties of Anglic but allowed greater scope in a loosely standardised variety such as Scots is all but complete (Parsley 1999).[14] Of itself this is not a relevant dialect difference, since the forms are panlectal in spoken Scots, being attested in Glaswegian, for example, by Miller (2003), but it may have relevance to future codification.

The Scots used in Robinson (1997) exhibits perhaps the clearest example yet of mixed orthographies. While writers such as Tom Scott and David Purves tentatively mixed the vowel practice of Middle and Modern Scots[15], Robinson goes further in ignoring the diachronic watersheds relevant to codification, also including the consonantal graphemes <sch> and <quh>, the latter of which, Mac Póilin (1999: 118) remarks, had hardly been used since the seventeenth century. To the resulting much more thorough mix of Middle and Modern Scots Robinson (1997) adds eye dialect, which might be considered a potential 'future Scots', representing as it does a rejection of contemporary practice without the justifying historicity of archaism. On a philosophical and functional level, the presence in the same texts of archaic spellings, which might be considered super-etymological, and quasi-phonetic diacritics intended as mimetic of minor articulatory differences similarly blurs boundaries.

While Robinson (1997) has provided the inspiration for the language of many publicly funded translations, its influence on writers outside the immediate circle of the grammar's author has been limited. One is tempted to ascribe this to what Kallen (1999: 159) terms 'the awkwardness of these proposals'. Moreover, as suggested above, increased heterogeneity may invite a modernising programme of linguistic democratisation that favours mimetic spelling strategies and rejects archaisms. A primary-school project funded by the Ulster-Scots Agency attempted an *ad hoc* reform of spellings based on Robinson (1997), but the revision process proved problematic.

---

[13] Nelson McCausland's amendment of 9 October 2007 to David McNarry's motion in the Northern Ireland Assembly suggestrs that Unionist unanimity on lip-service to language status may not yet have been achieved, however.

[14] Presumably this is owing to the small size of the language community, the simplifying dynamic of language contact, and the relative unavailability of literary Scots of whatever provenance.

[15] Purves extended use of the Scots digraphs <ei> [i] and <ou> [u] in preference to equivalent English digraphs that showed length by the doubling of letters; the latter sound in particular was often rendered <oo> in Modern Scots to avoid interpretation as a diphthong. However, Purves applied his reforms only to vocabulary not shared with Standard English.

Perhaps the only element in the mix of orthographies in Robinson (1997) to have found favour among local writers is the respelling of the definite article as *tha*, probably owing to its relative frequency.[16] Jim Fenton, who may be the sole contemporary writer of any stature, does not use it. The author of a volume of poetry[17] and an important dialect glossary, Fenton is remarkable from an orthographic perspective mainly for a tendency to eye dialect, and it is tempting to view that tendency as the hallmark of contemporary Ulster Scots. McClure (2000: 215–217) remarks that the eye dialect of the present-day, and relatively young, Scots poet Alison Kermack (1965–), now known as Alison Flett, is not used as a satirical sociolinguistic device in the manner of Tom Leonard and that the author's concern appears to be nation rather than class. Given the ongoing attenuation of the Modern Scots orthographic tradition, the advent of post-structural eye dialect is perhaps to be expected.

As with the differences between contemporary British and American English, variant spellings common in Ulster have little or no relevance to phonology but are the result of separate codification – or in this case the lack thereof. The only exceptions are evidence of Ulster vowel lowering in the sporadic respelling of <i> as <a>, pre-rhotic interdentalisation, which one might argue is adequately marked by the phonetic environment that causes it, and Hiberno-English loan realisations in such words as *coul'*, *houl'*, *oul'*, and *boord*, whose relevance to historical Ulster Scots in core areas might be disputed.

A key question in appraising the above with the aim of securing a sustainable future for Hiberno-Central must be whether the spoken and literary traditions are the same. Is a spelling system the servant and defender of the spoken language or itself an example of linguistic diversity that deserves protection? It is perhaps fortunate that we need not provide an answer. While it is possible to project divergent orthographic traditions through comparing the apples of the Ulster newspaper tradition with the pears of Scottish poetry, as soon as one compares like with like, one is struck not by divergence but by identity, and though the orthographic tradition of Modern Scots has broken down in Ulster, there is as yet no obvious replacement. The most prevalent combinations, based on Robinson (1997), are too various and contradictory for general use, and, although less difficult, Fenton's orthography is used only by Fenton.

A way forward from contemporary discord over orthography might be offered by the history of church reform. Before the widespread availability of vernacular Bibles, ordinary people were onlookers in theological debates played out by educated elites. Making the relatively slender corpus of traditional Ulster-Scots writing available through republication or via the Internet would allow readers to draw their own conclusions about the spellings employed by their forebears, what diachronic caesurae separated them from previous practice, whether they constituted a standard, and whether that standard was shared with Scotland. Republication might also encourage increased public interest in Hiberno-Central as a whole in a way that the doubtfully transactional Ulster Scots of Government advertisements has hitherto failed to do. A lesson of spelling debate in Scotland in the twentieth century has been that a reduced literary community, even of great intellectual vigour, is more prone to cliques and disagreements, rendering a standard correspondingly more difficult to maintain. It is to be hoped that the Ulster-Scots Agency will take the simple, overdue and relatively uncontroversial step of comprehensive republication soon.

[16] This is seen, for example, in the work of Charlie Reynolds (e.g. *Mae Granfeyther's Tunge*, [n.p.]: The Ullans Press. 2005) and Charlie Gillen (e.g. *Tha Wizard's Quill*. [n.p.]: The Ullans Press. 2005).

[17] James Fenton. *Thonner and Thon*. [n.p.]: The Ullans Press. 2000.

In his recent work *The World Without Us*, Robert Weisman (2007) describes the resurgence of nature across an earth freed from human activity. One feature of Weisman's thought experiment is that, as wild animals reassert themselves, domesticated animals vanish. Minority languages are akin to domestic animals in that they depend on repeated intervention for their survival. Perhaps the best example is Irish, which despite a high level of knowledge in the general population has very low rates of intergenerational transmission, depending instead on the school system. Debates concerning minority languages often centre on whether the state is doing enough to save a language.[18] It might be fruitful to consider how a minority variety can survive after the sort of disruptive event that happens only every few hundred years, however. The Second World War saw the decimation of Yiddish through the murder of its speakers, the destruction of German varieties east of the Oder-Neisse line through ethnic cleansing, the weakening of *Plattdeutsch* through the resulting influx of refugees, and an accelerated shift away from Alsatian by French citizens owing to the dialect's German associations. Current threats could easily have much worse results.

The lesson for those working for minority languages must be to work with nature rather than against it. An independent Hiberno-Central might well prove unsustainably small, even in the context of generous state backing and relative stability, and there is no great gain for linguistic diversity in separate codification. That Scots everywhere is used with reference to Standard English – even if the reference is to highlight a rejection of social mobility in an act of sociolinguistic solidarity – suggests the desirability of having an orthography that is at least compatible therewith, since world English itself must nowadays be considered a force of nature. A strategy of having one and a half orthographies may have a greater chance of success than having wholly separate norms for Scots and English, with a third standard imposed in Ulster.[19] It may well also be the case that the imperatives of minimum divergence from Standard English and pan-dialectal codification result in a firmer standard and a stronger language variety, even at the level of the individual dialect.

**References**

Aitken, A.J. ed. C.I. Macafee. 2002. *Older Scottish Vowels: A History of the Stressed Vowels of Older Scots from the Beginnings to the Eighteenth Century*. Edinburgh: Scottish Text Society.

Eagle, A. 2006. 'Aw Ae Wey'. Unpublished paper. Downloaded from http://www.scots-online.org/airticles/AwAeWey.pdf on 16 October 2007.

Fenton, J. 1995, 2000, 2006. *The Hamely Tongue. A Personal Record of Ulster-Scots in County Antrim*. [n.p.]: The Ullans Press.

---

[18] In some cases, such as that of Irish in Northern Ireland until the 1980s, and again since 2007, a minority language can be ignored or even suppressed, while in others, such as that of Scottish Gaelic, state intervention hitherto may have served only to slow language death to a more dignified pace.

[19] Ulster Scots would be considerably disadvantaged, even if a logical, scientifically tested orthography such as that proposed in McClure (1981) were adopted, since a majority of Scots texts encountered by its speakers would still originate in Scotland, while Scottish speakers would have much less incentive to learn how to read Ulster texts. In practice, ethnic and political considerations preclude the conscious adoption of a planned heteromorphic standard, and attempts to 'prove' the pedigree of language status using diverse historical elements may have resulted in constructs that are as impractical as they are inauthentic.

Kallen, J. 1999b. 'Review of *Ulster-Scots: A Grammar of the Traditional Written and Spoken Language*'. *English World-Wide* 20.1: 157–62.

Kloss, H. 1952. *Die Entwicklung Neuer Germanischer Kultursprachen*. München: Pohl.

Kloss, H. 1978. *Die Entwicklung Neuer Germanischer Kultursprachen seit 1800*. Second Edition, Düsselsorf: Pädagogischer Verlag Schwann.

König, W. (1978) (ed.) dtv-Atlas zur deutschen Sprache. Munich: Deutscher Taschenbuch Verlag.

Macafee, C.I. 2000. 'Lea the leid alane'. *Lallans* 57: 56–63.

Macafee, C.I. 2005. 'Scots and Scottish English'. In ed. Hickey, R. *Legacies of Colonial English: Studies of Transported Dialects*. Cambridge: Cambridge University Press. 59–81.

Mac Póilin, A. 1999. 'Language, Identity and Politics in Northern Ireland'. *Ulster Folklife* 45: 108–32.

McClure, J.D. 1981. 'The Spelling of Scots: A Phoneme-based System', *Scottish Literary Journal Supplement* 12: 25–29.

McClure, J. D. 2000. *Language, Poetry and Nationhood: Scots as a Poetic Language from 1878 to the Present*. East Linton: Tuckwell Press.

Miller, J. 2003. 'Syntax and Discourse in Modern Scots'. In eds. Corbett J., McClure, J.D. and J. Stuart-Smith. *The Edinburgh Companion to Scots*. Edinburgh: Edinburgh University Press. 72–110.

Montgomery, M. 1994. 'The Evolution of Verb Concord in Scots'. In eds. Fenton A. and D.A. MacDonald. *Studies in Scots and Gaelic*, Edinburgh: Canongate Academic. 81–95.

Montgomery, M. 2004. 'Ulster-Scots: Lost or Submerged?' In eds. Kelly W. and J. R. Young. *Ulster and Scotland, 1600–2000: History, Language and Identity*. Dublin: Four Courts Press. 121–32.

Murray, J.A.H. 1873. *The Dialect of the Southern Counties of Scotland*. London: Asher and Co. on behalf of the Philological Society.

Parsley, I.J. 1999. 'Notes on the Ulster-Scots Strong Verb'. Unpublished Paper.

Quirk, R. 1982. *Style and Communication in the English Language*. London: Edward Arnold.

Robinson, P. 1997. *Ulster-Scots A Grammar of the Traditional Written and Spoken Language*. [n.p.]: The Ullans Press.

Tait, J. 2002. 'Is Shetlandic a Language or a Dialect'. Unpublished, unpaginated paper accessed from http://myweb.tiscali.co.uk/wirhoose/but/wan/dialect.htm on 10 October 2007.

Todd, J. 1987. 'Two Traditions in Unionist Political Culture'. *Irish Political Studies* 2: 1–26.

Weisman, A. 2007. *The World Without Us*. London: Virgin Books.

# German-Speakin Swisserland: A Paitren for Dialect Uphaud?

*Andy Eagle*

## Innin

In discussions anent the uphaud o Scots, compare is aften made tae the seetiation o ither leeds. In Scotland it is aften the oncome o the history o Catalan[1] efter the deith o Franco in 1975 an the restoration o democracy. In Ulster it is aften the oncome o the history o Wast Frisie efter the Netherlands behaud it as a offeecial leed o Frisie in 1956,[2] in parteecular the Frisie Academy.[3] Here the sociolingueestic seetiation in German-speakin Swisserland is leukit at for tae conseeder whit micht coud be learnt frae that.

Modren Swisserland kent as *Confœderatio Helvetica* in the Laitin, efter the Helvetii – a auncient Celtic fowk that bid in the Alps, is a mony-leedit state[4] that haes its oreegins in the 13t century when three communities swuir a aith tae "thole nae juidge nor ken him in ony wey gin he excerceeses his office for reward or for siller or gin he isna o wir ain ilk or frae the glens."[5] Frae that, the Swiss is kent as *Eidgenosse*, that is: 'aith feres'. In the follaein centuries mair communities becam pairt o the confederation as allee'd or subject stewartries. Efter the French revolution the confederation fell unner the owerins o Napoleon an becam the Helvetic Republic that treatit aw stewartries e'enly. Efter the defeat o Napoleon that e'enliness bade sae aw stewartries haed the selsame richts. By 1815 Swisserland wis muckle as it is the day. The constitution o 1848 kent German, French an Italian as offeecial leeds. In 1938 Romanch wis kent an aw.

Here the terms *Staundart* an *dialect* will be uised. Wi staundart is meant the staundart written language an spoken forms that's a affcome o't. Wi dialect is meant the local spoken varieties that's no a affcome o the staundart. *Hochdeutsch* for ordinar beirs tae the oreegin o the variety in the upthrou kintra an the Alps, an is uised for aw the spoken varieties uised in central an soothren Germany, in Austrick an in Swisserland. For staundart German some fowk uises the term *Hochdeutsch*, uisin *Hoch* ('heich') in a cultural or eddicational wey, sae for tae evite ony raivelment *Hochdeutsch* winna be uised here.

Swiss German is the Alemanic dialects o German that's spoken in Swisserland an neebourin Leichtenstein an is sindert intae laich, heich an heichest Alemanic varieties. Some o thir is spoken ootwith Swisserland an aw. Swiss German can be conseedert kenspeckle acause aw German-speakin Swiss uises a hamelt dialect as thair foremaist mainer o speak, nae maiter thair social staundin or eddicational backgrund. Thir dialects thegither is kent as "Swiss German" (*Schwyzertütsch*). Nae social, economic or

---

[1] Molts Noms a un Sol Amor (Many Names for a Single Love): A study of the current position of the Scots language within a European and global context, focusing on the language revival of Catalan as a potential model for development. Eilidh Bateman, 2006. The Scots Language Society.

[2] Tho It wisna till 1980 that it becam a required subject in primar schuils an no till 1993 in seicondar schuils.

[3] Proposals for an Ulster Scots Academy: Consultation Document (www.dcalni.gov.uk/public_consultation_on_proposals_for_an_ulster_scots_academy.pdf)

[4] For mair aboot that see: Fisher (2001:105–122).

[5] *Wir haben auch in gemeinsamen Ratschlag und mit einhelligem Beifall einander gelobt, festgesetzt und verordnet, dass wir in den vorgenannten Thälern keinen Richter, der dies Amt um irgend welchen Preis oder um Geld irgendwie erkauft hätte oder der nicht unser Einwohner oder landsmann wäre, irgendwie annehmen oder anerkennen*. Oechsli (1901: 66)

eddicational factors gars fowk leuk doun on dialects forenent the staundart langage. Ower the mairch in Austrick an Germany no awbody speaks a dialect as thair foremaist mainer o speak. In thir kintras thare's been a historical shift in speak frae dialects tae the staundart, awbeit colloquial forms wi regional accents.

The staundart written language is a Swiss variety o Staundart German (*Heich German*), that is gey an seemilar tae, but no the exact same as the Staundart German o Germany. It haes twa-three orthographic differs an aften conteens Helveticisms, in parteecular thaim that's pairt o staundart Swiss German. Aw Swiss German-speakers can maister it mair or less perfit.

**The Oncome o the Written Staundart in Swisserland**

A affcome o Swiss independence wis that frae the early 16t century German-speakin Swiss haes been awaur o the *Swissness* o their written (an spoken) langage. Sin syne terms sic as *Eydgenossische Sprach*, *der Helvetier Tütsch*, *Helvetisch* an *Schwyzerisch* haes kythed. Frae the early 16t century, wi the settin furth o Luther's Bible, thare wis a muive awa frae the written langage bein close tae the spoken, tae the written form bein paitrent efter the written German frae Germany. The influence o the Electoral Saxon Chancery syne begoud tae spreid an that wis uised for the 1165 Zürich Bible. Mauger o that, it wisna till the 18t century that a widely acceptit written norm cam aboot. In 1876 the Pruce govrenment held the 1st Orthographic Conference for tae wirk tae shape a written staundart for the hale German Empire. In 1880, the dominie Konrad Duden set furth the *Vollständiges Orthographisches Wörterbuch der deutschen Sprache* ('Hail Orthographic Dictionar o the German Langage'), for ordinar kent as the *Duden*. In 1902, the *Duden*, wi a pickle newfangle maks, wis susteent by the govrenments o the German Empire, Austrick an Swisserland. The last multi-national spellin mendin wis in 1996.

Swiss German authors kens fine that for tae win tae a braid audience thay maun forhou their mither tongue or at least caw canny wi the uiss o Helveticisms. Leeteratur wi a Swiss theme aften conteens Helveticisms, tho, tae haud wi thir whaur thay dinna uphaud a Swiss theme is for ordinar thocht on as no bein richt an plain hashy.

**Uphaudin the Dialects**

In the 18t century it wis the langage o leeteratur, staundart German, that airtit lingueestic awaurness an syne by the time o the Helvetic Republic at the turn o the 19t century the dialects wis threitent when advocates o French revolutionary thochts wis threapin that it wis undemocratic for fowk tae speak mony sindry dialects an that aw equal fowk shoud aw speak the selsame wey. Short syne cam the stairt o compulsitor eddication an wi't a growin in the knabby naitur o Staundart German an the domains that it wis uised in. In the seicont hauf o the 19t Century it wis feart that the influence o the German Empire wad lead tae the dialects bein tint an by the late 19t an early 20t centuries the staundart wis uised in ceety shops an businesses an by mony middle cless faimilies in formal faimily seetiations lik at the denner table. In 1901 Ernst Tappert spaed that Zürich wad be the first hailly staundart-speakin ceety.

Frae thir 19t century oncomes it wis seen that the dialects wis threitent an in 1892 Friedrich Staub begoud tae ingaither maiter for his *Schweizerisches Idiotikon* acause he wis feart for the uphaud o the dialects. This fear for the dialects dwynin awa syne cairit on an is kent as the *Mundartwellen* ('dialect waws'). The first wis atween the 1900s an 1920s that stairtit oot frae Bern wi a renaissance o dialect leeteratur an the uiss o dialect in the Canton pairlament. That spreid tae Zürich in the 1930s an becam pairt o the intellectual fend (*'geistige Landesverteidigung'*) agin Nazi Germany. Some e'en gaed sae faur as tae propone a staundart written Swiss German tae tak the steid o the extant staundart. At the time fowk that spak staundart ootby its ordinar domains micht be thocht o as traitors, an in the canton o Zürich learnin dialect wis necessar for tae applee for ceetizenship. The affcome o siclike ettles wis the oncome o a tradeetion o veegilance an respect for the dialects that brocht aboot the third waw in the 1960s wi the uiss o dialects spreidin intae aw domains. That is seen as bein doun tae the upwart mobeelity o thaim that's ken o the staundart isna glib, wantin tae haud wi the mither tongue. Pitten anither wey, its aw doun tae the spreid o egalitarian conceits. Sicna growthe in the uiss o dialect haes gart some fowk threap that siclike micht be a threit tae fowk's competence in the staundart. E'en the *Verein Schwyzertütsch* ('Swiss-German associe'), foondit in 1937 as the *Bund Swyzertütsch*, nae langer feels it's necessar tae threap for mair uiss o dialect, but nou juist hauds wi scholarly airticles, the settin furth o dialect dictionars an leeteratur, an coorses for learners.

**Dialect Leeteratur**

Mauger o the fact that mony Swiss Germans disna aften write dialect an will aften warstle wi the spellin, thare's aye been a lang tradeetion o writin dialect that taks in muckle mair nor e'en mony Swiss fowk jalouses. No juist nairatives an poetry but detective stories, Bible translations, plays an nane-feection an aw. Thare's aye been a certain amoont o freedom whan it comes tae writin but thare's been nane-bindin rules for mair nor saxty year that haes sert aw the dialects weel.

In 1938 Adolf Guggenbühl an Eugen Dieth, thegither wi a pickle like-myndit fowk foondit the *Bund Schwyzertütsch*, tho e'en afore the oncome o that associe fowk wis ettlin tae shape a unifee'd orthography for Swiss German. The spreid o this orthography wis ane o the foremaist ettles o the associe. A year afore, in 1937, Eugen Dieth haed setten furth the *Schwyzertütschi Dialäktschrift*, a guidal for aw Swiss-German dialects that haed been wrocht by a 20-strang comatee o lingueests, teachers an writers. That wis a semple, near-haund exception-free, phonetic orthography that coud pit ower the parteecularities o ilka dialect. For the maist pairt it uises the same graphemes as Staundart German, but gin needit, a mair exact mynt at the soondin can be shawn by the uiss o diacreetics sic as a tilde for nasalisation an a grave accent for open vouels. It wis merkit that a braider representation coud dae athoot the diacreetics. Wi time, an throu uiss, thir haes been modifee'd. In parteecular, twa-three practices that fowk wisna fameeliar wi, for want o thaim in the staundart, wis drappit frae the 1986 2nt edeetion. The key statement o thir is: „*Schreibe wie du sprichst, wie du es hörst und empfindest.*" Write hou ye speak, hou ye hear an feel it. Gaun on, Dieth wrate that "ilka dialect can hae its ain 'wird picturs'.[6] Dinna be pitten aff by whit deviates frae the leuk o the staundart. Swiss German follaes its ain rules an athin this frame the sindry dialects gangs thair ain gate.[7]

---

[6] *Wortbilder*

[7] Oreeginal: *Jeder Dialekt darf seine eigenen Wortbilder haben. Stoße dich nicht an Abweichungen vom gegenwärtigen standardsprachlichen Schriftbild. Das Schweizerdeutsche folgt seinen eigenen Gesetzen, und innerhalb dieses Rahmens gehen die einzelnen Dialekte ihren eigenen Weg* (Dieth 1986: 22).

Dieth's orthography haes estaiblished itsel athort the feck o German-speakin Swisserland but the airts aboot Bern. Thare's aye been a lang tradeetion o writin the Bern dialects, sae fowk wis mair at hame wi the Bern tradeetion nor the calculate *Schwyzertütschi Dialäktschrift*. In 1967 the *Berner Schriftstellervereins* ('Berner Writers' Associe') haed a comattee writers, dialectologists an furthsetters, baith o leeteratur an schuil beuks, pit thir rules thegither an thay war syne setten furth by Werner Marti in the *Bärndütschi Schrybwys*. Thir rules follaed the preenciple 'write hou ye speak' an aw, but wi some inconceestancies. Tae the maist pairt, thir wis a balance atween phonetic realism an the fameeliarity o the staundart, but teuk tent o the pan-Swiss seetiation an, tae a certain amoont, haudin tae Eugen Dieth's *Schwyzertütschi Dialäktschrift* wis ettelt at.

**Diglossia**

Ferguson (1959: 336) descrieves diglossia as follaes:

> "DIGLOSSIA is a relatively stable language situation in which, in addition to the primary dialects of the language (which may include a standard or regional standards), there is a very divergent, highly codified (often grammatically more complex) superposed variety, the vehicle of a large and respected body of written literature, either of an earlier period or in another speech community, which is learned largely by formal education and is used for most written and formal spoken purposes but is not used by any section of the community for ordinary conversation."

In German-speakin Swisserland the dialects is for ordinar aye uised for the follaein:

Aw ordinar communin

The feck o braidcastin but news
Inbrocht programmes is aye pitten ower intae staundart German, aften programmes frae Americae that been pitten ower intae the German in Germany.

Fowk leeteratur an bairns' leeteratur
Bairns beuks that's wrtten in the staundart is for ordinar pitten ower intae dialect whan read loud oot bi paurents.

The staundart is for ordinar uised in the follaein domains, tho the dialects aften wins throu:

Seicondar an further eddication
Spoken dialect is tholed mair an mair in the clessroom whaur it disna relate tae the 'textbeuk'.
Airt, crafts, muisic, sport an releegious studies is for ordinar in dialect.

Meelitary commaunds
Thir micht weel be passed doun the chyne o commaund in dialect.

# German-Speakin Swisserland: A Paitren for Dialect Uphaud?

Kirk services
Dialect is uised mair aften than in the bygane an is ordinar for the likes o Sunday schuil, Bible studies – aw bes it uisin a Staundart German Bible. The Catholic Kirk for ordinar uises dialect acause efter Vatican II it wis the dialects that teuk the steid o the Laitin an no Staundart German.

Speeches in pairlament

Legislative bodies an public meetins
Dialect is aften uised at public meetins.

Televeesion an wireless news
Interviews wi public feegurs, politeecians, an experts etc. is for ordinar in dialect.
Local services is aye in dialect.

Prent adverteesin is for ordinar in the staundart.
Juist 27% o wireless an 42% o spoken televeesion adverteesin is in the staundart.
Spoken Poleetical adverteesin is for ordinar in dialect.

Newspapers, editorials an reports

Personal letters

Maist leeteratur

Whan speakin tae nane-speakers

**Threits tae the Dialects**

Awtho the poseetion o the dialects is strang the chief threits tae thaim the nou is aften identifee'd as:

Influence frae the staundart
Throu the growthe in domains o uiss, wirds taen frae the staundart is uised in steid o hamelt anes or is taen frae the staundart athoot bein pitten ower intae the Swiss-German lingueestic seestem. Alang wi that is the staundart impressin phonological, morphological, seentactic an semantic influences on divergent forms. A pickle examples o adoptit wirds no haudin tae the Swiss-German lingueestic seestem is: *Mädchenheim* > *Mädcheheim* an no *Meitliheim*, or *Brausebad* > *Brausibad* an no *Brusbad*.

Ill-wirdit offeecial language ("*Großratsdeutsch*")
That comes aboot whan a offeecial forms thochts, or writes a speech in the staundart an syne pits it ower intae dialect athoot eneuch tent. The affcome is a uggsome mixtur-maxtur o dialect an staundart that is naither fish nor foul.

Dialect levellin (Dialects influencin ilk ither)
That comes aboot throu fowk flittin frae ae dialect airt til anither. Growin fameeliarity wi ither dialects throu the mass-media is helpin conter that.

Unaseemilatit lend-wirds.
French haes aye been the foremaist soorce o fremmit wirds. Nou for ordinar English.

**Motivations for Haudin on tae the Dialects**

Aside the fact that awbody aboot speaks dialect, some identifee'd motivations is:

The pittin ower o the national chairacter an identity (We're no Germans!)

A speeritual hame, a sense o community identity in a globalised warld

Stylistic – the hamelt tongue, semple, clear, perjink, the leed o the hert, mair honest

Mair democratic – nae dialect is better nor ony ither, nae linguistic mairginalisation o fowk.

**Strenths an Waiknesses o the Seetiation**

A clear strenth o the Swiss German diglossia is the fact that there's nae *Swiss creenge* an dialects is aye uised by awbody for ordinar speak, whither at the schuil, wirkplace or interviews on the wireless an televeesion. Dialect levellin, awtho a threit tae the tradeetional dialects, is content throu sicna want o a *creenge*, the affcome for ordinar bein foondit on the extant dialects raither nor imports frae the staundart. It aye still hauds wi its tradeetional chairacter an bides merkit Swiss in naitur.

Mauger o the fact that the poleetical an eddicational authorities is interestit in uphaudin diglossia – ae waikness is that the concern for the dialects haes mair adae wi the superfeecial maiter o status nor lingueestic substance. Thare's nae thocht-throu langage policy for the dialects sae the affcome is a kin o eddicational mislippenin o the dialects whaur want o guidance anent uiss disna dae eneuch for tae conter middlin frae the staundart. The primar socialisation o Swiss German bairns is aye in dialect, an bairns learns *Schwyzertütsch* in the ordinar wey that a body learns a mither tongue. But at the schuil the bairns learns a hiely divergent staundart form as a conscious-learnt medium. No bein at hame in the staundart mony a bairn haes a ill conceit o the spoken staundart. Aw the same, throu schuilin in the staundart, thay're mair awaur o the richtness o its grammar an lexis. The want o a teacht awaurness o the richtness o dialect grammar an lexis disna help uphaud the canny sinderin o dialect an staundart. Sicna want o dialect awaurness conteenas ootthrou life athoot muckle communin or thocht amang Swiss German-speakers as tae whit is guid or ill dialect.

Maist knawledge, binna that learnt by verbal transmeesion, is for ordinar gotten frae beuks or jurnals written in the staundart. That aften leads tae terminology frae the staundart taen the steid o dialect lexis for many things sic as flora, fauna an ilka day graith. That loss o lexis, an the *laissez faire* approach tae dialect uphaud, aften allous the phonological, morphological, seentactic an semantic influences on divergent forms tak a haud an be cairit on tae the neist generation. Some fowk threaps that acause o the want o a proactive policy for dialect uphaud, the staundart is slawly cawin the feet frae unner the dialects. The affcome micht juist be Swiss soondin Staundart German.

**Forder readin**

Baur, A. 1990. 'Schweizerdeutsch: Woher und Wohin?' Zürich: Verlag Hans Rohr.
Dieth, E. 1986. 'Schwyzertütschi Dialäktschrift.' 2. Auflage, Aarau: Christian Schmid-Cadalbert.
Dürscheid, C. and M. Businger, eds. 2006. 'Schweizer Standarddeutsch' Tübingen: Gunter Narr Verlag.
Ferguson, Charles A. 1959. 'Diglossia'. *Word* 15.2: 325–40.
Fisher, A. 2001. 'Language and Politics in Switzerland'. In eds. Kirk, J.M. and D.P. Ó Baoill, *Linguistic Politics Language Policies for Northern Ireland, the Republic of Ireland, and Scotland*. Belfast: Cló Ollscoil na Banríona. 105–22.
Keller, R.E. 1982. 'Diglossia in German-Speaking Switzerland'. In ed. Haas, W. *Standard Languages Spoken and Written*. Manchester: Manchester University Press. 71–93.
Kropf, T. 1986. *Kommunikative Funktionen des Dialekts im Unterricht: Theorie und Praxis in der deutschen Schweiz*. Tübingen: Niemeyer.
Lerch, W. 1971. *Probleme der Schreibung bei schweizerdeutschen Mundartschriftstellern: Ein Beitrag zum Problem inadequäter Schreibsysteme. Beiträge zur schweizerdeutschen Mundartforschung*, Band XIX. Frauenfeld: Huber and Co. AG.
Marti, W. 1985. *Bärndütschi Schrybwys. Ein Wegweiser zum Aufschreiben in berndeutscher Sprache*. 2. Auflage. Bern.
Oechsli, W. 1901. *Quellenbuch zur Schweizergeschichte*. 2. Auflage. Zürich. 65–7.
Pezold, K. ed. 1991. *Geschichte der deutschsprachigen Schweizer Literatur im 20. Jahrhundert*. Berlin: Volk und Wissen.
Rash, F. 1998. *The German Language in Switzerland*. Bern: Peter Lang
Russ, C.V.J. 1987. 'Language and Society in German Switzerland. Multilingualism, Diglossia and Variation'. In eds. Russ, C. and C. Volkmar. *Sprache und Gesellschaft in deutschsprachigen Ländern*. München: Goethe Institut. 94–121.
Schwarzenbach, R. 1969, 'Die Stellung der Mundart in der deutschsprachigen Schweiz: Studien zum Sprachbrauch der Gegenwart'. *Beiträge zur schweizerdeutschen Mundartforschung*, Band XVII. Frauenfeld: Huber and Co. AG.
Trudgill, P. 1984. *Accent, Dialect and the School*. London: Edward Arnold
Zimmer, R. 1977. 'Dialekt – Nationalsprache – Standardsprache'. *Zeitschift für Dialektologie und Linguistik* 44: 145–57.

# Sustaining Minority Language Communities: The Case of Galician

*Bernadette O'Rourke*

## Introduction

It is generally agreed that there are somewhere between 5,000 and 6,000 languages spoken in the world today. Experts have, however, begun to predict changes in this picture. A small number of languages including Arabic, Chinese, English and Spanish are being used by an ever-increasing percentage of the world's population, while a great many others are set to die out. Just how many will disappear is widely debated, but according to the more pessimistic predictions of Michael Krauss (1992), over 4,000 will cease to be spoken. The most threatened languages are usually those used by people who in the past entered into political, economic or colonial relations which favoured the use of one or more dominant languages or language varieties. In language contact situations, where economic and political power is vested in one language group, the position of the other language tends to become 'minorized'. The rise or decline of any language cannot therefore be seen as a 'natural' phenomenon that occurs without human or social agency. .

In a significant report on the 'minorised' languages of Europe, which was carried out by the European Union in 1996, Nelde, Strubell and Williams note the following:

> The concept of minority by reference to language groups does not refer to empirical measures, but rather, to issues of power. That is, they are language groups, conceived of social groups, marked by a specific language or culture, that exist within wider societies and states, but which lack the political, institutional and ideological structures which can guarantee the relevance of these languages for the everyday life of members of such groups (Nelde et al. 1996: 1).

The minorisation of Galician, like many other European minority languages, is closely related to its historically subordinate position within a larger political entity. In more recent history attempts have been made to enhance the status of the language and to increase its relevance for its speakers. Decentralisation policies in Spain since the 1980s have provided a more favourable socio-political context for the language, along with Spain's other regional languages including Catalan and Basque. The form of regional self-government allocated to Galicia and the other autonomous communities within Spain has led to the emergence of the political and instrumental structures necessary to guarantee the relevance of Galician within the community.

## A Brief Sociolinguistic History of Galician

Galician is a member of the Romance family of languages and is spoken not only in Galicia but in a number of small enclaves along the borders with the neighbouring region of Asturias and Castilla-Leon as well as Extremadura, close to the Portuguese border further south. However, Galician only holds official status within the Autonomous Community of Galicia.

An analysis of the early sociolinguistic history of the language indicates the prestige that the language held up until the end of the Middle Ages (see Mato 1997; Monteagudo and Santamarina 1993; Mariño 1998; Monteagudo 1999). Until the twelfth century, Galician was broadly similar to the language variety spoken south of what constitutes part of the present political border between Galicia and Portugal. Linguistic differences between Galician and Portuguese only began to appear in the thirteenth and fourteenth centuries following the political independence of Portugal from the rest of the Peninsula. Since its beginnings as an independent Romance language in the early Middle-Ages, there was a gradual process through which Galician became consolidated as an everyday language in more informal registers. It was also the language used in early Galician literature. During this period the language was used by all social classes and was used in administration, economy, judicial systems and the church. As well as a flourishing literature, most renowned for its brilliant school of lyrical poetry (Monteagudo and Santamarina 1993: 120), most documents written in Galicia in the thirteenth and fourteenth centuries were also in Galician. Much prestige was attached to Galicia's lyrical poetry and its use for this genre of writing was used in the Castilian Court during the reign of Alfonso X (López Carreira 2005).

The thirteenth century marked the beginnings of change for the language. After the rise to the throne in 1230 of Fernando II, the then King of the neighbouring Castile, the medieval kingdom of Galicia came under increasingly Castilian control. Although certain varieties of Castilian began to be used by the autochthonous Galician-speaking population, it was not until considerably later that they adopted Castilian as part of their repertoires. While language contact with Castilian had no immediate consequences on the Galician language, these events marked the initial hold gained by Castile over the Galician territory.

In the fourteenth century, the coming to power of the Trastámara dynasty was an important turning point for the language. This period marked the decline of the native Galician nobility and their substitution by a Castilian ruling-class. Castilian began to replace Galician in formal domains and throughout the echelons of civil and military administration, making it the language of prestige in Galicia.

In the second half of the fifteenth century, the increased move towards the consolidation of political unity by the Catholic Kings furthered the subordination of Galicia as a periphery of a Castilian-based centre of power. Language shift on the part of the dominant classes to some extent began to filter down to the general population, increasing familiarity with Castilian amongst the population (Monteagudo and Santamarina 1993). Galician, however, continued to be the language used by the majority of the people.

While no official linguistic laws were passed during the reign of the Catholic Kings, there was an implicit link between the Castilian language and political and administrative power. This link was more explicitly stated in the eighteenth century during the strongly centralist ideologies characteristic of the Bourbon dynasty which followed and prohibited the use of Galician in the high functional domains of culture and education (Martin 2002: 21). In quantitative terms, these policies had little effect on the illiterate peasant population and the numbers of speakers of Galician remained unchanged (Recalde Fernández 2000; Bouzada Fernández 2003). Nonetheless, the exclusion of the language from formal domains such as education conveyed a poor image of its value to the community at large.

While there is little formal data on the number and socio-demographic distribution of Galician speakers at the end of the nineteenth and early twentieth century, indirect accounts would seem to suggest that over eighty percent of Galicians were monolingual speakers of the language (Fernández Rodríguez and Rodríguez Neira 1995: 52–3). Castilian was confined to the small number of urban centres in the region and was the language used by the bourgeoisie. Over ninety percent of Galicians lived in rural areas and this divide can be taken to loosely correspond to the linguistic divide between

Galician and Castilian speakers at the time (Rei-Doval 2007). Hermida's (1992) analysis of texts written at the end of the nineteenth century also identifies the visible divide between the Castilian-speaking upper social strata of Galician society and the Galician-speaking rural peasants.

The profile of Galician speakers at the turn of the twentieth century consisted of a predominantly rural, uneducated peasant population. The slow but gradual process of industrialisation in Galicia began to make Castilian the language of reference for commerce and progress. Galician continued to survive in rural areas where the centralist government took relatively little interest and had thus exerted less influence.

The unusually long period of linguistic sheltering of Galician speakers from a shift to Spanish can at least partly be explained by Galicia's geographic, socio-economic and cultural isolation up until the twentieth century. Galicia's geographically isolated and peripheral position in the extreme north- western corner of Spain was closely linked to a history of poor economic development. As a result, the number of Castilian-speaking migrants to the area was negligible. This is a very different situation to Basque and Catalan, where in-migration has altered the sociolinguistic contexts of these communities. The trend in Galicia has been more strongly on the side of out-migration to Europe and Latin America. Over one-million left the region between the mid-nineteenth and twentieth century (Villares 1984), the majority of whom were in all likelihood Galician speakers (Recalde Fernández 1997).

While low levels of education, poverty and rurality allowed Galician to survive several centuries of linguistic dominance as a subordinate of Castilian, as the twentieth century progressed these factors provided the rationale for future generations to abandon the language as they moved to Galicia's cities or abroad in search of work. As the society began to modernise during the twentieth century, Galician speakers became less isolated and came into more direct contact with areas in which Castilian was used and needed. As access to education and the media became more widespread amongst the rural population, so too did exposure to Castilian. The link between Castilian and progress, values associated with the modern world, became engrained in the minds of many Galician speakers. Along with socio-structural changes in Galicia, the coercive linguistic policies of the Franco regime between 1939 and 1975 also had a negative impact (Freitas 2008). While there was no official or explicit prohibition on the use of the language, as Ramallo (2007: 24) points out, Franco's regime established, de facto, a unique acknowledgement of Spanish and put into practice a surreptitious persecution of the peripheral languages, hindering cultural production in the Galician language.

The forty years of dictatorial rule in Spain shelved attempts initiated at the end of the nineteenth century to reverse the negative social meanings which has come to be associated with the Galician language and its speakers. The impulses which had brought language issues onto the public agenda in Galicia were, like in many other parts of Europe and Spain at the time, the result of the ideological orientation of ethnocultural movements. This new awareness of Galician had been concerned in the first instance with extending the functional domains of use for the language, followed by a process of corpus planning and the development of a language which could be used for literary purposes. An ethnocultural discourse was constructed which connected Galician speakers to a mythical past (Hermida 1992; Mariño Paz, 1998; Monteagudo 1999) and much of this imagery became part of language policy and planning initiatives put in place in the 1980s following Spain's transition to democracy.

## Predicting the Survival Prospects of Galician in a Contemporary Context

In determining the survival prospects of minority languages such as Galician, in studies on language maintenance and shift a range of macro-social events and factors have been identified (see, for example, Fishman 1976, 1991; Paulston 1994; Weinreich 1968). These include numerical strength of the group in relation to other minorities and majorities, social class, religious and educational background, degree of similarity between the minority and majority language, language attitudes, institutional support and patterns of language use (Romaine 1995: 40). In the literature on language maintenance and shift, there is not however widespread consensus about their effects on the survival prospects of a minority language. In some contexts certain factors have been found to hinder the process of language shift while in others, the same factors have been found to speed up the process. A number of typological frameworks also exist which explore the inter-related effects of these factors in determining the future of a minority language (see for example Edwards 1992; Fishman 1991; Paulston 1994). In the remainder of this article I will look at the complex ways in which a number of these factors are implicated in the fate of the Galician language.

## Socio-political Factors

Political independence or some form of autonomy has the potential to increase the sustainability of a minority language, leading to a shift in the balance of power back to the autochthonous community. This can enable the minority language community to take control of the institutions that affect the lives of its speakers and to achieve sustainable improvement (see for example Corson 1990; Cummins 1988). While political independence may not be enough in and of itself to guarantee the ethnocultural and ethnolinguistic distinctiveness of a group (Fishman 1991: 27–8), political organization is important in forming and implementing language policy and planning initiatives (Spolsky 2004: 15).

Decentralization policies in Spain since the 1980s, in line with changes in political ideologies which favoured a more pluralistic Spanish society, created a new context for Galician along with the others languages of Spain including Catalan, Basque and Valencian. In this new socio-political context, the Galician language enjoys constitutional protection under Article 3 of the 1978 Spanish Constitution and holds co-official status with Spanish within the Autonomous Community of Galicia. In Article 5 of the Galician Autonomous Statutes, approved in 1981, the status of Galician as Galicia's 'own language' (*lingua propia*) is confirmed and guarantee is given to its 'normal' and official use along with Spanish in all domains of public and cultural life. The new socio-political context therefore provides a supportive context for the language and its legal protection within the Autonomous Community of Galicia.

Compared with many other minority language cases where decisions about the future of these languages continue to be under the control of non-autochthonous centres of political power, Galicia's status as one of Spain's autonomous communities has devolved decision-making in key areas such as education, local media and public services. In comparison with other minority languages, in particular Irish, which is the official language of the Irish State, the constitutional status of Galician is considerably weaker. Galician is co-official with Spanish within the territorial confines of its Autonomous Community but Galicians, as citizens of the larger Spanish State are required to know the language of that state (Vernet 2007).

The privileged socio-political position of Irish compared to other minority language contexts has not however, been a guarantee for its revitalization. Despite the declaration of the language as the first official language of the Irish State, in practice English has continued to be the dominant language used for all parliamentary business and indeed for almost all official and non-official interactions. Therefore, declarations relating to the official status of a language must be looked at in terms of the symbolic significance of such statutory provisions rather than their immediate practical value. Irish is what Eastman (1984) refers to as an 'associated' language, where the language continues to be upheld as a constitute part of Ireland's heritage but is not widely used.

The 'associated' function of language as outlined by Eastman (1984) has clear parallels with the weak form of social mobilisation adopted by minority language groups which Paulston (1994) terms ethnicity. The undisputed status of the Irish Republic as an independent political entity has, as Paulston (1994) suggests, weakened the need for the expression of strong cultural symbols such as language. She also adds that political independence has removed the sense of urgency surrounding the language as a means of distinguishing 'us' from 'them' (Anderson 1991) which had been enforced by Irish cultural nationalists at the end of the nineteenth century.

In the Galician context, the continued presence of a dominant 'other' in the form of the Spanish State introduces some element of what Paulston (1994: 32) refers to as a more 'militant' form of ethnicity. In this context, Galician becomes symbolic of the power struggles between the minority and dominant culture. This struggle takes the form of ethnic movement (Paulston 1994) which is most clearly articulated around a coalition of nationalist parties in Galicia, the most prominent being the Galician Nationalist Party (*Bloque Nacionalista Galego*) for whom support has been on the increase since the 1990s (del Valle 2000). So while on the one hand changes in Galicia's socio-political situation since the 1980s has shifted some of the power away from the Spanish centre and given Galicia a certain degree of control over linguistic matters, there have been limitations to its devolutionary process. On the other hand, the continued presence of the dominant other has to some degree maintained the symbolic role of Galician in distinguishing it from other parts of Spain and sustained a certain degree of urgency around language issues in Galicia.

**Language Policy and Planning**

The declaration of a language as official is not of itself an essential act of language planning as it does not necessarily bring about increased language use (Cooper 1989: 101). The new constitutional status which gave co-official status to Galician within its Autonomous Community became more concrete through the development of specific language policies and language planning efforts. Through the inclusion the language in key public spaces such as public administration, schools and the media, status, corpus and acquisition planning efforts have been used to facilitate its acceptance within Galician society.

To fulfil its statutory aims of defending and promoting the Galician language, outlined in the Galician Statutes of Autonomy, in 1983 the Law for Linguistic Normalisation (*Lei de Normalización Lingüística*) was endorsed by the Galician Parliament. The main aim of the 1983 Law was to legalise the use of Galician, promote its use in all domains within Galician society and to reverse the historically-rooted process of linguistic substitution by Castilian which had begun to take place. While there have been amendments to various facets of the Law since 1983, it continues to constitute the core piece of Galician language legislation. The Law consists of six different parts and includes separate sections outlining linguistic rights, official use of the language, its use in education, the media, outside of Galicia and by the autonomous administration as well as the normalising function of the language. To oversee the fulfilment of the Law, a General Directorate for Language Policy (*Dirección Xeral de Política Lingüística* (DXPL)) was also appointed as the main government body charged with the recovery of the Galician language.

The status planning aspects of the 1983 Law have focused largely on the provision for Galician in education (Portas Fernández 1997). Linguistic policy in this area supports the progressive incorporation of Galician in the primary and secondary school curricula, with the aim of establishing bilingual programmes in all Galician schools. Outside of education, Galician language policy also makes reference to the promotion of Galician in other key societal domains including the media. In 1984, Galician Radio and Television was established to promote the spread of Galician language and culture (Casares et al. 2008; Recalde Fernández 1997). Explicit measures were also taken to increase the presence of the language in the area of public administration. Additionally, the Law of Public Function (*Lei de Función Pública da Galicia*) in 1988 as well as a modified version of the same law in 2008 made knowledge of Galician a compulsory requirement for access to public sector employment in Galicia. The Law for Linguistic Normalization also stipulates that all official documents in the Galician administration must be published in both Galician and Spanish.

The 2004 General Plan for Linguistic Normalization (*Plan Xeral de Normalización Lingüística* (PNL) constitutes a more recent policy document outlining specific measures and actions which need to be taken to make the 1983 legal stipulations a reality. It outlines a set of proposals on how to enhance the social use of Galician in seven key areas including adminstration, education, family and youth, economy, health, society and use of language outside the Galician community. While the PNL constitutes an important policy initiative which explictly formulates and lists a set of measures intended to guide language planning measures, it does not implicate any legal changes for the language.

Language policies such as those in place in Galicia are not autonomous processes (Ó Riagáin 1997; Romaine 2002) but exist in an environment with physical, geographical, political and socioeconomic components (Ager 1996: 11). As Spolsky (2004: 8) notes, because language and policy both exist in highly complex and dynamic contexts, the modification of any part may have effects on any other part. It thus follows that a range of non-linguistic factors (political, demographic, social, religious, cultural, psychological etc.) regularly account for any attempt to intervene in the language situation, and for subsequent changes to occur (*ibid.*). Ó Riagáin (2008) points out that it is necessary to examine state policies which relate to economic and social issues, particularly education as it is likely that in total, their consequences on language attitudes and use are of more importance than language policies *per se*.

As was highlighted earlier, education and public sector employment constitute two important areas which were targeted by language policies and planning initiatives in Galicia. These initiatives coincide also with a period of educational expansion more generally. The General Law on Education (*Ley General de Educación*) in 1970 made education free and obligatory for all six-to fourteen-year-olds in Spain and, since the 1980s, the number of school places greatly increased following institutional reform which further extended the school-going age. Recalde Fernández (2000) notes the potentially positive effect this has had on Galician, given that 98 per cent of the younger generation are now exposed to the language through the education system.

Language policy for Galician since the 1980s also coincides with socio-structural changes which had been taking place within Galicia over more recent decades leading to the transformation of a rural society into a more urbanised one (Rei-Doval 2007). By that time, the numbers engaged in the primary sectors of agriculture and fishing had begun to decline and in-migration to Galicia's main cities was increasing. More than half the population were engaged in the service industry and less the one fifth in the more traditional areas of agriculture and fishing. Public sector employment also increased in line with the provisions needed to meet Galicia's new autonomous administration, thus providing an occupational niche where language policy makes knowledge of the Galician language an explicit requirement (Monteagudo and Bouzada Fernández 2002).

While the expansion of education and socio-structural changes in Galicia meant that a large sector of the Galician population were being directly affected by the new language policies, the region's own political context created a less-favourable climate. Bi-party politics dominated in Galicia since the 1980s oscillating between Galician branches of Spain's two main political parties – the centre-left Socialist Party (*Partido Socialista Obrero Español*) and the conservative centre-right Popular Party (*Partido Popular*). The latter has tended to attract more support amongst the population. A key objective of the Galician administration has been to avoid language policies which might provoke social conflict. Official language policy in Galicia, particularly up until 2005, has tended to promote (although implicitly) the idea of 'harmonious bilingualism', that is the non-conflictive co-existence of Castilian and Galician within the community (see Regueiro Tenreiro 1999). This policy, reflected a political agenda aimed at maintaining the support of powerful sectors of Galician society, the majority of whom were Castilian speakers and amongst whom support for the autochthonous language has tended to be lowest (Monteagudo and Bouzada Fernández 2002). Therefore, by in large, language policies have been lukewarm and were developed in line with a non-conflictive interpretation of the sociolinguistic situation for the language (Lorenzo 2008). As a result language policy intervention has been low, and has tended to be concentrated in the educational sphere with little real revitalization of the language in other domains.

Even in the area of education, policy intervention has been low and as a result the specificities of the 1983 Law have not always been adhered to. The implementation of measures intended to serve the instructional role of Galician have been largely ineffective. A blind eye was often turned to failure on the part of schools to meet the stipulated bilingual requirement in their classes. Instead, the presence of Galician in the classroom tended to be based on individual teachers' preferences. According to Caballo Villar (2001) more than 90 percent of pre-school and initial stage primary education schools and over three-quarters of secondary schools were shown not to meet the stipulated requirements.

Since 1993, however, support for the politics of the Galician Nationalist Party (*Bloque Nacionalista Galego*) has significantly increased, thus bringing a third party into the political arena in Galician politics and adding a new dynamic to language issues in Galicia. In contrast to the official discourse of 'harmonious bilingualism', Galician nationalists tend to view the language contact situation between Galician and Castilian as conflictive and as one in which Galician speakers still remain in a dominated socio-economic position. Galician nationalists therefore tend to be highly critical of official language policy which they view as largely inadequate in reversing the process of language shift towards Castilian. In reaction to such criticisms, proponents of official language policy in Galicia condemn what they perceive to be a largely radical approach to resolving the Galician language problem on the part of Galician nationalists. The coming to power of a Socialist government in coalition with the Galician Nationalist Party for one term of office between 2005 and 2009 marked a brief period of political change away from the previous thirteen years of the more cautious language policies of the centre-right. During this time some attempts were made to regulate more stringently the use of Galician in classroom contexts and to ensure that the stipulated minimum of fifty percent of school subjects be given through the medium of Galician. However, the proposed legal amendment did not meet with widespread approval and was the subject of bitter attack by a small but powerful group of a pro-Spanish organisation within Galicia who euphemistically call themselves Galicia Bilingüe (Bilingual Galicia) but whose discourse is essentially anti-Galician. This group, which has greatly attracted the attention of the media, regards the proposed 2007 amendment as the imposition of Galician on those members of the population who prefer to use Spanish and therefore an infringement of their linguistic rights (O'Rourke, 2011).

This brought language issues centre stage during the 2009 regional elections in Galicia and which saw the return to power of the Popular Party. In his pre-electoral campaign, the new leader to the party, Alberto Núñez Feijóo, promised to abolish the contentious 2007 decree. Although his promise was not followed through, at the time of writing of this chapter, a draft of the amended decree was being made public which proposed a multilingual strategy in schools with a requirement that one third of all subjects be taught through Galician, a third Spanish and third in English. For pro-Spanish groups such as Galicia Bilingüe, this proposed amendment does not go far enough in guaranteeing the rights of Spanish speakers in Galicia. Conversely, for pro-Galician groups the amendment reduces the potential to improve the already precarious situation for Galician.

**Linguistic Proximity between the Minority and Majority Languages**

Linguistic proximity between languages in contact can have a positive effect on the process of language revitalization, facilitating relearning of the minority language amongst those members of the population who have already shifted to the dominant language. Such relearning has been made difficult in genealogically different language contact situations as in the case of Irish in contact with English and Basque in contact with Spanish. At the same time however, similarities between the minority and majority languages can also speed up the process of linguistic assimilation. Clyne's (1991) study of the English-Dutch language contact situation in Australia shows that linguistic similarities between the two immigrant language communities in fact increased the process of language shift to English amongst Dutch speakers. Linguistic similarities between contact language can also be used to justify the politically motivated process of what Kloss (1967) referred to as 'dialectalisation'. This process occurs when enough structural similarity exists between a dominant and a subordinate language to classify the latter as a substandard dialect. Such structural similarities can thus increase the process of language shift in favour of the dominant language.

There is a high level of intelligibility between Galician and its contact language, Castilian-Spanish. Both are Romance languages and their closeness in linguistic terms allows them to be classified as languages by extension or in Kloss' (1967) terms, 'ausbau' languages. Linguistic closeness between the two languages, justified socio-politically motivated claims that Galician was a sub-standard dialect of Spanish and speaking

Galician came to be equated with speaking 'badly' in Spanish. In more recent history and particularly in the context of a more explicit recognition and respect for Spain's linguistic diversity, questions about whether or not Galician is a language no longer appear.

As far as revitalization of the language is concerned, linguistic proximity undoubtedly has facilitated the acquisition of the language amongst second language speakers of Galician. According to most recent sociolinguistic surveys on the language, almost all Galicians report an ability to understand and speak the autochthonous language (Bouzada and Lorenzo 2005; González González et al. 2007). Even amongst young, urban, middle-class sectors of the population, where use of Galician has tended to be lowest, the majority reports high levels of spoken ability in the minority language.

The closeness in linguistic terms between Galician and Spanish also facilitates asymmetric bilingualism and equips speakers of both languages with at least a passive knowledge of the other speaker's language. Bilingual conversations in Galician and Spanish are therefore frequent with each interlocutor maintaining his or her language. While in the past, because of the underlying negative social meaning associated with Galician and its speakers, Galician speakers tended to accommodate their speech habits to the dominant language, Spanish. However, sociolinguistic surveys (see Fernández Rodríguez and Rodríguez Neira1996) would seem to suggest that this social norm has changed as a result of the more favourable language policies in place since the 1980s and in this new context, switches to Galician are tolerated by Spanish speakers. The underlying suggestion from survey research is that Galician speakers no longer feel obliged to converge to Spanish in interpersonal interaction and Spanish speakers have in fact become more accepting of Galician-speakers' maintenance of their language in a bilingual conversational context.

While similarities between Galician and Spanish may be encouraging language maintenance amongst existing Galician speakers and facilitating its acquisition amongst newcomers to the language, linguistic proximity may also be favouring the dominant language. This is not least because speakers of the dominant language, although more tolerant of Galician in conversational interaction, tend to remain passively accepting and this is not necessarily converted to active solidarity through actual language use. Linguistic proximity between the two languages allows for conversational interaction to take place but provides little incentive for Spanish speakers to switch to the minority language.

**Language Attitudes**

The relative success of linguistic policies and the positive reinstatement of the Galician language in Galicia since the 1980s are evident in changes in linguistic attitudes. On a five-point scale, where 1 represents most negative and 5 most positive attitudes, Galicians score a 3.6 average in their ratings of the language (Fernández Rodríguez and Rodríguez Neira 1996: 80). The majority of Galicians believes that everyone who lives in Galicia should know how to speak the autochthonous language. Over three-quarters say the language is an important symbol of Galician identity. Around eighty percent favour its increased use at societal level and over ninety percent believe that its use in public administration is equally or more appropriate than Spanish. About two-thirds express an explicit desire to have more radio and television programmes in Galician and almost as many favour its use in newspapers, street signs and advertising. More than half agrees that Galician should be the language used at school. These figures show that there is strong support for the 'normalisation' of the language in public spheres, areas from which it was absent for several centuries. Also positive for the language is the fact that language attitudes have become most favourable amongst the younger generation.

Language policy also appears to have eliminated prejudices against the language. For the majority of Galicians, the authochonous language is not seen as being in any way socially inferior to Spanish. The findings of sociolinguistic surveys on Galician point to a strong level of societal support for the language and point to a weakening, at least at certain levels of consciousness, of the coarser aspects of prejudice and sociolinguistic stigmatisation that have been working against the language for years (Bouzada Fernández 2003: 331). However, although quantitative studies of linguistic attitudes in Galicia show that explicitly negative attitudes have been eliminated, at other levels of consciousness, some more deep-seated prejudices still remain (Lorenzo Suárez 2008: 26). Certain discourses continue to exist, albeit in a more implicit way, highlighting some of these negative identities and prejudicial beliefs about the language. Adjectives such as 'rough', 'ugly', 'inferior', 'lacking culture' and 'stupid' are sometimes used to describe Galician at certain levels of consciousness (González González et al. 2003; Iglesias Álvarez 2002; Iglesias and Ramallo 2003; O'Rourke 2003, 2006). As well as the continued latent existence of some of the older prejudices associated with Galician, certain newer ones have also emerged. The association between speaking Galician and nationalism has, for instance, begun to introduce a new social norm restricting the use of Galician in certain social contexts (Iglesias Álvarez 2002; O'Rourke 2011).

**Number of Speakers**

Because the survival of a language is likely to depend on the degree to which it is used within a particular population, a large minority group is often in a better position by dint of numerical strength to make itself prominent and promote itself in support of its language (Romaine 1995: 40). There are more than two million speakers of Galician and for the majority of the population, Galician is the most frequently used language. Despite several centuries of language contact with a socio-politically and socio-economically dominant language, Galician never ceased to be the language of Galicians.

However, the numerical strength of the language conceals a number of important factors. In the literature on language maintenance and shift we are reminded that it is sociolinguistically naive to predict language survival solely on the basis of the number of speakers and who speaks a language is ultimately more important than how many speak it (see Dorian 1981; Romaine 1995). As can be discerned from the brief account of Galicia's sociolinguistic history outlined earlier, Galician passed from the status of a majority to a minority language once a Castilian-speaking elite established itself in significant numbers in Galicia, despite the fact that those numbers were small in comparison to the body of Galician speakers in the area. In a contemporary context, although the majority of the Galician population reports daily use of the Galician language a socio-demographic breakdown of Galician speakers provides a more revealing picture of the Galician sociolinguistic context. In general, Galician-speakers are characterised by their lower socio-economic status while Spanish speakers, although numerically weaker, tend to be socially and economically dominant (Fernández Rodríguez and Rodríguez Neira 1994, 1995)

Although demographically stable for centuries, there are signs of language shift in the direction of Spanish, particularly since the middle of the twentieth century. According to Dorian (1989: 39) it is possible for seemingly demographically stable languages to experience a sudden "tip", after which the demographic tide can begin to flows strongly in favour of some other language. Sociolinguistic data on Galician (see Fernández Rodríguez and Rodríguez Neira 1994, 1995; González González et al. 2007; Monteagudo and Lorenzo 2005) indicate that while Galician may be a long way from language death, the final stage in the process of language shift (Dorian 1981), the symptoms of language decline outlined by Fishman (1991), are becoming more evident in the decreasing number of younger speakers and decline in intergenerational transmission of the language within the home. The findings of sociolinguistic research indicate that the younger generation of Galicians shows lowest levels of habitual use of the autochthonous language with less than a quarter returned as active users. Paradoxically, this is a group where language attitudes and support for the language have been shown to be post favourable. Intergenerational mother-tongue transmission of Galician is also lowest amongst younger Galicians where almost half of the cohort has Spanish as opposed to Galician as their first language. In the last thirty years, the number of younger Galicians reporting Spanish as the first language in which they learned to speak increased to over half of the cohort (Monteagudo and Lorenzo 2005).

Socioeconomic and socio-structural changes in Galicia since the mid-twentieth century has led to increased migration from rural to urban contexts in search of work with the result that traditionally Galician-speaking strongholds are being eroded. The continued decline in so-called 'native' or first language speakers of the Galician language is to some extent being counteracted by an increase in the number of 'new speakers' of Galician, particularly amongst the younger generation through their exposure to the language in the education system. Policy provisions in the area of education have supported a bilingual strategy aiming to establish a context in which at the end of formal schooling, all Galicians are expected to have equal proficiency in both languages. The tendency has however been that the education system has had a 'castilianizing' effect on first language speakers of Galician from traditional Galician-speaking rural communities and is not 'galicianising' urban newcomers to the language so as to bring about any substantial increases in language use.

**Concluding Comments**

Over the past number of decades, much discussion in sociolinguistics and the sociology of language has centred on concerns over the survival prospects of lesser-used or minority languages such as Galician (see for example Dorian 1989; Edwards 2010; Fishman 1991; Grenoble and Whaley 1998; Hogan-Brun and Wolff 2003; King *et al*. 2008; Williams 2005). Researchers have been particularly interested in isolating the factors which best determine such survival. However, almost none of the factors cited in connection with language maintenance and shift is on its own a reliable predictor of the outcome of any particular situation of language contact (Romaine 1995). Although a number of these factors have been discussed separately in this article, there is considerable overlap amongst them and their effects cannot be understood in isolation. Socio-political changes have knock-on effects on the level of institutional support for a language and the degree to which language policy in favour of the minority language will be put in place. The numbers of speakers will also be affected by policy intervention but at the same time by other external variables such as the linguistic proximity between the two languages in contact, socio-structural and socio-economic changes.

The apparent strength of Galician in numerical terms conceals the vulnerability of a language which is largely made up of an aging and rural-based population. Migration to urban areas, particularly since the mid-twentieth century, has destabilised its demographic base, advancing the process of language shift, particularly amongst the younger generation. It could, nevertheless, be predicted that the numerical strength of Galician speakers as a minority group places it in a strong position to mobilize itself in support of the language, a position which has also been strengthened by recent changes in language policy.

Socio-political changes in Galicia since the 1980s in the context of Spain's transition to democracy have led to an ideological shift in favour of a more pluralistic society. In this context recognition is given to Spain's linguistic diversity and greater respect is awarded to the different languages of Spain, including Galician. Decentralisation has thus shifted some power away from the Spanish centre and given Galicia a degree of control over its own future, including its linguistic future. While regional autonomy as opposed to complete political independence can be seen to limit the powers of the Galician Autonomous administration, the continued presence of the dominant 'other' has to some degree maintained the symbolic role of Galician and sustained a sense of urgency surrounding language issues in Galicia.

Language policies for Galician have, however, tended to be lukewarm and have been developed in line with a non-conflictive interpretation of the sociolinguistic situation for the language. This has resulted in a low-intensity model with a strong focus on the educational sphere and with little real revitalization of the language in other domains. Even in the area of education, policies have tended to be weakly implemented. Although the positive reinstatement of the language in formal domains such as education has led to more favourable attitudes towards the language, particularly amongst the younger generation, this is not leading to any significant shifts in language use amongst these age groups. This is despite the fact that ability to speak Galician is high amongst the entire Galician population, even amongst those whose first language is Spanish. Such ability is related to the high level of intelligibility between Galician and Spanish and such closeness in linguistic terms allows for bilingual conversations to take place. Spanish speakers are now more ideologically supportive of the minority language and more tolerant of Galician speakers' right to maintain their language in conversational interaction. However, Spanish speakers less frequently become active users of Galician themselves, something which may reflect the weakly implemented bilingual policies which have tended to characterise the Galician sociolinguistic context.

In his analysis of language policy in Galicia, the newly appointed General Secretary for Language Policy in Galicia, Anxo Lorenzo Suárez, has suggested that the model of language planning adopted for the Galician language has been based on a false illusion of its linguistic vitality, leading to a distorted analysis of its demographic and territorial strength (Lorenzo Suárez 2008). Given that rural Galician-speaking population is being eroded, if Galician is to be sustained then a stronger focus on activating language use amongst the growing number of second language speakers of the language amongst Galicia's urban youth.

## References

Ager, D. 1996. *Language Policies in Britain and France: The Processes of Policy*. London: Cassells.
Anderson, B. 1991. *Imagined Communities*. London and New York: Verso.
Bouzada-Fernández, X.M. and A.M. Lorenzo Suárez. 1997. *O Futuro da Lingua. Elementos para un Achegamento Prospectivo da Lingua Galega*. Santiago de Compostela: Concello da Cultural Galega.

Bouzada-Fernández, X.M. 2003. 'Change of Values and Future of the Galician Language'. *Estudios de Sociolingüística. Linguas, Sociedades e Culturas* 3.2/4.1: 321–41.
Caballo Villar, M.B. 2001. 'Los educadores sociales en la animación sociocultural'. *Pedagogía Social. Revista Interuniversitaria*, n° 8 (segunda época). 199–207.
Casares H., Lorenzo Suárez, A. and F. Ramallo. 2008. *Lingua, sociedade e medios de comunicación en Galicia*. Santiago de Compostela: Consello da Cultura Galega.
Clyne, M. 1991 'German andDutch in Australia: Structures and Use'. In ed. Romaine, S. *Language in Australia*. Cambridge: Cambridge University Press. 214–8,
Cooper, R. 1989. *Language Planning and Social Change*. Cambridge: Cambridge University Press.
Corson, D. 1990. *Language across the Curriculum*. Cleveland: Multilingual Matters.
Cummins, J. 1988. 'From Multicultural to Anti-racist Education: An Analysis of Programmes and Policies in Ontario'. In eds. Skutnabb-Kangas T. and J. Cummins. *Minority Education: From Shame to Struggle*. Clevedon: Multilingual Matters. 127–57.
Del Valle, J. 2000. 'Monoglossic Policies for a Heteroglossic Culture: Misinterpreted Multilingualism in Modern Galicia'. *Language and Communication* 20: 105–32. .
Dorian, N.C. 1981. *Language Death: The Life Cycle of a Scottish Gaelic Dialect*. Philadelphia: University of Pennsylvania Press.
Dorian, N.C. ed. 1989. *Investigating Obsolescence: Studies in Language Contraction and Language Death*. Cambridge: Cambridge University Press.
Eastman, C. 1984. 'Language, Ethic Identity and Change'. In ed. Edwards, J. *Linguistic Minorities and Pluralism*. London: Academic Press. 259–76.
Edwards, J. 1992. 'Sociopolitical Aspects of Language Maintenance and Loss: Towards a Typology of Minority Language Situations'. In eds. Fase, W., Jaspaert K. and S. Kroon. *The Maintenance and Loss of Minority Languages*. Amsterdam: John Benjamins. 37–54.
Edwards, J. 2010. *Minority Languages and Group Identity: Cases and Categories*. Amsterdam: John Benjamins.
Fernández Rodríguez, M. A. and Rodríguez Neira, M. 1994. *Mapa Sociolingüístico de Galicia. Lingua inicial e competencia lingüística en Galicia*. Real Academia Galega: Vigo.
Fernández Rodríguez, M. A. and Rodríguez Neira, M. 1995. *Mapa Sociolingüístico de Galicia. Usos lingüísticos en Galicia*. Real Academia Galega: Vigo.
Fernández Rodríguez, M. A. and Rodríguez Neira, M. 1996. *Mapa Sociolingüístico de Galicia. Actitudes lingüísticas en Galicia*. Real Academia Galega: Vigo.
Fishman, J.A. 1976. 'The Sociology of Language'. In ed. Fishman, J. A. *Advances in the Sociology of Language*. Volume 1. *Basic Concepts, Theories and Problems: Alternative Approaches*. The Hague: Mouton. 217–404.
Fishman, J.A. 1991. *Reversing Language Shift: Theoretical and Empirical Foundations of Assistance to Threatened Languages*. Clevedon: Multilingual Matters.
Freitas, P. 2008. *A Represión Lingüística en Galicia no Século XX*. Vigo: Xerais.
Freixeiro-Mato.X.R. 1997. *Lingua Galega: Normalidade e Conflito*. Santiago de Compostela: Laiovento.
González González, M. *et al*. 2003. *O Galego Segundo a Mocadide*. A Coruña: Real Academia Galega.
González González, M. *et al*. 2007. Mapa Sociolingüístico de Galicia 2004. Vol. 1. *Lingua Inicial e Competencia Lingüística en Galicia*. Real Academia Galega: Vigo.
Grenoble, L.A. and L.J. Whaley, eds. 1998. *Endangered Languages: Current Issues and Future Perspectives*. Cambridge: Cambridge University Press.

Grillo, R.D. 1989. *Dominant Languages: Languages and Hierarchy in Britain and France*. Cambridge: Cambridge University Press.
Hermida, C. 1992. *A Revindicación da Lingua Galega no Rexurdimento (1840–1891): Escolma de Textos*. Santiago de Compostela: Concello da Cultura Galega.
Hogan-Brun, G. and S. Wolff, eds. 2003. *Minority Languages in Europe*. Houndmills: Palgrave Macmillan.
Iglesias Álvarez, A. 2002. *Falar Galego "no veo por qué"*. *Aproximación Cualitativa á Situación Sociolingüística de Galica*. Vigo: Xerais.
Iglesias Álvarez, A. and Ramallo, F. 2003. 'Language as a Diacritical in terms of Cultural and Resistance Identities in Galicia'. *Estudios de Sociolingüística. Linguas, Sociedades e Culturas*, Vol. 3.2/4.1. 255–87.
King, K.A, Schilling-Estes, N., Fogle, L., Lou, J.J. and B. Soukup. eds. 2008. *Sustaining Linguistic Diversity. Endangered and Minority Languages and Language Varieties*. Washington, DC: Georgetown University Press.
Kloss, H. 1967. '"Abstand" Languages and "Ausbau" Languages'. *Anthropological Linguistics* 9.7: 29–41.
Krauss, M. 1992. 'The World's Languages in Crisis'. *Language* 68: 4–10.
López Carreira, A. 2005. *O Reino Medieval de Galicia*. Vigo: A Nosa Terra.
Lorenzo Suárez, A. 2008. 'A Situación Lingüística do Galego: Unha Lectura'. *Grial*, 179. 19–31.
Mariño Paz, R. 1998. *Historia da Lingua Galega*. Santiago: Sotelo Blanco.
Martin, F. 2002. 'Patrimoine et Plurilingue et Faiblesse de l'État: L'émergence des Nationalismes autour de la Question Linguistique'. In eds. Boyer H. and C. Lagarde. *L'Espagne et ses Langues*. Paris: L'Harmattan. 17–40.
Monteagudo Romero, H. 1999. *Historia Social da Lingua Galega. Idioma, Sociedade e Cultura a través do Tempo*. Vigo: Galaxia.
Monteagudo Romero, H. and X.M. Bouzada Fernández. 2002. *O Proceso de Normalización do Idioma Galego 1980–2000*. Volume I. *Política Lingüística: Análise e Perspectivas*. Santiago de Compostela: Concello da Cultura Galega.
Monteagudo Romero, H. and A. Lorenzo. 2005. *A Sociedade Galega e o Idioma: A Evolución Sociolingüística de Galicia (1992–2003)*. Santiago de Compostela: Concello da Cultura Galega.
Monteagudo Romero, H. and A. Santamarina. 1993. 'Galician and Castilian in Contact: Historical, Social and Linguistic Aspects'. In eds. Posner R. and J.N. Green. *Trends in Romance Linguistics and Philology*, vol. 5: *Bilingualism and Linguistic Conflict in Romance*. Berlin: Mouton de Gruyter. 117–73.
Nelde, P., Strubell, M., and G. Williams. eds. 1996. *Euromosaic. The Production and Reproduction of Minority Language Groups in the European Union*. Brussels: European Commission.
Ó Riagáin, P. 1997. *Language Policy and Social Reproduction in Ireland, 1893–1993*. Oxford: Clarendon Press.
Ó Riagáin, P. 2008. 'Language Attitudes and Minority Languages'. In eds. Cenoz J. and N.H. Hornberger (eds.) *Encyclopaedia of Language and Education*, Second Edition. Vol. 6: *Knowledge about Language*. New York: Springer. 329–41.
O'Rourke, B. 2006. 'Language Contact between Galician and Spanish: Conflict or Harmony? Young People's Linguistic Attitudes in Contemporary Galicia'. In Mar-Molinero C. and M. Stewart. eds. *Globalization and Language in the Spanish-speaking World: Macro and Micro Perspectives*. Houndmills: Palgrave Macmillan. 178–96.

O'Rourke, B. 2011. *Galician and Irish in the European Context: Attitudes towards Weak 4and Strong Minority Languages*. Houndmills: Palgrave Macmillan.
Paulston, C. 1994. *Linguistic Minorities in Multilingual Settings: Implications for Language Policies*. Amsterdam: John Benjamins.
Portas Fernández, M. 1997. *Lingua e Sociedade na Galiza*. A Coruña: Bahia Edicións.
Ramallo, F. 2007. 'Sociolinguistics of Spanish in Galicia'. *International Journal of the Sociology of Language* 184. 21–36.
Recalde Fernández, M. 1997. *La Vitalidad Etnolingüística Gallega. Centro de Estudios sobre Comunicación Interlingüística e Intercultural*. 9. 1–39.
Recalde Fernández, M. 2000. 'Le Parcours Socioculturel du Galicien. Du Moyen Age au XXe siècle'. *Lengas* 47. 11–38.
Regueiro-Tenreiro, M. 1999. *Modelo Harmónico de Relación Lingüística. Estudio en Galicia*. Santa Comba: 3catorceeuro Ediciones.
Rei-Doval, G. 2007. *A Lingua Galega na Cidade do Século XX*. Vigo: Xerais.
Romaine, S. 1995. *Bilingualism*. Oxford: Blackwell.
Spolsky, B. 2004. *Language Policy*. Cambridge: Cambridge University Press.
Vernet, J. 2007. 'El Pluralismo Lingüístico'. In eds. Vernet J. and R. Punset. *Lenguas y Constitución*. Madrid: Iustel. 17–60.
Villares, R. 1984. *A Historia*. Vigo: Galaxia.
Weinreich, U. 1968. *Languages in Contact*. The Hague: Mouton.
Williams, G. 2005. *Sustaining Language Diversity in Europe: Evidence from the Euromosaic Project*. Houndmills: Palgrave Macmillan.

# Sustaining Minority Language Communities: The Case of Hungary

*Judit Solymosi*

Hungary has developed an unprecedented model to facilitate the preservation of the identity, the culture and the language of its minority communities. This model, the system of minority self-governments is included in the Hungarian constitution and specified in the 1993 *Act on Minority Rights* as a collective right of minorities.

This presentation aims to assess if, and in what respect, the system has proved successful in sustaining minority language communities.

Since the change of the political system in 1989–90, the subsequent Hungarian governments have built out a coherent system of minority protection on an extensive legal and organisational basis and with extensive financing from state resources.

The protection covers 13 minorities (Armenians, Bulgarians, Croats, Germans, Greeks, Poles, Roma, Romanians, Ruthenes, Serbs, Slovaks, Slovenes and Ukrainians), whose situation is rather different from the point of view of their size, the proportion of language speakers, the level of linguistic assimilation, the use of an archaic or a modern, standardised language, the distance from, and the simplicity of maintaining contacts with, their kin-states, or the existence of an institutionalised minority educational system.

However, they all have one thing in common: they typically live dispersed throughout the country, and constitute in general a minority even within their settlements. Statistically there are only 235 settlements, that is, about 7 per cent of all settlements in Hungary, where no one declared minority affiliation at the 2001 Census.

In such circumstances, arrangements of territorial autonomy are obviously impossible, but personal or cultural autonomy can provide effective means to sustain minority communities. This was the aim of the system of minority self-governments.

Minority self-governments are elected bodies that represent the interests of the given national or ethnic minority at local, regional or national level. These bodies have different competences ranging from simple consultation rights to strong blocking powers and even to transferred competences of autonomous decision-making. At all levels, minority self-governments enjoy financial state support for their operation.

Local minority self-governments are established for a four-year term through direct elections. Only those Hungarian citizens are entitled to take part at the elections who have previously registered in the minority voters' register kept (and destroyed afterwards) by the chief administrator of the Mayor's Office. The registration requires the declaration of the voter on his or her minority affiliation. These declarations remain secret. As local minority elections can only be held if the number of those registered reaches 30, the only data to be made public is the number of people registered.

Regional and national minority self-governments are elected in a system of electoral lists proposed by minority organisations. They are elected by the already elected members of the local minority self-governments ('electors') at a second round of elections, which is held in March of the subsequent year. This system makes it possible to avoid the creation of one-sided, 'one-coloured' bodies: the composition of the body may reflect the internal diversity of the given minority community. In this term, between 2006–10, the 13 minority communities have elected a total of somewhat more than 2000 local, 57 regional and 13 national minority self-governments.

Local minority self-governments have extensive consultation rights in all issues affecting the local minority population in their capacity as such, and also the right of consent (veto right) in the adoption of local municipal decrees which affect the minority community in the area of local public education, media, culture and the collective use of the mother tongue. Regional minority self-governments give their opinion on draft resolutions of the county assembly or the government of the capital city which affect minorities in their capacity as such, and they support state organs having the appropriate powers and duties in the professional supervision of secondary minority education.

National minority self-governments represent the given minority at national level. Being the partners of legislative and state administrative bodies, they have consultation rights in draft legislation whenever minorities are concerned. They have the right of veto in legislation concerning the protection of historical minority settlements and architectural monuments, in the adoption of government decrees concerning the preschool and school education of minority children and in approving minority schoolbooks.

Besides these consultative rights, minority self-governments are entitled to make autonomous decisions. These rights include for example the right to compile the list of minority forenames that can be given to babies, the right to decide on the minority's memorial sites, the dates of the minority's local and national holidays or the principles of how to use public radio and television broadcasting time at their disposal. However, the most important right concerns the right to found, to take over and to run cultural and educational establishments, schools, museums, libraries, scientific institutes, theatres or publishing houses. For running these institutions, they get the same state support as other public institutions.

Minority self-governments are powerful tools for political participation and for asserting minority rights. It is easy to understand that these functions can play an essential role in safeguarding the minority language. In a resolution concerning the implementation of the European Charter for Regional or Minority Languages, the Committee of Ministers recommended that Hungary should continue to develop the system of minority self-governments precisely in view of the valuable contribution it can make to the promotion of minority languages.

So, the question is whether the system has contributed to slowing down or stopping the process of language loss. The answer is 'yes' and 'no'.

Most of Hungary's 13 minority communities have reached a high level of linguistic assimilation. Language shift can be observed in these communities not only from the dialect-type languages to the standard language of the mother country, but also from the native minority language to the dominant use of Hungarian. The various dialects are not able to adapt and therefore their role in social communication is diminishing. The conscious use of the standard language is a relatively recent phenomenon which is characteristic primarily among intellectuals. In most minority families the language is no longer passed on to the next generation. The learning of the mother tongue starts 'artificially' from outside, in the kindergarten or at school.

It would be evident that bodies of minority self-governance could and should play an outstanding role in promoting the use of minority languages and in sustaining language communities.

However, from this point of view we can only talk of partial success.

The system has clear strengths and weaknesses. The greatest successes have been reached in the area of founding or taking over educational and cultural institutions. A survey among minority schoolchildren showed that the proportion of those pupils in minority schools whose mother tongue was the minority language varied between 5 and 10 per cent in the case of the German and Slovak children but reached 60 and 85 % in the case of the Croatian and Serbian pupils.

Such differences explain why Hungary has developed a system with three types of minority schools. Schools where the minority language is taught as a second language in 4 or 5 lessons a week constitute the most frequent type. The second type consists of bilingual schools where at least 50% of the subjects are taught in the minority language. The number of schools teaching all subjects in the minority language is rather low because of the lack of qualified teachers and the lack of children wanting to attend them.

According to the regulations, local or national minority self-governments are entitled to take over a minority school if they conclude an agreement respectively with the local municipal council, which, as a rule, is the maintainer of educational institutions, or with the minister of education, if the school has a regional or national coverage. In this way, minority self-governments will administer these schools and have thus the right to decide on the curriculum and the contents of the education, the teaching materials used, the teachers employed, etc.

From among the hundreds of minority schools existing in public education, minority self-governments have taken over so far one Croatian, three Slovak and two German schools. These are either bilingual schools or minority language medium schools. Three more educational institutions were founded by the minority self-governments themselves. Figures show that a total of 37 educational and cultural institutions are already run by the self-governments. These institutions constitute the most tangible result of cultural autonomy.

Let us go back to the three newly founded educational institutions. Some minority communities are so small that they do not have a network of schools, just one or two schools or even none. The Bulgarian, Greek and Polish communities have initiated a new form called complementary minority education. In this practical form of education, children belonging to minorities who attend different (non minority) schools in the morning, can participate in mother tongue education in four afternoon lessons a week. As normally there is a minimum number of pupils required for launching a minority school-group in a school, this form of complementary education makes participation in minority education possible also for those children whose number does not reach 8 within the same school district. The complementary instruction is accepted and recognised as part of the official educational system. The certificate the students get here entitles them to pass the so-called maturity exam in the given subject and to enter higher education. The advantages of this form of education can be summarised as follows: it does not require a minimum number of students, it can be organised for students studying in different schools, it has an established legal, professional and financial background, and it entitles the students to continue their studies.

Besides the endeavour to provide children with minority mother tongue education, another achievement of Hungary's recent minority policy is that it has reinforced the identity of people belonging to minorities.

However, this cannot be considered as a clearly, unambiguously positive process. For the past years, minority communities have been more and more willing to profess their minority affiliation, but their knowledge of the mother tongue has become weaker and weaker. Nearly all groups have suffered a loss of language speakers, although in most cases the number of their members has increased. The system has visibly strengthened individual and collective identity and contributed to sustaining minority communities, but it does not seem to be motivating enough for the preservation of the minority language. Minority self-governments prove to be in general more efficient in encouraging political participation than in enhancing the use of minority languages. The members of the minority communities do not often make use of their linguistic rights. Minority languages are hardly used in public administration, before courts or in managing the affairs of everyday life. People are not really determined to talk to each other in their native language in the street, in the shops, in the offices. The use of their mother tongue in public life seems useless to them. In some communities even the meetings of the minority self-government are run in Hungarian. In 2002, it was shocking to learn that one of the first decisions made by the newly elected Armenian National Self-government was to declare that the official language in which the meetings are to be held would be Hungarian.

If we compare the situation of the linguistic communities of Hungary with the situation of Irish and Scottish Gaelic, we can find some similarities such as the level of language loss, the shift in language use, the existing or planned protective and promotive legal provisions, or the lack of people speaking exclusively the minority language. However, there are also clear differences such as the existence of kin-States in the case of Hungary's minorities and the absence in Hungary of a minority language board and strategic minority language planning activities. Still the most striking difference is the lack of a clearly perceptible wish of the communities to revive their language.

What is then wrong with current arrangements and practice?

One problem is certainly connected to the fact that the provision of minority rights was not followed with a list of well defined duties for minority self-governments. For getting the state subsidy, it was enough for them to hold four meetings a year. A government decree on the differentiated funding of minority self-governments, entering into force in 2008, might bring a solution to this problem. However, the most important problem may be connected to the fact that electoral rules, although amended in 2005, still make abuses possible, and the wide rights enshrined in law as well as the accompanying state funding seem to be very tempting to many intruders. In a number of cases, the establishment of minority self-governments, instead of being a tool, has become an aim in itself; an aim to reach for getting secure state funding and a certain power and political influence. This is the essence of the phenomenon called ethno-business.

According to the opinion of the ombudsman of minority rights, the proportion of pseudo-self-governments may reach 6–10 per cent. No clear cultural and linguistic criteria are used for registering the voters, and no one is legally allowed to question or to check a person's affiliation to a national minority, as these data are considered to be sensitive. There are 119 settlements where minority self-governments have been set up in spite of the fact that during the 2001 census no one declared minority affiliation there. The former minority ombudsman compared the situation to the disbursement of welfare payments. He said it would be impossible to imagine somebody who should simply set out in the Mayor's Office that he was poor, and a public servant, who would immediately transfer him the welfare payment on this basis.

Whose task or responsibility is it ultimately to sustain a minority language community? In the concrete case, I think that communities themselves are the only entities that are able and morally entitled to decide who belongs to them and to eliminate intruders. In more general terms: I am convinced that communities built up of families play the key role in sustaining a language. The state can promote languages by different means but it cannot speak instead of the speakers. At a given stage of assimilation, education and support cannot replace a living linguistic environment. One can often hear that the school will take over the role of the families and the community, but the possibilities of the school are overestimated. The school is unable to hinder or to stop the assimilation process if communication in the majority language has become dominant also within the family and the community.

To reverse this situation, people should be motivated by the increased practical value of knowing the minority language. This could be, for example, the result of developing economic relations with the kin states. Awareness on the value of language knowledge in the international labour market should also be raised. It must not be overlooked that the most important function of a language is communication and co-operation between people.

It is worth quoting a member of the Slovak community who said: 'Hungary's minority legislation is exemplary, but it came too late'. This sentence gives us food for thought and the desire to learn from the efforts of other linguistic communities to revive their languages.

# Sustaining Minority Language Communities: The Case of Estonia

Tõnu Tender

In this paper, I would like to talk briefly about Estonia's language policy on minority or regional languages and dialects. At the beginning of the speech I would like to stress that I will handle some Estonian dialects (e.g. Võru dialect) in the context of minority language communities as well. Dialects are not 'minority or regional languages' in the meaning of the *European Charter for Regional or Minority Languages*. The Charter defines 'regional or minority languages' in Article 1 as 'traditionally used within a given territory of a State by nationals of that State who form a group numerically smaller than the rest of the State's population' and 'different from the official language(s) of that State'. It does not include either dialects of the official language(s) of the State or the languages of migrants.[1] It is quite complicated to define the terms 'language' and 'dialect' – the borders between them are not clear-cut anywhere and often depend on either linguistic approaches or political decisions. A dialect's prestige is not as high as that of a language. The high reputation of a language variety is the basis and precondition for its preservation.

### Estonia and Minority Nations: National Minorities

The history of Estonia and Estonians dates back to ancient times, but the Estonian state is young (established in 1918). As early as in 1925 the *(Estonian) National Minorities Cultural Autonomy Act* was passed. This act regards national minorities as Germans, Russians, Swedes and other ethnic groups, whose population in Estonia was more than 3000 people. The act stipulated the establishment of cultural self-governments and the possibility for national minorities to establish their schools and foster their culture as a whole. Not all minority nations who had the legal right to Cultural Autonomy made progress in establishing their cultural self-governments (e.g. Germans and Jews[1] were successful, but not Swedes and Russians). One explanation is that their compact population enabled most of their national problems to be solved through the local authorities.

The *Molotov-Ribbentrop Pact* (signed on 23 August 1939) divided Eastern Europe into spheres of influence and left the Republic of Estonia in the power of the Soviet Union. After the signing of the pact Adolf Hitler invited the Baltic Germans living in the Baltic States to relocate to Germany. The organised departure of the Baltic Germans from Estonia began. After the occupation and annexation of Estonia by the Soviet Union (1940) repression struck all ethnic groups. German occupation followed (1941–44),[2] during which Estonian Jews and Roma people were killed and Estonian Swedes left the country. In 1944 a large number of Estonians fled to the West to escape the approaching Soviet occupation. Estonia not only lost its independence, but also around 200,000 of its people one fifth of its population during World War II.

In 1944–90, the time of Soviet occupation, Estonia had no possibilities to implement its own immigration policy. During this period about 1.4 million persons who were

---

[1] Estonian State Commission on Examination of the Policies of Repression. *The White Book: Losses Inflicted on the Estonian Nation by Occupation Regimes, 1940–91*. Estonian Encyclopedia Publishers. 2005.
[1] The Estonian state was entered in the Golden Book of the Jewish National Foundation in 1926 as the highest acknowledgement for Estonia.
[2] See *White Paper: Losses inflicted on the Estonian Nation by Occupation Regimes 1940–91* (2005) reports of the Estonian State Commission on Examination of the Policies of Repression. Soviet Occupation 1940–41, German Occupation 1941–44 (2005) and Estonia 1940–45. *Reports of the Estonian International Commission for the Investigation of Crimes Against Humanity* (2006).

born outside of Estonia, mostly in the area of the previous Soviet Union, moved in and out of Estonia. Before the Soviet occupation Estonia was nationally a homogeneous state, but it became a land where representatives of more than a hundred ethnic groups live beside Estonians. For example Estonia was composed of 97.3% ethnic Estonians in 1945, but only 61.5% in 1989.

The figures of the 2000 census showed that the Estonia's population of 1,370,052 now had 142 nationalities (ethnic groups), including 930,219 Estonians (67.9%) and 351,178 Russians[3] (25.6%). Other largest ethnic groups were 29,012 Ukrainians (2.1%), 17,241 Byelorussians (1.3%), 11,837 Finns (0.9%), etc. The number of languages spoken as a mother tongue was 109, which was less than the number of ethnic groups: many nationalities have lost command of their mother tongue. This discrepancy between the numeric strength and the number of language speakers in ethnic groups indicates that they had undergone a language shift. First languages (mother tongues) spoken in Estonia divided as follows: Estonian: 921,817 (67.3%), Russian: 406,755 (29.7%), Ukrainian: 12,299 (0.9%), Byelorussian: 5,197 (0.4%), Finnish: 4,932 (0.3%), etc. A comparison of these figures with the census data shows that in all ethnic groups, including Estonians, the number of first/mother language speakers is smaller than the total number of the ethnic group. The only exception is the Russian language whose speakers outnumber ethnic Russians both in absolute and relative terms. For 97% of Estonian residents the first/mother language is either Estonian or Russian. The combined number of speakers of all the remaining 107 languages is just about 3%. The great majority of people who had no command of their mother language had lost it alre for Estonians and Russians) and thus the multitude of native languages is not

| Nationality (ethnicity) | | | Knowledge of national language | | | Difference between nationality (ethnicity) and knowledge of national language | |
|---|---|---|---|---|---|---|---|
| | number | % | | number | % | number | % |
| Estonians | 930,219 | 67.9 | Estonian | 921,817 | 67.3 | − 8,402 | − 0.6 |
| Russians | 351,178 | 25.6 | Russian | 406,755 | 29.7 | + 55,577 | + 4.1 |
| Ukrainians | 29,012 | 2.1 | Ukrainian | 12,299 | 0.9 | − 16,713 | − 1.2 |
| Byelorussians | 17,241 | 1.3 | Byelorussian | 5,197 | 0.4 | − 12,044 | − 0.9 |
| Finns | 11,837 | 0.9 | Finnish | 4,932 | 0.3 | − 6,905 | − 0.6 |
| Tatars | 2,582 | 0.2 | | | | | |
| Latvians | 2,330 | 0.2 | Latvian | 1,389 | 0.1 | − 941 | − 0.1 |
| Poles | 2,193 | 0.2 | | | | | |
| Jews | 2,145 | 0.1 | | | | | |
| Lithuanians | 2,116 | 0.1 | Lithuanian | 1,198 | 0.08 | − 918 | − 0.02 |
| Germans | 1,870 | 0.1 | | | | | |
| Others | 9,410 | 0.7 | Others | 7,276 | 0.6 | − 2,134 | − 0.1 |
| Unknown | 7,919 | 0.6 | Unknown | 9,189 | 0.7 | + 1,270 | + 0.1 |
| Together | 1,370,052 | 100.0 | Together | 1,370,052 | 100 | | |

Table 1: The Nationalities (Ethnic Groups) and their Knowledge of National Language by 2000 Census

[3] The Russian ethnic group consists of two subgroups differing from each other demographically and in their social behaviour: the historically established Russian minority estimated to be around 37,500, and the Russians relocated to Estonia after World War II and numbering over 300,000, according to the 2000 Census (See Katus, K. Puur, A. And L. Sakkeus. 2000. 'The Demographic Characteristics of National Minorities in Estonia'. In *The Demographic Characteristics of National Minorities in Certain Europen States*. Vol 2. Council of Europe Publishing. 29–80).

particularly noticeable in everyday life.[4]

Estonia paid more attention to national minorities after regaining independence in 1991. The *Constitution of the Republic of Estonia* and the *Language Act (1995)* guarantee prior to their arrival to Estonia and switched to the Russian language. The exceptions are Swedes and Finns: a significant part of them speak Estonian as first language. Among other nationalities the number of mother tongue speakers is very small (except for Estonians and Russians) and thus the multitude of native languages is not particularly noticeable in everyday life.[5]

The *Language Act (1995)* defines a minority language as a foreign language, which is indigenously used as the native language by an Estonian citizen. The act allows in certain conditions foreign languages and the languages of national minorities to be used.

The Republic of Estonia has signed the *Framework Convention for the Protection of National Minorities*. The Framework Convention (Article 14) guarantees representatives of ethnic minorities the right to be taught in their native language.

Estonia officially recognises minority nations 'national minorities' (Estonia has issued its clear definition, which is not defined in the Framework Convention) and their right for preserving their native language (see the new *National Minorities Cultural Autonomy Act* (*Vähemusrahvuse Kultuuriautonoomia Seadus*, 1993).[6]

> For the purposes of this Act, a national minority shall mean citizens of Estonia who reside in the territory of Estonia; maintain longstanding, firm and lasting ties with Estonia; are distinct from Estonians on the basis of their ethnic, cultural, religious or linguistic characteristics; and are motivated by a concern to preserve together their cultural traditions, their religion or their language, which constitute the basis of their common identity.[7]

The list of national minorities is not fixed in the Constitution of the Republic of Estonia. According to some experts (and Estonian legislation), there are three national minorities: Estonian Russians or Old Believers (*vanausulised peipsivenelased*) clearly distinguishable from the Estonian Russians who arrived in Estonia after the Second World War, Estonian Ingerians (Finns), and Estonian Swedes in Estonia today.

## The Status of Estonian Dialects or Regional Languages

Estonian legislation does not include a concept of regional language. Nevertheless, this topic has been discussed on several occasions, e.g. in 2004 when, based on an order issued by the Government of the Republic, a committee of specialists[8] was formed at the Ministry of Cultural Affairs with the task of determining the legal status of the Southern Estonian language (Võru, which has traditionally been considered a dialect of Estonian). The committee was not able to achieve consensus and the issue was closed without results, as the committee did not reach an agreement regarding the (regional)

---

[4] *Language Education Policy in Estonia – Language Policy Profile Report*. Country Report of Estonia, 2008. http://www.hm.ee/index.php?044904
[5] See note 4
[6] http://www.einst.ee/factsheets/cult_auton/
[7] http://www.coe.int/t/dg4/linguistic/Profils1_EN.asp
[8] *Order of the Government of the Republic* no. 27-k, 15.01.2004; the hairman of the committee was Minister of Culture, Urmas Paet.

language or dialect.

Estonian language policy on dialects or regional languages has been formulated in the *Language Act (1995)*, the last redaction of which took effect on 1 March 2007, and in the *Development Strategy of Estonian 2004–2010 (2004)*.[9] Estonian legislation defines dialects and the corresponding written language varieties that arise from them as 'special regional varieties of Estonian'. At the same time *The Development Strategy of Estonian 2004–2010 (2004)* considers their protection important, as follows:

> **6.1. Regional varieties of Estonian in Estonia**
> The spoken regional varieties of Estonian include Estonian dialects and the corresponding written varieties. Northern Estonian and Southern Estonian dialects show the largest number of differences. /.../
> **Objective**:
> to create conditions for the use of regional varieties of Estonian, their preservation as cultural treasure, as a development source of Standard Estonian, and the bearer of the local Estonian identity.
>
> **Tasks**:
> to create opportunities for teaching dialects in general educational schools and other educational establishments and to prepare such teaching materials;
> to support the use of dialects in the media and other culture by means of projects for the development of regional culture;
> to legally regulate the use of the regional varieties of Estonian in local administration, public signs, advertisements, notices, and advertising.'

The *Language Act (1995)*, last redaction of which took effect on 1 March 2007, provides the definition of the 'regional varieties' of Estonian:

> § 23 Language of Information of this Act states that:
> '(2) The Estonian text of public information can be supplemented with the text in the regional variety of Estonian or the translation into a foreign language, whereas the Estonian text shall be in the prevalent position and shall not be less viewable than the text in the *regional variety of Estonian* ('eesti keele piirkondlik erikuju') or the text in the foreign language.'

---

[9] Languages with a small number of speakers are always in danger of extinction even if there are no dramatic reasons because their users are always in the minority in global communication. To keep their languages useable, considerably more money per speaker is needed than in the case of languages with a large number of users. In such a situation, to preserve the language, i.e. developing all its functions, it is necessary to have a fixed plan and well distributed resources. The plan must be based on the national will to implement good intentions, and the will in its turn must rely on the understanding of the present language situation, the price of the plans and what will happen if the intentions in the strategy are not implemented. The strategy for the development of Estonian is a plan which connects all the activities necessary for the language itself, for using and preserving it, the people who use and develop the language and the state which through its legislation, administration and public relations must guarantee priority usage of Estonian on the territory of Estonia at present and in the future. The document was approved by the Estonian government on 5 August 2004. It provides a research-based description of the situation of Estonian, objectives that need to be achieved, the necessary steps, and institutions and people. The strategy is the first development plan of Estonian covering all the major areas of language use.

The language policy of the newly independent Estonia has been somewhat controversial regarding the issue of special regional varieties of Estonian. The special varieties of the Estonian language and multi-identity have been favoured as a cultural value, one of the sources for the development of standard Estonian and a medium of local Estonian identity. The state grants financial support to the activities of the Võru Institute[10] and the Estonian Bureau for Lesser Used Languages.[11] There are operating national (state) programmes financed from the state budget as 'Language and Culture of South Estonia, 2005–2009', 'Setumaa Cultural Programme', etc., supporting Southern Estonian regional varieties. Special regional varieties have been taught in general education schools (especially in the South of Estonia) and high schools and on summer courses; readers have been published and media publications produced in regional varieties, as well as special issues of magazines; radio and TV programmes have received support; support has also been granted for the writing and directing of plays in regional varieties, the publication of fiction and the organisation of poetry and home dialect days; and the Place Names Act has stipulated the use of the regional

Figure 2. Southern Estonian Dialects: Mulgi, Tartu, Võru (~ Võro) and Setu (~ Seto)[12]

[10] The Võru Institute was established by the Government of the Republic of Estonia in 1995. It belongs into the area of government of the Ministry of Culture, its activities are financed from the state budget and additional finances are applied for from various foundations and programmes. See http://www.wi.ee/index.php/welcome?lang=en-GB.

[11] The non-profit organisation Estonian Bureau for Lesser Used Languages (EstBLUL) was established in 2004. EstBLUL belongs to the trans-European organisation *European Bureau for Lesser Used Languages* (EBLUL). The members of EstBLUL include both the organisations of language communities (Yiddish, Roma language, Swedish, German, Finnish, Tatar and Russian; Setu and Võru language) as well as legal persons, see http://www.estblul.ee/EST/index.html.

[12] Source: http://et.wikipedia.org/wiki/Pilt:Lounaeesti_k_ja_keelesaarte_kaart_en.jpg

varieties of place names. However, attempts to promote regional varieties, especially those designed to attribute the status of regional language to some varieties, have been rejected. Dismissive attitudes have been justified by the relatively limited possibilities in terms of both human resources and finances[13] and sometimes even by the possible threat of separatism.

*The Implementation of the Development Strategy of the Estonian Language (2006)* highlights the problems in this area: legislation does not stipulate the use of regional varieties of Estonian in local public administration. There are also problems teaching regional varieties of the language since the national curriculum does not promote it sufficiently, and there is no way to grant additional qualifications to teachers of regional varieties.

Some leaders and friends of the Võro movement believed that Estonia should sign the *European Charter for Regional or Minority Languages*. Here I would like to emphasise that the Võru people (99% of them) consider themselves Estonians (not a separate nation). This means that being a Võru is not in conflict with being Estonian, and the Võru language would have gained the status of a regional language, if recognised by the Estonian State as a regional language and if Estonia had joined the Charter. At the same time, the Setu people consider themselves a separate nation.

Estonia has not signed the European Charter. According to Mart Nutt, the Member of the Riigikogu (Parliament of the Estonian Republic), the reasons are the possible cost of fulfilment of the requirements of Charter (the most important argument for many countries, including for Estonia); the danger of separatism; and the fear that attempts would be made on political grounds to extend the Charter to immigrant languages as well (the Charter does not protect the latter).

Although Estonia has not signed the European Charter and has not recognised Estonian dialects as regional languages, the Republic of Estonia attributes much importance to the continuous support for financing the activities in the field of dialects, according to possibility. Estonia supports the use of regional varieties of Estonian, their preservation as cultural treasure, as a development source of Standard Estonian, and the bearer of the local Estonian identity.

---

[13] For example, it has been stressed that Estonia would not be able to finance two languages sharing standard language status.

# Sustaining Minority Language Communities: The Case of Tatarstan[1]

*Marina I. Solnyshkina*

## Abstract

This paper briefly describes the history of Tatars in the middle Volga region, Russia, and examines the functions of the Tatar language. It gives an overview of Soviet and post-Soviet language policies and the legacy of these policies, focusing on the internal and external language attitudes towards Tatar and the asymmetry of functional domains where Tatar and Russian are used.

## Introduction

During the past several years, linguists have become more and more concerned about ethnolinguistic groups which are shifting from their original language to another offering more power or opportunities. The paper addresses the language ideologies and linguistic performance of Tatar[2] and the role which the language plays in ethnic self-identification and nationhood.

Tatar is considered to be 'endangered': that is to say that 'though it is ... still being learned by children, it will – if the present conditions continue – cease to be learned by children during the coming century' (cf. Krauss 1992).[3]

The Tatar community maintenance programmes, including language development strategies such as education, literature production, translation, etc., are aimed at the language's revitalization, its domain preservation and even its expansion. Tatar is alive as it still has many social functions, and there is a strong understanding in the society that the Tatar identity is constructed through linguistic performance.

---

[1] Here are some key facts about Tatarstan. Tatarstan is a subject in the Russian Federation, **Territory**: 67,836.2 sq. km.. **Location:** Russia, East-European Plain, the confluence of the Volga and the Kama. **Population** (2002 Census): 3,773,800. **Ethnic mix:** 48.5% Tatar, 43.3% Russian, 3.7% Chuvash, others 4.5%. **Total Tatar population** in the CIS 6,648,800. in Russian Federation 5,522,000, Tatars are Russia's second-largest ethnic group and the largest Muslim nationality. **The official languages:** Tatar and Russian; **Urban population**: 73.4% in 19 Cities, Kazan, Capital 1.2 million, Challi (Naberejni Chelny) 600,000; **Religion:** Sunni Islam, since 922; **Key industries**: oil production, petroleum industry, aircraft, mechanical engineering, instrument-making. **The first President:** Mintimir Shaimiyev, resigned his post on 22 January 2010, two days before his 73rd birthday. **The Acting President**: Rustam Minnikhanov.

[2] A Turkic language currently spoken in the Republic of Tatarstan by one quarter of its 3,773,800 residents. The Kazan Tatar language has three dialects: Eastern, Central, Western. The Western dialect (Misher) is spoken mostly by Mishars, Central is spoken by Tatarstan and Astrakhan Tatars ('Volga Bulgarians'), Eastern (Siberian) Tatar is spoken by some groups of Tatars in Tyumen Oblast of Russia, related to Chulym language. The Kazan Tatars speak a pure Turkic dialect (with a big complement of European and Arabic words) which became a literary one in the 15th century (iske tatar tele), because it is understandable to all groups of European Tatars as well as to the Chuvash and Bashkirs. Nowadays the literary language includes European and Russian words instead of Arabic.

[3] Krauss defines three categories of languages: *moribund:* 'languages no longer being learned as mother-tongue by children'; *endangered:* 'languages which, though now still being learned by children, will – if the present conditions continue – cease to be learned by children during the coming century'; and *safe:* languages with 'official state support and very large numbers of speakers'. See Krauss, M.E. 1992. 'The World's Languages in Crisis'. *Language* 68.1: 4–10

## The History of Kazan Tatars

The developed taxonomies of Tatars vary, but all of them include: Kazan Tatars ('kazanli'), Mishar Tatars ('misher'), Siberian Tatars ('seber ek'), Kriashens, Kasimov Tatars, Tiumen Tatars, Tobol Tatars, Tara Tatars (self-denomination Tarlyk (Darlik), Baraba Tatars, Bukharlyks, Astrakhan Tatars (Karagashly), Lithuanian Tatars (Polish or Belorussian Tatars), Teptiars, Crimean Tatars.[4]

Tatars all over the world regard the territory of Tatarstan as their historical birthplace and the centre of their cultural development. The Tatars enjoyed statehood in the form of the Bulgar Khanate, the Golden Horde and Kazan Khanate. They were later annexed by Russia under Ivan the Terrible, but the Tatars have always played a special role in the history of Russia. Certain traits of state structure and social life of Russia were influenced by the Golden Horde, while Russian culture experienced some influence on the part of Tatar culture. In general, Tatars have played a more prominent role in the history of the Volga Basin than other Turkic neighbors, and they are distinguished by their early move to agriculture, early conversion to Islam, early rise to statehood, early written culture and widespread literacy, early and strong bourgeoisie, and strong national press and intelligentsia (Graney 1999: 63).[5]

As late as the second half of the nineteenth century, Volga Tatars preferred to identify themselves, and to be identified by others, as Muslims.[6] Orthodox Christianity has been historically peceived by the Tatars as the religion and culture of the Russian conquerors. Christianisation is associated with the most tragic pages in the annals of Kazan Khanate. Only since late eighteenth century, after Catherine the Great's decree on religious tolerance, were Muslims no longer persecuted in Russia. Islam's influence on the re-emergence of the Tatar national and sociolinguistic identity is also convincingly demonstrated in *Religion And Identity in Modern Russia* (2005).[7] At the moment there are no religious frictions in Tatarstan.

## Language Ideologies and Policies in Soviet Union

In the Soviet Union the idea of the Russian language having a privileged role in the new Soviet state was rejected. During the early 1920s efforts were made all across the Soviet Union to educate children in their mother tongue, regardless of whether or not they spoke their mother tongue.[8] Until 1958, all Soviet children received education in their 'mother tongue'; afterwards, 'the use of the mother tongue was actively discouraged in the classroom',[9] and some languages were classified as non-viable.

---

[4] Iskhakov D. 1993. *Historical Demography Of The Tatars*. Kazan.

[5] Graney, K.E. 1999. 'Education Reform in Tatarstan and Bashkortostan: Sovereignty Projects in Post-Soviet Russia'. *Europe-Asia Studies* 51.4: 611–32.

[6] Khalikov, A.Kh. 1978. *Proiskhozhdenie Tatar Povolzh'ia i Priural'ia* (The Origin of Tatars of the Volga region and the Urals). Kazan. 13–5.

[7] Johnson J., Stepaniants, M., and Forest, B. eds. 2005. *Religion And Identity in Modern Russia*: The Revival Of Orthodoxy and Islam. Aldershot: Ashgate.

[8] Kreindler, I.T. 1989. 'Soviet Language Planning since 1953'. in ed. Kirkwood, M. *Language Planning in the Soviet Union*. London: Macmillan, in association with the School of Slavonic and East European Studies, University of London, 46–63.; Lewis, E. G. 1972. *Multilingualism in the Soviet Union: Aspects of Language Policy and its Implementation*. The Hague and Paris: Mouton.

[9] Lewis, E.G.1972. *Multilingualism in the Soviet Union: aspects of language policy and its implementation*. The Hague and Paris: Mouton..

Mastery of Russian has always been essential to success and 14–17% of classroom time was spent on teaching Russian; the number of non-Russian medium school subjects in the Russian Republic decreased from 47 in the early 1960s to 16 by 1982.[10] As a result parents did not encourage their children to invest their time and effort in learning no longer viable languages.

Under L. Brezhnev (1964–84), parents were encouraged to speak only Russian at home with their children in order to save them from the stigma of speaking Russian 'with an accent'. M. Gorbachev did not alter Soviet language policy although, like N. Khrushchev, he did not glorify Russian.

**Language Ideologies and Policies in Tatarstan**

Since 1990, Tatarstan's government has been legislating 'promotive' language policies trying to expand the functions of Tatar and put it on a more equal footing with Russian. B. Bowring (2007) states that Tatars being the most numerous minority in Russia have achieved, peacefully, a very high degree of autonomy.[11] The republic has adopted a number of crucial documents – the Declaration of State Sovereignty (30 August 1990), the Constitution (30 November 1992), the law 'On the Languages of the Peoples of the Republic of Tatarstan' (1992) and the Treaty with the Russian Federation on Delimitation of Jurisdictional Subjects and Mutual Delegation of Powers (15 February 1994).

The law *On the Languages of the Peoples of the Republic of Tatarstan (1992)* guarantees social, economic and legal protection to all the peoples of Tatarstan irrespective of their status. The state pledges to finance national and scientific programs on preservation, study and development of the languages of RT and provides for legal responsibility to break the law on the languages.

On 15 February 1994, the Russian Federation and Tatarstan signed the treaty[12] on the delimitation of responsibilities between the executive organs of the two entities, in which the federal centre confirmed the 'special status' of the Republic of Tatarstan. One of the targets of the Treaty was promoting the preservation and development of historical and national traditions, cultures, languages. Article III said that 'The State Bodies of the Russian Federation and the State Bodies of the Republic of Tatarstan jointly are authorised to:

> […] 16) co-ordinate the activities on the issues of health care, protection of family, maternity, paternity, childhood, education, science, culture, physical culture and sport; train national specialists for schools, educational, cultural institutions, mass media organisations and other institutions and organisations; provide pre-school and school organisations with native language literature; co-ordinate scientific research in the fields of history, culture of nations and their languages […]'.[13]

---

[10] *Ibid.* p. 50.
[11] Bowring, B. 2007. 'The Tatars of the Russian Federation and National-Cultural Autonomy: A Contradiction in Terms?' ***Ethnopolitics*** 6.3: 417–35. London. University of London, Birkbeck College.
[12] *On Delimitation of Jurisdictional Subjects. 1994. Treaty Between The Russian Federation And The Republic Of Tatarstan On Delimitation of Jurisdictional Subjects and Mutual Delegation of Powers between the State Bodies of the Russian Federation and the State Bodies of the Republic of Tatarstan.* Kazan. The Kremlin.
[13] *Ibid.*

On 19 April 2002, the State Council of Tatarstan adopted the revised version of the Constitution, which proclaims an individual, his rights and liberties the highest value and obliges the Republic of Tatarstan to accept, observe and protect human and civil rights and freedoms. The Tatarstan Constitution provides for such principles as universal suffrage, freedom of speech, freedom of conscience, right to participate in political parties and organizations, etc.

On 22 February 2007, the State Duma (the Russian Parliament) approved the treaty proclaiming that the candidates proposed by the Russian President for the office of the Republic's Presidency must speak the Tatar language.

**The Role of Language and Religion in Self-identification**

Rorlich (1999) highlights importance of collective memory in reconstructing the ethnic identity and writes that most Tatars assign the particularly prominent role to language and religion not only in identity construction, but in resurrecting and consolidating statehood as well.[14]

Wertheim (2003: 107) comes to the conclusion that, in Tatarstan, 'Language in particular is seen as representative of the nation, the barometer of the health of the nation, such that the impurity and decline of the Tatar language are seen as representative of the impurity and decline of the Tatar nation as a whole'. A typical expression of this theme states that '[...] a people without a language can not be a people in the true sense – its culture, literature, customs, and rituals can only live at a time when the native language is living' (Valiyev 1992).[15] A more explicit expression of the theme is found in an article entitled (quite straightforwardly) 'Tel saflïgï – millät pak'lege' [The purity of a language is the purity of a nation] (Fäsakhov 1994).[16] Fäsakhov first draws upon a prominent Russian cultural source as authority: 'The well-known Russian writer F. Dostoyevsky said 'A language – it is the people'. So if some kind of language exists and is in use, then the nation owning that language also exists [...]' Fäsakhov then continues. 'If that language, having become entangled with another language [...] begins to be diluted, then the fear for the existence of the nation is born, and the nation steps onto the path to extinction. Therefore the purity of the mother tongue [...] is perhaps the basic factor deciding the fate of a nation'. In the logic of this discourse, this is due to assimilation: 'A person who has lost his/her native language stops being a member of the nation [...] s/he has changed into a member of the nation whose language s/he knows and speaks. One or two generations after the Tatars who have forgotten their native tongue will be people who have become Russian [...]'. Therefore, 'the attempt to reanimate, cleanse and develop our native language is a battle for our nation's purity, safety, non-liquidation, and, in the end, for our independence'. The logic is clear and explicit: if a language is a people, and the language is lost, then the people will be lost as well – therefore language promotion and purification is necessary for survival of the nation'.[17]

---

[14] Rorlich, A.A. 1999. *History, collective memory and identity: the Tatars of sovereign Tatarstan. Communist and Post-Communist Studies*, V. 32, Issue 4, 379–196. Stanford University: Elsevier.
[15] Väliyev, R. 1992. 'Telebez khasta khälendä' [Our language is in a sick state]. *Shähri Kazan*, June 20, 3.
[16] Fäsakhov, K. 1994. 'Tel saflïgï – millät pak'lege' [The purity of a language is the purity of a nation]'. *Shähri Kazan*, December 9: 3–1.
[17] Wertheim, S. 2003. *Linguistic purism, language shift and contact-induced change in Tatar.* University of California, Berkeley dissertation. Available at http://ling.northwestern.edu/~wertheim/

## Multiculturalism in Tatarstan: Present Situation

The population of the Republic of Tatarstan consists of people of some hundred different ethnic groups. The 2002 census provides the following figures: 48.5% Tatar and 43.3% Russian, with Chuvash, Mari, Mordva, Bashkir, Ukrainians, Volga Germans, Jews, and a number of other ethnic groups comprising the remaining 8.2% of the population.[18]

In accordance with the Tatarstan Constitution, in June 2000, the Republic established the institution of the Commissioner for Human Rights.

Nowadays, there are 71 newspapers and 19 magazines published in the Tatar language, a republican newspaper *Suvar* and four regional newspapers in the Chuvash language. Regional n ewspaper of the Baltasi region is translated into the Udmurt language and, since O ctober 2002, a new newspaper *Tuganaylar* has been published for Tatar-Kriashens. On the territory of the Republic of Tatarstan, there are 30 TV companies, 20 of which broadcast programs in the Tatar and Russian languages, three in the Tatar language, and seven in Russian. From 41 republican radio stations, 15 broadcast programs in the Tatar and Russian languages, three in the Tatar language, and seven in Russian. From 41 republican radio stations, 15 broadcast programs in the Tatar and Russian languages, seven in the Tatar language and 17 in Russian.

23 organizations providing various types of help to migrants are active in the Republic of Tatarstan. Efforts are being made to improve the supply of minority language textbooks and teachers as well as to expand the availability of minority language teaching in public education.

100% of Russian children, 55% of Chuvash children, 71% of Udmurt children, 49% of Mari children and 8% of Mordvinian children receive schooling in their native languages. National and Cultural Centres host 28 Sunday schools providing schooling for more than 2000 children of smaller ethnic groups.

## Tatar-Russian Bilingualism: Present Situation

Bilingual Tatar speakers have a range of proficiency that can be organised according to level of language mixing, with pure Tatar on one end, pure Russian on the other end, and 'mixed' styles in between. Quite often speakers unconsciously use Russian words in Tatar discourse. A worse situation is observed in cases when elements of Tatar lexis are used in Russian syntactic patterns. These code-mixing and code-shifting as well as its accompanying structural alterations are a pathway of language attrition.

According to Wertheim (2003), a 1989 survey stated that only 36% of urban Tatars in Tatarstan used Tatar as a home language. This of course was before the re-establishment of Tatar-teaching schools, which have been expanded to be universal, even for Russian children, in Tatarstan.[19]

Tatarstan legislation regulates the spheres of Russian and Tatar as the state languages. The subject of special regulation is the usage of the state languages in the structures of the Republic power and management. The work of the State Soviet (Parliament), Cabinet of Ministers, President's Administration and other state offices,

---

[18] Russian Census. 2002. *Osnovnye Itogi Vserossiskoy Perepesi (The Main Results of the All-Russia Census)*. Moscow: Goskomizdat.
[19] Wertheim, S. 2003. *Linguistic Purism, Language Shift and Contact-induced Change in Tatar*. Unpublished PhD Thesis, University of California, Berkeley. Available at http://ling.northwestern.edu/~wertheim/

organizations and elected bodies, including clerical work, is to be done in Tatar and (or) in Russian.

The results of the poll conducted by Garipov (2002) aimed at the evaluation of the native language significance by the youth contained the question: 'What is the function of your native language?' and had a multiple choice of answers: a means of communication; a part of the cultural life of my nation; the foundation of the nation's cultural life development; and the guarantee of my ethnic community existence. Only 15% of the Tatar and 16% of the Russian youth chose that the native language is the guarantee of their ethnic originality. At the same time 32.5% of Tatars and 59% of Russians consider the native language no more than just a means of communication.

The second question: 'Which language would you like to master (Tatar, Russian, European languages, Turkic, Arabic)? Enumerate depending on your preferences' was answered as follows: both Tatars and Russians placed their native language first; Tatars ranked Russian second, and Russians ranked Tatar second. The preferences in foreign languages coincide: both Tatars and Russians place European languages before Turkic and Arabic.[20]

Whereas the Tatar and Russian languages are in principle equal, there is a distinct asymmetry in their functional domains and usage, particularly in urban Tatarstan. While Tatar usage has greatly increased since the declaration of sovereignty (due, in part, to language policy), Russian is still, by far, the dominant language, and the language of the public domain. The majority of newspapers, magazines, television shows, and radio programs are in Russian only, as are government proceedings and the majority of educational opportunities – for example, according to Lotfullin (2000),[21] there are presently five times more Russian medium schools than Tatar medium schools in Kazan.

## Creating a System of National Education

Hellner (1991) argues that a political unit does not possess vital capacity unless it is able to afford its national system of education.[22] Realizing the Law *On the Languages of Peoples of the Republic of Tatarstan*, the Parliament of the Republic worked out and adopted *The State Program of the Republic of Tatartan on Preservation, Study and Development of the Languages of the Peoples of Tatarstan (1994)*. Its 13 parts embrace scientific, organizational and administrative meaures to functional development of the state languages. A special attention is paid to the revival of the national Tatar medium system of education embracing all kinds of institutions from preschool to higher educational institutions.

The Program provides for functional widening of the Tatar language in Information Technologies. It is also planned to finance special editions of different types of bilingual and spelling dictionaries (Tatar-English, Tatar-German and Tatar-French).

The Soviet school used to serve the ideological purposes of 'rapprochement and

---

[20] Garipiv, Y.Z. 2002. 'Tendencies of national Language Development'. *Sociological Research*. 3–13. (in Russian).

[21] Lotfullin, M. 2000. 'Tugan teldä belem aluga shartlar tudïru kürsätkeche [An index of the establishment of conditions for learning in the native language]'. *Fän häm Tel* 4: 54–5.

[22] Hellner, E. 1991. *Nations and Nationalism*. Moscow. (in Russian).

[23] Garipiv, Y.Z. 1999. 'Ethnic Aspects of Education'. In *Urgent Problems of Education*. Moscow. 134–5 (in Russian).

integrity of peoples' and had the right to be ethnic only 'in form' with its content being 'socialistic' under the ideology of 'proletarian internationalism'.

Nowadays according to the character of bilingual educational process there are two types of schools in Tatarstan: 1) 'Ethnic school' with teaching in mother tongue from the first to the 11th year, the Russian language being studied as one of the subjects; 2) Russian medium Schools with teaching the Tatar language, literature and native culture up to seven hours per week.

In 1999, 63% of preschool Tatar children were brought up in Tatar while 10 years ago only 10.6% of Tatar children were educated in preschool Tatar medium institutions. 1220 of 2503 secondary schools were Tatar medium schools, 48% of Tatar children (34% of urban and 64.9% of country-side children) were educated in the Tatar medium secondary schools. 10 years before these figures were estimated at 12%.[23]

In 1960, the ratio of Tatars and Russians in Tatarstan higher educational institutions was 1:2, and since 1980 it has always been 1:1. In 1989/1990 school year Tatar students made up 45.6% while Russians made no more than 42.9%. Last year higher educational institutions were training 51% of Tatars. In 15 higher educational institutions of the republic 5,600 students (about 20% of all Tatar students) are trained in Tatar.

**The Tatar Language: The Situation outside the Republic of Tatarstan.**

Tatar is the second widely used language (after Russian) in Russian Federation: it is the medium of teaching in 2,166 schools and it is being taught as a discipline in 2,464 schools outside the Republic of Tatarstan.

The list of republican and oblast-based TV and radio companies broadcasting in Tatar includes: GTRK (State TV and Radio Company) Bashkortostan; GTRK Orenburg; GTRK Yamal, Commercial and industrial group *Eurasia, Kardashler* ('Compatriots'), Novosibirsk oblast the city TV channel *Young culture of Siberia,* Ulianovsk oblast radio company *Volga* (*TV-Kulatka*).

In 2003, six newspapers outside Tatarstan were published in Tatar: in the Orenburg oblast: *Yana Vakyt* ('New Times'), in the Perm krai *Khalyk Chishmese* ('Popular Spring'), *Tan* ('Dawn'), in the Samara oblast (*Berdemlek*), in St. Petersburg *Nur*, in the Ulianovsk oblast *Tatar*.

**Issues of concern**

Outside the Republic of Tatarstan the Tatar language attrition is extremely fast. Tatar families are losing the generation transferring the language and culture. Of all Russian Federation Tatars (5,558,000) only five – six% Tatar children are being educated in Tatar. 27% of Tatars outside the republic do not speak their native language[24].

The majority of Tatars (68%) are oriented at bringing up their children (grandchildren) in traditions of ethnic culture but half of them (53%) prefer to educate their children in Russian schools with Tatar being one of subjects.[25] This situation can be partially explained by low quality teaching in Tatar schools which does not guarantee University admission.

---

[24] Russian Census. 2002. *Osnovnye Itogi Vserossiskoy Perepesi (The Main Results of the All-Russia Census).* Moscow: Goskomizdat. 46.

[25] State Languages Functioning. 2007. *Sociolingvisticheskiye Problemy Funkcionirovaniya Gosudarstvennyh Yazakov Respubliki Tatarstan (Sociolinguistic Problems of the State Languages Functioning in the Republic of Tatarstan).* Kazan: Tatar Kniznoye Izdatelstvo. 20.

The Tatar teachers outside the Republic of Tatarstan lack the educational and methodological foundation meeting the European standards, they are disunited, do not have a union aimed at professional development, experience exchange and following the world standards in language teaching. The financial situation of the Tatar teachers outside the Republic of Tatarstan do not always allow them to participate in professional workshops and conferences usually held in the city of Kazan.

# Sustaining Minority Language Communities: The Case of Ukrainian in Southern Russia

*Alexander Pavlenko*

Russia has seen the competition of two types of language policy conventionally designated as 'eastern' and 'western' ones, the former considering linguistic variety as a tolerable phenomenon if not an advantage and the latter stressing the priority of the only dominating language of the state (cf. Kreindler 1984). Historically the 'eastern' approach used to be prevalent, dominating until late XIXth century when language policy in the Russian empire started to change. However those changes were not uniform throughout the country and mostly affected such western provinces as Poland, Ukraine, Finland and what is the Baltic states and Belarus' today. The policy of Russification was intensified in those lands, its principal element being the prohibition of the indigenous languages in education, publishing and theatre. It is worth mentioning, however, that in Asian Russia local idioms were enjoying relatively favourable conditions at the same time.

Some signs of democratisation in the field of language policy and therefore another shift towards the 'eastern' pattern started to appear in early twentieth century, especially after the revolution of 1905. The Soviet Union as the successor of the Russian empire continued to exercise the 'eastern' pattern of language policy which dominated before the October revolution. Democratisation of the last years of the empire went on after 1917. Due to the ideology of 'internationalism' chosen by the Bolsheviks the opposition to Russification was supported in the national regions by the young Soviet state from the very beginning.

Lenin's government proclaimed equality of all languages and the refusal from any compulsory state language (i.e. Russian). To this end measures were taken to provide the national territories with school teaching and publishing in the indigenous languages. The constitution of 1925 proclaimed the right for free and unrestricted use of all languages in administration, court, and social life. Positive results of the Soviet language policy in the 1920s are widely known. More than 80 ethnic groups had been using their native languages in all spheres of life by early 1930s. Many of these ethnic groups provided themselves with a written language and written literature only after the Revolution. But the mid 1930s saw the dramatic change of the language policy. Most of the activity in national language planning was abolished. In 1938 Russian was introduced in all national schools as a compulsory subject in the first form. All the alphabets newly created on the basis of the Latin prototype were substituted by the Cyrillic.

The 'naive' early years of the Soviet regime were followed by Stalin's centralizing and concentrating of power accompanied by general promotion of Russian as the title language of the country. Thus in the mid 1930s the USSR saw a complete switching to the 'western' pattern as more suitable for a centralised multilingual country.

Building of a new state structure in the southern part of European Russia began after the civil war in early 1920s. The borders of the administrative regions, territories and even those of some historical ethnic areas used to change very often in those days. In 1925 all the territorial and ethnic regions of south-western Russia were combined to form the new North Caucasus territory (the Russian for 'territory' as an administrative

Sustaining Minority Language Communities: The Case of Ukrainian in Southern Russia 301

division is *krai*), which had existed until 1935. An important constituent part of the above mentioned larger administrative unit was the then Don territory (in the times of monarchy the region (or the *oblast* in Russian) of the Don Cossack Army) which was renamed into Rostov region in 1937 (see Figure 1).

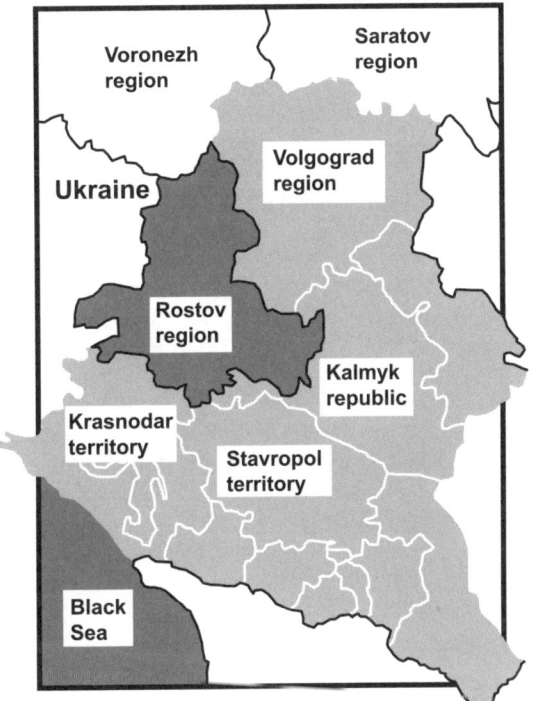

**Figure 1. Map of Present-day Rostov Region**
Consider some principal peculiarities of the language situation in this region. The Eastern-Slavic speech was and still is (although in a different proportion) represented here by four main types of varieties. They are:

1. The so-called Don or Don Cossack dialects of the Russian language, which used to occupy more than a half of the whole area in early twentieth century.
2. The dialects of the Ukrainian settlers which also used to occupy about a quarter of the total area at one time.
3. Mixed (mostly urban) Russian dialects which emerged as an amalgamation of certain varieties of Russian and Ukrainian along with few borrowings from Greek, Armenian and other languages. They occupy about a quarter of the area as well – mostly its southern part where the main urban centres (Rostov-on-Don and Taganrog) are situated.
4. Besides, there are some non-Cossack Russian dialects which had spread in the former Don Cossack Army region as 'dialect isles' with the influx of immigrants from other regions of Russia from the late eighteenth century (cf. Gab 1965: 8).

Besides Russians and Ukrainians there are certain groups of population speaking languages others than Russian and Ukrainian in Rostov region. They are Armenians, Kalmyks, Tartars, Gipsies, Koreans, Germans, Poles, and some others, Armenians being the most numerous of them. Their languages were hardly ever able to affect the grammar and phonology of the local Slavic dialects strongly, because of their Abstand and demographic disparity. However the Don Cossack dialects owe a lot to the earlier contacts with the Turkic languages for a considerable amount of lexical borrowings.

There has been much argument (and confusion) on the issue of geographical border between the Ukrainian and Russian languages. The assumption that a considerable part of the said border passes across today's Rostov region used to be taken by many for granted. In fact, the peculiarities of the language and cultural contacts between the Ukrainian immigrants and Russians (mainly Don Cossacks) in what is now Rostov region and the adjacent regions of Ukraine are such that it is incorrect to speak of any continuous border because of heavy ethnical, cultural, economical and language intermingling in the area (cf. Ovchinnikova, et al. 1975: vii; xii). Although Ukrainian is obvious to exist here in the form of dialect isles only, a false concept of a linear border between the languages is still sometimes referred to.

In this area it was the Russian and Ukrainian languages that affected one another most of all as the closest cognate ones. The case of south Russian Ukrainians is a good example of what may happen to an ethnic group in the course of unification proceeding in the form of convergence with another more numerous and more powerful group. In terms of language contact it is a kind of absorption of one ethnic idiom by another, the interaction of English and Scots being the closest parallel in the British Isles. In south Russia this process was caused by the demographic disparity of the mentioned ethnic groups and the closeness of their languages and cultures. At present most descendents of the first Ukrainian settlers, especially the urban dwellers, lost their original identity altogether and identify themselves as Russians as a result of ethnic assimilation.

However, nowadays in Rostov region of Russia the Ukrainian language, no matter how mixed or degraded it is, still exists as a means of oral communication of mostly elderly inhabitants of some rural areas. Besides being a vernacular, Ukrainian is also present in folklore – songs, verses and tales, but nothing is done to sustain the language within the communities and to elevate its social status. The twentieth century saw the gradual retreat of Ukrainian in south-western Russia, although there were times, as it will be said further, when the local authorities influenced by the Ukrainian nationalists used to have strikingly positive attitudes towards the Ukrainian language and were promoting it for several years however paradoxical it might sound today. Those historical facts become especially remarkable if we take into account today's uneasy relations between the Russian Federation and Ukraine, language policy being one of the dimensions of this uneasiness.

As is known the policy dubbed as 'Ukrainisation' was being carried out from 1925 to 1933 in the then North-Caucasus territory by the local communist authorities along with the activists of the Ukrainian national Renaissance. The campaign took in 35 areas of what today is Rostov region, Krasnodar and Stavropol' territories (see Picture 1) as well as a number of North Caucasian ethnic autonomies where there was a considerable Ukrainian population. This process was proceeding within the mainstream of the Soviet internal policy of that period, following rather the abovementioned 'eastern' pattern of language policy. It was being conducted by the local authorities along with the activists of the Ukrainian national movement. Those developments were implemented as a part of the said general approach in the ethnic policy and were based on the decisions of the communist party Central Committee and the Soviet government.

This policy was not by any means fortuitous and groundless in this part of Russia as the Ukrainian population here had grown considerably between the late eighteenth and the early twentieth centuries. The contribution of the Ukrainian settlers into the development of the virgin lands and creating local economy and culture was conspicuous. These lands started to be settled and developed by Russians and Ukrainians as a result of Russia's expansion in the Southern direction and joining the territories of the lower Don, the territories North of the Sea of Azov, and the North Caucasus (cf. Yefremov et al. 2003: 178–182).

According to the census of 1897 the Ukrainian population of the region of the Don Cossack Army amounted nearly to 720,000 or about 28%. Most Ukrainians lived in Taganrog and Donetsk areas (both shared between Russia and Ukraine today) where the Ukrainian population prevailed over the other groups. However Ukrainians were present more or less in all the other southern areas as well, especially in Cuban' territory. They had lived among Russians for a long time what resulted in the retreat of their indigenous language, with only 57% of those identifying themselves as Ukrainians still being the speakers of Ukrainian by early 1920s.

Practical work on Ukrainisation started in May 1925 and at the first stage this work was confined to introducing Ukrainian into school teaching. Later the authorities along with the activists initiated a number of long-term programmes aimed at raising the social status and the purity of local Ukrainian.

The most significant of those measures were as follows: opening a number of teachers' training colleges to provide primary schools with Ukrainian teachers; establishing a number of territorial and local newspapers in Ukrainian; transferring the chancellery from Russian to Ukrainian both in the centre and on the periphery and turning Ukrainian into a working language of administration. It was recommended to use Ukrainian in cultural life of the territory as widely as possible, to publish dictionaries, and to sustain language, literary and folklore societies. The significance of philological studies was also stressed as well as the urgent necessity of establishing a social and literary journal of the territory. Those plans were officially approved both in Rostov-on-Don and in Moscow and the measures adopted were to be implemented within three years. A special Board was established to coordinate the process of Ukrainisation in the North Caucasus territory.

Besides the other Ukrainian periodicals the territorial newspaper of the Communist party – 'The Chervonaya Gazeta' (*The Red Newspaper*) – was launched in 1926. Its circulation had reached 38,000 copies by 1930. Also a socio-cultural journal 'Novym Shliakhom' (*Along the New Way*) started to be published in Rostov-on-Don. Several local newspapers were published in Kuban' territory. A children's territorial newspaper 'The Lenin's Little Grandchildren' had an appendix in Ukrainian for some years (Tereschenko 2000: 65).

School education was being transferred to Ukrainian in many areas of the whole North Caucasus territory. Teaching staff training was carried out mostly in the educational institutions of Cuban' (today's *Krasnodar*) territory where the Ukrainian population was historically very considerable. Two Ukrainian teachers' training colleges were established in Krasnodar – the administrative centre of Cuban' territory. Another similar institution was established in the settlement of Poltavskaya. Besides, the Ukrainian studies were introduced in the pedagogical college in Taganrog which had been returned to the then Don territory by that time (previously belonging to Ukraine for a short period). Various reference books, textbooks and teaching materials were compiled in the North Caucasus Ukrainian Research Institute which was established in Krasnodar. The specialised 'Pivnichny Kavkaz' publishing-house (*The North Caucasus*) was founded in Rostov-on-Don in order to publish the materials elaborated by the Krasnodar Institute as well as fiction and poetry for adults and children. All these developments allowed thousands of schoolchildren to start their studies in Ukrainian in both urban and rural areas in the 1930–31 academic year.

Publishing in Ukrainian was actively supported financially and organisationally. Nearly all the literary heritage written in the Ukrainian language from the late eighteenth to early twentieth century was published in the form of cheap popular series for the broad range of readers. Ukrainian publishing-houses based in Kyiv, the capital of Ukraine, also provided the Russian regions in question with their editions as the North Caucasus territorial party committee based in Rostov-on-Don was controlling and directing the process of the Ukrainiasation in close co-operation with similar state organ in Ukraine where language planning and culture rebuilding were also evolving rapidly.

An important sphere in which the territorial authorities were most helpful and efficient was the development of the Ukrainian culture by means of establishing libraries, the so called houses of culture, cinemas, and radio networks. A Ukrainian travelling theatre was organised and financed, and the plan to provide it with a permanent building in Rostov-on-Don was adopted. The Ukrainian language societies and courses were being widely organised in all the areas under the Ukrainiasation. Besides, the municipal and regional authorities required all the civil servants and the chancellery to switch to Ukrainian. Those reluctant to do so underwent more or less strict punishment or were dismissed. (*ibid*. 66).

However the policy of the Ukrainiasation and its successful implementation in south-western Russia were negatively reconsidered by Moscow authorities in the end. In December 1932 Stalin sent to the regional Communist party and Soviet organs his order to stop the Ukrainiasation immediately as a harmful and erroneous policy. The regional authorities were also ordered to transfer all the media, and publishing back to Russian and to reintroduce teaching in Russian starting with the 1933/34 schooling year. Nearly a decade's efforts undertaken by the Ukrainian language-planners were abruptly cancelled in favour of strict centralisation and struggle against nationalism.

The key figures of the Ukrainisation were accused of nationalism what often meant a concentration camp or the death sentence at that time. The most active worker of the Ukrainiasation, the Peoples' Commissar for Education of Ukraine A.M.Skrypnik, committed suicide after being accused of perverting the party policy. The regional party and the government leaders of the North Caucasus territory were announced to be 'vraghi naroda' (*enemies of the people*) and underwent the repression as such. The wide scope and conspicuous results of the Ukrainiasation in South Russia make it quite understandable how many people belonging to different social strata must have suffered from the un-Ukrainiasation (many even losing their lives in its course).

The present-day condition of Ukrainian still spoken in several settlements of Rostov region and further South in Krasnodar territory can be characterised as an accelerating retreat. These communities are the remainders of the bygone massif of the Ukrainian speaking population which was formed as a result of the intensive Ukrainian colonisation of the Russian South. However, today it is the Ukrainian language – no matter how 'spoiled' it might be – that makes up the principal peculiarity of the above mentioned settlements. Ethnic identity of these Ukrainians is rather vague. They are certain to remember their roots but not all of them realise their being ethnic Ukrainians, long and close cultural, historical and linguistic ties with Russia and Russians being a cause of that. While the language of the migrants' descendants is still conserved in the rural areas, in the urban centres the situation is very different. Here the great-grandchildren of the Ukrainian settlers are also very numerous, family names being an obvious evidence of that, but their ethnic identity is already homogeneously Russian. A person feeling his or her 'Ukrainianness' here must be an enthusiast if not an eccentric.

However one must acknowledge that the results achieved by the activists of Ukrainisation were impressive. Language planning was among their principal interests. History does not know a 'subjunctive mood' however if there had not been Stalin's 'change of course' there might have been a vast Ukrainian-speaking area in the South of Russia.

Of course, the Soviet authorities were not just benevolent altruists and obviously were interested in creating the conditions for pacifying national movements where they were developing. The then North Caucasus territory was no exclusion. The authorities skilfully directed the energy and efforts of the local nationalists to building their national culture and language rather than campaigning for some other less inoffensive objectives.

Today when Ukraine enjoys the status of an independent state there has been established a Ukrainian consulate in Rostov-on-Don. Its activities also have a cultural dimension, i.e. an exchange in the fields of folklore, art, language, history, etc. Although this cannot provide any substantial support to the Ukrainian-speaking islets in the sea of Russian, local Ukrainians have obtained an additional channel to communicate with the country of their forefathers.

Of course, sad events similar to those concluding the Ukrainisation in the 1930s are very unlikely to happen again somewhere in Europe but those historical facts must be remembered reminding us how expensive the price of language and culture planning can sometimes be. Language activists today are sure to be safe of any repression, their principal objective and concern being the Herculean labour of reintroducing the lesser used languages basing on their own views, theories, and ethnic traditions also taking into account some international experience.

Striking similarities to the Russian and Ukrainian linguistic interaction either in South-Western Russia or in Eastern Ukraine can be found in Lowland Scotland where the language situation is characterised by a complex amalgamation of English and Scots. If we compare the Lowlands and the aforementioned Southern region of Russia, we will see some parallels, the main being such correspondence as 'Russian-English versus Ukrainian-Scots'. The former couple of languages is dominant in all respects. Scotland is a unique culture whose internationally famous national identity somehow manages to do without language-icons. The communities which are mainly Scots-speaking still conserve as such due to natural vitality of the idiom manifested both through language loyalty of the population and the efforts of the language activists. It is worth mentioning that Scots in Scotland has never experienced anything like the the Ukrainiasation of 1920s–1930s in the South of Soviet Russia.

Natural vitality of indigenous languages based on language loyalty and non-governmental language planning are important factors although they are far from being enough without energetic language policy carried out by the national authorities. An obvious conclusion follows – to raise the social status of Scots in individual communities and all over the country a wide campaign of 'Scotsisation' is necessary, fruitful Ukrainiasation of early twentieth century being an encouraging example.

Despite the titanic work done by the generations of Scottish scholars and men of letters, and relatively high level of autonomy Scotland has enjoyed within the UK the social status of Scots has remained without substantial changes. Language development in Scotland has being proceeding, so to speak, in a 'natural' way, rather evolutionary than revolutionary one.

The comparison with the former Soviet Union shows one more time that language planning demands active intervention of the state. In Scotland the lack of political will to promote Scots obviously results from the lack of interest towards the idea on behalf of the nationalist forces. Undoubtedly, this situation is caused by some widely known factors: firstly, the special role of the English language in the UK and in the today's world; and secondly the attractive idea of the unity of the Anglo-Saxon protestant culture (going back to the times of Reformation). Building up and disseminating another although closely related language must be considered not worthwhile just from the point of view of expected pay off. One more important factor is the presence of Gaelic far outweighing Scots in its *Abstand* and symbolic function.

Of course, Scotland was lucky not to experience that intensive interference in its culture as the former Soviet regions did being parts of a totalitarian empire. However now it is possible to certify that many indigenous languages of Russia and the present-day CIS countries rather gained than lost from that interference in the end.

## References

Gab, S.P. 1965. *Accents and Dialects of Rostov Region*. Rostov-on-Don: Rostov State University Publishing House. [in Russian]

Kreindler, I.T. 1984. 'The Non-Russian Languages and the Challenge of Russian: The Eastern versus the Western Tradition'. In ed. Kreindler I.T. *Sociolinguistic Perspectives on Soviet National Languages: Their Past, Present and Future* (Contributions to the Sociology of Language 40). Berlin: Mouton de Gruyter. 345–68.

Ovchinnikova, V.S. et al. eds. 1975. *Dictionary of the Russian Don Dialects*. vol. 1. Rostov-on-Don: Rostov State University Publishing House. [in Russian]

Tereschenko, A. 2000. 'Ukrainisation in North-Caucasus Territory' [1924–1933]. in *Donskoy Vremennik* (The Don Chronicle). Rostov-on-Don. 64–7. [in Russian]

Yefremov, A.S. et al. 2003. *A History of Lougansk Territory. Lougansk* (Ukraine): Alma-Mater. [in Russian]